Turning to the Other

Turning to the Other
Martin Buber's Call to Dialogue
in *I and Thou*

Donovan D. Johnson

WIPF & STOCK · Eugene, Oregon

TURNING TO THE OTHER
Martin Buber's Call to Dialogue in *I and Thou*

Copyright © 2020 Donovan D. Johnson. All rights reserved. Except for brief quotations in critical publications or reviews, no part of this book may be reproduced in any manner without prior written permission from the publisher. Write: Permissions, Wipf and Stock Publishers, 199 W. 8th Ave., Suite 3, Eugene, OR 97401.

Wipf & Stock
An Imprint of Wipf and Stock Publishers
199 W. 8th Ave., Suite 3
Eugene, OR 97401

www.wipfandstock.com

PAPERBACK ISBN: 978-1-5326-9913-9
HARDCOVER ISBN: 978-1-5326-9914-6
EBOOK ISBN: 978-1-5326-9915-3

Excerpt from THE LETTERS OF MARTIN BUBER by Martin Buber, edited and selected by Nahum N. Glatzer and Paul Mendes-Flohr, translated by Richard and Clara Winston and Harry Zohn, copyright © 1991 by Schocken Books, a division of Random House, Inc. Used by permission of Schocken Books, an imprint of the Knopf Doubleday Publishing Group, a division of Penguin Random House LLC. All rights reserved.

New Testament quotations are from New Revised Standard Version Bible, copyright © 1989 National Council of the Churches of Christ in the United States of America. Used by permission. All rights reserved worldwide. http://nrsvbibles.org/

Cover photograph, "Martin Buber (1878–1965), Philosopher and Theologian, Vienna, c. 1916," ©Museum of the Jewish People at Beit Hatfutsot, The Oster Visual Documentation Center. Used by permission of the Museum of the Jewish People at Beit Hatfutsot, Tel Aviv, Israel.

Manufactured in the U.S.A.   09/30/20

To Wanda and Briana, dialogical partners along the way

It all comes down to the one thing—utter openness to presence.

—*I and Thou* §46f

Contents

Acknowledgments | xi

The Conventions Used in This Book | xiii

Key Linking the Sixty-One Sections of I and Thou *with the German, Smith, and Kaufmann Pages* | xv

Chronology—The Life and Work of Martin Buber | xix

Chapter 1   Reopening *I and Thou* | 1
  1. Decline: The Reception of *I and Thou* has Reduced Buber's Message to an *It*
  2. The Nature of the Work—Three Readings
  3. Recovery
  4. Overview of this Book

Chapter 2   Buber's Spiritual Initiation | 13
  1. The Concept of Spiritual Initiation
  2. Buber's First Period of Withdrawal: His Spiritual Initiation
  3. Buber's Second Period of Withdrawal: His "Creative Illness"
  4. Buber's Experience and Ellenberger's Concept of Creative Illness
  5. Spiritual Initiation: Transmission of the Transcendent

Chapter 3   Buber's Task Finds its Rhetoric | 41
  1. Buber's Task: The Imperative to Bear Witness
  2. Indirect Communication: Buber's Means of Bearing Witness

3. Buber's Invention: His Rhetoric of Pointing
4. Breakthroughs toward a Dialogical Rhetoric
5. Buber's Rhetorical Tools Applied in *I and Thou* —An Overview

Chapter 4   Buber's Life in Dialogue | 54
1. Introduction
2. Buber's Loss of His Mother
3. Buber's Grandparents
4. Buber's Father
5. Buber's Wife, Paula Winkler Buber
6. World War I as Watershed—The Rev. William Hechler, the Young Mehe, Gustav Landauer
7. Gustav Landauer
8. Franz Rosenzweig
9. Conclusion

Chapter 5   Buber's "No" to Objectification | 95
1. Buber's Existential Edge
2. Buber's Distinction: Philosophy vs. Religion
3. Buber's Revaluation of *Erlebnis*
4. Conclusion

Chapter 6   Buber's "Yes" to the Way | 116
1. The Controversial Essay: "The Teaching of the Tao"
2. Buber's Concept of "The Teaching"
3. The Master
4. The Global Historical Perspective
5. The Core of the Teaching—"The One Thing Needful": The Unification of the Self
6. Buber's *Way*
7. Conclusion

Chapter 7   Exposition of *I and Thou*—Part One | 146
1. The Problem of Individuation and Alienation
2. Buber's Landmark Distinction: *I-Thou* vs. *I-It*
3. *I-Thou* in the Three Spheres of Existence
4. A Double Genealogy of *I-Thou* and *I-It*
5. Either/Or

Chapter 8   Exposition of *I and Thou*—Part Two | 173
    1. History as Cosmic Gyre
    2. Modernity, the Era of Profound Alienation, as Nadir
    3. Individualism: The Individualist [*Eigenwesen*] Versus the Person
    4. Existence on the Cusp of *Teshuvah*
    5. Crisis: *Teshuvah*—Reversal/Turning
    6. Process: Swinging between *Thou* and the *It*-World
    7. Crisis: The Reader Must Decide

Chapter 9   Exposition of *I and Thou*—Part Three | 219
    1. Finite *Thou* and Eternal *Thou*: Presence as "The One Thing Needful"
    2. Critique: *I-Thou* vs. Creaturely Dependency
    3. Critique: *I-Thou* vs. Christian Mystical Absorption
    4. Critique: *I-Thou* vs. Hindu Mystical Absorption
    5. Critique: *I-Thou* vs. Buddhist Mystical Absorption
    6. *I-Thou* and the Three Spheres of the Created Order
    7. *I* and *Thou*: The Role of Solitude
    8. Critiques: *I-Thou* vs. Scheler on Idols and *I-Thou* vs. Kierkegaard on "The Single One"
    9. *I-Thou*: The Dialogical Nature of Revelation
    10. *I-Thou* vs. *I-It* as the Dynamic in the History of Religions
    11. Conclusion

Chapter 10   The Open Challenge | 266
    1. Locating Buber's Timely Task
    2. Focusing on Buber's Message: The Dialogical Core
    3. Hearing Buber's Prophetic Call
    4. Conclusion

Appendix 1   Chart: The Three Global Traditions in "The Teaching of the Tao" (Chapter 6) | 285
Appendix 2   Buddhist Texts Quoted in *I and Thou* | 287
Appendix 3   *I and Thou* Expresses a Hebraic Vision | 289

Bibliography | 293
Index | 305

Acknowledgments

THIS BOOK WOULD NOT have been possible without two professors of dialogical reading, Otto Michel (1903–1993), Professor of the Evangelisch-theologische Fakultät and founder of the Institutum Judaicum at the Eberhard-Karls-Universität, Tübingen, Germany, who taught me to read the texts of the Johannine tradition in dialogical interaction with its Hebraic substrate, the Hebrew Bible; and Allan W. Anderson (1922–2013), Professor of Religion at San Diego State University, who taught me to read the Bible in dialogical interaction with the Hindu Scriptures.

On October 14, 2012, I participated in a discussion of *I and Thou* which became my call to engage with it more deeply and to turn to engage with Martin Buber. The text, the voice, and the person stand together as one in witness to dialogue, to encounter with others and with the eternal *Thou*.

Seven years with Buber—a project has become a lifestyle. Here there is no veil: Laban cannot exact another seven years from me as a Jacob before this consummation.

If it takes a village to raise a child, it takes a community to write a book. Taking up the task of writing that book is the means of discovering that community of support, finding the matrix in which the vision can find its legs and wings. Those who stand out in this community of grace and dialogue:

> Long-term supporters: Wanda Johnson, Briana Johnson, Eido Frances Carney, Joseph Hickey-Tiernan, Samuel Torvend, and Florence Sandler.

> Dialogical readers: David Chamberlain, Kathleen Byrd, Ted Johnstone, Bruce Johnson, MaryAnn Johnson, Doug Oakman, Jane Maynard, and John Petersen.

The Conventions Used in This Book

I HAVE KEPT TRANSLATOR Smith's *Thou* rather than going with translator Kaufmann's "You." When *I*, *Thou*, or *It* is used as one of the technical terms in Buber's discourse, I have used italics to distinguish such usage. Following Wood, one of Buber's major interpreters, I have numbered the sixty-one sections of *I and Thou* and assigned a lowercase letter to each paragraph in sequence within each section. Accordingly, a parenthetical reference such as (§60d) uses a section symbol and refers to the fourth paragraph of section 60. This convention makes the location cited definitive regardless of whether one has Smith's version, or Kaufmann's, or the original German at hand. Most other material from Buber that is quoted comes from published English translations; exceptions—my translations and modifications are noted in the footnotes. *Begegnung*, one of the key words in Buber's dialogical vocabulary, can be translated either as "encounter" or as "meeting." Contra Maurice Friedman, when I translate this word I use the word "encounter."

This book is a study of Martin Buber's *I and Thou*. Quotations from the text of *I and Thou* are my translations from Buber's original German unless otherwise noted. I have consulted the two published English translations of *I and Thou* in my work with the German text. It is worth noting the differences between these two translations.

The first, that by Ronald Gregor Smith, was published in 1937, fourteen years after *Ich und Du* was first published in Germany. Smith was a Scottish Protestant theologian who had studied and lived in Germany and he worked closely with Buber on this translation of *Ich und Du*. As Buber's major early translator into English, Smith undertook translating a number of Buber's major early works up until his untimely death in 1968 at the age of fifty-five. Smith's precision as a twentieth-century British theologian brings a crispness to the language that first introduced *I and Thou* to the English-speaking world.

Walter Kaufmann, the second translator, was a German by birth and a Jew by conversion. Kaufmann migrated to the US for his undergraduate studies. He completed his career as a Professor of Philosophy at Princeton University. His primary allegiance was to the discipline of philosophy, which made him critical of Buber and Buber's language at times. In 1969, Buber's son Rafael invited Kaufmann to undertake a new translation of *Ich und Du* into English. Kaufmann's native German served him well for this task, largely because of his ease with literally translating Buber's phrasing. Kaufmann chose to use capitalized "You" and "It" rather than Smith's italicized "*Thou*" and "*It*."

Key Linking the Sixty-One Sections of *I and Thou* with the German, Smith, and Kaufmann Pages

Section	German	Smith	Kaufmann
Part I			
§ 1	9	3	53
§ 2	9	3	53–54
§ 3	10	4	54
§ 4	10	4	54
§ 5	10–11	4	55
§ 6	11	5	55–56
§ 7	12	5	56
§ 8	12	6	56
§ 9	12–13	6	56–57
§ 10	13–14	7–8	57–59
§ 11	15–16	8–9	59–60
§ 12	16-17	9–10	60–61
§ 13	17–18	11	61
§ 14	18	11	62
§ 15	18–19	11–12	62–63
§ 16	19	12	63
§ 17	19–20	12–13	63–64
§ 18	20–21	13–14	64–65
§ 19	21–23	14–15	65–67
§ 20	23	15–16	67
§ 21	23-24	16	67–68
§ 22	24–25	16–18	68–69

Section	German	Smith	Kaufmann
§ 23	25–30	18–22	69–73
§ 24	30–31	22–23	73–75
§ 25	32	23–24	75
§ 26	32	24	75
§ 27	32–37	24–28	76–79
§ 28	37–40	28–31	80–82
§ 29	40–42	31–33	82–84
§ 30	42–44	33–34	84–85
Part II			
§ 31	47–49	37–39	87–89
§ 32	49–53	39–43	89–92
§ 33	53–57	43–46	92–95
§ 34	57–58	46	95–96
§ 35	58–62	47–51	96–100
§ 36	63–71	51–58	100–7
§ 37	71–74	58–61	107–10
§ 38	74–75	61	110–11
§ 39	75–79	61–65	111–15
§ 40	79–81	65–67	115–17
§ 41	81–84	67–69	117–19
§ 42	84–85	69–70	119–20
§ 43	85–87	70–72	120–22
Part III			
§ 44	91	75	123
§ 45	91–92	75–76	123–24
§ 46	92–94	76–78	124–26
§ 47	94–96	78–79	126–28
§ 48	96–97	79–81	128–29
§ 49	97–100	81–83	129–31
§ 50	100–13	83–95	131–43
§ 51	114–15	95–96	143–44
§ 52	115–18	96–99	144–48
§ 53	118–19	99–100	148
§ 54	119–20	100–1	148–49
§ 55	120–21	101–2	149–50
§ 56	122	102–3	151
§ 57	122–24	103–4	151–53
§ 58	124–26	104–6	153–55

Section	German	Smith	Kaufmann
§ 59	126–29	106–9	155–57
§ 60	129–32	109–12	157–60
§ 61	132–41	112–20	160–68

German text: Martin Buber. *Ich und Du*. Gütersloh: Gütersloher Verlagshaus, 1974.

Smith text: Martin Buber. *I and Thou*. Second edition. Translated by Ronald Gregor Smith. New York: Scribner's, 1958.

Kaufmann text: Martin Buber. *I and Thou*. Translated by Walter Kaufmann. New York: Scribner's, 1970.

Chronology—The Life and Work of Martin Buber

Decade	Political-Cultural History	Major Publications	Buber's Life	age
1878–1890	Vienna the capital of the Austro-Hungarian Empire 1867–1918		1878—Buber is born in Vienna on February 6	
			1881—Buber's mother abandons the family	3
			1881–92—Buber lives with his grandparents in Lvov	3–14
1890–1900			1892–96—Buber lives with his father in Bukovina	14–18
			1896–99—University years: Vienna, Leipzig, Zürich, Berlin	
			1898—Buber becomes a Zionist activist	
			1899—Buber meets Paula, they live together	
			1899—Buber meets Gustav Landauer	

Decade	Political-Cultural History	Major Publications	Buber's Life	age
1900–1910			1903—Buber breaks with Theodor Herzl	
		1904—Diss: Individuation in Cusa, Boehme	1904-08—Buber withdraws, intensively studies Hasidism	
			1904—Buber undergoes a spiritual awakening	26
			1904-17—Buber edits for Rütten & Loening	
			1905-06—Buber and his family sojourn in Florence	
		1906—*Tales of Rabbi Nachman*	1906—Buber family relocates to Berlin	
		1908—*Legends of the Baalshem*	1907—Paula formally converts to Judaism, they marry	
		1909—*Ecstatic Confessions*	1909-19—Buber gives a series of lectures in Prague	
1910-1920		1910—*Talks & Parables of Zhuangzi*	1914—Buber meets with William Hechler in May	
	1914—World War I begins July 28	1913—*Daniel*	1914—Buber meets with Mehe in July	
		1916—*Die jüdische Bewegung*	1916—Buber family moves to Heppenheim in April	
	1918—World War I ends November 11	1918—"My Way to Hasidism"	1916-24—Buber publishes monthly, *Der Jude*	41
	1919—Bavarian Soviet Republic	1919—"The Holy Way"	1919—Landauer is bludgeoned to death in May	
			1919-21—Buber withdraws a second time	

CHRONOLOGY—THE LIFE AND WORK OF MARTIN BUBER

Decade	Political-Cultural History	Major Publications	Buber's Life	age
1920–1930		1920—(ed) *Meister Eckhart's Writings*	1920—Buber meets with Franz Rosenzweig on December 4	
		1922—*Der grosse Maggid*	1922—Buber gives "Religion as Presence" lectures	45
		1923—*I and Thou*	1923–33—Buber lectures at University of Frankfurt	
		1926–1938—Translates Hebrew Bible: *Die Schrift*	1925—Buber and Rosenzweig begin translating Bible	
		1929—*Dialogue* [companion to *I and Thou*]	1929—Rosenzweig dies December 10	
1930–1940		1932—*The Kingdom of God*	1935—Nazis forbid Buber to teach publicly	
	1933—Nazis seize power in Germany	1936—"The Question to the Single One"	1938—Buber family moves to Jerusalem	
	1938—Nazis annex Austria	1937—*I and Thou* [Smith translation]	1938—Buber begins teaching at Hebrew University	
		1938—*What is Man?*	1939—Nazis seize Buber family lands in Poland	
1940–1950		1941—*Gog and Magog* [novel]		
		1942—*The Prophetic Faith*		
	1945—World War II ends on May 8	1945—*Moses*		
		1947—*Tales of the Hasidim*	1947—Buber's first visit to Europe after World War II	
	1948—Founding of the State of Israel			

Decade	Political-Cultural History	Major Publications	Buber's Life	age
1950–1960		1950—*Two Types of Faith* 1952—*Eclipse of God* 1954–62—Buber reworks Bible translation	1951–52—First visit to the US 1957—Second visit to the US 1958—Third visit to the US 1958—Paula dies in Venice on August 11	
1960–1965			1960–62—First president, Israel's Academy of Sciences 1965—Buber dies in Jerusalem on June 13	87

Chapter 1

Reopening *I and Thou*

> Reading is about how one opens the book.
> —Alexander Gelley

Martin Buber stands out as a spiritual thinker whose work has had a profound impact on twentieth-century thought. This impact came primarily through his breakthrough book, *Ich und Du*. This book, first published in December 1922, shortly before his forty-fifth birthday, became a seminal work, articulating an emerging philosophy of dialogue that helped shape an era of philosophical, theological, and religious thought.

The book became a kind of manifesto of what came to be known as Buber's philosophy of dialogue. It also became the foundation for a whole discourse of dialogue in communication theory, psychotherapy, and international diplomacy. It was quickly recognized as Buber's masterpiece; he considered it to be his most important work: "*I and Thou* stands at the beginning . . . everything else is only illustration and completion."[1]

It is one of a handful of works that stand out as modern classics because of the lasting value of its breakthrough insight. In 1937, fifteen years after its first publication, *Ich und Du* entered the English-speaking world as *I and Thou*. People continue to refer to it today to ground their understanding of its key distinction between *I-Thou* and *I-It*.

1. Decline: The Reception of *I and Thou* has Reduced Buber's Message to an *It*

Yet in the years since its first publication, a whole industry of commentary and appropriation has arisen in response to it. Its interpreters have worked

---

1. Buber, cited in Kohn and Weltsch, *Martin Buber*, 454.

assiduously to domesticate the book. In the process they have reduced it to being just another fragment in the mosaic of the existing culture; that is, they have reduced its contents to an "*It*." Buber's distinction between *I-Thou* and *I-It* and the book itself quickly became central icons of "the philosophy of dialogue." As a result, Buber's concerns that led to the book became flattened into a formula—"*I-Thou*" vs. "*I-It*"—and the philosophy of dialogue became packaged and commodified as an item in the twentieth-century marketplace of ideas. "*I-Thou*" became shorthand for practices of attentive, empathetic listening in conversation, the preferred alternative to treating one's interlocutor as merely another "*It*," a functional means to one's self-initiated ends.

Therefore, although Buber's thinking in *I and Thou* arose from a profound elementary experience, the language of this work quickly became reduced to a common currency so that "people began to talk of 'the *I-Thou* relationship' and 'the *I-Thou*'" as glibly as they might "talk of 'original sin' or 'the natural man,'" thus reducing Buber's thinking to "a few simple vivid concepts."[2] Buber himself wrote of the special period of the book's gestation and of the loss that would come about if he tampered with it once that period had passed.[3] At the heart of *I and Thou* Buber characterized this very kind of decline of entities in the realm of the human spirit, whether in the arts or in the human relation to the divine: "This is the exalted melancholy of our lot, that every *Thou* in our world must become an *It*."[4]

When commentators read *I and Thou* as the expression of Buber's mature thought, often they use it to divide his work into an early mystical phase completely divorced from a mature phase which they characterize as that of the true Buber, the exponent of dialogical philosophy. Prime among these interpreters is Paul Mendes-Flohr, the historian of modern German-Jewish intellectual culture. Mendes-Flohr divides Buber's thought into two intellectual phases, in which an about-face to the "dialogical" Buber is opposed to the immature stance of the "mystical" Buber.[5] Maurice Friedman, Buber's primary biographer, tends to concur with Mendes-Flohr. Yet his division of Buber's thinking into three parts—into mystical, existential, and dialogical phases—suggests a more fluid sense of Buber's intellectual development.

Buber himself interprets the development of his thinking by dividing it into his immature work before *I and Thou* and his mature work that

---

2. Kaufmann, "Buber's Religious Significance," 282–83.
3. Buber, "Replies to My Critics," 706.
4. Buber, *I and Thou*, §22a; see Buber, "Man and His Image-Work," 159–65.
5. Mendes-Flohr, *From Mysticism to Dialogue*.

emerged beginning with *I and Thou*. For Buber, the inescapable reality of World War I and its aftermath served as the catalyst of his mature thinking.[6] In a key piece of writing interpreting the development of his thinking titled "A Conversion," and dating to events in 1914, Buber emphasizes the discontinuity for which those events serve as a hinge.[7] Given Buber's use of the metaphor of conversion, it should be noted that conversion as transformation does not mean a complete upending of one's self-substance and conceptual tools. Rather, it marks a shift of orientation from one set of reference points to another, a shift that casts the contents of one's thinking and experiencing in a new light.

Buber takes up the discontinuity of his thinking again in his 1957 foreword to a collection of his essays.[8] We will consider this passage in detail in chapter 6 below, where we consider "The Teaching of the Tao" (1910), an essay presenting a number of Buber's core global spiritual insights, yet made controversial by his later comments in this foreword.[9]

Even though the younger Buber's emphasis on ecstasy gave way to the mature Buber's vision of life as the dialogical task of "hallowing the everyday," the latter still carries forward a mystical dimension. Buber apparently describes this mysticism of his maturity when he characterizes the spirituality of the Baal-Shem-Tov in his 1928 introduction to the great *zaddik*'s testament. It is

> a realistic and active mysticism, a mysticism for which the world is not an illusion from which man must turn away in order to reach true being, but the reality between God and him in which reciprocity manifests itself . . . . [This mysticism] preserves the immediacy of the relation, guards the concreteness of the absolute and demands the involvement of the whole being; one can . . . also call it religion for just the same reason. Its true English name is perhaps: presentness.[10]

It is indisputable that Buber's thinking evolved and was shaped in part by the historical events of his lifetime. Yet dividing a person's lifetime of thinking into phases, like dividing history into periods, imposes a structure from outside a person's actual lived experience and oversimplifies a complex process. It can obscure as much as it reveals. For an adequate interpretation, it is as important to see the continuities in a person's ways of thinking as it is

6. Buber, "Afterword," 214–16.
7. Buber, "Dialogue," 13–14.
8. Buber, "Foreword," xv–xvi.
9. Pages 116–45.
10. Buber, "Baal-Shem-Tov's Instruction," 180–81.

to see the discontinuities. From start to finish, the great nourishing ground of Buber's thinking, the aquifer of culture that he drew on, was his dual German-Jewish heritage.

The degree to which *I and Thou* is a Jewish work has been a matter of debate. One interpreter even wrote a book to advance the thesis that *I and Thou* is a thoroughly Jewish work.[11] Buber's interpreters have often responded to his dual heritage by dividing his works between his European-based "universal" writings and his Jewish-biblical writings. Yet as a German Jew, Buber drew on both parts of his dual heritage, both from the Judaism of Eastern Europe's Hasidic villages and from the philosophical discourse of the German-speaking universities. After pulling back from his early Zionist activism and undertaking a five-year period of intense immersion in Hasidic studies, Buber spent the years leading up to World War I contextualizing Judaism and defining its spirituality while developing his "universalistic," that is, nonsectarian, "philosophy of realization."[12] In this period both aspects of his work, his Judaism and his universalism, played off each other in a creative ferment that would be reframed and deepened by the traumas of the war years.

In a retrospective statement late in his life, Buber himself used the image of the threshold to stake out his position as liminal, as a stance existing in a space between the two cultures:

> I have sought, in a lifelong work, to introduce the Hasidic life-teaching to present-day Western man. It has often been suggested to me that I should liberate this teaching from its "confessional limitations," as people like to put it, and proclaim it as an unfettered teaching of mankind. Taking such a "universal" path would have been for me pure arbitrariness. In order to speak to the world what I have heard, I am not bound to step into the street. I may remain standing in the door of my ancestral house: here too the word that [the teaching] utters does not go astray.[13]

Buber's position is clear: he places his life work at the threshold between the "house" of his ancestral heritage and the "street" of global humanity. From this vantage, he can introduce Hasidic teaching to the modern world. Thus, we can imagine Buber occupying this liminal space, grounded in the riches

---

11. Breslauer, *Chrysalis of Religion*.

12. Buber continued giving his addresses on Judaism in Prague at the same time he was writing *Daniel: Dialogues on Realization*.

13. Buber, "Hasidism and Modern Man," 41–42; this version follows Avnon's reading in *Martin Buber*, 117.

of his tradition as his voice calls out to address us in our common humanity. In true dialogical fashion, he listens, he hears, and he speaks the word of this teaching to any and all who will listen.

In a summative essay published near the end of his life, Buber explains that his life's work is based on a central insight that is at once both Jewish and universal:

> Since about 1910 [my understanding of] the central truth of Judaism and Hasidism . . .—on this point, no doubt has touched me during the whole time—has its origin in the immovable central existence of values that in the history of the human spirit and in the uniqueness of every great religion has again and again given rise to those basic attitudes concerning the authentic way of man. Since having reached the maturity of this insight, I have not made use of a filter; I *became* a filter.[14]

To paraphrase Buber here, the central truth of Judaism has its origin in core values that have repeatedly given rise to the authentic way of human life, both throughout the history of the human spirit and in the particularities of every great religion. Buber's appeal to the image of the center here is at once both Jewish and universal. Following this passage he specifically discusses the teaching stories of Zen Buddhism, Sufism, and Franciscan Christianity alongside those of Hasidism as expressions of this "authentic way of man." This vision is at once both universal and particular, for it is built on the foundations of Judaism that are at the same time the foundations of authenticity in every great tradition. True to his notion of being, he did not manipulate the filter or nexus between this way and his audience—Martin Buber, the man himself, in his lived life, became that nexus. As he concluded, "I *became* a filter."

Regarding his stance within Judaism, Buber locates himself on the side of *Aggadah*, the side of stories and images and inspiration, as opposed to *Halakha*, the side of the law and its interpretation and application. He makes this clear in a passage in "The Holy Way" (1918) where, speaking across the divide between them, he addresses those on the side of *Halakha* whom he calls "the dogmatists of the law":

> Oh you who are safe and secure, you who take refuge behind the bulwark of the law in order to avoid looking into God's abyss! Yes, you have solid, well-trodden ground under your feet, whereas we hang suspended over the infinite deep, looking about us. Oh, you heirs and heirs of heirs who have but to exchange the ancient golden coins into crisp new bills, while we,

---

14. Buber, "Interpreting Hasidism," 221 (emphasis Buber's).

> lonely beggars, sit at the street corner and wait for the coming of the One who will help us. Yet we would not want to exchange our giddy insecurity and our untrammeled poverty for your confidence and your riches. . . . To you God is Being who revealed Himself once and never again. But to us He speaks out of the burning bush of the present, and out of the *Urim and Tummim* of our innermost hearts.[15]

In this dialogical passage Buber sets his spiritual thinking apart from that of the rabbis, the traditional systematic interpreters of Torah, identifying his position as an image-oriented, existential one. The foundational story of Moses' encounter with YHWH becomes existential through being lifted into the burning present, just as the discernment once practiced as divination by means of the *Urim* and *Tummim*, the ancient Hebrew oracle objects, now takes place in the immediacy of our innermost hearts.

In a late essay that confirms the meaning of Buber's *Aggadic* stance *vis à vis* the rabbis, he insists the purpose of the giving of the law on Mount Sinai was not to make the covenant people "good" but to lead them "beyond themselves into the sphere of the 'holy.' . . . Thus, every moral demand is set forth as one that shall raise the human people to the sphere . . . where the difference between the ethical and the religious is suspended in the breathing-space of the divine."[16] The absolute norm is actually relational; it is given to show the people how to "follow in His way," that is, how to live "before the face of the Absolute."[17]

In sum, Buber's complete enculturation in German academic life was part of his identity. Its counterpoint was his spiritual quickening, beginning with his early encounters with the Hasidim in their Central European villages and culminating in his spiritual initiation and his periods of intense study of Hasidic writings (1904–1909, 1919–1921). As a German-Jewish academic, Buber was perfectly equipped to bridge these two realms. Accordingly, the fact remains that one can choose to read *I and Thou* as a philosophical or sociological work and thus see it as the expression of a universal philosophy of dialogue. At the same time, one can choose to read the book as a theological work and thus see it as the expression of a Jewish religious philosophy.

I believe rather than dividing the development of Buber's thinking into contrasting periods or categorizing *I and Thou* as either Jewish or German, it may be more helpful to see his thinking in terms of its continuities and in

---

15. Buber, "Holy Way," 137.
16. Buber, "Religion and Ethics," 104.
17. Buber, "Religion and Ethics," 105.

relation to the crisis periods he underwent. Two crises stand out: first, his response to his rupture with Herzl in 1903, and second, his response to the murder of Landauer in 1919 at the climax of the war period. We will look closely at these two crises in chapter 2 below.[18]

2. The Nature of the Work—Three Readings

Taken together, three major readings of Buber suggest the profound range and depth of *I and Thou* as a multivalent testament to Buber's breakthrough. Each locates *I and Thou* in relation to a tradition, whether that of modern German social science, Taoism and the study of Taoism in the West, or Hasidism and the centrality of the *zaddik* figure in Hasidic tradition.

In one reading, Paul Mendes-Flohr locates *I and Thou* in the modern field of social science as the publication that inaugurated Buber's philosophy of dialogue. Mendes-Flohr found Buber's "'romantic discontent' with modernity" to be shared by many European intellectuals of Buber's generation and limned out an affinity between Buber's "celebration of I-Thou relations in the face of the insidious prevalence of I-It relationships and Tönnies' romantic conception of *Gemeinschaft* [community]—characterized by relations of mutual trust and care."[19] For Mendes-Flohr, therefore, Buber's philosophy of dialogue and his presentation of it in *I and Thou* amounts to "a grammar for the reconstruction of *Gemeinschaft*."[20]

In a second reading, Jonathan R. Herman presents *I and Thou* as a product of Buber's intense intercultural encounter with Chuang Tzu, "in a manner of speaking, the original dialogical philosopher some twenty-five hundred years ago."[21] Accordingly, Buber's formulation of the *I-Thou* relation is "a culturally transplanted accretion to Taoist mysticism, an organic growth of Chuang Tzu's philosophy in a new historical and spiritual context."[22] Herman's radical conclusion is that *I and Thou* can be read as the presentation of "a profound transformation of self before the text of *Chuang Tzu*."[23]

In *The Hebrew Humanism of Martin Buber*, first published in 1966, Grete Schaeder suggests a third reading when she puts the Hasidic tradition, and in particular the figure of the *zaddik*, at the core of Buber's dialogical vision. She points out that *Der Grosse Maggid* (*The Great Maggid*,

18. Pages 13–40.
19. Mendes-Flohr, *From Mysticism to Dialogue*, 9.
20. Mendes-Flohr, *From Mysticism to Dialogue*, 10.
21. Herman, *I and Tao*, 193.
22. Herman, *I and Tao*, 193.
23. Herman, *I and Tao*, 193.

to date still untranslated), first published in 1921, was the direct product of Buber's transitional years (1912–1919), and therefore it "occupies a central position among his works on Hasidism" and accordingly works as a kind of gloss on *I and Thou*.[24]

Beginning with Buber's spiritual awakening at the age of twenty-six when he received "the calling to proclaim [the "perfect man," the zaddik] to the world,"[25] Buber's life became more and more identified with the figure of the *zaddik*, the holy man who serves as leader of the Hasidic community. In "My Way to Hasidism" (1918), Buber traced the stages of "his gradual initiation into the being-tradition of the zaddik."[26] This initiation amounted to a "growing familiarity with the tradition of the zaddik from within."[27] This inner transformation lies at the core of *I and Thou*.

Schaeder sees Buber's change during the war years (1912–1919) not as a break with his earlier views but rather as a change in his emphasis "from the power of the zaddik to his service."[28] To Schaeder, Buber's misencounter with a young man who came to him for help in 1914 and its aftermath constituted a "shattering experience" which "finally placed Buber within the tradition of the zaddik."[29] Like the *zaddiks* who turned from "all esoteric knowledge, all ecstatic cleaving to God . . . to the daily involvement of [their] entire being, [their] being present for the sake of others," Buber turned "from realization that remained conceptual and literary to the presentness of the entire person for the sake of others."[30] The new element that emerged during this process, the "turning," marks Buber's existential shift from "the realm of thought to the 'realizing mode'"[31] Schaeder then quotes Robert Weltsch, who completed Buber's first biography, begun by Hans Kohn, to link Buber's identification with the *zaddik* figure to the emergence of his dialogical philosophy: "The origin of Buber's turning to dialogic thinking was at least partly in his immersion in the immediacy of Hasidic speech."[32]

Each of these three readings provides a very different context for understanding *I and Thou*, yet each in its own way presents a kind of

24. Schaeder, *Hebrew Humanism*, 300; Buber, "Autobiographical Fragments," 34; Buber's long preface to *Der grosse Maggid* was reprinted in part as "Spirit and Body of the Hasidic Movement," 113–49.

25. Buber, "My Way to Hasidism," 59.

26. Schaeder, *Hebrew Humanism*, 305.

27. Schaeder, *Hebrew Humanism*, 305.

28. Schaeder, *Hebrew Humanism*, 304.

29. Schaeder, *Hebrew Humanism*, 306.

30. Schaeder, *Hebrew Humanism*, 307.

31. Schaeder, *Hebrew Humanism*, 303.

32. Kohn, quoted in Schaeder, *Hebrew Humanism*, 306.

transformation as the dynamic core of the work. Transformation is the issue and the outcome of Buber's two periods of creative withdrawal, times of focusing inward which initiated him into the realm of the spirit and then later into the world of dialogue.

3. Recovery

If we work to approach Buber's book as *Thou*, we can see it as a testament not to a doctrine but to Buber's inner struggle which calls forth a new, deeper "I" within. For the book is much more than merely a philosophical statement—it is a white-hot distillation from the fire of Buber's imagination when it burned most brightly. It is the product of an intense process of intellectual struggle and marks Buber's breakthrough to a new level of resolution expressing this process, thereby functioning as a testament to Buber's life's work as a path-breaking thinker.

If *I and Thou* teaches us anything, it teaches us how to read—how to let the text before us become a *Thou* that confronts us so that "all talk about [the eternal *Thou*] is sacrificed to the voice that speaks to us."[33] Thus, if we take Buber as our teacher, we can develop an approach to the book that takes us beyond the packaged formulations to the nuances, the layers, the depth—the Presence—to which Buber points and invites us. *I and Thou* opens up the way to encounter "the Other"—and this includes text as well as person, cat, tree, or rock. Thus, *I and Thou* can teach us how to read *I and Thou*.

Steven Kepnes, in a study of Buber's thinking entitled *The Text as Thou*, uses the language of hermeneutics to trace how a text can become a *Thou*.[34] Yet Buber, using the compactness of poetic expression, presents just this transformative process within the heart of *I and Thou*. There he writes that we can learn to read a spiritual text (such as *I and Thou*) as "the word become life"—Buber's struggle and potentially ours—and "life become teaching"—an image of "how life is lived in the spirit, in the presence of *Thou*." As a testament to such a life lived in the spirit, the text stands before new readers "perpetually ready to become a *Thou* and thereby to open up the world of *Thou* once again—no, more than standing ready, it actually comes to them ever again and touches them" (§32h).

---

33. Kaufmann, "Buber's Religious Significance," 683.
34. Kepnes, *Text as Thou*, 19–78.

4. Overview of this Book

The chapters of this book amount to a series of forays into the world of Martin Buber and into the world presented to us by *I and Thou*. Taken together, these forays constitute a quest for understanding, which in dialogical terms is the quest for an adequate response to Buber's call to dialogue.

This introductory chapter has presented *I and Thou* as a spiritual treasure worthy of reclaiming from the cloud of familiarity that has reduced it to just another piece of cultural goods. Chapter 2 presents the two-part spiritual initiation of Martin Buber as the crucial development, the immediate context out of which *I and Thou* was created. The first was Buber's spiritual awakening in response to the testament of the founder of Hasidism when Buber was a young man. The second phase of this spiritual initiation took place when Buber was struck by the loss of his friend at mid-life. His struggle to come to terms with that loss resulted in the breakthrough expressed in *I and Thou*.

Chapter 3 lays out the nature of Buber's message: he felt compelled to proclaim it; at the same time, he had to develop unique, original means to do so. Buber's struggle with the depths in the face of his loss led him to develop these means, summed up in his metaphor of "pointing," and in the rhetoric he developed to express his message in his construction of *I and Thou*.

Chapter 4 presents *I and Thou* in the context of the relationships that punctuated Buber's life, some of which are chronicled in his "Autobiographical Fragments." The chapter begins with the early loss of his mother, which led to his concept of *Vergegnung*, "mismeeting," and his subsequent relationships with his paternal grandmother and his wife, Paula. His spiritual initiation through reading the *Testament of Rabbi Israel ben Eliezer*, the Baal-Shem-Tov, is linked to the influence of his paternal grandfather, Salomon Buber, a scholar of the Jewish *Haskalah*. Following on Buber's great mismeeting with his mother, subsequent mismeetings, such as with the Rev. William Hechler and then with a youth named Mehe, became occasions for Buber's further reflection and growth. Finally, Buber's friendships with Gustav Landauer and Franz Rosenzweig, both fellow German Jewish intellectuals, became the major remaining relationships that shaped and embodied his dialogical life.

Chapters 5 and 6 lay out some of the contexts of the book as they influenced the development and major motifs of Buber's thinking. First, chapter 5 explores the existential edge of Buber's thinking that intensified in the transitional years around World War I. This existential dimension developed along with his specifically Jewish thinking, so that his Judaism and his universalism dialectically reinforced each other. Buber's change of position on the role of *Erlebnis* (inner experience) in the spiritual life became a major pivot point in the development of his thinking. This and other changes in his thinking necessitate careful consideration of his controversial early treatise on Taoism in chapter 6 and of the concepts it developed: the teaching, the master, "the one thing needful," the Tao—all of which came into play in the evolution of Buber's understanding of Hasidic spirituality. These broad, free-ranging intellectual and cultural contexts all serve as reference points for the reading of *I and Thou*, and they all intersect in our construction of the meaning of the book.

Chapter 7, the exposition of part one of *I and Thou*, is informed by the metaphor of the journey. This metaphor helps us to see connections between Buber's spiritual initiation and what he points to when he takes us to his window to show us what he sees. As our guide on the journey, he begins by showing us two paths, two alternative opportunities of existence. The first is the dialogical fullness to which he beckons us, even though to some this realm appears to be a will-o'-the-wisp. The second is the world of *I-It*, the illusory, fractured, consuming stance that to Buber leads to ultimate destruction. Once these two loci are established, Buber traces the journey humanity has already taken from its beginnings in dialogical promise down to the present moment of our complicity with the *It*-world. He first traces this journey at the broad anthropological level, and then again at the level of individual psychospiritual development. Once he has brought us to the present moment, we are faced with a crisis: we must choose how to proceed on the journey, either to continue on the downward way or to radically change course—to turn so that we move toward the realization of our potential as dialogical beings. In this way part one leads us to this crisis.

Chapter 8 presents part two of *I and Thou* as Buber's exposition of the *agon* of human existence. Buber traces the decline of humanity into the depths of modern alienation, our being engulfed ever more deeply in the *It*-world. In the course of his exposition he begins to unfold the alternative to this destructive course as *teshuvah*, which is the turning to relating that opens the path to renewal and recovery. Buber then shows some of the dynamics of a life characterized by the chiaroscuro of continual *teshuvah*, turning toward the presence of *Thou* in each new circumstance. Once the horror and the hope offered by these two paths is laid out, we are presented with a dilemma designed to prompt us to make the existential choice between them: we must choose whether to continue down the path toward destruction or to turn toward relation in dialogue with others and with the eternal *Thou*.

Chapter 9 lays out part three of *I and Thou*, which focuses on the eternal *Thou* and on the nature of revelation. Part three begins with critiques of obstacles to the dialogical relation to the eternal *Thou*, both those created by modern spiritual thinkers—Schleiermacher, Otto, Scheler, and Kierkegaard—and those created by doctrines of absorption in Christian, Hindu, and Buddhist mystical traditions. Buber then revisits how the dialogical is manifested in nature, in interhuman existence, and in the realm of culture. *I and Thou* reaches a high point in Buber's exposition of his concept of revelation. For him revelation is that which first opened to him in his spiritual initiation and continues as an ongoing, universal reality. *I and Thou* as a whole serves as a manifesto of dialogical reality and it is this reality that Buber celebrates as an element of a larger proposed project: the revival of Hebrew Humanism.

Chapter 10 concludes this study of *I and Thou* by placing Buber's call to the dialogical life in our contemporary global context. Accordingly, it locates Buber between exile and homecoming, between tradition and modernity, and between East and West. It then sums up the dialogical core of his vision. Finally, it characterizes Buber's voice as a prophetic voice that allows us to properly see *I and Thou* as Buber's invitation to us to turn toward the other in a life of genuine dialogical existence within the shifting flux of our times.

Chapter 2

Buber's Spiritual Initiation

1. The Concept of Spiritual Initiation

BUBER'S SPIRITUAL INITIATION IS the master key for understanding *I and Thou*.[1] Initiation is particularly potent as a frame of reference for understanding Buber because it grounds the discourse of *I and Thou* in the concrete reality of Buber's development in relation to the Hasidic tradition, rather than allowing it to simply float untethered as a nebulous set of philosophical generalizations. It grounds the discourse in the specificity of Buber's humanity, his own inner struggle and development within his time, place, and circumstances. In *I and Thou*, Buber was not writing generalities to be reduced to platitudes; rather, he was presenting the process and outworking of his own hard-won spiritual development, his initiation into Hasidic spirituality in its white-hot immediacy.

The concept of initiation has been the subject of rich anthropological and psychological reflection for more than a century. Arnold Van Gennep's *Rites of Passage* (1909) highlights a three-part pattern that applies to the modern understanding of initiation: according to this pattern, the initiate separates from society, undergoes a period of inner struggle leading to transformation, and then returns to be reincorporated back into society. Joseph Henderson developed this model by positing an archetype of initiation and seeing the work of analytical psychotherapy as a kind of initiation as it facilitates an individual's move from one level of holistic self-understanding to another. In this work, the archetype of initiation gives the individual a framework, a reference point, and an impetus for the intentional work of

---

1. Grete Schaeder wrote of Buber's emergence as a spiritual teacher as "his gradual initiation into the being-tradition of the zaddik." See Schaeder, *Hebrew Humanism*, 300–9.

self-development.² Others, such as Arnold Toynbee and Henri Ellenberger, have written of this pattern of withdrawal, renewal, and return in terms that broaden our understanding of spiritual initiation and creative breakthrough, shedding further light on Buber's own process.

Toynbee has described the pattern of withdrawal and return, of a turn inward for a period of deep grappling with one's spiritual roots, followed by a shift back to the outer world and a sharing of the outcome of one's inner work, to explain how creative innovation becomes a major force that shapes the course of history.³ Toynbee presents the "withdrawal-and-return" of creative individuals as a "non-social experience" that functions as "the very source and fountain-head of creation in social affairs."⁴ He invokes a range of figures, including Moses and Confucius, even the hypothetical person who escapes from Plato's allegorical cave, as examples of this pattern. Through this process of withdrawal and return, such creative personalities are able to cut through the cake of custom and, by confronting the mere imitation of past paradigms and practices, to advance a society to a new configuration of meaning in facing its emerging issues. With this sketch of what appears to be a global phenomenon, Toynbee seems to be conceptualizing at the archetypal level, outlining the process as a kind of transcultural hero's journey.

Ellenberger brings the anthropological and the psychological discussions of initiation together in his historical study of the breakthroughs of Freud and Jung as the founders of depth psychology.⁵ Using language fitting for his clinical setting as a psychiatrist, Ellenberger developed this pattern of withdrawal, transformation, and return without reference to Van Gennep or Toynbee, calling it a "creative illness." Such "creative illnesses," according to Ellenberger's analysis, echo the primal reality of shamanic initiation into the spiritual world.⁶ Where Toynbee emphasized the cultural-historical impact of the phenomenon, Ellenberger, focusing on the inner development of Freud and Jung in particular in the gestation of their theories, builds on its transformative impact for the creative individual. The concept of creative illness is Ellenberger's answer to the question he poses: "Why could not illness disappear through a transformation into an idea?"⁷

---

2. Henderson, *Thresholds of Initiation*; see also Kirsch et al., *Initiation*.
3. Toynbee and Myers, *Study of History*, 3:248–77.
4. "Study of History," 130.
5. Ellenberger, *Discovery of the Unconscious*.
6. Ellenberger, "Maladie Créatrice," 330–32.
7. Ellenberger, "Maladie Créatrice," 329.

From the beginning, spiritual initiation has been practiced across the world's great religious traditions. For example, initiation as practiced during the early centuries of Christianity has a largely forgotten history, yet it is still carried forward in attenuated form in the process of the catechumenate, culminating in baptism as the rite of entry into the community of faith. Spiritual initiation is also carried forward today as the process of entering into diverse spiritual communities, whether Jewish, Christian, Muslim, Hindu, or Buddhist.

Spiritual initiation as a passing from one role in society to another begins with withdrawal from society, followed by a period of inner work and struggle on the part of the initiate that changes or transforms the initiate's inner, as well as outer, identity. The means of transformation may include an ordeal, a trial of the character of the initiate, as well as a shift within the person often characterized by the symbols of death and rebirth. This shift may be seen as a letting go, surrender, renunciation, or sacrifice of the initiate's self or self-understanding, and the entry into a new state of being. It is enacted in the transmission of spiritual power from the master to the initiate. Following the three-part pattern, the person who has undergone this transformation returns to society with a new sense of relation to the ultimate as well as a new sense of standing and vocation in the world.

Essentially, spiritual initiation is the participation in spiritual reality that is directly transmitted from a master to an initiate. Traditionally this has been brought about as the culmination of a period set apart for teaching and learning, a process of working toward spiritual realization to which both master and initiate commit themselves. The rite that often marks the culmination of this process is the initiate's entry into a new standing both in his inner life and in his relation to the spiritual community.

Mircea Eliade presents reading as a necessary modern mode of the initiatory process, because in this, as he puts it, "'crepuscular age' . . . we are condemned to learn about the life of the spirit and be awakened to it through books. Erudition is 'baptism by intellect.'"[8] Accordingly, "From the perspective of this new model of initiation, the transmission of secret doctrines no longer implies an unbroken chain of initiatory transmission; the sacred text may be forgotten over the centuries—all that is necessary is that it is rediscovered by a competent reader in order that its message becomes once again intelligible and present."[9]

In his 1957 postscript to *I and Thou*, Buber prescribes just such a practice of initiatory reading to his readers. Through repeated effort with

---

8. Eliade, quoted in Wasserstrom, *Religion after Religion*, 42.
9. Eliade, quoted in Wasserstrom, *Religion After Religion*, 41–42 (my translation).

a passage of spiritual writing, the reader moves from the distanciation of reading it as a text from another era to the immediacy of encounter in the present moment. The reader begins to hear the voice of the master in the text and to be present to its presence through the text. The central dynamism of this practice is *teshuvah*, "turning."[10] Buber gives specific instructions for this practice:

> Let [the reader] make present to himself one of the traditional sayings of a master ... and let him try, as best he can, to take and receive this saying with his ears—as if the speaker had said it in his presence, even spoken it to him. In addition, he must *turn* with his whole being toward the speaker, who is not at hand, of the saying, which is at hand. This means that he must adopt the attitude which I call the saying of *Thou* toward the one who is dead and yet living. If he succeeds—and of course his will and his effort are not sufficient for this, but he can undertake it again and again—he will hear a voice, perhaps only indistinctly at first, which is identical with the voice he hears coming to him through other genuine sayings of the same master. Now he will no longer be able to do what he did as long as he treated the saying as an object—that is, he will not be able to separate out of the saying any content or rhythm: he simply receives the indivisible wholeness of what is spoken.[11]

There are a few crucial elements of this practice: Buber bases it all on a "making present" of the master through his words, as did Eliade; the initiate's work in this making present involves *teshuvah*, "turning with one's whole being toward the speaker"; it involves "repeated effort": the receiver "tries, as best he can to take and receive this saying with his ears—as if the speaker had spoken it [directly] to him," addressed him with it; the receiver "simply receives" it in its "spokenness." There is a risk involved in this effortful practice, for the seeker may or may not succeed ("if he succeeds") at hearing the voice. Elsewhere, Buber makes clear that the working of "grace" is the decisive factor determining whether or not the transmission takes place.[12] This very practice was initiatory for Buber; as we shall see from his own testimony, early on he so read the testament of the great *zaddik* and founder of the Hasidic movement, the Baal-Shem-Tov, until he knew he

---

10. *Teshuvah*, which lies at the core of the vision of *I and Thou*, will be examined in detail in chapter 8 below, pages 194–208.

11. Buber, "Postscript," 128 (translation modified, emphasis added).

12. Buber, *I and Thou*, §14.

was directly addressed by the master. This awareness was the entrée to his original spiritual awakening.

Later, this approach to text became the foundation for the theory behind Buber's decades-long project of translating the Hebrew Bible into German, in which his goal was to convey the oral qualities of the original Hebrew in modern German. In "The How and Why of our Bible Translation," an essay written in 1938 during the transitional period of his flight from Nazi Germany and settlement in Israel, Buber amplified his sense of this very reading process.[13] Buber writes that he had an easy familiarity with the Hebrew Bible as a child. Then, exposure to German translations of Scripture during his youth and early adulthood alienated him from it for a number of years. A chance encounter with the Hebrew text got him back to reading it aloud, a practice through which he was freed from the text as writing and could take it as *miqra*, "calling," "what is spoken."[14] Through this practice, "the book was melting in the voice." Buber's goal as reader was "by an experiment risking one's entire being . . . to re-awaken the spoken word."[15] Buber quotes the words of Franz Rosenzweig to express the intended effect of this practice of reading:

> Everywhere the human traits [of Scripture] can, in the light of a lived day, become transparent, so that suddenly they are written for this particular human being into the center of his own heart, and the divinity in what has been humanly written is, for the duration of this heartbeat, as clear and certain as a voice calling in this moment into his heart and being heard.[16]

Thus, Buber testifies to the power of a particular practice of reading to bring about the dialogical moment, and to *teshuvah*, "turning," as its transformative essence, which had been the inner essence of his own initiation into spiritual life.

Buber's spiritual initiation consisted of two intense periods when he withdrew from his active public life to turn inward and focus on his reading of Hasidic material in quest of his spiritual roots. Each of these phases was precipitated by a significant personal loss. The first of these two periods, from 1903 to 1909 (when Buber was twenty-five to thirty-one years old), was precipitated by Buber's rupture with Theodor Herzl, the founder of modern political Zionism who was eighteen years his senior and an early mentor figure. The second period came more than a decade later at the end of World War

---

13. Buber, "How and Why," 205–19.
14. Buber, "How and Why," 208.
15. Buber, "How and Why," 213, 212.
16. Buber, "How and Why," 215, quoting Rosenzweig, "Scripture and Luther," 59.

I, extending from 1919 to 1922 (when he was aged forty-one to forty-four).[17] This latter period of withdrawal was precipitated by the brutal political murder of Gustav Landauer, Buber's close friend from his student days.

Buber characterized this second phase of withdrawal as the time at the end of his watershed years when "all the experiences of being that I had ... became present to me in growing measure as *one* great experience of faith."[18] Through this process he could "enter into an independent relationship with being."[19] The fully initiated Buber had come to the position which he characterized as that of the person who "stands in the dual basic attitude that is destined to him as a man: carrying being in his person, wishing to complete it, and ever-again going forth to meet worldly and above-worldly being over against him, wishing to be a helper to it. [In this stance,] being true to the being in which and before which I am placed is the one thing that is needful."[20]

2. Buber's First Period of Withdrawal: His Spiritual Initiation

Buber's involvement in the Zionist movement and his subsequent withdrawal from it led to his first transformative breakthrough. His accounts of these events show how Theodor Herzl became a foil for his initiation: Buber's relationship with Herzl, their disagreement which emerged over time, and their final parting of the ways spurred him toward his inner quest for his spiritual roots in Judaism. When Buber became active in the Zionist movement in 1898, he became a follower of Herzl. This involvement drew him back to his Jewish cultural roots after his having been immersed in secular academic life during his student years. In 1898–1899, Buber organized a Zionist student group in Leipzig, and in 1899–1900, another one in Berlin. Then, at the high point in their relationship, Herzl appointed him editor of the Zionist publication *Die Welt*. Yet differences between Buber's vision of Zionism and Herzl's became obvious to Buber when they reviewed a map of Palestine together in the spring of 1901.[21] Through Buber's work with Herzl as the leader of the Zionist movement, he saw Herzl both in public and up close. He came to know Herzl as a troubled man who had a narrow political focus and could not brook any disagreement within the movement. The

17. Buber, "Replies to My Critics," 689.
18. Buber, "Replies to My Critics," 689.
19. Buber, "Foreword," xv.
20. Buber, "Foreword," xvi.
21. Friedman, *Martin Buber's Life and Work*, 1:61–62.

rupture finally came when Herzl took autocratic action at the Sixth Zionist Congress in Basel in August 1903. Buber later wrote an account of their final meeting in which he could see that the man who had been his hero began to take on the proportions of a tragic figure.[22] At the Congress Buber made his decisive break with Herzl.[23]

In a letter Buber wrote to Paula during the Congress, he described his rupture with Herzl as a terrible shock. Then, he introduced the focus that characterized his next six years: "The shock I have experienced is perhaps the worst in my life. . . . One thought dominates me: *I want to bring absolute purity and greatness into my life at all costs.*"[24] Herzl's leadership and their falling out had made Buber aware of the difference between a leader and a teacher: "Unhappy, certainly, is the people that has no leader, but three times as unhappy is the people whose leader has no teaching."[25] Through these events Buber was primed: he had become ready for the ultimate teacher who, it turned out for him, was Yisroel ben Eliezer, known as the Baal-Shem-Tov, the eighteenth-century *zaddik* who founded the Hasidic movement.

In an essay entitled "On Modern Initiation into the Spiritual," Murray Stein discusses what he calls Buber's "spontaneous spiritual initiation."[26] He suggests Buber's recoil from Herzl led to his new openness which was necessary for his initiation because, as he put it, a positive outcome of such initiations "mainly depends on an inner openness to the 'call.' This readiness to receive the transcendent Other creatively may well increase amidst painful experiences of rupture and loss of significant others . . . . The crisis that ensues from such loss may open the way for the key transformation in a person's life."[27] For Stein, Buber is a paradigmatic case of loss leading to the openness that is necessary for spiritual initiation.

Buber returned home to Berlin from the Congress, withdrew from his public involvements, and turned inward in order to more deeply pursue his spiritual roots. As he later explained: "At twenty-six, I withdrew myself for five years from activity in the Zionist party, from writing articles and giving speeches, and retired into the stillness; I gathered, not without difficulty, the

---

22. Buber, "Autobiographical Fragments," 16–19.
23. Herzl died of heart disease less than a year after this event.
24. Martin Buber to Paula Winkler, August 25, 1903, in Buber, *Letters*, 100 (emphasis added).
25. Buber, in Friedman, *Martin Buber's Life and Work*, 1:73.
26. Stein, "On Modern Initiation," 96–99.
27. Stein, "On Modern Initiation," 99.

scattered, partly missing [Hasidic] literature, and I immersed myself in it, discovering mysterious land after mysterious land."[28]

This period of withdrawal and study was motivated by his desire to know Judaism with "the immediate knowing, the eye-to-eye knowing of the people in its creative primal hours."[29] Grete Schaeder observed that it was through these years of intensive focus and study that Buber "attained the personal 'reality' of a great Jewish teacher."[30]

Thus, it was that in 1904, when he was twenty-six, Buber underwent a spontaneous spiritual initiation. It was the most intense spiritual encounter of his life, his supreme meeting with the eternal *Thou*. He wrote an account of this event in 1918, confirming its continuing significance for him at the end of the war years.[31] According to this account, when he was a student and had been pulled in different directions by the lure of modern European culture, "I had neglected my Hebrew, which had become close to my heart as a boy."[32] Yet in his mid-twenties he returned to Hebrew afresh, penetrating to its deeper meaning, "which cannot be adequately translated, at least not into any Western language."[33] He spent time reading in Hebrew,

> at first again and again repelled by the brittle, awkward, unshapely material. Gradually overcoming this strangeness, I began discovering its character and seeing its essence with growing reverence. Then one day I opened the *Tzava'at Harivash*, [*The Testament of Rabbi Israel Baal-Shem*, a collection of the sayings of Israel ben Eliezer, the founder of Hasidism] and these words flashed out at me: "May he completely grasp the nature of intentness [German *Eifer*, Hebrew *zerizut*]. May he raise himself up from his sleep in intentness, for he has become set apart and has become another person and is worthy to create/testify [*zeugen*] and has taken on the quality of the Holy One, blessed be He, when He created [*erzeugte*] His world."[34]

When Buber read these words that day, it was as if the voice of the master was calling out to Buber as his listener, inviting him to a life of transformation.

Buber's spiritual initiation in this encounter begins with an invitation. As part of this invitation, the master names the characteristics of the

---

28. Buber, "My Way to Hasidism," 59–60.
29. Buber, "My Way to Hasidism," 58.
30. Schaeder, *Hebrew Humanism*, 238.
31. Buber, "My Way to Hasidism," 58.
32. Buber, "My Way to Hasidism," 58 (translation modified).
33. Buber, "My Way to Hasidism," 58 (translation modified).
34. Buber (my translation), quoting from Ba'al Shem Tov, *Tzva'at HaRivash* 1:20.

transformed life. In response to the master's call, the person becomes his intentness, embodying *teshuvah*, the turning of one's whole being to God. This moment is an awakening, a making holy, a "becoming another." In this transformation, he takes on the nature of the Creator at the moment of creation: he becomes "worthy to create" as a co-creator, a partner with God the Creator, and to testify to the Presence. Both the nature and the power of the person are taken to a new level.

Buber later featured this passage written by the Baal-Shem-Tov in his translation of selections from the *Testament* which he published under the title "The Baal-Shem-Tov's Instruction in Intercourse with God,"[35] and he added this note on *zerizut*, "fervor," or "the state of intentness": "[It] is the divine attribute of 'readiness,' the power to effect what is allotted to one who is created in the image of God. One awakens each morning ... in the pure state of likeness to God, and on each morning it is up to him, as it was in the primal time, whether he will realize or undercut what has been allotted to him."[36] This intentness, this "readiness to realize," means standing like a hair trigger before the immediate circumstances one is allotted as a being in the image of God. This is *teshuvah*.

In Buber's account of his initiatory experience, he next describes the impact of this call, how the Baal-Shem-Tov's words deeply engaged his whole being in that moment of reading:

> Then it was that, overwhelmed in that instant, I experienced the Hasidic soul. The primally Jewish came upon me, in the darkness of exile flowering to new conscious expression: the image of God in man, grasped as action, as becoming, as task. And this primal Jewish reality was a primal human reality, the substance of human religiosity. Judaism as religiosity, as "piety," as *Hasidut* opened to me then. The image out of my childhood, the memory of the *zaddik* and his community, rose up and illumined me: I understood the idea of the perfect man [*der vollkommene Mensch*, "the fully realized, whole person"]. And I became inwardly aware of the call to proclaim it to the world.[37]

With these words Buber explains what transpired with him: the transformation he was reading about widened to include him. In an instant he was overcome with the sense that his soul had become the Hasidic soul. His Jewish identity was quickened as that Hasidic soul, the primal essence

35. Buber, "Baal-Shem-Tov's Instruction," 185.
36. Buber, "Baal-Shem-Tov's Instruction," 214n1 (translation modified).
37. Buber, "My Way to Hasidism," 59 (my translation). Bracketed words present Dan Avnon's helpful amplifications of this passage (Avnon, *Martin Buber*, 82–83, 237n4).

of Judaism, came over him: he became conscious of the image of God in himself, not as an entity but as a dynamism: "as action, as becoming, as task." Yet, he sensed this reality as at once both Jewish and universal, as the quiddity that he calls "religiosity."[38] He uses a series of synonyms which build as intensifiers, the last shifting into Hebrew: *Hasidut*. At this point, as he entered into the transformation spoken of by the master, he saw into the meaning of a vivid memory that arose for him from his childhood visits to Hasidic villages, that of the *zaddik*, the spiritual leader, in the midst of his community, as the fully realized, whole person. Buber's sense of self was engulfed in the sense of Jewish spirituality that came over him. For him this reality became concrete in the figure of the *zaddik*. As a result, this visionary moment of encounter became his call to bear witness to the human encounter with the eternal *Thou* before the world.[39]

This account of Buber's spiritual initiation shows two things: first, that his tradition-specific spiritual grounding in Hasidism is at one with the universal in his spiritual experience,[40] and second, it shows that from the beginning he sensed an imperative to bear witness to the spiritual reality to which he at that moment first awakened.

The elements of this event became the seeds which bore fruit in his writing of *I and Thou* sixteen years later. First, he sensed himself as "created in the image of God" and he took this reality not as static ontology but as dynamic imperative—"as deed, as becoming, as task." At the same time, he saw this reality as at once both specific to Judaism, "primal Jewish reality," and universal, "a primal human reality, the substance of human religiousness." As he writes it, the vision of the *zaddik*, the Hasidic master, as perfected or completed human being (or "central man," the term Buber used in "The Teaching of the Tao"[41]) opened to him at that moment—both as a goal to attain and as a message to proclaim. Accordingly, this initiatory encounter set Buber on the path of the spiritual life; the imperative to proclaim to others the possibility of such an encounter would eventuate in the means to do so, the language that came to him to express it in *I and Thou*, in the years ahead. This event, and the language he used to express it in this account in 1918, is strongly echoed in a unique and striking first-person paragraph at the heart of *I and Thou*,[42] and

---

38. Buber later asserted the centrality of "religiosity" (*Religiosität*) in his 1913 lecture, "Jewish Religiosity," 79–94.

39. Avnon comments: "The perfect man" is the one "whose life is oriented to the task of translating 'the Adam as created in the image of Elohim' into actual, realized human life" (*Martin Buber*, 83).

40. Buber, "My Way to Hasidism," 58–60.

41. Buber, "Commentary," 72–73, 76–77. See chapter 6 below [x-ref].

42. Buber, *I and Thou*, §36c.

it became the foundation for a major passage expounding Buber's concept of revelation at the climax of the book.[43]

Maurice Friedman makes it clear: this account of his spiritual initiation as a Hasid marks "one of the truly decisive moments in Buber's life.... The combination of summons and sending, of revelation and mission, to which Buber later pointed in *I and Thou*, came for Buber as a single moment of meeting."[44] Buber surely has this moment in mind when he refers to the "supreme encounter" in *I and Thou*.[45] From this time onward this moment stands as the spiritual reference point for Buber on the path that becomes his life of faithfulness.

In this event, reading has become a catalyst of spiritual awakening for Buber, a transforming moment of revelation. In "The Foundation Stone" (1943), his essay on the founding of Hasidism, he returns to this pivotal moment and explains its dynamics, beginning with an exhortation to his readers to "listen" to the text: "Only listen to a saying such as this which made me, over forty years ago, into a Hasid of the Baal-Shem-Tov: 'He takes unto himself the quality of fervor....'" Buber continues, "Who before the Baal-Shem-Tov... has spoken to us thus? I say: to us, for this is what is decisive: he who has heard him feels as though his speech were addressed to him."[46] Here Buber returns to his own experience of initiation to underscore the power of a text to address its readers directly, just as when one person addresses another as *Thou*. He goes on to disavow that the master's teaching is "a teaching enclosed in itself, high above our existence, [transmitting] only a ray from the higher worlds, nor is it merely an instruction that shows our soul the path of ascent."[47] Instead, the teaching, as the master's voice coming by means of the text, "is a help for our concrete life—our life itself is uplifted through the speech directed to us if we listen to it. Reality calls forth reality; the reality of a man who has lived in intercourse [*Umgang*] with the reality of being in its fullness awakens the reality in us and helps us to live in intercourse with the reality of being in its fullness."[48] This is spiritual transmission, the passing of spiritual quickening from master to student.

This method of reading as turning to a text as *Thou* involves a kind of mental ascesis. In the introduction to his translation of selections from the *Testament of Rabbi Israel Baal-Shem*, Buber asserts, "If one really wishes to

---

43. Buber, *I and Thou*, §60.
44. Friedman, *Martin Buber's Life and Work*, 1:97.
45. Buber, *I and Thou*, §46e, §60a, §61h.
46. Buber, "Foundation Stone," 70–71.
47. Buber, "Foundation Stone," 71.
48. Buber, "Foundation Stone," 71.

take in the words of the Baal-Shem in this text, one will do well to forget all that one knows of history and all that one imagines one knows of mysticism and, reading, hearken to a human voice that speaks here and now to those who here and now read."[49] With these words Buber expresses the turn from *I-It* to *I-Thou*, the opening of oneself to a text as to a voice that addresses one as *Thou*.

In an essay titled "Dialogue," which Buber published in 1929 to clarify the central concepts of *I and Thou*, he presents a generic account of transformation that does not refer explicitly to his own initiation but yet applies to it. This passage refers to initiation, the initiation that breaks through stereotypes to open the initiate up to the immediacy of dialogue between the above and the below. This step in the process of initiation takes place as "that decisive hour of personal existence when we had to forget everything we imagined we knew of God, when we dared to keep nothing handed down or learned or self-contrived, no shred of knowledge, and were plunged into the night."[50] This forgetting, this letting go of perceptions, is the core of the stripping process the initiate must undergo in order to approach the Face. The plunge into the night is the death that is the prerequisite for the spiritual birth that follows. Buber's next words mark this rebirth and suggest the subject of consciousness that comes with it: "When we rise out of [the night] into the new life and there begin to receive the signs, what can we know of that which—of him who gives the signs?"[51] In the position of the twice-born we can know "only what we experience . . . from the signs themselves. If we name the speaker of this speech God, then it is always the God of a moment."[52] Yet through a process of learning to listen, to read, to interpret, "out of the givers of the signs, the speakers of the words in lived life, out of the moment Gods there arises for us with a single identity the Lord of the voice, the One."[53]

In this process of learning to perceive the One, each event of lived experience can come to be taken as another moment in the divine-human dialogue. Such perceiving became the substance of Buber's mature vision, which he voiced repeatedly as universally dialogical: "God speaks to man in the things and beings that He sends him in life; man answers through his actions

---

49. Buber, "Baal-Shem-Tov's Instruction," 181 (my translation).
50. Buber, "Dialogue," 14–15.
51. Buber, "Dialogue," 15.
52. Buber, "Dialogue," 15.
53. Buber, "Dialogue," 15.

in relation to just these things and beings."[54] Every moment of existence has become full as a divine message, calling for a full human response.

While Buber calls his spiritual encounter through reading a "conversion to Hasidism"—this encounter "made me . . . into a Hasid of the Baal-Shem-Tov"[55]—he makes clear, given his cultural orientation, he could not become a traditional Hasid:

> I knew from the beginning that Hasidism was not a teaching which was realized by its adherents in this or that measure, but a way of life, to which the teaching provided the indispensable commentary. But . . . I could not become a Hasid. It would have been an impermissible masquerading had I taken on the Hasidic manner of life—I who had a wholly other relation to Jewish tradition. . . . It was necessary, rather, to take into my own existence as much as I actually could of what had been truly exemplified for me there, that is to say, of the realization of that dialogue with being whose possibility my thought had shown me.[56]

As a result of the encounter, he fulfills his legacy in a new way. He reconstructs both the Hasidic tradition as it came down to him and his own life in response to it as a revelation of authentically relating to being.

As part of the overall transformation taking place in the young Buber, he continued to focus on the intense study of Hasidism for the next five years, thus building a foundation for his lifelong work as an interpreter and disseminator of the spiritual world of the Hasidim. In all of this work he was inspired by his image of the *zaddik* as the completed person, as the ideal holy human being, the true helper of mankind.

Thus, Buber's sense of the summons to proclaim the spiritual life that began with his spiritual initiation is what he carried through to fullness in his writing of *I and Thou*, as he attests in his postscript:

> When I drafted the first sketch of this book . . . I was impelled by an inward necessity. A vision which had come to me again and again since my youth, and which had been clouded over again and again, had now reached steady clarity. This clarity was so manifestly suprapersonal in its nature that I at once knew I had

---

54. Buber, "Spinoza," 94; see Buber's other references to human life as divine-human dialogue: "Dialogue between Heaven and Earth," 221; "Replies to My Critics," 710; "Prejudices of Youth," 51.

55. Buber, "Foundation Stone," 70.

56. Buber, "Hasidism and Modern Man," 24.

to bear witness to it. Some time after I had received the right word as well, and could write the book again in its final form.⁵⁷

Beginning then and continuing through his second period of withdrawal, Buber's vision came to steady clarity and he could present it in his book. The nature of this vision was such that "I knew at once that I had to bear witness to it." Elsewhere he confirms the direct connection between the "openings" that came to him and the imperative to bear witness to them: "Where I may draw out of primal depths that have opened to me as he who I am, I must acknowledge it."⁵⁸ Moreover, the work of proclaiming the vision became central to his existence: "I have . . . let myself be led . . . again and again by the task that has overcome me in the midst of life and will no longer let me go. [My] 'security' stands in the command of the task alone."⁵⁹

This first period of withdrawal was his spiritual initiation. It was the second, more profound, crisis of loss, the murder of Buber's friend Gustav Landauer, that brought his spiritual development to its full expression ten years later. This second period of withdrawal was a creative struggle or "illness," to use Ellenberger's word, through which Buber forged the tools that were adequate to express his spiritual vision.

3. Buber's Second Period of Withdrawal: His "Creative Illness"

Buber had his life-changing spiritual awakening in 1904 but, as we have seen, for a long time he lacked the language with which to carry out its mandate to bear witness to it in the world. His crisis of loss at the murder of Landauer and the resulting period of withdrawal completed his equipping for this task.

I and Thou is the product of an intense period in Buber's life, the period that capped off what Buber marked as the great watershed in his intellectual development. I see this period as the second, culminating phase in which Buber's initiation into Hasidic spirituality comes to fruition in his work as a witness to it. Writing in retrospect near the end of his life, Buber summed up the transformative experience of the years around the First World War as having a single impact, one to which he sensed he had a responsibility to bear witness:

---

57. Buber, "Postscript," 123.
58. Buber, "Replies to My Critics," 703.
59. Buber, "Replies to My Critics," 702.

> All the experiences of being that I had during the years 1912–1919 became present to me in growing measure as *one* great experience of faith. By this is meant an experience that transports a person in all his component parts, his capacity for thought certainly included, so that, all the doors springing open, the storm blows through all the chambers.... I have ... no doctrine ... to offer. I must only witness for that meeting in which all meetings with others are grounded....[60]

Like the biblical Job in his confrontation with the whirlwind, Buber withstood the stormy blast of those years, the blast that sifted his whole being. This blast reached its climax with the death of Landauer and the impact of this death on Buber. In the first years of grieving following his loss of Landauer, Buber was able to move through his initial shock and disorientation to a deeper sensitivity to dialogue and to his expression of it as a total orientation in *I and Thou*. As a result, it is to this blast and its aftermath, taken together as divine-human dialogue, that Buber subsequently stands as witness.

Buber's deep grief over the loss of Landauer and over the brutality of his murder precipitated his second period of withdrawal from May 1919 to early 1922. Landauer's brutal murder meant not only the loss of a friend and mentor in whom Buber had confided over the course of their twenty-year friendship; it was also a trauma that deeply impacted Buber because of his capacity to "imagine the real."[61] Stricken with grief, Buber turned inward. Three years later, he had produced *I and Thou*.

Friedman makes clear that *I and Thou* was forged in the white heat of Buber's response to Landauer's death: "We cannot understand the road to *I and Thou* adequately without examining the ... terrible events of [the war] period. The most important of these, not just for *I and Thou* but, one suspects, for the whole of Buber's life to come, was the murder of Gustav Landauer."[62] Buber's grief in response to this loss threw him into a period of creative withdrawal like that outlined by Toynbee and delineated by Ellenberger.

---

60. Buber, "Replies to My Critics," 689–90, 691 (emphasis his); compare this first-person account with Buber's more general statement on the impact of the unconditional in "Herut," 153: "The unconditional affects a person when he lets his whole being be gripped by it, be utterly shaken and transformed by it, and when he responds to it with his whole being..."

61. Buber and Rogers, "Dialogue between Martin Buber and Carl R. Rogers," 168; see also, Buber, "Elements of the Interhuman," 81.

62. Friedman, *Martin Buber's Life and Work*, 1:245. It is important to note that Friedman's claim and my thesis are exactly the same here. Yet Friedman does not develop the connections and implications of this trauma. These connections and implications are the core of my argument here.

The events of 1918 and 1919 which led to Landauer's demise were stark. Germany was in political chaos after being defeated in the war. The new revolutionary republic of Bavaria that arose at the end of the war was made very unstable by the in-fighting of political factions on the left, the socialists and the communists, who were vying for control. In November 1918, Landauer went to Munich to serve as an official in the new revolutionary republic. At Landauer's behest Buber went to Munich for a week the following February. There he participated in intense deliberations among the leftist factions in their struggle over the control of Bavaria.[63] Landauer served as a minister of state for a week that April. When the regime he served was then overthrown by the Communists, concerned friends across Germany arranged a safe exit from Bavaria for him, but at the last minute he refused to leave.

By May 7, Buber had not heard from Landauer. He wrote to their friend Fritz Mauthner expressing his deep concern about the lack of news from Landauer. At that point Buber had run out of hope. He and Paula stood ready to go to Meersberg to tend to Landauer's children if that would be helpful. He ended his letter by expressing his agitation over Landauer's perilous situation: "During these days and nights I myself have been wandering through *sheol*."[64] Buber's use of "Sheol," the biblical term for the realm of the dead, captures the intensity of his distress at the mere thought of a mishap to his friend Landauer.

It was later disclosed that when the German army swept in on May 1 and retook Bavaria, Landauer had been imprisoned and then brutally bludgeoned to death by right-wing troopers the next day in the prison courtyard.[65] He was forty-nine years old.

For many years Buber was silent about the brutal murder of his friend and the weight of grief that he bore in response to it. Friedman stresses the intense impact this loss had on Buber:

> Buber's response to the news of Landauer's death was probably, next to his 'conversion' and the early separation from his mother, the most important single event in his life. Yet this is one "autobiographical fragment" that Buber could not write. [Even forty years later] in 1960 he was still too close to this event to be able to write about it.[66]

---

63. Friedman, *Martin Buber's Life and Work*, 1:249.

64. Martin Buber to Fritz Mauthner, May 7, 1919, in Buber, *Letters*, 244 (translation modified).

65. Lunn, *Prophet of Community*, 338–39.

66. Friedman, *Martin Buber's Life and Work*, 1:257. Each of these three major events

Yet, there were moments in the long years after Landauer's death when Buber let his guard down. These moments suggest the immense power of this loss and its impact on Buber's life. Near the end of his life, he confided to Grete Schaeder the deep meaning of this loss for him: "I experienced his death as my own," revealing that this loss had a lifelong impact.[67]

In the spontaneity of a dialogue with Carl Rogers at the University of Michigan in 1957, Buber linked his loss of Landauer to the deepening of his sensitivities in interpersonal encounter. Rogers asked Buber, "How have you lived so deeply in interpersonal relationships and gained such an understanding of the human individual?" Buber responded:

> In 1918 I felt ... that I had been strongly influenced by ... the First World War ... because I could not resist what went on, and I was compelled ... to live it. ... You may call this *imagining the real*. ... This imagining [reached its climax in] a certain episode in May 1919 when a friend of mine, a great friend, a great man, was killed by the antirevolutionary soldiers in a very barbaric way, and now again once more—and this was the last time—I was compelled to imagine just this killing, but not in a [visual] way alone, but ... with my *body*. And this was the decisive moment, after which, after some days and nights in this state, I felt, 'Oh, something has been done to me.' And from then on, meetings with people, particularly with young people, became ... different. [From then] on, I had to give something more than just my inclination to exchange thoughts and feelings. ... I had to give the fruit of an experience.[68]

Here Buber links the brutality of the war with that of Landauer's murder. He makes clear that the impact of this violence was visceral—Buber "had to feel in his own body every blow that Landauer suffered in that courtyard where he was beaten to death."[69] He relates this experience to his concept

---

referred to by Friedman precipitated a crisis of loss for Buber. According to Buber's "Autobiographical Fragments," discussed in chapter 4 below, pages 55–59, 73–75, his mother's disappearance when he was a young child precipitated Buber's lifelong sense of a great void. This sense of abandonment at the loss of his mother shaped his turn to dialogue and relation as core values. His sense of guilt and his soul-searching in response to his mismeeting with the young Mehe and Mehe's subsequent death on the front at the beginning of the war led to his "conversion," his shift from an otherworldly to a this-worldly spirituality. And his loss of Landauer was the final blow in this series of losses. It provoked the process that led to *I and Thou*.

67. Buber, quoted in Schaeder, "Martin Buber," 24.

68. Buber and Rogers, "Dialogue between Martin Buber and Carl R. Rogers," 168 (emphasis Buber's).

69. Friedman, *Martin Buber's Life and Work*, 1:257.

of "imagining the real," which he elsewhere defined as "the capacity to hold before one's soul . . . what another man is at this very moment wishing, feeling, perceiving, thinking, and not as detached content but in his very reality, that is, as a living process in this man."[70] The image of a major loss as a "deep wounding" was more than a mere metaphor for Buber. Clearly the shock was something he had to live with for quite some time. The immediate kinetic impact of this active imagining of the violence inflicted on his closest friend led to a deepening of Buber's outlook. This experience of mortality intensified his sense of the deep urgency of each interpersonal encounter and of the great responsibility to address the other in terms of his meeting with destiny. This long-term effect is the product of Buber's work of mourning, distilled during his years of withdrawal following the murder.

Buber spoke at Landauer's memorial service shortly after the murder.[71] Later that year he gave a talk in Frankfurt called "Landauer and the Revolution" that concludes with an image of Landauer as crucified: "In a church in Brescia I saw a mural whose whole surface was covered with crucified men. The field of crosses stretched to the horizon, and on all of them hung men of all different shapes and faces. There it seemed to me was the true form of Jesus Christ. On one of those crosses I see Gustav Landauer hanging."[72] Buber is most likely referring to the painting entitled *I Martiri dell'Ararat* in the San Giovanni Evangelista Church that he may have encountered during his year-long sojourn in Italy in 1907–1908. Here his memory of the image of his friend overlaid this work of art. He fuses Landauer with Jesus, whom Buber regarded primarily as a prototypical Jew. Both Jesus and Landauer had been brutally killed for putting their values into action. When Buber spoke at the funeral of Landauer's daughter Charlotte, eight years later (in 1927), he referred to Landauer's murder. To him it was an image of the modern era as a low point in history. He connected her life to the "barely graspable meaning of Gustav Landauer's death. . . . a death in which the monstrous, sheerly apocalyptic horror, the inhumanity of our time has been delineated and portrayed."[73] Buber's intense characterization of Landauer's death as a symptom of the spiritual abasement of modernity, expressed here in a heartfelt aside, adds depth to his critique of modernity, a major element of the central section of *I and Thou*.

---

70. Buber, "Distance and Relation," 70.

71. This talk is excerpted in Friedman, *Martin Buber's Life and Work*, 1:247.

72. Buber, cited in Friedman, *Martin Buber's Life and Work*, 1:255; see also Buber, "Landauer und die Revolution."

73. Buber, cited in Friedman, *Martin Buber's Life and Work*, 1:256.

Buber later summed up the overall impact of his twenty years of friendship with Landauer in this imperative drawn from Landauer: "Thou shalt not hold thyself back" [*Du sollst dich nicht vorenthalten*].[74] Just as Landauer had not held himself back as a political activist, so Buber learned not to hold himself back in giving voice to his dialogical vision.

The utopian vision Buber and Landauer shared, and which evolved over the course of their friendship, found expression in "The Holy Way," an essay Buber wrote in 1918. He dedicated it to Landauer's memory when it was published after his death in 1919. He identified the audience for it in its subtitle: "A Word to the Jews and to the Nations." Here Buber writes that the task of Jews is to overcome the most fateful assimilation: "the assimilation to the Occidental dualism that sanctions the splitting of man's being into two realms, . . . the truth of the spirit and the reality of life."[75] The goal of this overcoming is "the realization of the Divine on earth . . . not within man but between man and man. . . . Though it does indeed have its beginning in the life of individual man, it is consummated only in the life of true community."[76] The development from individual to community expressed here is the distinctive mark of the vision of social renewal Buber had shared with his closest friend. This vision bore fruit in *I and Thou*, which Paul Mendes-Flohr characterized as primarily a book of social theory, "a grammar for the ethical regeneration of *Gemeinschaft* [community]."[77]

Grief theory confirms the authenticity of Buber's response to his loss. Following a loss, the bereaved person tends "to continue in an ongoing and meaningful, but intangible, relationship with the deceased individual."[78] This relationship "often remains a focal point for the rest of the survivor's lifetime."[79] This continuing bond requires a reworking of the relationship for the sake of maintaining a continuing sense of connection with the deceased loved one. Buber, true to this dynamic of grieving, had a lifelong response to Landauer's death. As we have seen, he first spoke at Landauer's memorial service and then at that of Landauer's daughter eight years later. He also took up his role as Landauer's literary executor and editor over the course of the ten years following Landauer's death, editing Landauer's works as well as his correspondence. These included Landauer's translation

---

74. Buber, quoted in Schaeder, "Martin Buber," 28. This imperative becomes a refrain in Buber, "What is to be Done?," 109–11.

75. Buber, "Holy Way," 108–9.

76. Buber, "Holy Way," 113.

77. Mendes-Flohr, *From Mysticism to Dialogue*, 19.

78. Winokuer and Harris, *Principles and Practice*, 31.

79. Winokuer and Harris, *Principles and Practice*, 34.

of *Meister Eckhart's Mystical Writings* into Modern German (1920), Landauer's *Man Becoming* (1921), and *Gustav Landauer: His Life in Letters* (1929). He also published and wrote works of his own—"The Holy Way" was dedicated to Landauer when it was published in late 1919, and *Paths in Utopia* (1947), inspired by Landauer, celebrated their shared socialist vision—in fidelity to the values he and Landauer shared. In all of these ways, Buber was a conscious bearer of Landauer's legacy.

Thus, Buber's work of mourning in the months and years following Landauer's death deepened his sense of the tragic in life and of the urgency, the call to decisiveness, and the destiny-shaping power of each present moment. His withdrawal and immersion in the study of Hasidism for a second time was a natural early response to the loss. It deepened his encounter with the nurturing and healing roots of his spiritual heritage that had precipitated his spiritual awakening in 1904. Given this grounding in his spiritual heritage, the road to recovery then opened up an intense period of breakthrough and productivity, and the result was the manuscript of *I and Thou* as a pivotal book, the testament to his own spiritual emergence, and the foundational expression of his mature philosophy of dialogue.

4. Buber's Experience and Ellenberger's Concept of Creative Illness

Buber's period of withdrawal in grief after Landauer's death remarkably epitomizes what Ellenberger describes as a "creative illness." To consider Buber's grief as an instance of Ellenberger's concept helps to form a more complete picture of the process that led to *I and Thou*.

Recalling Stein's observation that one's "readiness to receive the transcendent Other creatively may well increase amidst the painful experiences of rupture and loss,"[80] we can see how Buber's withdrawal following Landauer's death in 1919 occasioned the transformation that resulted in *I and Thou*.

Further, the use of Ellenberger's illness metaphor to characterize this culminating phase of Buber's inner development coheres with the nature of grief. Studies of loss and grief show that a person's grief is like an illness or "deep wound."[81] As we have seen, Buber's description of the initial impact of Landauer's death shows this wounding was for him a bodily reality that involved a deep inner wounding as well.[82] As with any wounding, there is a

---

80. Stein, "On Modern Initiation," 99.
81. Winokuer and Harris, *Principles and Practice*, 26.
82. Buber and Rogers, "Dialogue between Martin Buber and Carl R. Rogers," 168.

natural, sometimes lengthy healing process. Yet the person is forever changed by the wound: the scarring that remains permanently marks the survivor.

Buber's largely autobiographical essay, "Afterword: The History of the Dialogical Principle," links his own inner process with the broader historical context as he construes it.[83] The story he lays out in this short account includes a number of elements that connect his sense of his own process with Ellenberger's phenomenon of "creative illness." In what follows we will trace Buber's account in conjunction with Ellenberger's analysis.

According to Ellenberger, a period of creative withdrawal begins when an individual turns inward for an extended period of time to address and resolve a major issue that he has devoted himself to fathoming.[84] At that point, the person's inner search "can take the shape of depression, even neurosis."[85] In Buber's case, it was not depression or neurosis but grief which served to throw off his psychic equilibrium.

Buber states he withdrew for a period of time. He specifies he had a two-year period from late 1919 to late 1921 in which he did not work on anything but Hasidic material. This focus was part of a process of his "spiritual ascesis," as he called it, a narrowing down which he imposed on himself as part of his turn inward.[86] In his account Buber uses the Greek word *askēse* (the root of the word "asceticism"), originally meaning "training" or discipline, to explicitly denote this period as one of withdrawal and disciplined narrow focus for "spiritual purposes."

Ellenberger points out that an extended time of intense preoccupation with an idea or issue can lead up to and even precipitate a period of creative withdrawal.[87] In Buber's "History," he specifies the focus for this intense inner work, that which had become his lifelong issue: "the question of the possibility and reality of a dialogical relationship between the human being and God . . . of a free partnership in a conversation between heaven and earth whose speech in address and answer is the happening itself, the happening from above and the happening from below."[88] This vision first seized him in his youth, but by about 1904, the time of his original spiritual awakening, it became the supporting ground and driver of his thinking. In short, "This question became my innermost passion."[89] Buber continues his

83. Buber, "Afterword," 209–24.
84. Ellenberger, *Discovery of the Unconscious*, 447–48.
85. Ellenberger, *Discovery of the Unconscious*, 447.
86. Buber, "Afterword," 215.
87. Ellenberger, *Discovery of the Unconscious*, 447, 889.
88. Buber, "Afterword," 213.
89. Buber, "Afterword," 213 (translation mine).

story, laying out the steps that led to *I and Thou*. He states he mentioned "the myth of *I and Thou*" as early as the introduction to his second book on Hasidism, *The Legends of the Baal-Shem*, in 1907. From this early envisioning of *I and Thou*, his thinking led him "ever more seriously toward the common, that which is accessible to all."[90] That is, he was searching for the universal language that would present the truth of his encounter with the Presence so all could understand it. As he put it, "Since I have received no message which might be passed on . . . but only had the experiences and attained the insights, my communication had to be a philosophical one. It had to relate the unique and particular to the 'general,' to what is discoverable by every man in his own existence."[91] With these words, Buber denotes the existential dimension as the locus of his discourse.

Buber began to clarify his thinking through his work at interpreting Hasidism in the fall of 1919: when he was writing his book *The Great Maggid and His Followers*, he developed his key concept of "encounter."[92] After finishing this pivotal work on Hasidism, he wrote a rough first draft of *I and Thou*. He initially envisioned it as the first of five volumes laying out a systematic anthropology of religion—yet over time he shifted away from this larger project.[93]

In the postscript to *I and Thou* he makes clear how the vision he was grappling with when drafting *I and Thou* in late 1919 was the fruit of a long incubation and that this vision came with an impelling need to proclaim it: "When I sketched the first draft of this book, an inner necessity was driving me. A vision that pursued me from my youth onward, although at first repeatedly growing dim, had then attained a constant clarity. This vision was so blatantly of a transpersonal nature that I knew at once that I had to bear witness to it."[94] These words echo the original sense of mission that came to Buber at the time of his spiritual awakening: "And I became inwardly aware of the call to proclaim it to the world."[95] The time had come for him to realize that mission. Significantly, he uses the word "vision" and presents the vision as *pursuing* him over the decades.

According to grief theory, in the process of responding to loss, grieving individuals oscillate between a loss-oriented focus where acute, active

---

90. Buber, "Afterword," 214 (translation mine).
91. Buber, "Replies to My Critics," 689.
92. Buber, "Afterword," 215; see "Spirit and Body," 122–23.
93. Buber, "Nachwort," 308: this statement was omitted in the English translation; see "Afterword," 215.
94. Buber, "Postscript," 123 (translation mine).
95. Buber, "My Way to Hasidism," 59 (translation modified).

grieving is prominent, and a restoration-oriented focus where they take up the ongoing responsibilities of their everyday lives.[96] In Ellenberger's analysis, this pattern is a major characteristic of creative withdrawal as well. The person may adjust his life circumstances to allow the time for this withdrawal, which can last for up to three years or more. During this period the person may maintain his normal professional activity and family life while at the same time suffering from inner feelings of utter isolation, even abandonment—such as Buber did following the loss of Landauer.[97] At this time in his life, Buber did almost all of his work as a scholar and editor in the solitude of his study in his home in Heppenheim. Thus, his circumstances fostered the isolation which Ellenberger describes; yet at the same time, he continued to be engaged in the household with his wife Paula and their two children.

Winokuer and Harris characterize the impact of loss in a way that fits the phases of the process of creative illness, which Ellenberger outlines thusly:

> The trauma, shock, and anguish of a major loss assault an individual's fundamental assumptions about the world. Meaning-making can result through reinterpretation of the negative events as opportunities to learn . . . about one's self or life in general, as a means of helping others, or contributing to society in some way that is related to the experience that occurred.[98]

In relation to the survivor's world view, the loss is an "assault on an individual's fundamental assumptions." This challenge to one's basic assumptions necessitates the extremely difficult task of reworking one's inner models of reality. It precipitates a new departure in the person's search for meaning. According to Ellenberger, because the person struggles "in utter spiritual isolation and has the feeling that nobody can help him," he must plunge into the unknown and figure out how to fathom the depths of the issue that grips him. Yet, throughout this process, he relentlessly pursues the thread of his dominant concern.[99] In this way, Landauer's death, coming when it did, shook Buber until it provoked him to deepen and reorient his thinking. Buber worked through the abyss that opened under him with his loss until he was able to reinterpret and reconstruct the blow into his emerging sense of dialogical reality. Thus, he struggled with his loss until he could make the loss into his opportunity to learn, and he thereby developed a deeper sense

---

96. Winokuer and Harris, *Principles and Practice*, 29–32.
97. Ellenberger, *Discovery of the Unconscious*, 447–48.
98. Winokuer and Harris, *Principles and Practice*, 36.
99. Ellenberger, *Discovery of the Unconscious*, 889.

of the nature of dialogue. The drafting of *I and Thou* became the screen upon which he worked this out. In this way, the book became for him a means of helping others and contributing to society while giving him a new standing as a survivor of Landauer's death.

According to Ellenberger, when a grieving person breaks through to a new level of understanding, he may experience this as his "liberation from a long period of suffering"; however, it is also an illumination. He becomes possessed by a new idea which he regards as a revelation.[100] The breakthrough to a new level of insight becomes the turning point in the process and opens up a rapid return to involvement in the outer world.[101]

In late 1921, Buber struck up a friendship with Franz Rosenzweig, who was his equal as a German-Jewish thinker, although eight years his junior. Rosenzweig invited Buber to deliver a series of lectures at the Freies Jüdisches Lehrhaus, the Independent Jewish Study Center, in Frankfurt, and Buber surprised himself by accepting the opportunity. Accordingly, Buber prepared and delivered eight lectures on "Religion as Presence" in the winter of 1922. The focus and coherence required for this effort gave him the necessary language that catapulted him into composing the final version of *I and Thou* that spring. As Buber stated in the postscript to *I and Thou*, "Then when I achieved the appropriate language with which to express the vision, I was free to write it down in its final form."[102] Buber later claimed he was in an exalted state of mind when he wrote the final draft of *I and Thou*: "At that time I wrote what I wrote in an overpowering inspiration. And what such inspiration delivers to one, one may no longer change, not even for the sake of exactness."[103]

Ellenberger points out that because the person has undergone such an intense spiritual adventure, he "attributes a universal value to his own personal experience": he takes what he has learned through his own lived experience as a great truth of universal value which must be proclaimed to mankind.[104] Like others who have undergone a period of creative withdrawal, Buber claims that the principle of dialogue as ontological is universal by nature:

> In all ages, it has clearly been intuited that the reciprocal essential relation between two beings signifies a primal opening of Being. . . . And it has repeatedly been intuited that when one steps into essential reciprocity, the human being becomes

---

100. Ellenberger, "Maladie Créatrice," 330.
101. Ellenberger, *Discovery of the Unconscious*, 448, 889.
102. Buber, "Postscript," 123.
103. Buber, "Replies to My Critics," 706.
104. Ellenberger, *Discovery of the Unconscious*, 673; 450.

revealed as human. That is, in this way he arrives at the authentic participation in Being that lies in store for him and that therefore the saying of *Thou* by the *I* stands at the origin of all individual human becoming.[105]

Only when he was finishing the third and last part of *I and Thou* in the spring of 1922 was Buber able to break out of his constricted focus, his "ascesis of reading." It was then he began to see "the almost uncanny similarity with which people of the time, in spite of diverse styles and traditions, had set off on comparable quests for the buried treasure of dialogical thinking."[106] His own "quest for the buried treasure" had been his period of withdrawal and ascesis which made possible his book, *I and Thou*.

> I had known precursors such as Feuerbach and Kierkegaard in my student days . . . Now a growing number of people in the present generation surrounded me who to varying degrees were focused on the one thing that had ever more become my "life-theme." I already had a sense of this in the distinction between a reifying stance and a making present in *Daniel* in 1913 which was the seed of the distinction between *I-It* and *I-Thou* in *I and Thou*. The latter was no longer grounded in the realm of subjectivity but in "the between." This is the decisive transformation that came to fullness for a number of thinkers during the period around the First World War. The commonality of our thinking emerged out of the fundamental shift in the human situation of that era.[107]

With this account, Buber put his own transformation in the context of a larger, emerging cultural pattern, that brought about by the universal change of circumstances resulting from the First World War.

Ellenberger points out that, as a result of the person's solitary struggle to understand, he has won a boon to share with humanity: he "is convinced that he has gained access to a new spiritual world, or that he has attained a new spiritual truth . . . a universal truth . . . that he will reveal to the world."[108] In the process he has been transformed through a deep-reaching metamorphosis: he has become the person who can and must do the work of disseminating the gift, the key concept he has uncovered. The discovery becomes the basis of his life's work, for his task becomes to explain and

---

105. Buber, "Afterword," 209 (my translation).
106. Buber, "Afterword," 215–16 (my translation).
107. Buber, "Afterword," 216 (my translation).
108. Ellenberger, *Discovery of the Unconscious*, 889–90.

elaborate the vision that has come to him.[109] Like others who had undergone a period of creative withdrawal, Buber returned from it with a new book, *I and Thou*, and a new basis for his further work, the work of elaborating his hard-won vision. Some time after completing *I and Thou*, Buber stated "it became clear that much was needed to complete the picture but that that work had to find its own place and form. As a result, I wrote a number of shorter pieces" to clarify and develop the breakthrough vision expressed in *I and Thou*. "Later, further material, whether anthropological foundations or sociological consequences, came to me as well."[110]

In Ellenberger's history of the unconscious, Freud and Jung were two of those who, as the outcome of such a process, produced the breakthrough books that became the foundations of their mature theories and made possible their contributions to human advancement. As persons who have undergone a creative illness, an initiatory period without a guide or mentor, such persons become pathfinders who lay down means for others to pursue a similar path.[111]

For a time Buber considered making the following words the motto of *I and Thou*, showing that he saw the book as the distillation and manifesto of his newly emerging vision and as the foundation for his continuing work: "This book presents the beginning of **a way** that I intend to continue in and in which I intend to lead others."[112] Buber's use of the word "*Weg*," way or path, here emphasizes the existential, concrete, lived quality of his work as witness, as opposed to the abstractness of a merely conceptual-discursive philosophical construct.

Thus, Buber underwent a period of creative withdrawal, characterized by both the preoccupation and the breakthrough Ellenberger described, which was the process that led to *I and Thou*. For Buber, the death of his closest friend, Gustav Landauer, precipitated this period.

5. Spiritual Initiation: Transmission of the Transcendent

In a late summative statement Buber shows how he was ready to transmit his spiritual awakening to others at mid-life. He writes of his having "matured to a life" through the experiences of his watershed years.[113] This was the comple-

109. Ellenberger, *Discovery of the Unconscious*, 448–50, 673.
110. Buber, "Postscript," 123–24 (my translation).
111. Ellenberger, *Discovery of the Unconscious*, 890.
112. Buber, unpublished motto of *Ich und Du*, quoted in Horwitz, *Buber's Way*, 55.
113. Buber, "Replies to My Critics," 689.

tion of his initiation, his struggle to win "a relationship to being . . . only after long and diverse but always productive journeys through decisive personal experiences."[114] This process brought him "from a timeless and languageless sphere into the sphere of the moment," the immediacy of dialogical existence, "where between one tick of the clock and the next everything depends on perceiving what is being said to one, now, in one of the innumerable languages of life, and on answering in a language appropriate to the situation."[115] This completion of his transformation brought forward the imperative to proclaim it: "I stood under the duty to insert the framework of the decisive experiences that I had at that time [1914–1919] into the human inheritance of thought."[116] Buber continues: "[M]y communication . . . had to relate the unique and particular to the 'general,' to what is discoverable by every man in his own existence. . . . I am convinced that it happened not otherwise with all the philosophers loved and honored by me . . . after they had completed the transformation [i.e., their spiritual initiation]."[117] With these words Buber may have had Plato's famous passage on initiation in mind:

> There is no writing of mine about these matters, nor will there ever be. For this knowledge is not something that can be put into words like other studies. Acquaintance with it must come rather after a long-continued intercourse between teacher and student in joint pursuit of the subject, when, suddenly, like a blaze kindled by a leaping spark, it is born in the soul and at once nourishes itself.[118]

With Platonic initiation, as with Buber's, the knowledge that is transmitted cannot be expressed in words. This knowing comes through long, focused effort and it manifests itself as "a leaping spark" which goes from master to initiate, a flame which becomes self-sustaining in the soul of the initiate. In this regard, Buber's prescribed method of spiritual reading as the reader's entering into dialogue with a master was autobiographical.[119]

The grounds of Buber's initiation lay in the life of the Baal-Shem-Tov, the man whose life was a vehicle for transmitting the Hasidic teaching to his disciples so they could become his successors. Buber shows the moment

114. Buber, "How and Why," 211.
115. Buber, "How and Why," 211.
116. Buber, "Replies to My Critics," 689.
117. Buber, "Replies to My Critics," 689.
118. Plato, *Letters* 341c (translation modified). Friedman points out that this passage was a repeated reference point for Buber, *Martin Buber's Life and Work*, 1:311. See Buber, "Religion and Philosophy," 41.
119. Buber, "Postscript," 128.

of transmission in the story of Rabbi Susya and his disciples on a day between Rosh Hashanah and Yom Kippur: "He raised his eyes and heart to heaven and freed himself from all corporeal bonds. Looking at him awakened in one of the disciples the impulse to the turning, and the tears rushed down his face; and as from a burning ember the neighboring coals begin to glow, so the flame of the turning came over one man after another."[120] The transmission occurred when the *zaddik*'s gesture awakened a spontaneous impulse to *teshuvah*, turning, and the flame jumped from the master to his disciples. Buber comments: "It is this kind of influence that I have pointed to as that handing on of the mystery that is above words."[121]

According to Buber, the spiritual structure of the Hasidic movement "was founded upon the handing on of the kernel of the teaching from teacher to disciple, but not as if something not accessible to everyone was transmitted to him, but because in the atmosphere of the master, in the spontaneous working of his being, the inexpressible How descended swinging and creating."[122] This initiatory transmission of the depths of life in the spirit transcended words, yet words were Buber's medium. His challenge was to turn the verbal medium into a vehicle for that which transcends it. The rhetorical tools that he found, invented, and applied were thus necessarily based on indirect communication. These tools are summed up in two metaphors: "bearing witness" and "pointing." We now turn to consider Buber's task to transmit his spiritual awakening to others and his very deliberate use of these tools to fulfill it.

---

120. Buber, "Spirit and Body," 146.
121. Buber, "Spirit and Body," 147.
122. Buber, "Spirit and Body," 148.

Chapter 3

Buber's Task Finds its Rhetoric

1. Buber's Task: The Imperative to Bear Witness

To BEAR WITNESS IS to testify regarding an experience one has had. In Buber's case, to bear witness is to testify to the reality of spiritual encounter, of *I-Thou* encounter, as he first came to know it in his response to reading the testament of the Baal-Shem-Tov. Buber's testimony to encounter takes written form as his own testament, his public declaration expressing his life stance, his relation with what he has found to be of ultimate importance. The major components of this testament are Buber's "My Way to Hasidism" and his "History of the Dialogical Principle," which we have examined above,[1] and *I and Thou*.

Buber makes clear that bearing witness, not abstract thought or argument, is the relevant means of communicating what he is attempting to proclaim. The depths that have opened to him are rooted in the concreteness of his individual human existence.[2] Such realities are accessible only by direct apperception, not through abstract concepts, as he himself has stated: "Everything else may be discussed purely speculatively, but not our own existence.... Here witness is made."[3] The immediacy of one's own personal existence requires witness, not discursive reasoning. Accordingly, the reality of dialogical mutuality is not subject to proof but, rather, to bearing witness, and the witness one bears has its effect because it is dialogical, the expression of an *I* to a *Thou*. It calls the one to whom witness is borne to witness to it as his or her own immediate apperception: "The existence of mutuality between God and man cannot be proved, just as God's existence cannot be proved. Yet the one who dares to speak of it bears witness, and

---

1. Pages 20–22, 34–37.
2. Buber, "Replies to My Critics," 703.
3. Buber, "Interrogation of Martin Buber," 18.

calls forth the witness of the one to whom he speaks."[4] Thus, witness is dialogical, for the voice of the witness calls forth its interlocutor's inner attestation to the reality of which it speaks.

As Grete Schaeder points out, "It was not Buber's task to transmit a message like the prophets or to admonish and censure in God's name, but rather to demonstrate that the experience he had and the path he took were accessible to others. He therefore had to find a conceptual language to convey the subtle texture of his nonconceptual experience to make it comprehensible to others."[5] This search became Buber's rhetorical task.

Buber's purpose is to bear witness to an experience so that others can know that that experience is accessible: "To bear witness to an experience is my basic intention, but I am not primarily concerned with exhorting men; rather, with showing that experience to be one accessible to all in some measure, in some form."[6] In other words, as we have seen above, "Since I have received no message which might be passed on . . . but only had the experiences and attained the insights, my communication [had to relate] to what is discoverable by every man in his own existence."[7] His witness had to be such that it resonated with the inner life of his readers. Buber was clear about this in his "History of the Dialogical Principle": "From this exceptional sequence [of his own spiritual initiation], thought led me now, ever more seriously, to the common, to that which is accessible in the experience of all."[8] Buber's search for the common was a search for the language to express the foundations of spiritual life at the level of humanity, the foundations of spiritual existence that are true for *all* human beings, not just those who identify with a particular spiritual heritage or who participate in a particular community of faith.[9] Buber describes the definitive sense of the dialogical nature of his task in bearing witness with these words: "If I am asked where the mutuality is to be found . . . all that remains to me is indirect pointing to certain events in a human life, which can scarcely be described, which experience spirit as encounter; and in the end, when this indirect pointing is not enough, there is nothing left for me but to appeal, my reader, to *the witness of your own mysteries*—somewhat buried, perhaps, but yet still accessible."[10] Buber

---

4. Buber, "Postscript," 137.

5. Schaeder, *Hebrew Humanism*, 148.

6. Buber, "Interrogation of Martin Buber," 18.

7. Buber, "Replies to My Critics," 689; see page 34.

8. Buber, "Afterword," 214 (my translation).

9. See Buber, "What is Common to All," 89–109; Buber, "Replies to My Critics," 692–93, 701.

10. Buber, "Postscript," 127 (translation modified, emphasis mine); on Buber's appeal to the reader's own inner witness or attestation, see also Buber, *Good and Evil*,

expects his reader to test the truth of that to which he testifies by holding it up for comparison with the truth of the reader's own inner life. For Buber, attestation is of the most inward kind.

2. Indirect Communication: Buber's Means of Bearing Witness

Because the *I-Thou* relation is a primal lived reality, it is visible at a level other than that of the *I-It* world. Buber's foundational distinction between lived reality and rational-conceptual thought necessitates a special rhetoric. He makes this clear:

> When a man's speech wishes to show, to show forth reality, obscured reality, it will not be able to avoid the paradoxical expression insofar as it touches on the reality between us and God. The lived [and not the conceived] reality of encounter is not subject to the logic forged in three millennia; where the *complexio oppositorum* rules, the law of contradiction is silent.[11]

Pointing to the *I-Thou* encounter requires indirect communication. Thus, Buber had to use unusual rhetorical tools to make this otherwise unknowable reality present to his readers. Along with Kierkegaard, Buber "needed a form of rhetoric which would force people back onto their own resources, to take responsibility for their own existential choices, and to become who they are beyond their socially imposed identities."[12] Yet Buber does not take his rhetoric to the extreme that Kierkegaard did in order to challenge his readers to turn and face the transcendent. Where Kierkegaard used multiple pseudonyms and irony in his rhetoric of indirect communication, Buber uses pointing. His primary modes of bearing witness include such devices as a few carefully selected axiomatic formulations, multiple voices in dialogue within his text, and poetic-metaphorical imagery.

3. Buber's Invention: His Rhetoric of Pointing

Buber uses the metaphor of pointing to identify the nature of his rhetoric in testifying to concrete human existence and the *I-Thou* relation. Pointing is a kind of gesture made in dialogue through which the person doing the

---

117–18.

11. Buber, "Replies to My Critics," 701.
12. McDonald, "Søren Kierkegaard," para. 11.

pointing directs the attention of his interlocutor toward something present but unnoticed by the interlocutor. The metaphor of pointing thus sums up the rhetoric of Buber's witness: "That which there has been to say was . . . *a pointing*, an indication of reality."[13]

Buber claims, "I have no teaching. I only point to something. . . . I take him who listens to me by the hand and lead him to the window. I open the window and point to what is outside. I have no teaching, but I carry on a conversation."[14] At first glance, Buber's claim to have no teaching seems disingenuous. Yet it serves to highlight his rhetorical move of pointing. To take his auditor/reader and "lead him to the window" requires that the person follow Buber to Buber's window. This following already puts the person in a dialogical relation with Buber, who thereby "carries on a conversation" with him.

The outlook at the window is akin to what Paul Ricoeur calls the world before the text. Ricoeur's analysis helps to give us a sense of the dialogical dynamic here. A text presents a world, what Paul Ricoeur calls "the world of the text."[15] The reader who learns to approach the text as *Thou*, that is, with the stance of the *I* in the primary word *I-Thou*, appropriates, enters into, the world that the text presents as a proposed world. This proposed world "is not *behind* the text, as a hidden intention would be, but *in front of* it, as that which the work unfolds, discovers, reveals."[16] Ricoeur continues, expressing in his terms the dynamics of Buber's *I-Thou* encounter, *Begegnung*, in the act of reading: "Henceforth, to understand is *to understand oneself in front of the text*. It is not a question of imposing upon the text our finite capacity of understanding, but of exposing ourselves to the text and receiving from it an enlarged self, which would be the proposed existence corresponding in the most suitable way to the world proposed."[17] The instrument of pointing is the trope signifying Buber's discursive method. Like the finger of the person doing the pointing, what is at stake is not the instrument. The instrument only functions properly if it helps the interlocutor to see beyond it to what the person pointing intends for him to see. This seeing, when undertaken by the whole person, involves *teshuvah*, turning as an awakening, a transformation of all of the perspectives of the one who looks.

In an essay on Buber's ethics, Maurice Friedman confirms how *I-Thou* is self-authenticating, and therefore stands apart from linear discourse:

---

13. Buber, "Replies to My Critics," 701 (emphasis added).
14. Buber, "Replies to My Critics," 693.
15. Ricoeur, "Hermeneutical Function," 143.
16. Ricoeur, "Hermeneutical Function," 143 (emphasis his).
17. Ricoeur, "Hermeneutical Function," 143 (emphasis his).

> The ultimate check of the authenticity of an *I-Thou* relationship is the verification that comes in dialogue itself. Therefore, Buber does not *prove* his moral philosophy. Rather, he points to the concrete meeting . . . in which alone it can be tried and tested. Not only the context of ethics, but also the formal nature and basis of ethics itself must be validated, verified, and authenticated in "the lived concrete."[18]

In this way the interlocutor's confirmation from within becomes his part in *I-Thou* dialogue with Buber.

Buber presents pointing as the alternative to linear conceptual discourse for two major reasons. First, it best fits the nature of that to which Buber is referring, the *I-Thou* relation. To refer to it by means of any field of discourse is to reduce it to nonrelational categories. Second, the nature of the era in which Buber and his interlocutors live requires this indirect rhetoric. This era of modernity is the time of "the eclipse of God," in which the obviousness of *I-Thou* is overlooked, hidden in plain sight. "I have no teaching. I only point to something. I point to reality, *I point to something in reality that had not or had too little been seen.*"[19] Buber fully lays out this problem of modern spiritual obtuseness in his extended critique of modernity in part two of *I and Thou*.

Pointing, the act of communication by gesture, draws from the depths of Buber's Hasidic roots. It keeps his message in the realm of lived life, even through the use of conceptual abstractions. It puts us, as Buber's readers, in the position of the seeker who goes as a pilgrim and learns from the *zaddik* simply by watching how he laces his boots.[20] The *zaddik*, like Enoch the cosmic cobbler, stitches together heaven and earth simply by his living his life as a *zaddik*.[21]

4. Breakthroughs toward a Dialogical Rhetoric

Buber consistently sides against the abstractness of conceptual thought and for the unmediated concreteness of the transcendent encounter—yet this reality is by its nature riven with paradox: "I have, indeed, no doctrine of a primal ground (*Urgrund*) to offer. I must only witness for that meeting in which all meetings with others are grounded, and you cannot meet the

---

18. Friedman, "Bases of Buber's Ethics," 199.
19. Buber, "Replies to My Critics," 693 (emphasis added); see also 690, 692.
20. Buber, *Tales of the Hasidim*, 1:107.
21. Buber, "Foundation Stone," 84–85.

absolute."²² With these words Buber presents the paradox of grounding without ground, meeting without meeting. He takes this further by characterizing the clash of mental construct with unmediated experience as the great paradox: "The primary reality is the working of the Absolute on the human spirit. The human spirit stands up to the Overwhelming [*dem Übergewaltigen*] through the power of its gaze; thus the human spirit experiences the Absolute as the great Over-Against, as the *Thou* as such [*als das grosse Gegenüber, als das Du an sich*]."²³ When the absolute/unconditional works on the human spirit, it enters human experience ("the power of its gaze")—and thereby human discourse—as encounter with "the *Thou* as such" (*das Du an sich*, echoing Kant's *das Ding an sich*). Hasidic legend gave Buber one way to formulate this paradox—as myth: "the myth of *I* and *Thou*" is the myth "of the one calling out and the one being called out to, of the finite that enters into the infinite and of the infinite that requires the finite."²⁴ In this formulation we see Buber's breakthrough to his great innovation, the fruit of his struggle in the months following Landauer's death, the coming to the fore of the *I-Thou* relation in his thought as the foundation of his discourse, the axiom and framework of his witness.²⁵

A second breakthrough in Buber's months of struggle was his formulation of the duality of the primal words *I-Thou* and *I-It*, a formulation he intended to use not to build a comprehensive system but to point back to that which was overlooked, the concrete experience of his reader:

> The theme that was dictated to the thinker experiencing here was not suited to being developed into a comprehensive system. It was, in fact, concerned about the great presupposition for the beginning of philosophizing and its continuation, about the duality of the primal words. It was important to indicate this duality.²⁶

Buber, as "the thinker experiencing," received, discovered, as an imperative theme or philosophical foundation, the axiom of the duality of *I-Thou* and *I-It* as the two primal positions of concrete human experience. It is true Buber had made an early distinction between "orienting," a reifying stance, and "realizing," a making present, in *Daniel*;²⁷ yet now this

---

22. Buber, "Replies to My Critics," 691.

23. Buber, "Herut," 150 (my translation).

24. Buber, "Afterword," 214 (my translation); Buber is here quoting from his 1907 introduction in *Legend of the Baal-Shem*, 13.

25. Buber, "Replies to My Critics," 689.

26. Buber, "Replies to My Critics," 692.

27. Buber, *Daniel*, introduced on 64; developed throughout the second and third dialogues, 61–99.

distinction has evolved to become the foundational distinction between *I-It* and *I-Thou*. His breakthrough here was to identify the two stances as the primal word pairs *I-It* and *I-Thou* and to locate the *I-Thou* encounter no longer in the subject or subjectivity but in "the between."[28] Encounter was about neither subject nor object but rather about the between, the interface where subject meets subject.

The *I-Thou* encounter now stood out as the treasure which Buber had recovered for mankind: "Although it is the basic relationship in the life of each man with all existing being, it was barely paid attention to. It had to be pointed out; it has to be shown forth in the foundations of existence. A neglected, obscured, primal reality was to be made visible."[29] Buber makes clear that this theme, the primal reality of the concrete, relational nature of human existence, had become lost: "it was barely paid attention to," it was "neglected" and "obscured." In the face of this loss or forgetting, the imperative stood forth for Buber: "It had to be pointed out; it has to be shown forth in the foundations of existence; [it] was to be made visible." That is, "The thinking, the teaching had to be determined by the task of pointing. Only what was connected with the pointing to what was to be pointed to was admissible."[30] With these last words, "Only what was connected with the pointing to what was to be pointed to was admissible," Buber's rigorous self-discipline as a witness/thinker/writer stands out.

Buber's focus as a thinker and teacher, as one who was summoned to be a witness to life in the spirit and who then articulated the metaphor of pointing, sums up the nature of his life task. The metaphor of pointing conveys Buber's overall discourse as a witness, his rhetoric as one who must use indirect communication to get his readers to see what he knows—the reality they are overlooking thanks to their cultural blinders.

In a very telling confession, Buber revealed the nature of his task as a writer from another angle. In a letter to the American philosopher Malcolm Diamond, he wrote that he does not make a rational or historical argument for relational reality, for that would lead his readers astray. Rather, he seeks to directly address his reader as *Thou*, to engage the reader in the reality of which he speaks: "In the final analysis, I do not appeal . . . to historical prototypes . . . but to the actual and possible life of my reader. *The intention of my writings is really a wholly intimate dialogical one.*"[31]

28. Buber, "Afterword," 216.
29. Buber, "Replies to My Critics," 692–93.
30. Buber, "Replies to My Critics," 693.
31. Martin Buber to Malcolm Diamond, September 19, 1957, in Buber, *Briefwechsel aus sieben Jahrzehnten*, 3:438 (translation and emphasis mine). This letter is not included in the English edition, *Letters of Martin Buber*. See Buber, quoted in Friedman,

5. Buber's Rhetorical Tools Applied in *I and Thou*—An Overview

I and Thou showcases the range of Buber's gifts as a master rhetorician. As we have seen, Buber's struggle with his grief during that second dark, lonely period became his struggle to bring what he had undergone in his spiritual awakening to full expression. This act of testifying was the life task to which he had been called. During the months after Landauer's murder, the struggle to accomplish this task became inseparable from the gestation and bringing to light of his testament, *I and Thou*. Therefore, his struggle to find the means to express his awakening resulted in his creation of the rhetorical tools for this task and in their application in the writing of *I and Thou*. We now turn to consider how the task of witness that requires indirect communication and pointing became embodied in the vision and the rhetoric of *I and Thou*.

Using dialogical means to convey his message, Buber deftly moves among multiple voices in his discourse. Most commonly he lays down the foundations of his dialogical vision with the authoritative or vatic voice. Occasionally, a negating voice clarifies Buber's ideas by telling what they are not. From time to time, the voice of an interlocutor breaks in, graphically marked off from the rest of the text through the use of dashes, to advance the exposition through dialogical questions and comments. A debunking voice also arises to critique modernity's preoccupation with the *It*-world. At another point an ironic voice indirectly critiques the reductionistic stance of the modern *It*-world mentality. Throughout the text a poetic or literary voice uses metaphors and literary allusions to make a point. Finally, Buber's personal voice sounds forth, through which he presents his own experiences of dialogical reality.

Buber provides the straightforward exposition of definitions and distinctions in the authoritative or vatic voice, such as in the laying out of the differences between the *I-It* stance and the *I-Thou* stance at the beginning of *I and Thou* (§§1–9). Working in short declarative sentences, he successively offers the characteristics, workings, power, and limits of each stance. As part of this exposition he uses negations, statements showing how certain *ersatz* perceptions and concepts are not adequate for understanding his points. For example, at the outset he defines "primal words" by using a pattern of negation and affirmation: "not . . . but . . . " (§§1c, 2a, 2b). Occasionally, as in §10m, he uses questions to advance the exposition. And from time to time, as in §11, he uses the first-person pronoun. He also uses poetic images such as *Weltnetz* ("world grid," §11b) or *Himmelkreis*

Encounter, 335.

("firmament," §11b) and metaphors such as "chrysalis" and "butterfly" (§22c and again in §§53c and 61), and even negations (§11b) to reinforce the distinction between *I-It* and *I-Thou*.

In this exposition Buber plays with word roots such as *gegen-*, as in *Gegenwart* ("Presence") and *Gegenstand* ("object"). In §16a, then in §17a–d, he develops the differences between the two to elaborate his opening distinction between *I-Thou* and *I-It*. At times he takes a reproachful tone to expose the illusory use of the *It*-world (§18a–c). He appeals to the evolution of language (§23b–c), of perceptions, such as of the moon (§23d), of concepts such as *mana* (§23e), and even the sense of the self (§23f). To show that *I-Thou* is more primal, basic, and authentic than *I-It*, he traces the genealogy of the distinction, first in human cultural evolution (§§24–27b), and then in the development of the human individual from prenatal existence to maturity (§§27a–28c). The exposition builds to a climax at the end of part one: there Buber presents two stark alternatives—the reader must choose between the stance that operates in the *It*-world and the stance that opens to the world of *Thou* (§29b–c). In the last words of part one, Buber uses the vocative *Du*, an insistently dialogical device, to reach out and touch the reader intimately, to confront the reader with the decision at hand: "And in all seriousness of truth, <u>you</u>: without *It* a human being cannot live; but whoever lives only with *It* is not a human being" (§30g). Kaufmann translates Buber's *du* here as "listen." He notes that Buber uncharacteristically uses this *du* as the idiomatic German pronoun of address to express intimacy such as that between lovers or close friends.[32]

Buber explicitly incorporates dialogue into the text of *I and Thou* by inserting the interjections of a second voice, the voice of an anonymous interlocutor—a modern "everyman"—which is introduced by a dash at the beginning of a paragraph break, followed by a reply in Buber's voice, also set off with a dash. There are twelve such breaks in the text (§§13, 21, 25, 26, 35, 37, 39, 41, 42, 48, 50, and 57).[33] Following Wood's analysis, these interlocutor passages serve at times to break the logical sequence of ideas (§§21, 26, and 41), to initiate a new line of exposition (§§13, 35, 39, 41, 42, and 57), or to stimulate the further development of a theme in the course of its exposition (§§25, 37, 48, and 50).[34]

These explicitly dialogical moments serve to propel Buber's exposition forward. While they are anonymous, they work much like Daniel's explicitly named interlocutors in the five dialogues that comprise Buber's *Daniel*:

---

32. Kaufmann, *I and Thou*, 85n5.
33. Wood lists all but the one at §25; see Wood, *Martin Buber's Ontology*, 28.
34. Wood, *Martin Buber's Ontology*, 28.

Dialogues on Realization. They also echo the student auditors recorded in the transcript of his eight lectures on "Religion as Presence" at the Frankfurt Lehrhaus who freely asked questions during his lectures. Yet, there is more of a dramatic sense in *Daniel* where the interlocutors in the dialogues are named and each character introduces extradiegetic actions and events. In the Lehrhaus lectures, Buber responded to his auditors' questions with a spontaneity that shows him thinking out loud to formulate an understanding. By contrast, the interlocutor in *I and Thou* mostly asks questions that elicit further clarification or the explication of an issue in the unfolding exposition. Most often the interlocutor expresses a common-sense attitude or shows a common misunderstanding which Buber then corrects. Several of the interlocutors' twelve passages ask Buber to comment on the underside of his presentation, such as the question about hate as the underside of love (§21); or about early humanity's "hell" as opposed to its enjoyment of the *Thou* (§26); or the introduction of Napoleon as a person being consumed by his cause in contrast to Socrates, Goethe, and Jesus (§41).

Buber's responses to the interlocutor typically come in an authoritative, vatic voice that, as a rejoinder to the interlocutor, moves the exposition forward. In response to the longest of the interlocutor passages where a series of eight long questions amounts to a reaffirmation of the *It*-world as the *status quo* (§35a), Buber retorts, calling the questioner a *Redender*, a "windbag" (§35a). He then proceeds to offer his counterpoint, much as he asks his readers to do with their own choices and lives. By contrast, when the next question assumes the constancy of the common-sense I, Buber's exposition of the counterpoint is more gentle: "Let us test, let us test ourselves, to see . . ." (§39b). Buber can even respond autobiographically, as he does in response to a question about mystical discourse as testimony to oneness: "I do not know of a single kind, but of two kinds of events in which duality is no longer perceived. In their discourse mystics often mix them up, as I too once did" (§50g). Thus, Buber's shifts in his use of the interlocutor allow his book to be explicitly dialogical, dramatizing the issues at stake with a sometimes avuncular, sometimes admonishing, but always vatic tone. Buber's use of this voice tends to turn the text into a teaching dialogue.

Buber uses an oppositional, debunking voice when he critiques elements of a wide range of positions in order to clear space for the authentic reality of true dialogue. The longest section of the text critiques doctrines of mystical absorption across three major traditions: Hinduism, Christianity, and Buddhism (§50). Late in *I and Thou*, Buber critiques modern thinkers whose sympathies are close to his own but whose ideas must be distinguished from the radical dialogical vision of *I and Thou*: Max Scheler (§58) and Søren Kierkegaard (§59).

The expository voice reaches its most ironic pitch when it presents the opposing perspective as its own: one passage at the end of part one considers the realm of *Thou* from the point of view of a person who is fully at home in the *It*-world (§30e–f). For such a person, starting from the benefits and comforts of the *It*-world:

> *Thou* moments appear as strange lyric-dramatic episodes with a seductive spell, but dangerous in tearing to the extreme, loosening the proven nexus, leaving behind more questions than satisfaction, convulsing one's sense of certainty—thus uncanny, dispensable. Why not . . . why not . . . why not . . . ? . . . One simply needs to fill each moment with experiencing and using and it ceases to burn (§30e–f).

Buber seems relentless in driving home this point of view—until the last sentence turns it on its head: "Without *It* a human being cannot live; but whoever lives with *It* alone is not human" (§30g).

At times, Buber uses poetic metaphors to convey the spontaneous inbreaking qualities of the presence of the *Thou*, such as when he refers to the Presence as sunlight catching on a tree branch (§50j). He also describes the realized state of living in the Presence as a steady moon on a cloudless night (§61h). Similarly, he uses poetic imagery to sketch the figure of the atheist at his garret window lifting his heart with longing in the darkness to the unknown *Thou* (§59a). Other metaphors he uses include the traces of realized lives that fade to fragmentary images in the minds of their successors (§32h) and the realizing person who in the swirl of his living speech rises up to the starry heavens of the spirit (§32h). He also refers to moments of silent grounding which are intuited as the flight of a musical note in a vast cosmic musical score (§28d). He invokes our global poetic heritage when he quotes from a Hölderlin poem (§36i), alludes to a handful of Goethe's short lyrics (§40g), refers to a version of a Chinese poem (§32f), recounts classic Hindu tales (§§38 and 50l), and discusses Dante's *Paradiso* as poetry (§52h).

In this text, which is primarily a testament to the transformation of his own perspectives, from his spiritual awakening to his being brought to a steady stance in the *I-Thou* relation, it is no accident that Buber implicitly and at times explicitly alludes to his own experiences, experiences he explicitly presents to his readers in first-person narratives in his other writings. Thus, §36 draws heavily on Buber's own experience of his spiritual initiation in 1904, even making extensive use of the first-person pronoun, and §60 also directly parallels his earlier account of his spiritual initiation.[35] Elsewhere, Buber refers to his experience with his cat (§52a–b) and with

---

35. Buber, "My Way to Hasidism," 59–60.

a chunk of mica where he uses the vocative to evoke its presence (§52f).[36] In addition, Wood reads Buber's gruesome account of nightmarish night thoughts (§43) as autobiographical.[37] In addition to these passages and his rejoinders to the interlocutor, mentioned above,[38] there are also other, more implicit autobiographical references in *I and Thou*.

For example, in one section Buber draws from his own reflections, using the first-person pronoun to conduct a thought experiment around the perception of a tree (§10). First he sketches a long series of mental actions regarding the tree from the *I-It* stance (§10a–f). Then he describes how the tree exists from the *I-Thou* stance (§10g–l, also §24d). He concludes this thought experiment with a dialogical series of questions and answers to bring home the nature of the *I-Thou* stance (§10m). In the next section, he extends this exposition to taking up one's stance in relating to another human being as *Thou* (§11a–g).

The most dramatic shifts of voice occur for climactic effect. As we have seen, at the end of part one the outlook of a partisan of the *It*-world is expressed (§30e). Here the realm of *Thou* can seem uncanny, even threatening to a person determined to be at home in the *It*-world. At the end of part two the stakes are raised, for such an *It*-bound person's fate is shown to be even more terrible. In this case, such a person, introduced again as second person, as *Du*, "you,"—"As when *you*, in darkest midnight, lie tormented by a waking dream . . . and *you* think in the midst of *your* anguish . . ." (§43a, emphasis added)—is thrown into deepest soul-searching and consciously takes up the nightmare of having to make a choice between two enormous false alternatives (§43). Thus, these culminations of both part one and part two are designed to throw readers off balance. They create a sense of vertigo at the idea of the *It*-world, designed to nudge readers to take the risk and turn to *Thou*, the decision which the culmination of part three and the book as a whole call for.

The overall structure of *I and Thou* in itself is a mark of Buber's rhetoric. Robert Wood makes the observation that the three parts of *I and Thou* into which Buber divided it fit the pattern of a symphony in three movements.[39] In the classic symphony structure, the first movement establishes the motifs that run throughout the whole work. The second movement, by contrast, presents a complication and a struggle that must be worked to resolution; and the third movement takes the theme and complication given

---

36. This passage is a reworking of an account in *Daniel*, 140–41.
37. Wood, *Martin Buber's Ontology*, 85.
38. Pages 48–50.
39. Wood, *Martin Buber's Ontology*, 29, 32.

and developed in the first two movements and brings them to a new level and resolution. Similarly, *I and Thou* begins with Buber's classic exposition of the differences between the *I-It* stance and the *I-Thou* stance. The second part is the agonistic movement in which Buber lays out the problem of modernity as excessively *It*-oriented, the struggle necessary to overcome the *I-It* stance, and the transformation that is achieved through the dynamic of *teshuvah*, turning. The third part develops the human sense of the divine, rejects *ersatz* approaches along the way, and concludes with a serene vision of the divine-human dialogical process.

Buber's rhetorical power is dazzling. Yet, rather than distracting his readers, it underscores his purpose: it displays the power and authenticity of the dialogical life, even as it invites us to participate in it.

Chapter 4

Buber's Life in Dialogue

Full mutuality is not inherent in human living together.
It is a grace for which one must always be ready and
which one receives without any guarantees.

—Postscript, *I and Thou* #5[1]

1. Introduction

It is natural to expect a particularly strong resonance between Buber's own experiences of encounter and what he teaches about the nature and meaning of the *I-Thou* encounter. In fact, the emergence of Buber's philosophy of dialogue is inseparable from his own experience of dialogue, his own meetings and mismeetings. Buber's concrete lived experience, his encounters with others and with the world and his reflections on them, were the fertile soil out of which his thinking emerged. Consequently, the substance of *I and Thou* becomes clearer when we see it in relation to these concrete events of Buber's own life story.

Buber points out that a master's teaching is not a matter of mere doctrines or precepts, but rather of the *quidditas*, the *how* of the master's lived life. The reality of this insight is summed up in the testimony of a disciple of the Baal-Shem-Tov, Rabbi Leib the Wanderer: "I did not go to the master in order to hear Torah from him, but to see how he unlaces his boots and laces them up again.[2]

Buber distills the *how* of the master's life down to dialogical presence: "The presence of a person who is simply and immediately present" is the

---

1. Buber, "Postscript," 131 (my translation).
2. Buber, *Tales of the Hasidim*, 1:107; see also 1:169: The master is one who "becomes so entirely a Torah that one can learn from his habits and his motions and his motionless clinging to God."

essential element that makes one's life itself into "the teaching," into what is worthy and naturally transmissible.

> More powerful and more holy than all writing is the presence of a person who is simply and immediately present.... Those who are transformed through his teaching are forthwith, one and all, apostles—even though they do not repeat anything of it, nor even proclaim the name of the teacher; as transformed men, they are apostles through their existence, and whatever they do is done in apostleship, through the essence of his teaching which they express therein. In the life of his friends, in the life of all who meet him, and thus to distant generations, immediacy is transmitted.[3]

This concreteness of the master's life has value for understanding Buber's own teaching as well. We gain access to the *how* of Buber's lived life by looking at his encounters, some of which he presented and some of which he suppressed.

Buber makes a foundational distinction between full, authentic dialogue and mere inter-human interaction that is qualitatively less than this. To address one's "other" as *Thou* is to step into direct relation to the other with one's whole being; this stepping into engagement involves self-disclosure, receptivity, vulnerability, and action. It means taking the risk of opening oneself to change by the other and thereby realizing one's innate potential in a new way. By contrast, to bring less than one's whole self and thus not to risk oneself in the interchange with another person is to miss the opportunity for full encounter. Buber names such missed opportunities *Vergegnungen*, "mismeetings." Buber's own life included both meetings and mismeetings, and the latter themselves can have value, for the failures, mistakes, shocks, and losses in a life can become occasions for transformation and creativity, as we saw with Buber's loss of his good friend Gustav Landauer. Buber's encounters and relationships, his meetings and mismeetings, and his soul-searching and reflection in response to them, give us glimpses of his inner development.

Buber declined to write a fully developed autobiography—he claimed he lacked "the kind of memory necessary" for this.[4] Yet, near the end of his life he did put together a collection of twenty short vignettes for the summative volume *The Philosophy of Martin Buber* (1967). Half of these had originally been written over the years as *exempla*, as narratives illustrating various

---

3. Buber, "Productivity and Existence," 7 (translation modified).
4. Buber, "Autobiographical Fragments," 3.

points in his philosophical essays.⁵ For the anthology he selected these key stories as "moments that have exercised a decisive influence on the nature and direction of my thinking."⁶ With this statement he made explicit the direct relationship between his concrete experience and his ideas.

It is no accident that when these autobiographical fragments were later published separately, they were entitled *Meetings*, for they focus on key relational moments in Buber's life. Many of them became instructive because they were mismeetings that spurred Buber to creative dialogical reflection and inner transformation. Accordingly, Maurice Friedman has treated these short accounts as teaching stories, inviting readers to close consideration of these autobiographical fragments:

> These "events and meetings" are in the fullest sense of the term "teaching" and perhaps, in the end, the most real teaching that Martin Buber has left us.... Some of the most profound of Buber's hard-won insights are contained within them like a vein of gold in marble. They await extraction by those who wrestle and contend with them until they are compelled to divulge their secret.⁷

Buber's autobiographical writings extend beyond those collected for the anthology and include other moments of his experience, whether explicitly identified as such or not. They include his accounts of the development of his thinking, such as "My Way to Hasidism,"⁸ the account of a recurring dream in "Dialogue,"⁹ and the largely autobiographical narrative, "The History of the Dialogical Principle."¹⁰ In addition, Buber's correspondence provides rich documentation of the lived concrete quality of his relationships. Letters, written to address an individual person at a particular moment, complement Buber's more formal autobiographical statements, given their more *ad hoc*, private, and interpersonal nature. Accordingly, we will focus on biographical sources as well as some of Buber's autobiographical statements and a portion of his correspondence. We will see how his own concrete experience of meetings and mismeetings and his reflections in response to such moments come into play in shaping his understanding and exposition of dialogical reality.

This chapter begins by examining how Buber's dialogical experience developed out of the soil of his early familial relationships: his early loss of

5. Buber, "Autobiographical Fragments," 3–39.
6. Buber, "Autobiographical Fragments," 3; Kepnes, *Text as Thou*, 104–19.
7. Friedman, "Introduction," 13–14.
8. Buber, "My Way to Hasidism," 47–69.
9. Buber, "Dialogue," 1–3.
10. Buber, "Afterword," 209–24.

his mother, which led to his concept of *Vergegnung*, "mismeeting," and his subsequent relationships with his paternal grandparents, his father, and his wife Paula. Then we turn to three encounters that significantly shaped his development during the period around the First World War, a time of transformation leading to the emergence of his dialogical philosophy. These include two mismeetings during his early adulthood, specifically with the Reverend William Hechler and a young man named Mehe, followed by a critical letter from Gustav Landauer. Finally, we take an extended look at his well-documented relationship with his fellow German Jewish intellectual, Franz Rosenzweig, as the embodiment of his vision of the life of dialogue in its fullness.

2. Buber's Loss of His Mother

The first of the short pieces comprising Buber's "Autobiographical Fragments" is entitled "My Mother."[11] This is an account of one of his earliest memories, his experience as a four-year-old one year after his mother, the actress Elise Wurgast Buber, had abruptly and without notice abandoned the family for a Russian officer and Buber had been taken to the country home of his grandparents. His family maintained silence about his mother but at one point a neighbor girl told him as they stood on a balcony looking out into empty space, "No, she will never come back."[12] The emptiness of the space before him on that balcony became the visual image of his abandonment and loss, of the absence of his mother. Buber stood there, taking in the finality of this loss, this abandonment, in silence. This verbal-visual image of abandonment "remained fixed in me; from year to year it cleaved ever more to my heart, but after more than ten years I had begun to perceive it as something that concerned not only me, but all men."[13] As Christine Downing put it, he came "to recognize the archetypal aspect of that separation ... how the primal separation from the mother ... issues in a lifelong longing for connection, for being fully affirmed, fully met."[14]

Buber wrote that, in coming to terms with this loss some ten years later, the term *Vergegnung* (mismeeting) came to him "to designate the failure of a real meeting" between persons.[15] He met his mother one time some twenty years later, after he had become a husband and father. He wrote of that

11. Buber, "Autobiographical Fragments," 3–4.
12. Buber, "Autobiographical Fragments," 3.
13. Buber, "Autobiographical Fragments," 4.
14. Downing, "Meetings and Mismeetings," 89.
15. Buber, "Autobiographical Fragments," 4.

unsuccessful visit, "I could not gaze into her still astonishingly beautiful eyes without hearing from somewhere the word *Vergegnung* as a word spoken to me."[16] Here the vivid visual image of the maternal gaze after two decades of its absence is countered by the verbal image which overwrites it with the searing meaning of the four-year-old's experience of the void. The untimely rupture of the child's natural bond with his mother could not be repaired in this belated experience. Looking all the way back to this earliest memory, Buber writes of its decisive, formative power for his thinking: "I suspect that all that I have learned about genuine meeting in the course of my life had its first origin in that hour on the balcony."[17] This breaking of relationship, with its attendant lifelong anguish and grief, served as the counterpoint, the foil to his central concept: authenticity in the *I-Thou* encounter. Thus, his early, traumatic loss, this breaking off of one of life's most fundamental relationships, became a significant event that structured and provoked his lifelong quest for unity and wholeness in dialogue.

Buber was attracted early to literature and the arts, as well as to accounts of mystical experience, as means of feeding his soul in his search for this unity and wholeness. His schooling and his work as a university student grounded him in the German academic world, while his family life connected him with the village culture and spirituality of Central European Jewry. The work of his professors in Berlin, especially Wilhelm Dilthey, recapitulated the line of German thought that evolved from the mysticism of Meister Eckhart into the idealist philosophy and the Romanticism of Hegel and Hölderlin. Buber's 1904 doctoral dissertation at the University of Vienna, "The History of the Problem of Individuation—Nicholas of Cusa and Jakob Boehme," was inspired in part by his friend Gustav Landauer, who was the first to translate Eckhart into modern German. After he completed his education, Buber began a very productive period as an editor and writer with a broad range of cultural publications. He published two collections of Hasidic stories in 1906 and 1908. He then edited an anthology of worldwide accounts of mystical experience in 1909, two collections of Chinese stories in 1911 and 1914, and an essay on the Finnish epic, *The Kalevala* in 1914.

An existential thrust stands out in a series of essays written around 1914 that Friedman described as "among the earliest and finest expressions of existentialism in this century."[18] Buber's lectures on Judaism during this period (1909–1914), and his major early work, *Daniel: Dialogues*

---

16. Buber, "Autobiographical Fragments," 4.
17. Buber, "Autobiographical Fragments," 4.
18. Friedman, "Introduction to the Torchbook Edition," viii.

on Realization (1913), also present this existential vision. The lectures on Judaism incorporated strong existential elements, while *Daniel* stood apart from the discourse of Judaism and became the first of his more general philosophical writings. *Daniel's* dialogue with an unnamed female interlocutor (49–59) addresses the theme of the mother.[19] All of this writing and editing, from his dissertation to *Daniel*, can be read as a series of broad-ranging soundings in Buber's quest for a spiritual resolution to the vacuum that opened up when he was three years old.

The trauma of early mother loss was foundational for Buber. It set the tone of existential anguish that ran through his life and thought. Like the grain of sand that comes to rest on the mantle of an oyster's shell, producing a pearl, the primal experience of mother-loss became formative for Buber's vision of contingency in dialogue. The anguish of contingency as a fundamental element of the human condition, expressed in the image of the abyss, stands out, for example, in Buber's mature thought: "I [stand] on a narrow rocky ridge between the abysses where there is no sureness of expressible knowledge . . ."[20] Buber embraced this sense of contingency, expressing its centrality for him in his insistence on the lived concrete as the core of religious life.

Thanks to this abrupt abandonment by his mother, from an early age Buber had an acute sense of his mortal vulnerability. Thus, at a primal level, he knew "that his personal 'trauma' was intimately bound up with the creative center of his being."[21] Buber expressed his sense of this nexus of frailty and power in lines he penned near the end of his life in 1963:

> All that we are is God's work:
> Splinter it must; it may reassemble itself.
> Timorous weakness and intrepid might
> Are from primordial time bound to one another.[22]

3. Buber's Grandparents

Buber's relationship with his grandparents, Salomon and Adele Buber, became the fertile soil within which his interpersonal life developed in his

---

19. Buber, *Daniel*, 49–59.

20. Buber, "What is Man?," 184. "[The life of faith] is a narrow way between two abysses, such as I once encountered in the Dolomites," Buber, quoted in Friedman, *Encounter*, 336.

21. Schaeder, "Martin Buber," 11.

22. Buber, previously unpublished quatrain quoted in Schaeder, "Martin Buber," 11.

early years. When the marriage of Buber's parents had failed, he was taken at the age of three to live with his grandparents, who raised him until he returned to his father's house in Vienna at the age of fourteen. The grandfather was a wealthy landowner who had mines and farms and lived on a large country estate near Lemburg, the capitol of the Polish-speaking province of Galicia in the Austrian empire of that time.[23]

The first years of young Martin's education consisted of private tutoring, overseen by his grandmother. According to "My Grandmother," one of Buber's autobiographical fragments, Adele Buber had read the classics of German Romantic literature in her teens. In dialogical fashion, she made a lifelong practice of copying out passages that spoke to her and writing replies to the words of the "great spirits" in her copybooks. Her belief that "a language-centered humanism was the royal road to education" led her to steep Martin in classical German culture and nourish his inclinations and talents as a person of the word.[24]

While Adele Buber oversaw the couple's practical affairs, Salomon Buber devoted himself to the study of the Aggadic side of rabbinical literature, producing authoritative critical editions of the Midrashim, commentaries on the Torah that combined textual exegesis and relevant teaching stories. For these projects, he occasionally enlisted the skills of his young grandson, who had become something of a prodigy with languages. Buber later characterized his grandfather as the last great scholar of the Haskalah, a central European movement of Jewish intellectuals to synthesize the Hebrew Scriptures with the rationalism of the European Enlightenment. He dedicated his first book on Hasidism, *The Tales of Rabbi Nachman*, to his grandfather with warm words of acknowledgment and affection: "To my grandfather Salomon Buber the last teacher [*Meister*] of the old Haskalah I offer this work on Hasidism in reverence and love."[25]

Alongside his scholarly work, Salomon Buber practiced the traditional Jewish custom of praying three times a day, and he did this shaking with fervor. In a letter many years later, Buber wrote that his grandfather "used to take me with him into his *Klaus* [Hasidic prayer room], where he, the *enlightened one*, prayed exclusively among Hasidim—from a prayerbook full of *kavvanot* [mystical intentions, fervor]."[26] Salomon Buber also took the young Martin on his visits to Hasidic communities of *zaddik*s and their

---

23. Lemburg is now Lviv in western Ukraine.
24. Buber, "Autobiographical Fragments," 4–5.
25. Buber, "Zueignung," n. p.
26. Martin Buber to Franz Rosenzweig, October 1, 1922, in Buber, *Letters*, 290 (emphasis in the original).

disciples in the nearby country villages of Sadagora and Czortkow. These visits on which Martin accompanied his grandfather came to him as a primal memory in his crucial initiatory encounter, as we have seen in chapter 2: "The image out of my childhood, the memory of the zaddik and his community, rose up and illuminated me."[27] This memory in association with the Baal-Shem-Tov's statement about intentness ("fervor") arose directly from his pious grandfather's fervor that Buber had experienced during the years in his home as a young boy.

Thus, Salomon Buber introduced his grandson to the world of scholarship and the translation of the Hebrew Scriptures on the one hand, and to Jewish spirituality in the form of the Hasidic community and of passionate piety on the other. The grandfather's influence was foundational for Buber's life work as a reader of Hasidic texts and as a translator of the Hebrew Scriptures.

The impact of Salomon Buber on Martin Buber's life and life work is perhaps best summed up in a letter of tribute Buber wrote to his grandfather in 1900 on the occasion of the grandfather's seventy-third birthday:

> That your loving kindness, dear grandfather, which has so often lent me comfort and joy and steadiness, shall long be preserved for me is the glowing hope of my heart. The tirelessness and singleness of your creation has often led me back to myself when I have scattered myself in many directions. . . . I cannot show my thankfulness and my love to you better than when I—in my spheres—emulate your manner and place my life, like yours, in the service of the Jewish people. You have drawn forth and utilized treasures from the spiritual life of the Jewish past; as a young man who longs still more for the deed than for knowledge, I have in mind working together with and helping to create the Jewish future. But both are ruled over by the spirit of the eternal people and in this sense I can perhaps say that I shall continue your lifework.[28]

With these words the twenty-two-year-old acknowledged both the dialogical power and the focused purpose of his grandfather and vowed to continue his grandfather's legacy in a life of service. Just as the grandfather worked with the treasures of the Jewish past, the grandson vowed to help create the Jewish future as a continuation of the grandfather's work. Here

---

27. Buber, "My Way to Hasidism," 59.

28. Martin Buber to Salomon and Adele Buber, January 31, 1900, translated in Friedman, *Martin Buber's Life and Work*, 1:39; see Buber, *Letters*, 70.

Buber expresses the power of his legacy and anticipates how his own life's work will affirm it in fidelity to the spirit of his grandfather.

4. Buber's Father

Buber's father, Carl Buber, was a counterpart to his grandfather who added another piece to the dialogical life of his son. Like the grandfather, Carl Buber was a landed property owner and community leader who focused his efforts on applying horticultural science to maximize the productivity of his farms; he was also involved in phosphate mining and oil extraction.

During his childhood, Buber spent his summer vacations with his father; at age fourteen he moved back to live with his father on the father's estate in Bukovina, where he stayed until he began his university studies in Vienna. Buber's move to his father's house took him from the Hasidic piety of the folk Judaism to which life with his grandfather had exposed him to the liberal Judaism of his father's community, that of the Reform temple in Lemburg. The fourteen-year-old Buber marked this shift by once and for all giving up the practice of wearing the *tefillin* for prayers. In a letter to Franz Rosenzweig on the eve of Yom Kippur in 1922, Buber gave an account of a powerful spiritual experience he had had shortly before his move to his father's house. Buber wrote that in his innermost heart he felt the mood of the eve of Yom Kippur and linked the intensity of that moment in 1922 with his experience of the last Yom Kippur he spent with his grandfather. He characterized that experience as having "an intensity such as I have not felt since."[29] Buber experienced the immediacy of his father's relating through the father's involvements with his stock, his crops, and the people in his employ when the young Buber accompanied him. Carl Buber was also "an elemental story teller."[30] These experiences and these gifts were part of what the younger Buber drew on in his relating, his thinking, and his writing.

Carl Buber was a practical man and a rationalist, yet he closely followed his son's career as a writer. At one point he wrote to steer his son away from his interest in Hasidism and the Kabbalah, since such subjects "can only have a mind-destroying and evil influence, and it is a pity to waste your abilities on such a sterile subject and consume so much labor and time, useless to yourself and the world."[31] Later, he wrote that he did not understand *Daniel*,[32] then that he was very concerned when he read Buber's "My Way

---

29. Martin Buber to Franz Rosenzweig, October 1, 1922, in Buber, *Letters*, 290.
30. Friedman, *Martin Buber's Life and Work*, 1:13.
31. Carl Buber to Martin Buber, February 6, 1908, in Buber, *Letters*, 114.
32. Carl Buber to Martin Buber, June 7, 1913, in Buber, *Letters*, 148.

to Hasidism."[33] Yet, on the whole, he eagerly and proudly followed Buber's successes as a published writer up until his death in 1935.

5. Buber's Wife, Paula Winkler Buber

Buber's relationship with Paula Winkler, with whom he lived from almost the day they met when he was twenty-one until she died fifty-nine years later, was the most important relationship of his life. In the constancy of their mutual love they worked out the interpersonal space within which deep, authentic dialogue could take place. Their dialogical intimacy became the foundation and core of Buber's understanding of relational reality. Buber drew on the power of this relationship when he wrote *I and Thou*.

The consolidation of the relationship between Martin Buber and Paula Winkler took place over time. They first met as classmates in a Germanics seminar at the University of Zürich in the summer of 1899. Their romance began shortly afterward at a dance party in the Alps. Paula had been raised in a Catholic family in Munich. Before she came to the university she had completed a teacher training program and had lived in an artist's colony in Southern Tyrol. Paula gave birth to their first child, Rafael, one year after they first met; their second child, Eva, was born one year later. During that second year Paula left the Catholic Church. Once their finances were stabilized by the success of Buber's first book, *The Tales of Rabbi Nachman*, published in 1906, the family relocated from Vienna to Berlin. Paula converted to Judaism in January 1907. Her conversion caused a complete and permanent break with her family. On April 20 of that year, the two were officially married.

Paula Winkler was a fitting counterpart to Martin Buber. She has been characterized as both "clever and strong-willed" and as at once "down-to-earth and ethereal."[34] Grete Schaeder wrote that Paula was "his equal, indeed his superior, in poetic talent and articulateness."[35] According to Schaeder, at the time they met, hers "was the stronger and more mature personality."[36] Their compatibility stood out to Paula: she "was aware of [a] childlike streak in his nature, but she was also aware of a spiritual faculty that, like her own, reached back to the depths of more primitive ages. [She] understood his achievement . . . completely and spurred him on."[37]

---

33. Carl Buber to Martin Buber, end of 1917, in Buber, *Letters*, 226.
34. Schaeder, "Martin Buber," 9.
35. Schaeder, "Martin Buber," 10.
36. Schaeder, "Martin Buber," 10.
37. Schaeder, "Martin Buber," 10.

From the outset, Paula deeply loved Buber. This is clear from her developing commitment to Zionism, Buber's cause, in the early years of their life together. Within weeks of their first meeting, Buber spoke at the Third Zionist Congress in Basel. Paula's account of this speech shows the impact it had on her as well as the depth of her love for him and for his cause:

> I experienced a human voice speaking to me with wonderful force. At times it was as if it were a child speaking shyly, hesitantly, tenderly, timidly, not sure it would meet with understanding. And now and then the delicate blush of an unsullied soul spread over this person's countenance. One moment it was as if my heart stood still, touched by sanctity. And at other moments it was as if he spoke with brazen tongues, as if all the bells in this world were clanging above me. This was no longer an individual human being; with primordial violence the tremendous longing, wishes, and will of a whole people poured over me like a raging torrent.[38]

These words reveal her sensitivity to his shy, vulnerable side, as well as to his passion and the power of his vision—and her full-hearted openness to him.

Two years after they met, in the fall of 1901, Paula wrote to Martin of the deepening of her commitment to Zionism: "I have a new desire. I must tell you this, because I did not have it formerly. I would like to be active with you in the cause of Zionism—no, I will be. I have the feeling that I can and must do something for it."[39] A day later, she wrote further, "Don't think, dearest, that I am not with you with my whole being. I truly am, have never been so intensely so. I am growing toward your cause; you must and will see that. It will be mine and also that of our children."[40] During that same period Paula published two essays in *Die Welt*, the Zionist weekly, when Buber was its editor: "Reflections of a Philo-Zionist" (6 Sept. 1901) and "The Jewish Woman" (8 and 15 Nov. 1901). With these essays she publicly announced her commitment to their shared cause and her emotional identification with Judaism.

Paula was a salutary influence in Buber's life, a healing presence that countered the emotional rupture caused by his early abandonment by his mother. The love Paula and Buber shared and the intimacy of their dialogical relationship were nurturing to his soul. Maurice Friedman assessed the healing power of this relationship in strong terms: Through Paula Winkler, Buber became more courageous and self-confident, stronger and firmer. This was

---

38. Paula Buber, cited in Schaeder, "Martin Buber," 10.
39. Paula Buber to Martin Buber, October 18, 1901, in Buber, *Letters*, 78.
40. Paula Buber to Martin Buber, October 19, 1901, in Buber, *Letters*, 79.

the decisive relationship of his life. [This relationship] made possible a life of trust in which Buber found again the strength to go forth to meet the unique and unforeseeable person or situation as his Thou."[41]

In their private, intimate correspondence—limited to the few times they wrote to each other when Buber was away from home—we glimpse Paula's solicitude toward Martin on the one hand, and on the other hand we see his emotional vulnerability toward her in their relationship. In an early letter to him when he was away at the Zionist Congress in Basel, she addressed his creative restlessness in response to the cause: "I have fond feelings for your great work—I would never want to spoil it for you. But I would like to slip myself between you and the little everyday bothers, like a sheltering cloud. That is why I so wish I were with you."[42] Here she sees their togetherness as a means of comforting him. At the same time, Buber's letter expressed his eager participation in the congress.[43]

In a letter to Paula when he was away in Vienna in 1901, Buber frankly confided his inner struggle and turned to her for nurture, comfort, and strength:

> Every moment here I am struggling with every fiber of my being to bear up against all my restlessness, against all my cares, against all my knowledge, against all my deprivation, against everything that is trying to crush me.... Your letters are the only source of strength for me. Everything else is too much intertwined with cares and restiveness. Your letters are absolutely the only thing. Aside from them, perhaps the thought that there is a mother in you, my faith in that. Now I know: ever and always I have been seeking my mother.[44]

With these words Buber explicitly expressed the reality of his wounding in response to his mother's abandonment and placed himself in openness before the healing power of Paula's presence.

In a later tribute to Paula Buber, Hugo Bergmann wrote how Paula's dialogical presence rescued Buber from disaster, helping him to keep the focus he needed to fully realize his creative calling:

> Paula Buber warded off the great dangers that threatened the young Buber. The powerful gifts of Buber were set within the literary milieu of the turn of the century, which were fully

---

41. Friedman, *Martin Buber's Life and Work*, 1:52, 1:337.
42. Paula Buber to Martin Buber, August 14, 1899, in Buber, *Letters*, 66.
43. Martin Buber to Paula Buber, August 15, 1899, in Buber, *Letters*, 66.
44. Martin Buber to Paula Buber, October 25, 1901, in Buber, *Letters*, 79.

aestheticizing and unbinding, and his gifts would have become for him a fatality, he would have been the victim of his early fame, had not Paula Buber been at his side at that time, had she not liberated him from deception and lies and pointed him toward the difficult way of work, of responsibility, of truth.[45]

An unpublished note Buber penned a year later shows the outworking of his vulnerability and her caring, how the solidity of their relationship fostered the formation of the *I* of the *I-Thou* relationship for Buber:

> Not until you came to me did I find my soul. And if from that hour forth my soul has been sorely oppressed and cast into fetters—is not a poor child in peril of death infinitely greater in worth than all dreaming? And if my soul should remain barren until the end—am I not even so of infinitely greater worth than the golem to whom the Word has not yet been spoken? For before you came to me, that is what I was, a creature of dreams and a golem. But when I found you, I found my soul. You came and gave me a soul. Therefore is not my soul merely this: your child?[46]

The interchange here between *I* and *Thou*, between agency ("When I found you, I found my soul") and receptivity ("you gave me a soul"), suggests the foundation of self-making in reciprocity, which is at the center of the *I-Thou* relationship as articulated in *I and Thou*: "I become through [my addressing] the *Thou*; becoming *I*, I say *Thou*" (§14c).

A major dimension of the dialogical intimacy that Martin and Paula shared was the realm of their literary creativity. They first came together in the Germanics seminar because of their shared aptitude for language, literature, and the imagination. The mutually subjective side of their intimacy is suggested by the nickname they used for each other: "Mowgli." The fact that each used it for the other shows their identification with each other and with the realm of the literary imagination. The name itself comes from the central figure in Rudyard Kipling's collection of animal stories for children, *The Jungle Book*. Mowgli, raised by wolves in the jungles of India after being abandoned by his parents, embodies the fusion of natural and human worlds in the life of the imagination.[47] Both Buber and Paula were gifted writers. She published collections of short stories and a novel under the pen

---

45. Hugo Bergmann, cited in Friedman, *Martin Buber's Life and Work*, 1:338–39.
46. Buber, unpublished note cited in Schaeder, "Martin Buber," 10–11.
47. See Schaeder, "Martin Buber," 11; Paula used the name to address Buber in some of her letters—see Paula Buber to Martin Buber, October 19, 1901, in Buber, *Letters*, 78, and Paula Buber to Martin Buber, November 17, in Buber, *Letters*, 79–80.

name Georg Munk. Over time they collaborated extensively with each other on their individual projects.

In a letter to Paula in 1901, Martin expressed his struggle with his surging creativity and turned to her for support in reining it in to good purpose:

> I must pull myself together with all my strength and in the next few months, or rather weeks, must accomplish something. Otherwise, I shall lose the last remnant of my artistic initiative . . . What's missing is a great effort. That is what counts now. You must understand, dearest, that this is a matter of life and death. What is at stake is simply my art: if I let myself go, I go to seed—that is definite. Then I can go on shaping myself as a university lecturer and as a decent individual in general. But it will all be over with the making of living things.[48]

Paula wrote to him as well during that period, responding to his drafts and sharing the process of her own writing project.[49]

Buber's efforts as a creative writer were the central focus of his work. His passion as a Zionist was for the renewal of cultural Zionism, bringing about a Jewish Renaissance through literature and the arts. He saw his writing as his means of making his contribution to this cultural rebirth. His break with Theodor Herzl at the sixth Zionist Congress in 1903 was over their differences of vision: Buber's focus was cultural while Herzl's was political. At that time Buber withdrew from the public political cause, but he continued with his more private work, which was to serve the cultural cause of his original vision.

Paula, as a master of narrative, was especially helpful to Martin in his early recasting of Hasidic tales. His letters to Paula in December 1906, when he was staying in Berlin and she remained in Austria, show that she collaborated with him by rewriting some of the traditional stories published in his first book, *The Tales of Rabbi Nachman*, which came out that year.[50] Then, in his second collection, *The Legend of the Baal-Shem* (1908), some of the stories were also rewritten by Paula during their yearlong sojourn in Italy in 1907. Schaeder wrote, "A good many of Paula's renditions of the Hasidic legends and tales were printed almost without alteration;

---

48. Martin Buber to Paula Buber, July 26, 1901, in Buber, *Letters*, 73.

49. Paula Buber to Martin Buber, November 17, 1901, in Buber, *Letters*, 79–80.

50. Martin Buber to Paula Buber, early December, 1906, *Briefwechsel*, 1:249–52. These four letters were not included in the English edition of Buber's letters.

others were rather heavily edited, Buber tightening and shortening them, or revising the conclusions."[51]

Martin's powerful relationship with Paula was the bedrock in concrete lived experience which undergirded the development of his dialogical philosophy and which shaped his exposition of *I and Thou*. As Friedman put it, this relationship was "an influence probably more decisive for the development of his *I-Thou* philosophy as a whole than any [other] events and meetings."[52] In contrast to the decisive mismeeting of his life, the disappearance of his mother when he was a small child, Martin's marriage to Paula was "the crucial *meeting*" of his life: "The existential trust that underlies *I and Thou* and all of Buber's mature works would have been unthinkable without his relationship to Paula. [His] thinking did not emerge from his individual being but from the 'between' which he knew first and foremost in his marriage."[53]

From early on Buber wrote expressive poems to Paula as part of their dialogue. The spirit of their collaboration is expressed in his dedication of a number of his writings to her, as in *I and Thou* (1923) and *Tales of the Hasidim* (1949), his culminating contribution to his work on the Hasidic tradition.

The epigraph which Buber used in the original edition of *I and Thou* and which comes from Goethe's *West-östliche Divan*, a collection of poems inspired by the Persian Sufi poet Hafez, can be read as a concealed dedication to Paula. Buber quoted the first half of a quatrain expressing the words of the Cupbearer to the Poet:

> So, by waiting, I have finally received from you:
>
> God's presence in all the elements.[54]

Walter Kaufmann suggests that the second half of the quatrain from Goethe confirms this intent:

> How you give it to me in such a lovely way!
>
> Yet most lovely of all is that you love.[55]

For Buber, the first two lines of the quatrain acknowledge the gift of divine presence in the everyday, the grace of *I-Thou* relating, specifically that in

51. Schaeder, "Martin Buber," 13.
52. Friedman, *Martin Buber's Life and Work*, 1:336.
53. Friedman, *Martin Buber's Life and Work*, 1:337–38 (emphasis original).
54. Goethe, *West-östliche Divan*, 9.21, lines 1–2 (my translation).
55. Goethe, *West-östliche Divan*, 9.21, lines 3–4 (my translation); see Kaufmann, "I and You," 27n.

his intimacy with Paula. The last two lines, clearly in Martin's mind but not written into the epigraph, implicitly acknowledge Paula's part in his creative discovery of the dialogical vision. They also point to her love at the heart of this inspiration.

Moreover, the contents of *I and Thou* reflect the intimacy of their relationship at a number of points. His passage teaching about the nature of love (§19b)—"love is *between* I and *Thou*," "love is the responsibility of an *I* for a *Thou*," "the blessedly secure person is the one whose life is embraced by the life of the beloved"—draws on his relationship with Paula. The crucial passage at the heart of the book on coming to decision befits the nurturing and grounding presence and decisiveness of Paula that informed their relationship (§36b–c). The longing expressed in *I and Thou* as inherent in the human condition is linked with "the eternal feminine" (§27d–e). It finds its fulfillment in the marital relationship: Buber draws on the poetry of Genesis 49 to present marital intimacy as the epitome of *I-Thou* when it transcends itself, "When a man is intimate with his wife, the longing of the eternal hills wafts over them" (§56c).

In 1929, Buber dedicated *Dialogue*, his long essay written as a companion piece to *I and Thou* and published as a small book, to Paula with a dialogical quatrain as the essay's epigraph. These four lines of Buber's poetry celebrate their life together as an ongoing dialogue.[56] Here again, the words of this dedication put Martin's dialogical life with Paula at the heart of his philosophy of dialogue.

The poem Martin penned in Paula's copy of his *Tales of the Hasidim* in 1949 after fifty years of their life together expresses the long-term intensity of their mutuality as creative writers. The reworkings of the phrase "I and thou" [*ich und du*] in lines 4, 8, and 16 also reaffirm their relationship as the dialogical core of his life.[57]

Maurice Friedman best sums up the character of Paula and her role in Buber's life and work:

> Buber's dialogical thinking could have grown only out of his marriage to this strong and really "other" woman, this modern Ruth who left her family, home, and religion, and finally even her country and people, for him. The fundamental reality of the life of dialogue—that it is a confirmation and inclusion of otherness—was understood and authenticated in the love

---

56. Buber, quoted in Friedman, *Martin Buber's Life and Work*, 1:338.
57. Buber, quoted in Schaeder, "Martin Buber," 12.

and the marriage, the tension and the companionship, of his relationship to Paula.[58]

In risking all to love him, Paula became the paragon of dialogical living that made *I and Thou* possible.

6. World War I as Watershed

In his inaugural lectures at the Hebrew University in Jerusalem in 1938, Buber marked the period around the First World War as a watershed [*eine entscheidende Wendung*] for his thinking.[59] He then sketched the development of his thinking before this major shift. It consisted of two phases, each of which was an outgrowth of the sources of his intellectual-cultural heritage. The first shows his debt to the mysticism behind the idealistic-romantic philosophy of German academic culture: "Since 1900 I had first stood under the influence of German mysticism from Meister Eckhart to Angelus Silesius, according to which the primal ground of being [*der Urgrund des Seins*], the unnamable, impersonal godhead, comes to 'birth' in the human soul."[60] The second draws on his Jewish religious heritage: "then I had stood under the influence of the later Kabbala and of Hasidism, according to the teaching of which a person can achieve the power to unite the world-transcending God with his world-indwelling *shekinah*."[61] Buber shows the early synthesis he was able to forge out of these two very different cultural strands: "Thus, there arose in me the idea of a realizing of God through the human; humanity appeared to me as the being through whose existence [*Dasein*] the Absolute, resting in its truth [*Wahrheit*], can achieve the quality of reality [*Wirklichkeit*]."[62] This early human-centered view of Buber's was close to that of Ludwig Feuerbach, who wrote, "Man for himself is man in the ordinary sense; man with man—the unity of I and Thou—is God."[63]

It was this view, this product of his early idealism, that was effaced in him during the war period. As he put it in the lecture, using geological metaphors, the shift in his thinking during the war period took him from

58. Friedman, *Martin Buber's Life and Work*, 1:336.
59. Buber, "What is Man?," 184–85 (my translation).
60. Buber, "What is Man?," 184–85 (my translation).
61. Buber, "What is Man?," 185 (my translation).
62. Buber, "What is Man?," 185 (my translation); compare with the "rest," "stillness" of Taoism in Buber, "Afterword," 87.
63. Quoted by Friedman in Buber, "Afterword," 214n; see Feuerbach, *Principles of the Philosophy of the Future*, 71.

this early view as "the broad high plain of a system that encompasses a series of unquestionable statements about the absolute" to his later standpoint, that of a "narrow ridge [*ein schmaler Grat*] . . . a narrow rock ridge between the abysses where there is no certainty of expressible knowledge but only the certainty of encountering that which is hidden, the Enduring [*Begegnung mit dem verhüllt Bleibenden*]."[64] His orientation had shifted from the certainty of a unitive world view to an existential stance, lacking all certainty but that of encounter on an uncertain path. The war's impact on Buber was a small piece of a much larger shift to a new post-war cultural horizon that was opening up across Europe.

The Rev. William Hechler

A measure of Buber's development during the war period is suggested by the contrast between a dialogue he had just before the war and the aftermath to this dialogue, a moment of insight years later, after the war. Buber's account of this dialogue in "Autobiographical Fragments" presents it as another fruitful "mismeeting" [*Vergegnung*].[65] It was a mismeeting because it culminated in Buber's evasive response to a man; it was fruitful because years of reflecting on it led Buber to a definitive insight—his delayed response to the man. Buber's account of this dialogue and its aftermath in one of his "Religion as Presence" lectures, and later as one of his autobiographical fragments, helps to frame the war as the watershed of his thinking. The aftermath shows a moment in the emergence of his new thinking that was part of the creative ferment that led to *I and Thou*.

William Hechler, a British clergyman who was a lifelong Christian Zionist and a follower of Theodor Herzl, visited Buber in Berlin one afternoon in May of 1914. He brought with him a complex chart of the details of the apocalyptic vision of the biblical prophet Daniel. He pointed to a place on the chart and identified it as the present moment in history, then announced that a great war was coming. When Buber accompanied the old man to his train at the end of the visit, Hechler stopped him at an intersection and asked, "Dear friend, we are living in a great time. Tell me, do you believe in God?" Buber responded by reassuring him that he need have no concern in that regard.[66] Given the theological-historical framework from which Hechler had asked the question, Buber could not freely give him a yes or a no, so this moment of rupture in their dialogue, this

64. Buber, "What is Man?," 184 (my translation).
65. Buber, "Autobiographical Fragments," 23–25.
66. Buber, "Autobiographical Fragments," 24.

moment of mismeeting, left him uneasy. Consciously and unconsciously, Buber deeply pondered this moment.

Then, seven years later on a train ride in the fall of 1921, an answer to Hechler came to Buber out of the blue[67]:

> If to believe in God means to be able to talk about him in the third person, then I do not believe in God. If to believe in him means to be able to talk to him, then I believe in God. . . . The God who gives Daniel such foreknowledge of this hour of human history, this hour before the "world war," that its fixed place in the march of the ages can be foredetermined, is not my God and not God. The God to whom Daniel prays in his suffering is my God and the God of all.[68]

Hechler's question in its traditional Christian theological framework, confronting Buber as it did as the two men walked together to Hechler's train, left Buber inarticulate and uneasy. Seven years later on a train ride of his own, Buber was able to complete the disrupted dialogue. While this insight would have made Hechler uneasy, it gave Buber a deep sense of satisfaction and resolution.[69]

Rivka Horwitz raises the question, "What happened . . . ?"[70] What caused Buber to move from his uneasy nonanswer to Hechler before the war to his pivotal insight after it? The answer lies in three moments during the period of the First World War. These moments were crucial in the development of Buber's mature existential stance. They grew in intensity from a conversation in 1914 to a letter in 1916 to a murder in 1919. All three of these moments are linked by a common element: military violence. Buber highlighted the first, the conversation, as one of the "moments that have exercised a decisive influence on the nature and direction of my thinking."[71] He suppressed the second, the letter and the events which surrounded it. And he spoke obliquely of the impact of the third, the murder. Each of these disturbing moments contributed to Buber's development and each laid the foundations for his mature thought.

---

67. Buber, "Religion as Presence," 103–5, gives this 1921 date in contrast to 1914, which is the date given in "Autobiographical Fragments," 24–25.

68. Buber, "Autobiographical Fragments," 24–25.

69. Buber, "Religion as Presence," 105.

70. Horwitz, *Buber's Way*, 174.

71. Buber, "Autobiographical Fragments," 3.

The Young Mehe

In attempting to understand this part of Buber's development, we begin with his conversation with a young man in 1914 and its aftermath. Buber first published an account of this event in his essay entitled "Dialogue."[72] The account presents a crucial instance of mismeeting from which Buber learned by reflecting on it and adjusting his perspectives. When the account is seen in its original context in the essay, it illustrates his point, his radical affirmation of concrete lived experience as the nub of encounter: "The concreteness of the world is the part of creation which is entrusted to me, to each human being. . . . We are addressed in the signs of the life which happens to us."[73] With these words, Buber introduces the event as a sign, characterizing it poetically as "an everyday event, an event of judgment, judging with that judgment from closed lips and steady gaze such as the ongoing course of things loves to render."[74] Buber begins this account by describing how for him his youthful practice of "religion," of breaking through "the firm husk of everyday reality" and entering a state of ecstasy—beyond time, space, and even the sense of self—divided reality in two: the realm of everyday life and the realm of transcendent experience.[75]

The illegitimacy of such a splitting of reality was brought home to Buber by this everyday event: one day in 1914, after a morning of such "religious" exaltation, a young man named Mehe came to him seeking guidance. Buber received him without being fully present to him. He "conversed candidly and attentively with him," but neglected to discern the questions that Mehe carried within but did not ask. Soon after this meeting Mehe entered the German army, then he was killed on the front shortly after the beginning of the war. Mehe died "out of that kind of despair that may be defined partially as 'no longer opposing one's own death.'"[76]

When a friend of Mehe's informed Buber of his death, Buber took it as a judgment: he had failed to engage fully in the depths of genuine dialogue that his hour with Mehe had offered. Buber's reflection on the meaning of that hour hints at his guilt: "He had come to me not incidentally, but borne by destiny, not for a chat but for a decision. He had come specifically to me, he had come specifically at this hour. What do we expect when we are in despair and yet go to another human being? To be sure, a presentness by means of

---

72. Buber, "Dialogue," 13–14; later included out of context in "Autobiographical Fragments," 25–26.

73. Buber, "Dialogue," 13, 14 (my translation).

74. Buber, "Dialogue," 13 (my translation).

75. Buber, "Dialogue," 13 (my translation).

76. Buber to Friedman, quoted in Friedman, *Martin Buber's Life and Work*, 1:188.

which it is affirmed that nevertheless there is meaning."[77] Buber goes on: "I know that in the claim [made by the other] I am addressed and must respond in responsibility, and I know who speaks and demands a response. I do not know much more than this. If this is religion, then religion is simply *everything*, the bare lived All in its possibility of dialogue."[78]

When Mehe departed from this consultation with Buber, he had not yet resolved to live; Buber recognized after the fact that, had he truly engaged with the young man in response to his crisis, he might have helped him toward greater decisiveness. Buber later wrote that "'trust in the world because this human being exists' is the most inward achievement of education."[79] Buber had failed to reach this level of engagement with Mehe when the young man had come to him as a troubled seeker.

Through a period of introspection, Buber responded to his sense of failure in this mismeeting by taking it as a judgment upon himself. As a result, he made an about turn, changing his life. As he explicitly states,

> Since then I have renounced that "religious" which is nothing but exception, self-removal, dropping out, ecstasy—or it has renounced me. I possess nothing but the everyday out of which I am never taken. The mystery no longer discloses itself; it has withdrawn or it has made its dwelling here where everything happens as it happens. I know no fullness other than the fullness of each mortal hour in its claim and responsibility.[80]

In his deliberative response to that hour, elaborated in "Dialogue," Buber did more than turn from a life-dividing practice of religion as escape from everyday life; he also began to practice more deeply the embrace of the present. He began to view every mortal hour as "the mystery" and, in the "fullness of claim and responsibility" which each moment brings, he more fully embraced "the One."[81]

Buber's point here is his conversation with Mehe, like each event of everyday life, provided an opportunity for encounter with the Eternal *Thou*. At the same time, it served as a painful, symbolic, and ultimately transformative instance of mismeeting. Its potential as encounter was

---

77. Buber, "Dialogue," 14 (my translation).
78. Buber, "Dialogue," 14 (my translation, emphasis his).
79. Buber, "Education," 98.
80. Buber, "Dialogue," 14 (my translation).
81. Buber, "Dialogue," 14–15 (my translation). Buber's climactic use of "the One" here resonates at multiple levels: it suggests "the one thing needful" as well as "the One" of Plotinus, and "being itself." Buber's shift to the seamless web of self-presence to the present moment will be more fully examined in chapters 5 and 6 below.

contingent upon his self-transforming response. In this way, the event reveals not only a particular turning point in Buber's life but it also highlights the principle that every moment can become an opportunity, a turning point, even after the fact.

7. Gustav Landauer

Another major factor in Buber's development during World War I was the impact of his relationship with Gustav Landauer, his closest friend. Buber and Landauer, who was eight years older than Buber, met in Berlin in 1899 when Buber was a twenty-one-year-old student. Both were participants in *die neue Gemeinschaft* (the New Community), a group Landauer helped to form to explore alternatives to the depersonalization that had emerged in modern industrial society. Landauer was a mystically oriented utopian socialist activist and a pacifist. He supported Buber's choice of his dissertation topic and later influenced the methods Buber employed in his translation of Hasidic writings. Friedman writes: "Next to his marriage, Buber's friendship with Landauer . . . was probably the decisive relationship in his adult life."[82] Two formative moments stand out in this twenty-year friendship: the intense dispute the two had in 1916 over the meaning of the war and Buber's traumatic loss when Landauer was brutally murdered in 1919.

In 1906, Buber moved to Zehlendorf, Landauer's neighborhood in Berlin, to live near his friend; after Buber moved to Heppenheim near Frankfurt ten years later, he and Landauer sometimes crossed Germany to visit each other for days at a time. The two shared a commitment to utopian socialism as well as aesthetic sensibilities and an interest in mysticism. However, they diverged over whether World War I was a step toward achieving their shared utopian vision. On one hand, Landauer saw the war from the beginning as a disaster and a crime against humanity.[83] Buber, on the other hand, maintained the idealistic outlook that had developed as part of the *Zeitgeist* in *fin de siècle* Germany by at first believing that the war was plowing the soil for the germination of a new age of universal brotherhood. To begin with, the two agreed to disagree regarding the war, even when they spent some days in discussion together at Buber's home in early May of 1916. Yet on May 12, within days of this visit, Landauer wrote a scathing letter to his friend in response to some of Buber's recently

---

82. Friedman, *Encounter on the Narrow Ridge*, 46.
83. Schaeder, "Martin Buber," 25.

published essays.[84] In this long letter Landauer challenged Buber's position and drew a line in the sand regarding their collaboration.

The letter has an avuncular tone, that of a mentor-like friend writing to a younger colleague. By turns it affirms their relationship, attacks Buber's illusions, rues his naiveté, and expresses hope that he will change.

Landauer begins by warmly confirming their visit and their relationship, "this communion [*Gemeinschaft*] that existed before the war and will survive it."[85] Then, referring to lines in two of Buber's recently published essays that idealize the war in terms of German nationalism, manifestations of which Landauer refers to as the "war Buber" [*Kriegsbuber*], he writes that these lines

> are very painful to me, very repulsive, and very close to incomprehensibility. Contrary to all your objections, I call the stance here a kind of aestheticism and formalism and I say that you—even in spite of yourself—have no right to speak out about the political events of the present, the world war, nor to paste these confused events into your sage and pretty generalities: the result is completely jejune and outrageous. I confess that my blood boils when I read how you place "the German of today" alongside the Greeks of Periclean Athens and the Italians of the Renaissance . . . .[86]

Landauer makes clear that "formalism" here means Buber's identifying German nationalism and the events of the war with the abstract social ideals which he and Landauer share. Landauer's damning reference to "aestheticism" refers to this misuse of their ideals through a subjectivity that lacks a self-critical capacity, a subjectivity linked to *fin de siècle* German idealism and embodied in the *Erlebnis*-mysticism Buber had originally shared with fellow members of the *neue Gemeinschaft* in Berlin. In Landauer's view, Buber's pro-war ideology masked the face of the war as the evil actuality that it was. Repeatedly Landauer spells out that Buber is denying the great chasm that lies between his idealism and the depravity of the war:

> The "spirit of Europe" that you find manifesting itself now in this war is a "communal spirit" of laceration, a completely lifeless construct. . . . Truly, this is no intuitive synthesis but rather a deformity. You want to make the turbid [reality of war] into a unity

---

84. Gustav Landauer to Martin Buber, May 12, 1916, in Buber, *Letters*, 188–92.

85. Gustav Landauer to Martin Buber, May 12, 1916, in Buber, *Letters*, 188 (my translation).

86. Gustav Landauer to Martin Buber, May 12, 1916, in Buber, *Letters*, 189 (my translation).

through the sheer power of contemplation.... You contemplate the squalid reality [of war] and declare it a miracle; observing it, you paste it into a pre-existing pattern. I gladly grant that the desire to see greatness lies behind this; but desire alone is not sufficient to make turbid baseness into greatness. "Virility, manliness, courage, sacrifice"—yes, these are all there, but not in the actions, not in the content, not in the meaning of this crime. Not through war do we learn how to nurture community.[87]

The implications here are clear. Contra Buber, to Landauer the stark contrast between the lacerating violence of war and the ideal of global harmony could not be stronger. Buber has not critically examined his naïve social and spiritual ideals deeply enough to see how he blanketed the perverse reality of war with them, for in his affirmation of unity Buber naïvely held onto these ideals at the expense of the rest of reality. He pasted the ideal of oneness onto the reality of German violence when he needed to critically examine the limits of idealism, see the falsity of nationalistic war ideology, and identify evil for what it is. All of this strikes at the heart of his subjective sense of unity, both as inner harmony and as universal peace. This letter strikes another serious blow against Buber's early *Erlebnis*-mysticism.

Landauer closes his letter by reproaching Buber for exalting "the nationalistic German empire-builders"; yet Landauer holds out hope for him as well, as he moves to the future tense in his conclusion:

> It is a pity that you have gone so astray regarding this war. How great a pity it is, you will later realize in face of the consequences that now lie hidden.... For your own sake you will have to reinterpret, to adumbrate, to circumscribe, to take back, and to regret. You will once again be able to distinguish the higher representations of the German spirit—among whom Swiss such as [Carl] Spitteler must be counted—from the "Germans of our day," from the ideologues of German imperialism. In the future you will not go along with a German war against the other peoples of Europe, nor with a war of Europe against itself, as you now do in your profound confusion and entanglement.[88]

With these hopeful words Landauer concludes his passionate, admonishing letter of counsel to his younger friend.

---

87. Gustav Landauer to Martin Buber, May 12, 1916, in Buber, *Letters*, 190–91 (my translation).

88. Gustav Landauer to Martin Buber, May 12, 1916, in Buber, *Letters*, 192 (my translation).

Buber deliberately suppressed this letter and never spoke of this rift with Landauer.[89] We can only speculate about his response to this awkward moment in this his deepest friendship, but soon afterwards Buber began attacking Germany's war effort and he no longer connected it with utopianism. In fact, this moment may have marked his shift toward greater support of Zionism as the means of achieving the vision. Paul Mendes-Flohr concludes: "Landauer's letter . . . was a pivotal factor in Buber's turn from his *Erlebnis*-mysticism to the philosophy of dialogue. In Buber's writings subsequent to the spring of 1916, we notice three new elements: an explicit opposition to the war and chauvinistic nationalism; a reevaluation of the function and meaning of *Erlebnis*; and a shift in the axis of *Gemeinschaft* from consciousness (i.e., subjective-cosmic *Erlebnis*) to the realm of interpersonal relations."[90] While the dialogue with Mehe challenged Buber's early practice of splitting reality into an ideal beyond the concrete everyday world, from an entirely different angle, Landauer's letter challenged his uncritically identifying the utopian dream with the actual sordid violence of war. Together these moments forced Buber to find his way anew in the darkness, the unprecedented conditions spawned by a world at war.

Moreover, Buber's strong inclination up to this point to cast his quest for unity in terms of the subjective-universal of *Erlebnis*-mysticism modulated to a different and deeper sense of oneness, one that focused more on "the between." His discourse shifted from a sense of oneness in the universal and the general to oneness as the concrete particularity of the present moment.

These developments worked together to move Buber further away from the framework of *Erlebnis*-mysticism and they also helped lay the foundation for the emergence of his mature philosophy of dialogue. Buber had reconfigured his utopian ideals more along the line of Landauer's, although for Buber those ideals were to be achieved through his emerging work as an educator, while Landauer threw himself into the fray and ultimately sacrificed his life in the cause of revolutionary struggle.

Just as Buber never spoke of the rift he had had with Landauer during the war, he was also for the most part silent about the brutal murder of his friend and the weight of grief he bore in response to it. We have looked closely at the impact of Landauer's death in chapter 2. When we consider Buber's loss of Landauer and his response to it alongside the encounter with Mehe and the letter from Landauer, we see how Buber's

---

89. Mendes-Flohr, *From Mysticism to Dialogue*, 101–2; see also Friedman, *Martin Buber's Life and Work*, 1:398; but see Lunn, *Prophet of Community*, 246–47.

90. Mendes-Flohr, *From Mysticism to Dialogue*, 102.

mourning in the months and years following the murder further deepened his sense of the tragic in life and of the urgency, the call to decisiveness, and the destiny-shaping power of each present moment. His immersing himself in the study of Hasidism was a natural first response to the loss, a retreat to the roots of his spiritual heritage for nurture and healing. Given this grounding in Hasidism, a path toward recovery then opened up for him. He entered an intense period of productivity and the result was a conceptual breakthrough, expressed in *I and Thou*. This book became the foundation of his mature philosophy of dialogue. The events of the war as a period of transition had put Buber firmly on a new footing which took expression in his philosophy of dialogue.

We turn now to a different relationship that expresses Buber's dialogical life in its fullness: his relationship with his fellow German Jewish intellectual, Franz Rosenzweig. Like his friendship with Landauer, this friendship also had its tragic side, one which the two friends came to bear together in their years of collaboration. That tragedy was Rosenzweig's premature decline and death over the course of their eight years of friendship. Yet the grounds of this friendship were different: Buber was able to plumb the depths of the dual heritage he shared with Rosenzweig in a way that had not been possible during his younger years in his relationship with Landauer.

8. Franz Rosenzweig

Buber's dialogical relationship with his good friend and fellow German Jewish intellectual Franz Rosenzweig is inseparable from the emergence of his dialogical vision and his embodiment of it in a life of dialogue. That relationship was Buber's most significant relationship next to those with his wife Paula and Gustav Landauer. Maurice Friedman has characterized this relationship in strong terms: "The kinship between the two leading Jewish philosophers and existentialists of the twentieth century was recognized by both men in a fruitful personal and intellectual interchange that made their friendship one of the most memorable episodes in recent Jewish history."[91] The published letters between these two friends reveal just how fruitful and powerful that dialogical relationship actually was.

The young Rosenzweig first briefly encountered Buber in 1914. They met again seven years later due to Rosenzweig's initiative. In November of 1921 Buber acted on moral grounds to break ranks with his collaborators and withdraw his support for a *Festschrift* for which Rosenzweig was editor. Buber's taking this moral stand impressed Rosenzweig: he determined

91. Friedman, *Martin Buber's Life and Work*, 1:283.

to meet Buber. At the beginning of December 1921, he and his wife Edith visited Martin and Paula Buber at their home in Heppenheim. Their long conversation that day was the beginning of a deep friendship. The visit began over coffee, then extended for some hours as Buber and Rosenzweig developed a strong rapport and it ended with their reviewing some Hasidic texts together.[92] Within days of the visit Buber wrote Rosenzweig that the visit "left me with the sense of a lasting relationship."[93]

The level of engagement, of mutual trust and respect, even their differences of temperament and viewpoint, became apparent in this first extended conversation in Heppenheim. It became the foundation upon which their friendship evolved both through their face-to-face dialogue and through their letters back and forth in the ensuing years.

Tragically, in November of 1921, at about the time when their relationship was taking root, Rosenzweig began to develop symptoms of what was soon diagnosed as amyotrophic lateral sclerosis (ALS, or Lou Gehrig's disease). He was thirty-five years old. This degenerative condition completely constrained his life. At first he expected an imminent death, yet he lived seven more years as a declining paralytic, for most of that time confined to his room. He died in December of 1929, just two weeks before his forty-third birthday.

The exchange of letters between Buber and Rosenzweig precipitated by that first visit extended over the remaining years of Rosenzweig's life. These letters amount to a partial transcript of their dialogical relationship. As such, this correspondence serves as a unique window into mutuality in dialogue as Buber practiced it.

Because Buber and Rosenzweig lived thirty-five minutes apart by train in an era before the widespread use of the telephone, much of their dialogue took place as face-to-face conversation at Rosenzweig's house in Frankfurt, which occurred with regularity when Buber was in town to give lectures. Yet in between these visits, a significant part of their dialogue took place as written correspondence. A good portion of this correspondence has been published.[94] The at times vigorous back-and-forth pattern of these letters between Frankfurt and Heppenheim reveals both high and low points in their relationship as well as their respect for each other and the lengths to which they went to cultivate their friendship. The letters convey both the formality of the genre of letter writing in that

---

92. Rosenzweig described the visit in detail in a letter to his protégé, Rudolf Hallo. See Franz Rosenzweig to Rudolf Hallo, early December 1922, Rosenzweig et al., *Briefe*, 461–64.

93. Martin Buber to Franz Rosenzweig, December 8, 1921, in Buber, *Letters*, 262.

94. See Buber, *Letters*; Rosenzweig et al., *Briefe*.

cultural context and the intimacy of direct, frank self-disclosure that was characteristic of their style of relating. Grete Schaeder, the editor of Buber's published correspondence, put these letters in context:

> Buber's exchange of letters with Rosenzweig is the deepest and most important that he conducted. And not simply letters of the one or the other partner but rather the exchange, which often took place on a daily basis—only this can convey an adequate impression of the intensity and significance of their fellowship [*Gemeinschaft*].[95]

In the course of their correspondence they addressed a series of issues over which they shared a common concern: first the lecture series entitled "Religion as Presence" which Buber delivered at the Frankfurt Lehrhaus[96]; followed by a second lecture series in the winter of 1922; then the galley proofs of *I and Thou* that September; and then their colloquy on the place of *halakha*, the law, in Jewish life, and finally their joint project of translating the Hebrew Scriptures into German.

Buber's Lehrhaus lectures

On Rosenzweig's way home from their get-acquainted visit it occurred to him to invite Buber to lecture at the Frankfurt Lehrhaus.[97] Buber's letter of December 8, 1921, in response expressed his surprise at his own willingness to accept Rosenzweig's invitation: "To my own astonishment, from the first moment I have had a positive feeling about your suggestion for a lecture (for having to decline such invitations has almost become a custom with me). For this I essentially have your visit and the sense of a connection that has remained with me since then to thank."[98] Buber went on to delimit the focus of the proposed lecture series. He characterized it as corresponding to "the prolegomena to a work with which I am now engaged [i.e., *I and Thou*]."[99] The result was a series of eight lectures titled "Religion as Presence" which Buber gave at the Lehrhaus from January 10 to March 11, 1922.

95. Schaeder, "Martin Buber," 41.

96. The Freies Jüdisches Lehrhaus, "the Independent Jewish House of Study," was a center for Jewish adult education in Frankfurt which Rosenzweig founded and directed until his illness forced him to resign.

97. Franz Rosenzweig to Rudolf Hallo, early December 1922, *Briefe*, 461–62.

98. Martin Buber to Franz Rosenzweig, December 8, 1921, in Buber, *Letters*, 262 (my translation).

99. Martin Buber to Franz Rosenzweig, December 8, 1922, in Buber, *Letters*, 262 (my translation).

Rosenzweig's invitation became a pivotal moment in Buber's development: it led to a new kind of commitment for Buber, confirming Landauer's earlier pull on Buber toward a life of action. The lecture series, together with a sequel which anticipated the extension of Buber's planned masterwork on religion, "established Buber's central position in the Lehrhaus, [taking] him, in his middle forties, out of the solitude of his Heppenheim study" and back into the public arena.[100]

Not only did Buber's Lehrhaus lectures of 1922 become the focus of the early correspondence between Buber and Rosenzweig; they also functioned as a run-up to his finalization of *I and Thou*. The lectures themselves were an experiment in pedagogy, introducing dialogue into the lecture format: in the intimacy of the small group, for the first time Buber took questions during his lectures, establishing the give-and-take of genuine dialogue which then became a key element of the distinctive Lehrhaus approach to instruction.[101] Furthermore, the dialogical format that emerged in Buber's teaching at the Lehrhaus beginning in the winter of 1922 had a significant impact on his thought and style in the writing of *I and Thou*, even to the extent that he incorporated a dialogical device, an interlocutor's voice, into the text in thirteen different passages.[102]

The lectures became an important step toward the completion of *I and Thou*: they gave Buber the occasion to organize and present what was emerging in his thinking as the foundations of his philosophy of dialogue. As Buber himself pointed out, his Lehrhaus lecture series had a formative impact on his writing: "Once I had developed the course of thought through giving the series of lectures at the Lehrhaus . . . I was able to complete the final version of *I and Thou*."[103] That spring Buber reworked lectures four, five, six, and eight to complete parts one and three of the manuscript.[104]

Together, both his Lehrhaus lectures and his relationship with Rosenzweig helped put Buber in a stronger position to synthesize his emerging dialogical philosophy. Rivka Horwitz affirms the dynamic role of Buber's

---

100. Nahum Glatzer in Friedman, *Martin Buber's Life and Work*, 1:297.

101. Buber, "Religion as Presence," 19–129. Buber's dialogical process with students here bears an uncanny resemblance to what he describes as the dialogue between teachers and students in Hasidic communities. See Buber, *Tales of the Hasidim*, 1:8–9. This passage is discussed on page 131 below.

102. See Wood, *Martin Buber's Ontology*, 28.

103. Buber, "Nachwort," 308–9. This sentence was omitted in the English translation—see "Afterword," 215.

104. Rivka Horwitz, in her book *Buber's Way to I and Thou*, published the transcripts of the lecture-dialogues along with her extended commentary on them, laying out the strong parallels between the lectures and *I and Thou*; see Horwitz, *Buber's Way*, 33–37.

living dialogue with Rosenzweig in his creative process: because *I and Thou* as "Buber's book on dialogue was written in the midst of a most significant living dialogue . . . the dialogical theory voiced in *I and Thou* was itself formulated, not in the solitude of a monologue but, at least in the last stages of its development, in a living dialogue between Buber and Franz Rosenzweig."[105]

Ongoing Lehrhaus work

After the winter lecture series and Buber's work finalizing his manuscript of *I and Thou* in the spring of 1922, the correspondence between Buber and Rosenzweig picked up in late July and became a flurry of letters; of these, twenty in all were published, and the series lasted until the beginning of October. These letters reveal a healthy give-and-take as their friendship deepened. They illustrate both personal and professional dimensions of their lives.

In late July, Rosenzweig wrote Buber that, given his degenerative condition, he would like Buber to be part of the ongoing Lehrhaus program.[106] Buber replied with alacrity: "Of course I will take up the lecture [series] if I can thereby fulfill a personal wish of yours."[107] After a back-and-forth on Buber's proposed topic, "The True Life,"[108] Buber reported a breakthrough in his thinking about the sequel to *I and Thou*, because he then envisioned *I and Thou* as a prolegomena to a five-volume work on the anthropology of religion. Buber thus proposed a four-lecture series, "The Basic Forms of Religious Life," to focus on sacrifice, mystery, and prayer. He closed his letter with, "On the topic, I await your candid—shall I say, friendly candid?—advice"[109]

In his next letter Rosenzweig proposed Buber as a second teacher for his young protégé Rudolf Hallo.[110] Buber replied, commenting on his deep affinity for Rosenzweig's book *The Star of Redemption*.[111] He then went on, sketching more of his concept for his projected five-volume opus on global

---

105. Horwitz, *Buber's Way*, 25, 183.

106. Franz Rosenzweig to Martin Buber, late July, 1922, in Buber, *Letters*, 267–68.

107. Martin Buber to Franz Rosenzweig, July 28, 1922, in Buber, *Letters*, 268 (translation modified).

108. Franz Rosenzweig to Martin Buber, July 30, 1922, in Buber, *Letters*, 268–69; Martin Buber to Franz Rosenzweig, August 2, 1922, in Buber, *Letters*, 269–70.

109. Martin Buber to Franz Rosenzweig, August 15, 1922, in Buber, *Letters*, 270.

110. Franz Rosenzweig to Martin Buber, August 19, 1922, in Buber, *Letters*, 271–72.

111. Rosenzweig had begun writing *The Star of Redemption*, his magnum opus, when he served on the front during the war in August 1918 and completed it after his return home five months later. It was published in 1921.

religion.[112] Rosenzweig responded to Buber's fine-tuning of his proposed lecture topics by laying out how he had wrestled with the boundaries of universal religion as he was formulating his book while at the front during the war.[113] Buber replied, introducing Taoism as an example of the blurred boundaries between religion and magic; he then expressed the wish to talk in more detail about this when they next got together.[114]

Three days later, on August 27, Rosenzweig wrote, beginning with the disclaimer that "what follows is no longer spoken from the 'director of the Lehrhaus'" in order to personally address his thinking to Buber.[115] He asserted that the distinction between prayer and incantation was a matter of the location or stance of the person making the utterance. Then he took up institutions—teaching, houses of worship—as having the function of "preparation, clearing the way, building construction" toward the ends of "improvement and turning in Praxis."[116] With these points he was working out two key elements of his thinking, creation and redemption, which had been the cornerstones of his book, *The Star of Redemption*.

Then, just before September 14, Rosenzweig wrote Buber a note preparing him for his shock at seeing Rosenzweig's physical decline at their next visit: "In addition to walking, my speech has just been destroyed."[117] He ended by characterizing his condition as the "tragicomic signs of our rendezvous." He wrote to put Buber at ease, encouraging him in advance of their next visit to focus on their intellectual concerns, not his physical condition.

Up to this point in this series of letters we see Rosenzweig's reaching out and Buber's openness toward their personal friendship. Rosenzweig wrote as the ailing director of the institute—not without humor at his own debility—and Buber wrote, sharing his creativity and spiritual explorations. These letters thus show both the process of the two friends becoming increasingly more open and trusting with each other and how they moved in concert on the task of educating, which they shared.

---

112. Martin Buber to Franz Rosenzweig, August 21, 1922, in Buber, *Letters*, 272–73.

113. Franz Rosenzweig to Martin Buber, August 22, 1922, in Buber, *Letters*, 273–74.

114. Martin Buber to Franz Rosenzweig, August 24, 1922, in Buber, *Letters*, 274–75.

115. Franz Rosenzweig to Martin Buber, August 27, 1922, in Buber, *Letters*, 276–77 (translation modified).

116. Franz Rosenzweig to Martin Buber, August 27, 1922, in Buber, *Letters*, 277, 276 (translation modified).

117. Franz Rosenzweig to Martin Buber, undated, in Buber, *Letters*, 277–78 (translation modified).

Correspondence over the printer's proofs of *I and Thou*

The printer's proofs of Buber's book were a further matter of intense give-and-take between the two men, much of which is evidenced by their vigorous correspondence about them in September of 1922.[118] In the first of these letters, written just before September 14, shortly after Buber sent Rosenzweig the printer's proofs of part one of *I and Thou*, Rosenzweig responded with a strong critique of it. He began with a disclaimer: "This is not at all an easy task for me." Then he objected that Buber's simple distinction between *I-Thou* and *I-It* was too restrictive and suggested adding "HE-It" and "We-It" as further categories. He also criticized Buber's use of the word "relation" [*Beziehung*] as a central term. He ended his critique by asserting his own basic stance: "I am a very unselfish knight of the It, now more than ever"; then he added an affirming claim: "I am now truly still *interested* only in I and Thou." Rosenzweig's straightforwardness in this first response to the manuscript is remarkable.[119]

Horwitz commented on this letter: "Rosenzweig uncompromisingly demands several basic principles of dialogical and biblical thinking which he finds missing or distorted in *I and Thou*, but which become cornerstones of Buber's thinking in later years."[120] It is significant to note that, although Buber did not substantially revise his manuscript in response to this critique from Rosenzweig, Rosenzweig's point of view shaped the evolution of Buber's thinking as he worked out the implications of the dialogical principle from that time forward. At the same time, this letter shows how the manuscript itself became an occasion for the deepening of their relationship.

Buber began his letter in reply on September 14 with ingratiating words: "I thank you from the heart for your great, magnificent criticism."[121] Next he expressed his wish that, having more of the text of *I and Thou*, Rosenzweig would see that his conception of the *It*-world was not so narrow. Buber then promised to adjust the title and preface according to Rosenzweig's advice. Buber ended the letter with a reaffirmation of his gratitude and a request "for more of the same" critical response to the rest of the book. He characterized his response to Rosenzweig as "inadequate,"

---

118. Correspondence between Martin Buber and Franz Rosenzweig, August 15–October 1, 1922, in Buber, *Letters* 279–90.

119. Franz Rosenzweig to Martin Buber, mid-September, 1922, in Buber, *Letters*, 278–80.

120. Horwitz, *Buber's Way*, 226; see also Casper, "Franz Rosenzweig's Criticism," 139–59.

121. Martin Buber to Franz Rosenzweig, September 14, 1922, in Buber, *Letters*, 280–81 (my translation).

yet assured Rosenzweig that that was the tip of the iceberg: "... (while my heart sounds in all its depths with inexpressible response)." The tenor and substance of this letter show Buber's openness and vulnerability toward his friend. Then, one day later in a subsequent note, a note which accompanied the final portion of the printer's proofs, Buber made a somewhat self-deprecating parry to Rosenzweig's thrust, characterizing the book as "a brief and rough-hewn beginning" of what he intended to be a five-volume work.[122] Clearly he was not going to reconceptualize the book at that point, yet we see him working here to recontextualize it in terms that seriously took Rosenzweig's critique into account.

On September 20 Rosenzweig responded to the complete text of *I and Thou*. He now characterized his reading as more than conceptual, as a kind of "living with" the text:

> I have now spent days dwelling in your book, and it has gone for me as it actually *should* for a reader: the alienness of the first day has faded away, I have become an acclimatized inhabitant and that which is most remote from me (prosaically stated: what I regard as untrue) has most attracted me—even charmed me, most more than the pieces of your household furnishing which I have come to be at home with. (It occurs to me, that it was just this way for you when you read *The Star [of Redemption]*: [the parts most remote for you] moved you more deeply than that to which you most closely related.[123]

While Rosenzweig's first response to part one was conceptual, he here shows a more intimate response to the book, treating it as a realm or proposed world he has entered into, one where he is drawn to explore, even the parts of it which are most foreign to him. He has moved from *I-It* to *I-Thou* as a reader of the book.

Rosenzweig's letter went further. This dialogical reality and response evoked his meta-level reflection on the dialogical relation between the thoughts of the two thinkers that was implicitly about his dialogical relationship with Buber: he raised the question of "what it means ... that 'another' 'also' [sic] thinks." Then he expressed the balance between difference and communion in genuine dialogical relating:

> Different starting point, different grounds for having to think, different contents that enter into one's thinking, different what

---

122. Martin Buber to Franz Rosenzweig, September 19, 1922, in Buber, *Letters*, 282 (my translation).

123. Franz Rosenzweig to Martin Buber, September 20, 1922, in Buber, *Letters*, 285 (my translation).

one overlooks, differences (least different of all) in what one repels; in short, different people—and yet a commonality that is not "objective," not a matter of "aims" to which different "paths" lead. Rather, the commonality belongs already to the path itself, even though it consists of different paths.[124]

Here Rosenzweig referred to Buber and to himself as two thinkers; then, developing a yarn analogy, he contrasted his first response to the book with this, his second response:

When two think like this, it happens that their thoughts, like two entangled skeins of yarn, meet a hundred times, and must part again a hundred times—must part *in order to* be able to meet again. If one wants to untangle them, one must find the ends, the free ends. . . . From the free ends, they can be untangled; that was what I tried last time [i.e., in Rosenzweig's letter of 14 September]. This time I had to let them lie entangled as they are and proceed along the windings with my heart, stopping again and again at every meeting and every twist.[125]

With this letter Rosenzweig has with deliberation modulated from his earlier focus on the concepts in Buber's text to reflecting on his dialogical relationship with Buber, his fellow thinker. Through his expansive reflections here he has enacted the move from *I*-It to *I-Thou*, the move to which *I and Thou* invites its readers. In this he proved himself to be the book's ideal first reader.

In Rosenzweig's letter two days later, having finished reading the book, he described his reading of it as an experience "in which nearness and remoteness *both* rose within me to the highest pitch."[126] He commented that he took the argument as a whole, savoring both where he disagreed as well as where he agreed: "In conclusion it does not really matter whether I can or cannot follow you on this or that specific point. Not when the ambivalent feeling of stepping away matches that of stepping toward as it does here."[127] Rosenzweig ended by using a rich architectural metaphor to express the nature of reading in relation to Buber's book: "It is difficult to say from outside

---

124. Franz Rosenzweig to Martin Buber, September 20, 1922, in Buber, *Letters*, 285 (my translation).

125. Franz Rosenzweig to Martin Buber, September 20, 1922, in Buber, *Letters*, 286 (emphasis original, translation modified).

126. Franz Rosenzweig to Martin Buber, September 22, 1922, in Buber, *Letters*, 286 (emphasis original, translation modified).

127. Franz Rosenzweig to Martin Buber, September 22, 1922, in Buber, *Letters*, 286 (my translation).

or even from the entrance whether the firmament still peeps in through the dome of the temple; even in the Pantheon in Rome, one has to walk a good distance in toward the center in order to know."[128] The Pantheon, like Buber's book, opens to the sky, yet the reality of this operculum or aperture can only be known by the one who moves to the center or heart of the edifice where the line of sight changes to make that to which it opens visible. Rosenzweig's first response to Buber's book was to read it from the edge of the edifice; his second response was to see it from closer to its center.[129]

Some days after these two letters responding to the book as a whole, Rosenzweig wrote Buber a short note out of concern because he had not received a reply to this second response: "Your emphatic silence in response to my letter of Friday makes me fear that you have taken offense at it. If that is the case, please tell me and do not remain silent. I am not so overly sensitive that I could not take a sharp reply, but also not so thick-skinned that I would not feel silence more sharply than any reply, even if it be the sharpest words—and that cannot be your intention."[130] Rosenzweig's whole focus here is on tending to the relationship. The note is at once a query and an affirmation of Rosenzweig's connectedness to Buber in their relationship. This necessary part of the whole range of relating is in full play here.

On September 28, six days after Rosenzweig's second letter responding to the book, Buber finally answered his friend. This letter shows Buber's part in tending to their relationship. Buber began by raising the issue of the intention behind his period of silence. At the core of this exposition he referred again to their initial extended conversation, holding it up as a prototype of the "pure utterance" that is the object of messianic longing.

> How could you ever think that I was practicing "emphatic silence" toward you—... you must have noticed that in my interaction with you, from about the second half-hour of your visit in Heppenheim on, I have maintained pure communication such as, in a kind of messianic wish-dream, one could wish one could maintain with all persons. As in the kingdom [of God], there is no taking offense, and silence is either *absolute* silence or not being able to speak. That I have not answered your letter of Friday was simply due to the fact that at this point in the

---

128. Franz Rosenzweig to Martin Buber, September 22, 1922, in Buber, *Letters*, 287 (translation modified).

129. Buber later applied Rosenzweig's Pantheon metaphor to the difference between merely studying the *mitzvot*, the commandments, and fulfilling them in one's actions (Buber, *Letters*, 287n3).

130. Franz Rosenzweig to Martin Buber, no date [late September 1922], in Buber, *Letters*, 288 (my translation).

dialogue to be sure presumably I could have spoken further but could not have written further.[131]

Following this very personal exaltation of their dialogical relationship, Buber descended to the mundane in a perhaps unnecessary moment of defensive dissimulation. In response to Rosenzweig's heartfelt sense of urgency, Buber took up the matter of his daily work at correspondence. "You should know that I am always amazed when I have written a real letter; for weeks at a time, I often merely succeed in 'managing' my correspondence, twenty, thirty items in a usual day, none without an attempt to make the addressee present, but also none with an authentic giving of my being."[132] Yet here again he ended by very intimately revealing the personal impact that their dialogue through letters was having on him: "You are one of the few persons with whom I have been able to 'exchange' letters in this decade. Often you draw me out of the cave; sometimes it is stronger."[133]

The next day Rosenzweig replied with his own affirmation of the dialogical nature of their relationship. Here he provided evidence that Buber may actually have been offended. Yet, at the same time, he revealed himself as vulnerable, confessing his suspicion of offense, his "twinges of guilty conscience," his "uneasiness in the writing":

> How could I have thought [you were offended]? Simply because the first word I received from you after my letter was that extremely agitated card... which did not mention receipt of the letter with even a word. Moreover, to be sure, because something of a guilty conscience predominated in me precisely because of the excessively unencumbered *ad hominem* language. Perhaps you noticed that this was due primarily to a certain uneasiness in the writing.[134]

Then he made his affirmation of "the truth that exists *between* us" and the voluntary risk-taking that genuine self-disclosure entails: "The truth that exists *between* us is much too closely linked with the truthfulness that is *within*

---

131. Martin Buber to Franz Rosenzweig, September 28, 1922, in Buber, *Letters*, 288 (emphasis original, my translation). Compare Buber and Rosenzweig, "Revelation and Law," 109.

132. Martin Buber to Franz Rosenzweig, September 28, 1922, in Buber, *Letters*, 288 (my translation).

133. Martin Buber to Franz Rosenzweig, September 28, 1922, in Buber, *Letters*, 288–89.

134. Franz Rosenzweig to Martin Buber, September 29, 1922, in Buber, *Letters*, 289.

us for me ever to want to tell you a 'naked' truth, one for which the messenger who delivers it would not be ready to pay with his own life."[135]

He ended with a further affirmation—that his openness to Buber extended to his willingness to give up cherished beliefs: "There are persons for whose sake one would gladly disown his own ideas, insofar as one is at all able to do so. You must know that for me you are one such person."[136]

Two days later on October 1, the Eve of Yom Kippur, Buber responded to Rosenzweig's heartfelt letter with a disclosure of his own heart, the sharing of a deep memory of the Eve of Yom Kippur when he was a young teenager.

> There is something serious that I must tell you: that in my innermost heart . . . I strongly feel the mood of *erev*, the sense that today is the Eve of Yom Kippur. This feeling probably comes . . . because I experienced this day between my thirteenth and fourteenth year . . . with an intensity such as I have not felt since. . . . All this was not simply in the past; it is. Yet it is with me as it is and much frailty but no more a lack.[137]

He then appealed to Rosenzweig for heartfelt understanding and gave him a traditional Jewish New Year's blessing: "May your heart understand me! [In Hebrew:] May a good year be sealed to you!"[138]

This series of letters around the manuscript of Buber's breakthrough book quickly moved from intellectual objectivity to the interpersonal dimension of their deep friendship. The dialogical reality to which *I and Thou* invites its readers—its questioning, its hesitations, its silences, its affirmations—is all embodied in the exchange between Buber and Rosenzweig in these letters. This enactment is a testament to the authenticity of Buber's hard-won vision of dialogue as it is expressed in the book.

Dialogue over the role of law in Jewish life

A further phase of the relationship between Buber and Rosenzweig consisted of their dialogue regarding the role of the law, the *mitzvot*, in Jewish life. When Buber's 1919 lecture, "Herut: On Youth and Religion," the last in a series of Buber's lectures on Judaism, was published in 1923 in Buber's collected *Speeches on Judaism*, it provoked a lengthy response titled "The

---

135. Franz Rosenzweig to Martin Buber, September 29, 1922, in Buber, *Letters*, 289 (emphasis original, translation modified).

136. Franz Rosenzweig to Martin Buber, September 29, 1922, in Buber, *Letters*, 289 (translation modified).

137. Martin Buber to Franz Rosenzweig, October 1, 1922, in Buber, *Letters*, 290 (translation modified).

138. Martin Buber to Franz Rosenzweig, October 1, 1922, in Buber, *Letters*, 290 (translation modified).

Builders" which Rosenzweig wrote early in the summer of 1923. This response took the form of an essay-letter addressed to Buber and it was first published in the eighth issue of *Der Jude* in August 1924.[139] Buber never wrote a formal reply to this letter-essay but it evoked a series of letters back and forth between the two of them on the issue. Buber published seven of his letters in this correspondence as "Revelation and Law" seven years after Rosenzweig's death.[140] The two took fundamentally different positions: while Rosenzweig was moving toward the complete observance of Jewish law, Buber continued to insist he would obey any given law as commandment only when he sensed it was directly addressed to him in any given present moment by the eternal *Thou*.

At the end of "The Builders" Rosenzweig expressed his intent that the essay would "open up a dialogue."[141] In his letter of June 24, 1924, Buber urged Rosenzweig to publish this essay expressing that the law was to be internalized so as to be expressed through the will as obedience in action; yet Buber reasserted his contrary commitment "to stand ready ... for the unmediated word and its hour."[142] Buber then demurred on writing a formal reply, claiming that the general reader would read such a reply "without obligation," which would contradict the depth of his reply, upon which "I would have to stake my very being."[143] In a letter he wrote two weeks later on July 5, Buber raised the issue once again: "I must not acquiesce to the laws and the statutes blindly, but I must ask again and again: Is this addressed to me, rightfully to me? ... I cannot go on with this exposition, incomplete though it is. Make it adequate by completing it in the rightness of your heart."[144] With these words Buber shows how dialogue with a specific focus always stands open-ended and incomplete, even when the participants have run their course with it.

This dialogue embodies a dynamic element central to genuine dialogue, the duality of holding one's ground while at the same time reaching out to the other in an open-ended search for commonality in the midst of difference. It also shows how taking the other participant in the dialogue seriously as *Thou* is inseparable from taking equally seriously the actual question at stake in the dialogue.

139. Buber, "Herut," 149–74; Rosenzweig, "Builders," 72–92.
140. Buber and Rosenzweig, "Revelation and Law," 109–18.
141. Rosenzweig, "Builders," 92.
142. Martin Buber to Franz Rosenzweig, June 24, 1924, in Buber, *Letters*, 314–15 (translation modified).
143. Martin Buber to Franz Rosenzweig, June 24, 1924, in Buber, *Letters*, 315; Buber, "Revelation and Law," 112.
144. Martin Buber to Franz Rosenzweig, July 5, 1924, in Buber, *Letters*, 317; Buber, "Revelation and Law," 114–15 (my translation).

The Buber-Rosenzweig translation of the Hebrew Scriptures

Buber's collaboration with Rosenzweig on the project of translating the Hebrew Bible into German began in 1925 in response to a request by the publisher Lambert Schneider, and it became the culmination and apotheosis of their dialogical relationship.

Rosenzweig's progressive paralysis limited him to pointing at typewriter keys until near the end of his life, when he had to communicate with his wife by blinking an eyelid to input his part in the project. Their goal was to produce a translation that was accessible to native German speakers but kept visible the alien nature of the Hebrew original, one that kept true to both the rhythm of oral recitation and the reality of the ancient Hebrew thought-world. Their method was intrinsically dialogical, with Buber writing annotated draft translations followed by Rosenzweig's responses and annotations, augmented by weekly conferences when Buber was in Frankfurt. At times their correspondence over a single word went on for several weeks. Buber devoted "most of his time to the indescribably difficult and time-consuming task of working together" with the increasingly incapacitated Rosenzweig. This collaboration "filled Rosenzweig's final years with satisfaction and meaning."[145] Four years of their intense work together (1925–1929) produced a translation up to Isaiah 53. After Rosenzweig died, Buber persevered for thirty-two years, completing the project in 1961, in part as a tribute to their friendship.

The central purpose of their translation was to recover the oral quality of the original Hebrew text. Maurice Friedman eloquently expresses their shared vision that the Bible is preeminently a dialogical book:

> The writtenness of the Bible lies on it like a light garment. In the moment when the psalms are prayed, the laws obeyed, the prophecies believed, they at once lose their monological muteness, find voice, and call the eternal Partner to dialogue. But the human partner, too, is constantly summoned to dialogue. Continually, the psalms awaken men to prayer, the laws awaken men to obey, the prophecies awaken men to belief. Even the epic is secret dialogue which, under the husks of its epic past, is carried over into full anecdotal presentness and what is awakened to deed, hope, love, becomes knowledge, teaching, revelation.[146]

Thus, the Buber-Rosenzweig translation of the Hebrew Bible serves as a monument not only to their shared dialogical vision but also to their relationship as an authentic life in dialogue.

---

145. Friedman, *Martin Buber's Life and Work*, 2:56.
146. Friedman, *Martin Buber's Life and Work*, 2:62.

Rosenzweig's influence and the legacy of the relationship

The relationship between Buber and Rosenzweig had a decisive influence on Buber and the direction of his thinking. Rivka Horwitz emphasizes this influence: "Buber's visits to Rosenzweig were characterized by a mutual give and take. Buber, the more well-known of the two, was nevertheless open to Rosenzweig's reactions to and criticism of his work. We do not know of any other person who influenced Buber as directly and forcefully as did Rosenzweig."[147] Like Buber's move from his early celebration of the German side in World War I to pacifism in response to Landauer in 1916, his shift to an overtly anti-mystical stance was encouraged and consolidated through his interaction with Rosenzweig. Rosenzweig's strong opposition to mysticism helps to frame some of Buber's express statements that do not consistently square with the rest of his views regarding spirituality. In a letter in early 1923, Rosenzweig gave an account of that first extensive conversation with Buber in Heppenheim in December 1921, emphasizing what to him was their accord contra mysticism: "Mystical eccentricity is hateful to me . . . . In [his] rejection of mysticism I am in complete agreement with Buber. There can be no harsher critic of the former 'famous' Buber than he himself, not only privately but also publicly."[148]

In another letter a year later, Rosenzweig again focused on Buber's repudiation of mystical ecstasy when he wrote of that first conversation:

> In the course of the conversation . . . I suddenly realized that Buber even spiritually was no longer the mystical subjectivist for which he was revered by people; but rather, even in the realm of the intellect, he was becoming a solid and reasonable man. I was rather astonished and impressed by the great sincerity with which he approached every topic.[149]

Clearly, their dialogue helped to bring out the nonmystical side of Buber's thinking—yet it did not completely efface the mystical part of his disposition. In fact, Buber's mysticism strongly remained as an undercurrent throughout his life, as we shall see in chapter 5.

The relationship between Buber and Rosenzweig shows the outworking of Buber's dialogical vision in concrete terms in his own life. Through their correspondence and their work together as men living in response to the eternal *Thou*, as educators, and as people of the word, we see the development of Buber and Rosenzweig's relationship and its vicissitudes. Over the course of the eight years of their friendship they made their

---

147. Horwitz, *Buber's Way*, 240.

148. Franz Rosenzweig to Eugen Mayer, cited in Horwitz, *Buber's Way*, 185.

149. Franz Rosenzweig to Rudolf Hallo, early December 1922, Rosenzweig et al., *Briefe*, 461; Horwitz, *Buber's Way*, 189.

affirmations, grappled with their differences, discovered their shared vision, and completed their common work.

9. Conclusion

In this chapter we have seen how Buber's relationships and his encounters were of a piece with what he developed and articulated as his philosophy of dialogue. We see what *I and Thou* points to in the concrete terms of Buber's own lived experience. We see how, particularly in terms of Buber's philosophy of dialogue, his life in all its concreteness was the ground out of which he spoke. We see how in his lived experience he knew both the *I-Thou* and the *I-It* as he engaged with his family, his acquaintances, and his friends—how, as he frequently iterated in *I and Thou*, "it is the exalted melancholy of our condition that every *Thou* in our world must become an *It*"—yet at any point we can choose to turn back to the *Thou*.[150] These accounts of his life and his correspondence help us to understand how we too live in a chiaroscuro world dappled by our shifts between *I-Thou* and *I-It*, between meeting and mismeeting.

We must now take a final preparatory step before turning to the text of *I and Thou* itself. In the next two chapters we will identify a few key reference points in Buber's thought-world. These reference points will allow us to establish a conceptual frame with which we can better understand what Buber brings out in *I and Thou* as the foundational exposition of his mature philosophy of dialogue. Therefore, we now turn to explore a few elements of Buber's existential and spiritual outlook that some of his interpreters have relegated to immature phases of his thinking and that, therefore, they discard from his mature dialogical vision. In strong disagreement with those interpreters, it is these very elements that I see as underlying his thinking as a whole from start to finish and as undergirding his vision as an expression of our common human spirituality.

---

150. Buber, *I and Thou*, §22a, §25a, §32b, §52d.

Chapter 5

Buber's "No" to Objectification

"It all comes down to the one thing—utter openness to presence" (§46g). To Buber, "presence" is the *fons et origo* of meaning and value. Access to presence requires the turning of the whole person to the other in dialogical immediacy. Such turning to the other is the move from the *I-It* stance to the *I-Thou* stance. Presence is the direct, unmediated interface of self and other. It involves an intuitive sense which is at once apperception and constitutive ontology. As such, the intuition of being precedes cognition and rational thought. Yet it can become "the ground of thought's arising."[1]

To Buber, the history of Western thought is the history of the erosion of presence, of the replacing of the direct intuition of being with forms of mediation. The forms of mediation work to objectify the world. They include the shift from the concrete to the abstract, from the particular to the general, and from the intuitive to the rational. The forms of mediation have mushroomed over the course of the development of Western culture.

Buber locates the breakaway from the primal binding to the absolute, the givenness of presence, in the rise of autonomous reason in the thinking of the ancient Greek philosophers.[2] He traces the trajectory of this breakaway autonomy into the present era through such thinkers as René Descartes. He pits the Cartesian idea of ratiocination as the foundation of thought against the Pascalian act of witness. Referring to Pascal's testimony—"FIRE. God of Abraham, God of Isaac, God of Jacob, not of the philosophers and scholars. Certainty. Certainty. Feeling. Joy. Peace."[3]— Buber writes: "When Pascal in a volcanic hour made that stammering distinction between God and God he was no genius but a man experiencing

---

1. Avnon, *Martin Buber*, 46.

2. Buber, "Religion and Ethics," 100–1.

3. This was Pascal's famous "Memorial," the note he wrote on a parchment and wore for the rest of his life stitched into the lining of his coat.

the primal glow of faith; but at other times he was a theological genius and dwelt in a specifying religion, out of which the happening of that hour had lifted him."[4] Here, regarding Pascal whom he affirms, Buber distinguishes between the thinker's dialogical witness to the unmediated presence and the other, mediated moments of his life.

Buber found Kierkegaard to be a major ally. Kierkegaard's language and sensibility became particularly compatible resources in Buber's effort to articulate and to uphold the raw, unpremeditated immediacy of concrete, particular, intuited reality. Kierkegaard's existential thinking provided necessary tools required in the struggle to reverse the culture-wide drift toward mediated existence. Buber reworked these tools, making them his own.

1. Buber's Existential Edge

Buber grounded his thinking in the immediacy of existence, an immediacy that first came home to him in his spiritual initiation. This immediacy is the counterpart to the distancing that comes with conceptualizing and speculative thought, which can be summed up as objectification. Buber reminds us, "Everything else may be discussed purely speculatively, but not our own existence. . . . Here witness is made."[5] This grounding in immediacy to which Buber points has a strong parallel in Kierkegaard's thought. Consistent with Buber's radical embrace of "the lived concrete," his opening distinction between *I-it* and *I-Thou* in *I and Thou* is anthropological, in the sense of being centered in the reality of human existence. All of Buber's work is closely tethered to this concrete human perspective. Consideration of this foundation of his work will provide an important reference point for understanding *I and Thou* and its intellectual context.

Buber's core distinction between the *It*-world and the realm of *Thou* places him alongside the thinkers of existence, rather than with the rational-conceptual systematic philosophers whose goal is to map out coherent systems of thought. Yet, like any of the so-called existentialists, Buber rejected anyone's categorizing him as an existentialist because his thought cannot be reduced to a philosophy, a system, or an "ism." His thinking is his original grappling with being as an individual and, as such, it cannot be reduced or systematized or categorized. Statements he made to his interpreters near the end of his life make clear the nature of his stance as a thinker.[6] Thus, it is helpful to place him on the side of the ontological thinkers as opposed to

4. Buber, "Question to the Single One," 57–58
5. Buber, "Interrogation of Martin Buber," 18.
6. Buber, "Interrogation of Martin Buber," and Buber, "Replies to My Critics."

cosmological thinkers according to Paul Tillich's "Two Types of Philosophy of Religion."[7] Yet this distinction is limited due to the deliberate, radically concrete scope of Buber's reflections, as he emphasizes:

> I am not authorized to philosophize by any metaphysical essences, neither of "ideas" nor of "substance" nor even of the "world reason," but must as a thinker concern myself alone with man and his relations to everything. . . . Reason as an object of my thought is important for me only insofar as it dwells in man as a property or function. [Reason] cannot replace the smallest perception of something particular and unique with its gigantic structure of general concepts, cannot by means of it contend in the grasping of what here and now confronts me.[8]

With these words Buber disavows reason as a means of knowing beyond its "corrective" function "to set right an error in my sense perception"; he limits his knowing to his own concrete experience. He points "to the lived and not conceived meeting with God [and] the lived reality of meeting is not subject to the logic forged in three millennia. . . . It is not of God but of the meeting that we speak."[9] Thus, he contrasts the "lived reality of meeting" with the attempts to conceptualize it, which are always only approximations of it. He limits himself to phenomenological reflections on it; he cannot pontificate on metaphysical reality.

In a summative statement Buber reaffirms his role as a witness to the encounter with the eternal Other:

> It has . . . not been to "theology," but rather to the experience of faith that I owe the independence of my thought. . . . My philosophy . . . serves an experience, a perceived attitude that it has been established to make communicable. . . . I have no doctrine of a primal ground (*Urgrund*) to offer. I must only witness [to] that meeting in which all meetings with others are grounded.[10]

With these words Buber sets his thinking as a witness to the experience of faith apart from the great speculative systems such as Neoplatonism as seen, for example, in the work of Meister Eckhart.[11]

Buber explains his work by emphasizing its focus is relational because the concrete existence of the person is by its nature relational:

7. Tillich, "Two Types," 10–29.
8. Buber, "Interrogation of Martin Buber," 53–54.
9. Buber, "Replies to My Critics," 700–1.
10. Buber, "Replies to My Critics," 690–91.
11. See Buber, "What is Man?," 184–85.

> The dialogical principle is an ontological one because it is concerned with a basic relationship between man and being; hence with the being of man, since this is grounded in his relationship to being. This principle is to be regarded as existential only as it is necessarily realized in the sphere of existence of the person. . . . I call my philosophy "dialogical philosophy" . . . but feel myself as standing perhaps between an existential thinking in Kierkegaard's sense and something entirely different, something which is still out of sight. . . . I welcome every philosophy of existence that leaves open the door leading to otherness; but I know none that opens it far enough.[12]

Here he locates his existential thinking in relation to Søren Kierkegaard and then points beyond Kierkegaard to, as he perceives it, his own greater openness to "the other."

Buber's relationship with Kierkegaard had a profound influence on him, so much so that he wrote about him more than any other European thinker. Kierkegaard's *Fear and Trembling* had a lasting impact on Buber from the time he first read it as a teenager; late in his life, almost sixty years later, he wrote a critique of its argument.[13] Furthermore, Buber addressed Kierkegaard as if in dialogue with him in at least seven of his writings, often taking on elements of Kierkegaard's thought with some of his harshest criticisms. The dialogical nature of his most extensive essay on Kierkegaard is underscored by its title: "The Question to the Single One."[14] It is important to recognize that Buber freely criticizes Kierkegaard where he disagrees with him, in part because his stance in the world has deep similarities with that of the Danish thinker. At one point he even refers to Kierkegaard as "my brother in faith." "Holy insecurity" and the "narrow ridge" became key metaphors for the character of Buber's thinking across his lifetime. Friedman links Buber's "holy insecurity" with Kierkegaard's *Angst* as the given condition of human existence.[15] For both Buber and Kierkegaard, authentic living is taking risks in response to sacred obligations, that is, living a life that is open and vulnerable in the face of radical uncertainty.

In *Daniel: Dialogues on Realization*, his early book of existential philosophy, Buber used the voice of his eponymous discussant to proclaim in vatic language the way of "holy insecurity":

---

12. Buber, "Interrogation of Martin Buber," 22–23.
13. Buber, "On the Suspension of the Ethical," 115–20.
14. Buber, "Question to the Single One," 40–82.
15. Friedman, *Martin Buber's Life and Work*, 1:108.

> This is the kingdom of God: the kingdom of danger and of risk, of eternal beginning and of eternal becoming, of opened spirit and deep realization, the kingdom of holy insecurity.... Here is your task: to create ... fulfilled unity out of tension and stream, such as will serve the polar earth. ... You must descend ever anew into the transforming abyss, risk your soul ever anew, ever anew vowed to the holy insecurity.[16]

These words characterize the existential realm as "the kingdom of God" and place the individual in it as a hero where he is to create unity out of his powers in order to serve the earth. His task is marked by continual descent to transformation, continual risk, and continual commitment. At that stage in Buber's thought, risk and uncertainty were the hallmarks of a "realizing life." As such, they were essential components of his "philosophy of realization."

Buber used the metaphor of "the narrow ridge" to mark the emergence of the existential that came with the great change in his thinking during the First World War:

> Since my own thoughts regarding ultimate things took a decisive turn during the First World War, I have at times described my standpoint to my friends as the "narrow ridge." By this I wanted to express that I did not dwell on the broad upland of a system that encompasses a series of sure statements about the absolute, but rather on a narrow mountain ridge between two abysses where there is absolutely no sureness of expressible knowledge but only the certainty of meeting with the hidden Enduring One.[17]

In words that prefigured Buber's image of the "narrow ridge," Kierkegaard delineated the dynamics of existential faith. At the heart of *Fear and Trembling*, one of his pivotal works, he introduced his key figure, "the knight of faith":

> The knight of faith renounces the universal in order to be the particular.... He knows that higher up [above the security of the universal] there winds a lonely path, narrow and steep ... the knight of faith is kept awake, for he is under constant threat and can turn back to the universal at any moment. The knight ... walks alone with his dreadful responsibility.[18]

This passage characterizes the person of faith as a knight, a hero, in terms that resonate with Buber's highest values: renunciation, the concrete particularity of human existence, the solitary nature of existential commitment,

16. Buber, *Daniel*, 95, 98–99.
17. Buber, "What is Man?," 184 (my translation).
18. Kierkegaard, *Fear and Trembling*, 103, 105, 107.

and the sense of his life of faith as a journey through the world on a narrow ridge, "a lonely path" that winds "narrow and steep." Most importantly, for both Kierkegaard and Buber, the knight of faith embodies the "absolute duty to God [in which] the single individual . . . stands in an absolute relation to the absolute."[19] For both of them the finite individual's putting all into the venture with the absolute is the *sine qua non* of spiritual existence.

Just as for Kierkegaard, "the true knight of faith is a witness, never a teacher,"[20] so it is for Buber, although Buber's witness is explicitly dialogical: "I have no teaching. I only point to something. I point to reality, I point to something in reality that had not or had too little been seen. I take him who listens to me by the hand and lead him to the window. I open the window and point to what is outside. I have no teaching, but I carry on a conversation."[21] This role which Buber identifies for himself is the grounds for his "rhetoric of pointing" discussed in chapter 3.

Walter Kaufmann confirms the existential nature of Buber's thought; for Kaufmann, Buber is the arch-existentialist. He concludes his summative essay on Buber's religious significance with this observation:

> If we find the heart of existentialism in the protest against systems, concepts, and abstractions, coupled with a resolve to remain faithful to concrete experience and above all to the challenge of human existence [and the ability] to listen to the challenge of another human reality as it has found expression in a text . . . one might well conclude that in reality there is only one existentialist, and he is no existentialist but Martin Buber.[22]

That is, if we set aside Buber's resistance to categories, we can see how his affinities with existential thought stand out.

Buber expresses his existential stance in a remarkable autobiographical confession: "I . . . am . . . a man endangered before God, a man wrestling ever anew for God's light, ever anew engulfed in God's abysses."[23] For him, the life of faith has the character of what he identifies as the high points of Jewish tradition: "All three movements—the prophetic, the Essenic-early Christian, and the kabbalistic-hasidic—share a resolve to make man's life not easier but more difficult, while at the same time inspiriting and exalting it."[24] Both sides of this chiaroscuro life of faith which he shares with

---

19. Kierkegaard, *Fear and Trembling*, 108.
20. Kierkegaard, *Fear and Trembling*, 107.
21. Buber, "Replies to My Critics," 693.
22. Kaufmann, "Buber's Religious Significance," 685.
23. Buber, "Autobiographical Fragments," 22.
24. Buber, "Jewish Religiosity," 92.

Kierkegaard are perfectly expressed in this late restatement of his autobiographical confession: "I possess no security against the necessity to live in fear and trembling; I have nothing but the certainty that we share in the revelation."[25] Here "holy insecurity" is the resolute acceptance of whatever arises for one in concrete existence because one takes this immediacy as "speech," as one's being addressed by the Transcendent.

Buber's thinking begins and ends with the "concretely human," what he calls *gelebte Wirklichkeit*, "the lived concrete" or "lived actuality."[26] All of his discourse about God is deliberately a phenomenology of the human faith-encounter with God. Thus, his perspective is radically anthropological. Given this base, for Buber, to take account of "the Other" of human encounter, experience, and interpretation is a crucial part of his discourse.

2. Buber's Distinction: Philosophy vs. Religion

In following through with what he laid down in *I and Thou*, Buber put great effort into two essays, "Dialogue" and "Religion and Philosophy,"[27] that strongly reinforced "the lived concrete" as the reality upon which all hinges. "Dialogue" became a companion piece to *I and Thou*, one which points to "the ontic basis of the *I-Thou* relation."[28] In this essay Buber grounds dialogical reality in the concreteness of lived life:[29]

> I know as a living truth only the concrete world which constantly, in every moment, is reached out to me. I can divide it into its component parts, I can compare them and distribute them into groups of similar phenomena, I can derive them from earlier and reduce them to simpler phenomena; and yet when having done all this, I have not touched my concrete world reality. Not analyzable, incomparable, irreducible, now, happening once only in its present moment, it confronts me with a horrifying gaze.... The true name of the concrete world

---

25. Buber, "Replies to My Critics," 699.

26. Buber, *I and Thou*, §50m–q.

27. Buber, "Dialogue," 1–39. Buber first published "Dialogue" in a periodical in 1929; two years later he expanded it and published it as a book; Buber, "Religion and Philosophy," 27–46. Buber first wrote this essay for a lecture in Frankfurt in 1929 and later expanded it for a presentation in New York in 1951.

28. Schaeder, *Hebrew Humanism*, 177.

29. "Concrete world reality" (*das Weltkonkretum*) or "my concrete world reality" (*mein Weltkonkretum*) in Buber, "Dialogue," 12.

>is this: the creation which is entrusted to me, to each person. In it the signs of address are given to us.[30]

He clears the space for this concrete grounding by ruling out modes of awareness that involve conceptual thought and the mystical quest. Opinions, ideas, conceptual content, discussion, the activity of the observer or onlooker—all are set aside for the sake of the dialogical stance. Using a vignette, Buber presents a person thus predisposed to dialogue and characterizes him in terms of his presence to his concrete, emerging situation: he is "calm [*gelassen*], receptive to whatever may come; his being seems to say, to be ready is not enough, one must also actually be *there* [*wirklich da sein*]."[31] Thus, the dialogical moment is the moment of breakthrough in which the immediacy of our concrete, conditioned reality is held in tension with that which transcends it: in this moment, the awareness of being limited in one's viewpoint as a concrete-historical human being coexists with the awareness of mutually overcoming this limit *along with* one's interlocutor.[32]

Buber's concern about the threat of Jewish assimilation to "Occidental dualism" is a direct expression of his insistence on the unmediated concreteness of the spiritual encounter.[33] This concern is well framed in his late collection of essays in *Eclipse of God*, subtitled *Studies in the Relation between Religion and Philosophy*. Buber distinguishes between religion as the *concreteness* of the encounter between the human and the transcendent and philosophy as the abstracting power that pulls the thinker into splitting the realm of mere ideas from the actuality of lived life. In "Religion and Ethics" he sketches the history of the decline from concrete oneness with the Absolute, the Axial insight, down to the radical relativism of the present era. He argues that primal human thought was grounded in "the binding of the radical distinction between good and evil to the Absolute" and that this was "the teaching of a universal continuity of meaning" across antiquity.[34] Then, the rise of autonomous reason in Greek thought had a corrosive effect on the unity of the ancient teaching, bringing about the relativizing of all values. Buber traces the development of this corrosive process across history into the twentieth century. Given this

---

30. Buber, "Dialogue," 12–13 (translation modified).

31. Buber, "Dialogue," 3 (translation modified; Buber italicized "there." Note that in my bracketed insertion of the original German I use italics to mark the German but here, to show that Buber's "da" ["there"] was in italics, I reverse that.). For a comparable moment expressed in *I and Thou*, see §28d.

32. Buber, "Dialogue," 6–8.

33. Buber, "Holy Way," 108–9.

34. Buber, "Religion and Ethics," 99–100.

broad historical framework, the central essay of the collection, entitled "Religion and Philosophy," lays out the opposition between the abstracting activity inherent in philosophizing and the lived concrete quality of the living divine-human encounter. Close consideration of this essay helps to limn out several key elements of Buber's position.

Buber claims the duality of *I* and *Thou* is fulfilled in the religious relationship. Because "*I* and *Thou* exist only in and by means of *lived concreteness*," the religious relationship "arises out of the original situation of the individual, his living before the Face of Being." Accordingly, the religious relationship consists of "the unfolding of the existence that is lent to us."[35] The finite immediacy of "lived concreteness" has as its counterpart the eternal *Thou*, the Absolute or Unconditional. Through this bond held in dialogue, the primal "situation of the individual," his "living before the Face of Being," is sustained and becomes his destiny in relationship, "the unfolding of the existence that is lent to us."[36] That is, the eternal *Thou*, the Creator, is the One who at once both lends us our existence and enters into living dialogue with us.

Accordingly, Buber defines faith as "the entrance into genuinely reciprocal meeting in the fullness of life between one active existence and another."[37] The entrance into this reciprocity consists of "binding oneself in relationship with" the eternal *Thou*, who is described in Buber's terms as "an undemonstrable and unprovable, yet even so, in relationship, knowable Being, from whom all meaning comes."[38] Relating to the eternal *Thou* as binding recalls the *adekah*, the patriarchal story of the binding of Isaac (Gen 22:9), the prototypical moment of self-giving to the Creator. From Buber's modern perspective, this absolute self-giving to the Absolute (echoing Kierkegaard's "absolute duty to God [in which] the single individual... stands in an absolute relation to the absolute") takes place in an apophatic context: there is no objective correlative to the incomprehensible eternal *Thou*. As Buber famously asserted in *I and Thou*, The eternal *Thou* "can be rightly addressed, but not expressed" (§48c).

Buber next takes up the concept of the "way of God" found in the Old Testament and the Gospels to illustrate the nature of religious thinking.[39] He sees the "way of God," not as commandments or ethical principles but as "the way of God in and through the world," which means, "God's becoming

---

35. Buber, "Religion and Philosophy," 32 (emphasis added). This central statement makes clear why Buber did not regard himself as a philosopher.

36. Buber, "Religion and Philosophy," 32.

37. Buber, "Religion and Philosophy," 33.

38. Buber, "Religion and Philosophy," 33.

39. Buber, "Religion and Philosophy," 33.

visible in His action." This manifesting is the "prototype" for the human "imitation of God." Surprisingly, Buber here makes an explicit parallel between this manifesting of God and the Chinese *tao*: "Similarly, the Chinese Tao, the 'path' in which the world moves, is the cosmic primal meaning. But because man conforms this his life to it and practices 'imitation of the Tao,' it is at the same time the perfection of the soul." The tao, like the eternal *Thou*, "from whom all meaning comes," is "the cosmic primal meaning."[40] The Taoist act of conforming one's life to the tao, the practice of imitating the tao, which is the perfection or completion of the soul, is the counterpart to the absolute self-giving to the Creator in dialogue. This is the heart of biblical religion, as Buber sees it.

Buber continues: the goal of the religious quest is "the attainment of a condition freed from intention." He equates "intention" here with "arbitrariness," the willfulness, the self-affirming striving of the autonomous individual. The counterpart to this willfulness is "unarbitrary life 'in the Face of God'" or *Gelassenheit*, self-surrender.[41] For this alternative life, the goal may be "salvation," but the means is the "way" itself, the unarbitrary life, that is, living in the presence of God freed from self-willed intention.

Buber portrays the history of religions as a continual struggle to break through the manifestations of "religion"—the tendency towards human constructions, towards stale autonomy—in order to move to the dialogical, to "lived concreteness as the meeting place between the human and the divine."[42] Buber elaborates on the nature of "the actually lived concrete" as the locus of this divine-human encounter: "The actually lived concrete is the 'moment' in its unforeseeableness and irrecoverableness, in its undivertible character of happening but once, in its decisiveness, in its secret dialogue between that which happens and that which is willed, between fate and action, address and answer."[43] The "moment" in its uncharted uniqueness is the "place" of the "secret dialogue" in which each person's destiny unfolds. Buber emphasizes that such concrete moments are the crux of divine-human dialogue: "The religious essence in every religion, its highest certainty, is the certainty that *the meaning of existence is open and accessible in the actual lived concrete*, not above the struggle with reality but in it. Meaning is to be

---

40. Buber, "Religion and Philosophy," 33.

41. Buber, "Religion and Philosophy," 34. Buber was familiar with this concept through his work on Eckhart; see *I and Thou* §48a; also Buber, "Dialogue," 3; Buber, "Kavana," 98–108.

42. Buber, "Religion and Philosophy," 35.

43. Buber, "Religion and Philosophy," 35.

experienced in living action and suffering itself, in the unreduced immediacy of the moment . . . the spontaneity of the mystery."[44]

To Buber, each person's role is to "go out" to the encounter with God in such moments: "Only he reaches the meaning who stands firm, without holding back or reservation, before the whole might of reality and answers it in a living way. He is ready to confirm with his life the meaning which he has attained."[45] This "going out" [*ausgehen; ausziehen*] is one of Buber's key terms in *I and Thou*.[46] In this "going out," this "stepping forth," the believing person exercises the courage of faith:

> When our existence between birth and death becomes incomprehensible and uncanny, when all security is shattered through the mystery. This is . . . the essential mystery, the inscrutableness of which belongs to its very nature; it is the unknowable. Through this dark gate . . . the believing man *steps forth* into the everyday which is henceforth hallowed as the place in which he has to live with the mystery. He *steps forth* directed and assigned to the concrete, contextual situations of his existence. That he henceforth accepts the situation as given him by the Giver is what Biblical religion calls the "fear of God." . . . [H]e endures in the face of God the reality of lived life, dreadful and incomprehensible though it be. He loves it in the love of God, whom he has learned to love.[47]

This passage begins with the existential condition within which we find ourselves, the mystery, the "dark gate" through which we pass to "go out," step forth, to our destiny. The act of stepping forth to enter fully into one's circumstances is the act of faith. This stepping forth is dialogical, for in it one is "directed and assigned to" one's concrete reality. The verbs that follow in the passage show that this stepping forth is of a piece with what comes with it: the one who steps forth *accepts* his circumstances as part of his divine-human dialogue. This acceptance—"Whether field of work or field of battle, he accepts the place in which he is placed"[48]—is more than raw capitulation to the unavoidable: it is radical receptivity, the open receiving of one's circumstances *as* the divinely "uttered," given part of the divine-human dialogue. The religious person "is certain that in the course of this his mortality he can meet God in God's very giving and in his, man's,

---

44. Buber, "Religion and Philosophy," 35 (emphasis added).
45. Buber, "Religion and Philosophy," 35.
46. Buber, *I and Thou*, §46f, §50h, §61q.
47. Buber, "Religion and Philosophy," 36–37 (emphasis added).
48. Buber, "Religion and Philosophy," 38.

receiving of the concrete situation."⁴⁹ He *endures* concrete lived life "in the face [the presence] of God." He *loves* this life "in the love of God." Stepping forth, accepting, enduring, loving—these are the elements of his response in his dialogue with the eternal *Thou*.

Buber adds two images to bring home the sense of this life of faith. First, he uses the metaphor of the orchestra to explain more fully the roles of the human *I* and the eternal *Thou* in this dialogue: "In lived concreteness . . . consciousness is the first violin but not the conductor."⁵⁰ If we imagine ourselves to be the conductor of the symphony, we are back to asserting our arbitrary, self-willed autonomy. If we perform as first violin in concert with the eternal *Thou* as our conductor, then the symphony is complete. Music is produced, music that is the synergy of our willingness, practice, and abilities with what emerges as our circumstances. The corollary is that we find deep fulfillment in the resulting music along with our role in producing it, thanks to the lead of the conductor. "Only through genuine intercourse with a *Thou* can the *I* of the living person be experienced as existing."⁵¹ In this working together, harmony sounds forth.

Second, Buber invokes the covenant metaphor in a fresh way. He shifts to the concept of covenant, which works as a spontaneous and immediate way of characterizing the dialogical bond between the human and the eternal *Thou*. Our concert with the eternal *Thou* can be seen as "the covenant of the absolute with the particular, with the concrete."⁵² Buber has moved from one dialogical metaphor to another, from that of the symphony to that of the covenant. In this case, the person of faith is both a participant in the dialogue and a witness to it. "Standing in the concrete situation and even witnessing to it, man is overspanned by the rainbow of the covenant between the absolute and the concrete."⁵³ When we find ourselves in this position as participant and witness, the rainbow of the covenant appears to us as the sign, as the arc linking the absolute and the concrete, heaven and earth.

So far in this chapter we have considered Buber's insistence on setting aside all of the elements of thinking that turn awareness into a mediated construct. We have seen how, for the sake of this goal, Buber appropriated the language and tools provided by the existentialism of Kierkegaard

---

49. Buber, "Religion and Philosophy," 39.

50. Buber, "Religion and Philosophy," 39.

51. Buber, "Religion and Philosophy," 40. Compare *I and Thou* §15c: "I become by means of the *Thou*; becoming *I*, I say *Thou*."

52. Buber, "Religion and Philosophy," 41.

53. Buber, "Religion and Philosophy," 41.

in particular. And we have seen Buber's contrast between philosophy and religion as his means of clearing the space for the unadorned immediacy of living in the face of the Transcendent. We now turn to another, crucial element of Buber's project of stripping away the clutter, his revaluation of *Erlebnis*, lived experience.

3. Buber's Revaluation of *Erlebnis*

Buber makes clear that the splitting of reality into subject and object lasts only so long as the power of abstraction is at work.[54] He points out that the subject side of that split has mushroomed as a problem in recent centuries, taking such manifestations as "the psychologizing of the world," which he saw as a modern form of Gnosticism.[55] Concomitantly, in the development of his own thinking, he went through a significant about-face regarding *Erlebnis*, subjective experience. To that issue we now turn.

The evolution of Buber's concept of *Erlebnis* ("lived experience") is an index of the development of his thinking in the crucial years around the First World War. As such, it shows at a broad conceptual level the shift that was taking place at that time, a shift Buber only hinted at in his account of his "conversion" in response to his encounter with the young Mehe in 1914.

Buber's early interest in mysticism was his part in a long history of the development of idealism in German thought. As a university student Buber read Meister Eckhart around 1900 when his friend Gustav Landauer was producing an anthology of Eckhart's writings in modern German. Eckhart, the great mystical theologian of the late thirteenth and early fourteenth centuries, was one of the first thinkers to write and to preach in Middle High German, thus serving as a major waypoint in the evolution of the German language as well as of philosophical discourse in German. Eckhart's thought itself is part of a trajectory of Greco-Christian mysticism that began with the New Testament, incorporated Plotinus's speculative theories, passed through the writings of Pseudo-Dionysius, and reached its full flowering in Eckhart's sermons. Buber's doctoral dissertation on Nicholas of Cusa and Jakob Boehme, completed in 1904, was an exploration of the development of individualism within this idealistic-mystical tradition. A passage from a talk on Boehme that Buber gave for the *neue Gemeinschaft* in 1899 shows how he expressed this version of German idealism as his sense of unity:

---

54. Buber, "Religion and Philosophy," 32.
55. Buber, "On the Psychologizing of the World," 144–52.

> Today we are closer to Boehme than we are to the teachings of Feuerbach, to the ideas of St. Francis of Assisi, who called the trees, birds, and stars his brothers and sisters, and nearer yet to the Vedanta. [Boehme] desires a deeper unity. It is not enough that the I unites itself with the world. The I is the world.... God is the unity of all powers.[56]

At that point, to Buber all things were one for those who had eyes to see this oneness and this oneness was a mystical sense which one could identify as "God." Buber's outlook at that time was monistic and his allusion suggests he may have then felt an affinity with Advaita Vedanta, the nondual form of Hindu philosophy.[57]

During his student years Buber moved from one university to another—Vienna, Zurich, Leipzig, Berlin—to attend lectures by some of the foremost thinkers of the day. In this moving about he followed centuries of German academic practice. He went to Berlin in part to study with Wilhelm Dilthey, a pivotal interpreter of cultures who focused on *Erlebnis* and the hermeneutical method of recovering *Erlebnisse* through interpreting written accounts of the past. True to the state of knowledge of his time, Dilthey's project was to recapitulate the history of human cultural knowledge. He sought to develop a comprehensive method of interpreting culture as the human sciences [*Geisteswissenschaften*] for which he could claim a validity parallel to that of the study of nature in the natural sciences. His goal was understanding [*Verstehen*] and in his view, the key element that would open one to any given cultural world, no matter how remote, was *Erlebnis*. The attractiveness of *Erlebnis* as a key to understanding the past also made sense to the young Buber.

Erlebnis is the noun form of the German verb *erleben*, from the root word *leben*, "to live," and it means "to experience" in the sense of "to undergo." Thus, the word *Erlebnis* is translated as "lived experience" or "living experience," the inner, subjective sense of experience. It is the individual's conscious perception of a meaning-event-entity taken as reality. Buber came to distinguish this idea of making experience into an object of consciousness from what he calls "lived reality," "the concrete," the immediacy of subject and world in dialogical interaction discussed earlier in this chapter.

In the first years following the completion of his doctorate, Buber worked as an editor in various publishing ventures. During this period he put together and published a number of anthologies reflecting his broad-ranging

---

56. Buber, "Über Jakob Boehme," 252–53.

57. Huston, *Martin Buber's Journey to Presence*, traces Buber's intellectual journey from this abstract monism to the dialogical theism of his mature thinking.

interests along the lines of Dilthey's hermeneutical project. These anthologies included collections of teaching stories about the great *zaddiks*, the masters of Central European Hasidism: *The Tales of Rabbi Nachman* (1906) and *The Legend of the Baal-Shem* (1908); as well as some of the first collections of classical Chinese stories to appear in German: *Talks and Parables of Chuang Tzu* (1910) and *Chinese Ghost and Love Stories* (1911); followed by his German edition of the *Kalevala*, the national epic of Finland (1914).

One of Buber's anthologies of that period, *Ecstatic Confessions* (1909), was a collection of accounts of mystical ecstacy brought together from a wide range of human cultures and religious traditions. This collection, among the first global anthologies of spirituality to be produced, shows the breadth of Buber's quest for expressions of the ultimate. His essay introducing this collection of spiritual accounts defines ecstasy as the experience [*Erlebnis*] of oneness beyond the manifold multiplicity of everyday life.[58] Yet even at this early point in his intellectual development, this exposition of the ecstatic experience of oneness already concludes with three looming questions: first, what is the nature of this *Erlebnis* of oneness? Second, is this experience an intuition of the unity of the self or is it truly a sense of the unity of all things? Third, how does one shuttle between ecstasy and everyday life?[59] Buber observed that the very existence of accounts of ecstasy suggests that ecstasy is not an end in itself—the person who has experienced ecstasy has a need to confess it, to share it as an experience in the language of experience so the account of the experience might make some sense to the ecstatic's more earth-bound contemporaries. This publication shows both his attraction to and his skepticism regarding the mystical experience of oneness as an end in itself. He was ambivalent about it at an early point in his mature development.

During the period leading up to the First World War (1909–1914) Buber wrote a series of six major lectures on Judaism, along with a number of more general essays, which together reflect his evolving thinking. In these years he was shifting between his early philosophy of "realization" which culminated in *Daniel* (1913) and his emphasis on the meeting between man and the other that is over against him, a meeting which can never become an identity of being—thus germinating the seeds of his later philosophy of dialogue. Maurice Friedman has identified several of the essays Buber wrote during this time, including "The Commentary," which Friedman titled "The

---

58. Buber, "Ecstasy and Confession," 1–2.
59. Buber, "Ecstasy and Confession," 11.

Teaching of the Tao," as "among the earliest and finest expressions of existentialism in this century."[60]

Buber grew critical of the concept of *Erlebnis* as his own spirituality deepened during the crisis of the war years. His major shift during World War I away from idealistic philosophy and mystical experience to his dialogical philosophy of encounter led to his locating *Erlebnis* squarely in the *It*-world. What became important to Buber in this shift was the difference between the solipsistic, self-enclosed nature of one's sense of unity which he came to identify with *Erlebnis*-mysticism (and later with absorption-mysticism in *I and Thou*, §50) and the existential stance of vulnerable openness to encounter with the truly other. He emphatically avowed this distinction again and again throughout his mature years. In a late clarifying statement he attributed this distinction to a radical self-correction in his own intellectual development:

> The concept of meeting ... arose, on the road of my thinking, out of the criticism of the concept of *Erlebnis*, to which I adhered in my youth, hence, out of a radical self-correction. "*Erlebnis*" belongs to the exclusive, individualized psychic sphere: "meeting" [*Begegnung*], or rather, as I mostly prefer to say, precisely in order to avoid the temporal limitation, "relationship" [*Beziehung*] transcends this sphere from its origins on. The psychological reduction of being, its psychologizing, had a destructive effect on me in my youth because it removed me from the foundation of human reality, the "one-to-another." Only much later, in the revolution of my thinking that taught me to fight and to gain ground did I win reality that cannot be lost.[61]

In sum, *Erlebnis* is a passive acquiescence to oneness; *Beziehung*, the foundation of human reality, is struggle and vulnerability before the other. *Erlebnis* becomes a self-enclosed or intrapsychic reality while *Beziehung*, by contrast, is deliberate, continual openness to contingency over against that which is other in the world—and the ultimate Other, the eternal *Thou*.

As early as 1919, when he was still coming to terms with his sufferings of the war years, Buber made a clear distinction between the transforming nature of a real encounter with the Unconditional and the individual's celebration of a moment of *Erlebnis* as a kind of psychological self-deception. First he showed the nature of real encounter:

> The Unconditional has its effect on a person when he lets himself in his whole being be seized by it, be utterly shaken, be

---

60. Friedman, "Introduction to the Torchbook Edition," viii.
61. Buber, "Replies to My Critics," 711–12.

transformed by it—when he responds to it with his whole being: with his mind, by perceiving the Divine in its symbols; with his soul, by his loving the All; with his will, by his passing the test of the Unconditional in his life actions.[62]

Then he showed the illusory, nondialogical nature of *Erlebnis*:

> But it may happen, by some odd perversity, that an individual falls into the delusion that he has surrendered himself to the Unconditional while in fact he has withdrawn from it from the ground up: he reduces the event of having been touched by the Unconditional to his having had an "experience" [*Erlebnis*]. In his whole being he remains unmoved and untransformed, but he has indulged in a sublime hour. He lacks the ability to respond [*er kennt die Antwort nicht*]; he knows only a "mood" [*Stimmung*]. He has psychologized God.[63]

With *Erlebnis*, transformatively responding to the Other has given way to expropriating the moment of encounter for oneself. In this lecture, as in his statement about self-correction, Buber emphatically distinguishes between *Erlebnis* as a psychologizing, the embracing of a mood on the one hand, and *Begegnung* as a transforming encounter with the unconditional one, the Other. This distinction is crystal clear to Buber because of the specific character of his own development from the one to the other. Yet for those whose course of development is different from Buber's, the contrast between the two may not stand out with such clarity.

Buber had expressed his repudiation of *Erlebnis* as early as his "Religion as Presence" lectures at the Lehrhaus in the winter of 1922, which were the lead-up to his completion of *I and Thou* that spring. In responding to a question from the audience, he elaborated on the function of *Erlebnis* for those who would collect exotic experiences, stating clearly how for him Erlebnis had become toxic:

> For what has been called "living experience" [*Erlebnis*] really means the opposite. It means that life is subjectivized, that, out of a great continuum, out of a great constancy [*Stetigkeit*, continuity], a space-time constancy in which we stand and into which we are inserted, life is transformed into an extracting, a pulling out of things for the use and to the taste of our subjectivity in such a way that the constancy is utterly torn apart and nothing remains but erratic moments—not even events that are inserted into being but "experiences" [*Erlebnisse*], treasures

---

62. Buber, "Herut," 153 (my translation).
63. Buber, "Herut," 153 (my translation).

> of the soul, as people call them. And religion is made into one of those treasures, so to speak, into an actual distillation of this elevated life.[64]

Following Dilthey, Buber had learned that what had served him well as a tool, a means of access to diverse moments of subjectivity, could become a fetish, a means of focusing on a part of reality at the expense of the whole. He then saw this fetishizing as an instance of the modern deformity, the reduction of the world to the subjectivity of the individual psyche which he called "the psychologizing of the world."[65] To him, this, the subjective side of the *It*-world, the modern nightmare (see *I and Thou* §43), was the major obstacle to the realm of *Thou* in the modern world.

In this "Religion as Presence" lecture Buber went on to argue for a major implication of *Erlebnis* as fetish: it is idolatry, the exaltation of the *Ersatz*, and therefore it destroys what is truly religious:

> This, then, is the final farewell to interconnectedness, to actuality, to something in which one stands, in which one is enfolded and interwoven. Here religion is totally taken over into transience, disconnectedness, the tearing into fragments of moments of the soul. Of the fictions into which the religious has been made, this is the most fictive of all. It is no longer the assigning of the religious to some sphere, it is annihilation, the annihilation of the religious.[66]

Whereas in the preceding passages Buber used psychologizing to express the nature of the great reduction of the Other, in this passage he presents the nature of the reduction in terms of amassing decorative artifacts as one's possessions. Buber sees this in terms of damage: "a great constancy"—the oneness of being—is pulled apart, torn into pieces, for the sake of an exalted fragment, an "experience"—*Erlebnis*.

As a result of this shift, Buber now took *Erlebnis* as the sense of oneness within the self, in contrast to the meaning and nature of encounter with the eternal *Thou*. Ecstasy, *Erlebnis*-mysticism, was thus an *Ersatz* form of spirituality, functioning as a false mainstay in the traditions of mystical quest, esotericism, and depth psychology, but lacking grounding in the concreteness of existence in the manifold world of society and creation. *Erlebnisse* had come to serve as memories to collect, as a kind of

---

64. Buber, "Religion as Presence," 50 (my translation); Buber used a similar line of analysis in his interpretation of his shift of thinking in response to Mehe (Buber, "Dialogue," 13–14).

65. See Buber, "On the Psychologizing of the World," 144–52.

66. Buber, "Religion as Presence," 50 (my translation).

bucket list of highs to achieve. Buber had moved from seeing ecstasy as an exalted moment of oneness to seeing being as a oneness that is constant, even as the individual person is subject to the contingencies of facing the Other as *Thou* beyond the self.

Buber's critique of modernity had its roots in the language and values of the philosophical movement known as *die Lebensphilosophie*. This movement reclaimed the value of the vital, the subjective, and the irrational in response to the modern domination of thinking by the rational, the scientific, and the empirical. The first major proponents of *Lebensphilosophie* were Buber's professors in Berlin, Wilhelm Dilthey and Georg Simmel; one of its major antecedents was Friedrich Nietzsche. Buber reevaluated the place of *Erlebnis* in the life of the spirit and he did so using what began as a foundational pattern of Nietzschean analysis: the tension between Dionysian vitality and Apollonian order. According to Nietzsche, Dionysian vitality must erupt repeatedly to break through the constant human gravitation toward sterile, objectified order. Buber brought this framework into the context of his Hebrew humanism by applying it to his concept of religiosity, the vivid life of the spirit brought forth by the call of the prophets to challenge again and again the settled religion of the priests and interpreters of the law. This dialectical pattern was the undergirding of his critique of *Erlebnis*.

Accordingly, the continual tendency to settle for order, for rational, controlled, received religion, for unitive mysticism—"the relation of an *I* to a *Thou* [is] the way in which the religious of all ages have understood their religion even if they longed most intensely to let their I be mystically absorbed into that Thou"[67]—must ever and again be called into question, denounced in the name of radical, total commitment to the Unconditional, which is "the one thing needful." Buber's critique of *Erlebnis* functions as a modern moment in the long history of prophetic denunciations and calls to renewal.

Buber later expressed this same dynamic as the opposition between gnosis and *devotio* in a 1954 essay.[68] There he pointed out that gnosis, like *Erlebnis*, is a state of mind that "involves no commitment" because "there stands over against the gnostic self nothing with any higher right, nothing that can demand of it, visit it, redeem it: the gnostic redemption comes from the liberation of the world-soul in the self."[69] With gnosis there is no commitment because there is no responsibility, no accountability to an Other—all has been internalized and the result is a closed, completed inner transaction.

---

67. Buber, "Religion and Modern Thinking," 79.
68. Buber, "Supplement," 242–54.
69. Buber, "Supplement," 244.

Buber presented *devotio* as the contrasting alternative to gnosis. He defined *devotio* as "the unreserved service, practiced in the life of one's mortal hours, to the Divine made present as over against one and ever again as over against, the Divine . . . to whom, in the language of the *vita humana* wholly turned toward Him in the everyday, one can say *Thou*, that is, dare to stand toward him in freely serving over-againstness."[70] Unreserved service is the state of complete surrender in obedient love. This state incorporates several elements at the core of Buber's dialogical vision: making present, wholly turning toward the divine, the grounding of the person in everyday life, the powerful act of standing up to God, and the fundamental reality of over-againstness—recognizing we are counterparts in a dialogical moment: servanthood freely undertaken in response to a gracious God.

Buber contrasted the self of *devotio* with the gnostic self: "One who so serves never and nowhere understands his self as *the* self—that unto the innermost depths of contemplation he still and ever again knows himself, rather, as *this* self over against the infinite Self, and thus relates himself to Him."[71] No matter how deeply the person of *devotio* goes in contemplation, he never confuses his sense of self with *the* self—the self of a boundless, all-inclusive oneness of gnostic ecstasy or absorption mysticism. With *devotio* he always remains the finite, created self *over-against*—that is, standing in relation to his Creator, the transcendent, the eternal Other.

Devotio, the struggle in history for the reality of faith, "the single bridge over the chasm of being," thus sharply contrasts with the gnosis which lifts "the historical-biographical out of its contingency and into the spiritual realm."[72] To Buber this gnosticizing is evil because it decontextualizes and universalizes the concrete-historical human struggle. It tears the lived life of faith "out of the historical-biographical ground in which it has taken root."[73]

The person taking the stance of *devotio* lives on the cutting edge of life and death: "In all of his service he holds his bodily death, his faithful mortality, in his hands as the most human of all presences and just thus, time after time, steps before the Eternal."[74] In such turning, surrender, service, the person of *devotio* continually steps before the Eternal, fully present because he stands with his mortality in hand, constantly putting it on the line in self-offering to the One who created it. Taking this stance is opening oneself completely to the Creator: self-preservation is no longer one's central concern. The concrete, earthly grounding of this stance is

70. Buber, "Supplement," 244.
71. Buber, "Supplement," 244 (emphasis original, translation modified).
72. Buber, "Supplement," 246 (translation modified).
73. Buber, "Supplement," 249 (translation modified).
74. Buber, "Supplement," 244 (translation modified).

clear: "A man defines and identifies himself only in his concrete action, his praxis. His Lord may be on all sides of him—in that this man serves Him, He is over against him."[75] That is, this life is the truly lived life. To freely take the stance of full self-giving in service to the Unconditional is to step fully into the Presence.

To sum up our consideration of *Erlebnis* as a bellwether of Buber's move from his early vision of unitive ecstasy to his later existential-dialogical philosophy, we see that what at first served him as a major tool of understanding he came to see as an impediment to relating to the divine as the unconditioned, unconditional Other. Thus, its shift in function for Buber marks a deepening of Buber's thinking that is consistent with the deepening of his spirituality, a deepening that was precipitated by the anguish he suffered and struggled with in the course of the First World War and its aftermath.

4. Conclusion

In conclusion, Buber insists our situation as human beings is inescapably concrete, contingent, and vulnerable. In fact, he asserts, we must embrace this very nature of our existence if we are to enter into dialogue with others and with the ultimate Other. Yet he knows only too clearly that we will invent and do almost anything to escape, deny, or hide from this our condition. As we have seen in this chapter, he presents us with our concrete reality and exposes our manipulations against it by contrasting abstraction and the "lived concrete," philosophizing and religiosity, *Erlebnis* and *Beziehung*, and gnosticizing and *devotio*. These counterparts, so named, are reference points in the dramatic struggle Buber presents in *I and Thou*.

This chapter lays the groundwork for understanding *I and Thou* as it was shaped by the conceptual and cultural tools Buber acquired and reworked in the course of his development. His early exposure to existential thought bore fruit in an existential edge to his work that intensified with the struggles of the war years and his loss of his friend Gustav Landauer. The "lived concrete" as Buber's expression of this existential edge affirmed his emerging values of this-worldliness and of life as fully lived when it is lived in the tension of ongoing dialogue with the Unconditional.

Buber's existential outlook led to his revaluation of mysticism and *Erlebnis* as he passed beyond the period of his youthful idealism. His tendency to think in terms of either/or was clearly manifest in the opposition he saw between *Erlebnis*-mysticism and the life in dialogue. This opposition which became clear to him during the watershed war years was part of his revaluation of the spiritual life.

75. Buber, "Supplement," 244–45 (my translation).

Chapter 6

Buber's "Yes" to the Way

THIS CHAPTER, LIKE CHAPTER 5, lays groundwork for understanding *I and Thou* as it was shaped by conceptual and cultural tools that Buber acquired and reworked in the course of his development. Here we consider his early essay, "The Teaching of the Tao." This essay represents a moment in his lifelong effort to attend to the whole range of human spiritual life. Signs of this lifelong focus on global spiritual traditions go back to an early essay on the Buddha (1907) and include two globe-encompassing anthologies, *Ecstatic Confessions* (1909) and *Chinese Tales* (1910), a five-volume work on the basic forms of religious life which he first envisioned in 1916 and which led to *I and Thou*,[1] and his appointment as Professor of Comparative History of Religion at the University of Frankfurt in 1930.[2]

There is no doubt Buber's 1910 essay in response to Taoism grew out of his early idealistic thinking and was an expression of his lifelong project of synthesizing diverse spiritual traditions. Yet the parallels between his interpretation of ancient Taoist texts and his interpretation of Judaism and pre-modern Hasidism show some of the deeper continuities that undergirded both his earlier and his later thinking. On the one hand the early treatise on Taoism represented an early stage of his religious thinking. Yet on the other hand it presents elements—such as the concepts of "the teaching," the master, and the spiritual life as the single concrete reality—which served as his framework from that early essay through his mature years. Therefore, the exposition of *I and Thou* in the next three chapters will be richer and deeper for our having examined these elements here.

1. Buber envisioned *I and Thou* as the prolegomena to this ambitious project; yet he never pursued the other four volumes once *I and Thou* was completed. See "A Plan Martin Buber Abandoned" in Kaufmann, *I and Thou*, 49–50; Martin Buber to Hugo Bergmann, May 13, 1922, in Buber, *Letters*, 266; Martin Buber to Franz Rosenzweig, August 15, 1922, in Buber, *Letters*, 270.

2. Friedman, "Martin Buber and Asia," 411.

We shall see how both in "The Teaching of the Tao" and in *I and Thou* the achieved unity of the whole person and the Chinese concept of *wu-wei* became central elements of the life transformed by the practice of turning to the Other, the *Thou*.

1. The Controversial Essay: "The Teaching of the Tao"

Buber's essay "The Teaching of the Tao" stands as a signpost pointing both back to Buber's original quest for oneness in *Erlebnis*-mysticism and forward toward his deeper sense of the oneness of being.[3] The mature Buber envisioned this sense of oneness as a binding of the person to the constancy of the Absolute in the concreteness of each present moment. The essay was written during a period of intense productivity when Buber was in his early thirties. During that time he had written his early collections of Hasidic teaching stories and was beginning his decade of lectures on Judaism. He was also editing a global anthology of mysticism and a second collection of Chinese stories. Not much later he produced his book of dialogues on the philosophy of realization. Amid this diversified flurry of activity, "The Teaching of the Tao" stands out as his first and most comprehensive attempt to construct a global synthesis of human spirituality.[4] As such, it provides important background for some of the key elements of the philosophy of dialogue in *I and Thou*. It also provides a context for Buber's general references to global cultural history in *I and Thou*.[5] This short treatise was originally published in 1910 as the afterword to Buber's anthology of Taoist teaching stories (the first such anthology to be published in German), derived from the classic Chinese work, the *Zhuangzhi*, and entitled *Talks and Parables of Chuang-tzu*. When this essay was republished in 1957 in English as an item in *Pointing the Way*, a collection of Buber's early essays, it was given the title "The Teaching of the Tao."

---

3. In this chapter the essay will be referred to as "The Teaching of the Tao," the title used in Maurice Friedman's translation; references in the notes will be to it as "Commentary," the title used for Jonathan Herman's translation in *I and Tao: Martin Buber's Encounter with Chuang Tzu*. Herman's translation corrects Friedman's; his study is immensely helpful for understanding Buber's relation with Taoism in the context of modern philology.

4. Other major essays by Buber that discuss spirituality in a global context include "Judaism and Mankind," 22–33; "Spirit of the Orient and Judaism," 56–78; "Religion and Ethics," 95–111; and "Interpreting Hasidism," 218–25.

5. Such references include §32h, §36h, §36i, §45, and §61n.

Buber wrote a short foreword to *Pointing the Way* as a caution regarding "The Teaching of the Tao" which had been written almost fifty years earlier. This cautionary statement put the essay at the center of the controversy regarding the evolution of Buber's views regarding *Erlebnis*. Consideration of this carefully crafted statement will further deepen our understanding of that intellectual transformation. In his foreword, Buber singled out "The Teaching of the Tao," the earliest of the eight pieces in this collection that had been published before his watershed years, as the one essay in the collection that he could not "stand behind today." Yet he included this essay in the collection because, "in connection with the development of my thought [it is] too important to be withheld from the reader." He then gave the reader instructions for reading this essay: "while reading it" the reader should "bear in mind that this small work belongs to a stage that I had to pass through before I could enter into an independent relationship with being." In short, Buber intended the piece to be read for the sake of understanding the background, the early "mystical" phase of his development that led to his mature thought, but not as an expression of that mature thought in itself.[6]

Buber continued his foreword, using language similar to that in "A Conversion," his earlier account of his shift from *Erlebnis*-mysticism to dialogue.[7] He defined mystical philosophy and mystical experience as he understood them before the development of his mature "independent relationship with being." To him mystical philosophy is "the belief in a unification of the self with the all-self, attainable . . . in levels or intervals of . . . earthly life." Such mystical philosophy as a belief is usually accompanied by a genuine "ecstatic" experience—or by the desire for it. He next defined "ecstatic" experience as

> the experience of an exclusive and all-absorbing unity of [one's] own self. This self is then so uniquely manifest, and it appears then so uniquely existent, that the individual loses the knowledge that "this is my self, distinguished and separate from every other self." He loses the sure knowledge of the *principium individuationis,* and understands this precious experience of his unity as the experience of *the* unity.[8]

Buber's point here as elsewhere is that the primary characteristic of the unitive experience is the sense of boundlessness, a state of awareness without

---

6. Buber, "Foreword," xv.
7. Buber, "Dialogue," 13–14; see the discussion in chapter 4 above, pages 73–75.
8. Buber, "Foreword," xv (emphasis original).

reference points and therefore with no means of knowing its scale or scope.[9] Earlier he had expressed the ambiguity accompanying this sense of boundlessness by using the powerful analogy of hearing the ocean in a seashell: "We listen to our inmost selves—and do not know which sea it is that we hear roaring."[10]

Again, as in his discussion in "A Conversion," Buber marks the mystic, the person who has had such an experience, as one for whom life has been divided in two because of the experience. To the mystic there is the "lower" everyday life and there is the "higher, true life." The mystic "is naturally inclined . . . to regard everyday life as an obscuring of the true life":

> He constantly *flees* from [everyday life] into the experience of unity, into the detached feeling of unity of being, elevated above life. But he thereby *turns away* from his existence as a human being . . . . He no longer stands in the dual basic attitude [the dialogical stance] that is destined to him as a human being . . . In the "lower" periods he *regards* everything as preparation for the "higher." But in these "higher hours" he *no longer knows* anything over against him: the great dialogue between *I* and *Thou* is silent; nothing else exists than his self, which he *experiences* as *the* self.[11]

Here, Buber claims that in exalting the experience of ecstasy the mystic tears it out of the fabric of being while at the same time rejecting the fundamental *I-Thou* stance, thus closing off the possibility of dialogue. With these words Buber emphasizes that the mystic is an escapist, one who spurns everyday earthly existence for the sake of an experience of solipsistic *Erlebnis*-mysticism. Buber sums up this splitting of life in two by the mystic as "an exalted form of being untrue."[12]

Buber's portrayal of his own early participation in such *Erlebnis*-mysticism in "A Conversion" (1929), his account of the transformation he underwent in response to Mehe, shows in concrete terms the nature of what he came to disavow about mysticism.[13] There he presented mystical experience as an experience which would begin with contemplation until suddenly and unexpectedly there is an in-breaking of another order of reality which lifts the person out of normal everyday life, as if the temporal

---

9. See Buber, "Ecstasy and Confession," 1–11.

10. Buber, "Ecstasy and Confession," 11.

11. Buber, "Foreword," xv–xvi (emphasis added to highlight the actions that Buber attributes to the ecstatic mystic).

12. Buber, "Foreword," xvi.

13. Buber, "Dialogue," 13–14.

flow itself has been ruptured: "first the firm world structure, then the still firmer self-certainty of the person is atomized; then the unsubstantiated person that one barely continues to be becomes surrendered over to fullness." In this event there has been a shift from "customary existence with its give-and-take 'over there'" to "rapture and enlightenment and ecstasy 'over here,' timeless and without succession." With this experience, one's own being is divided in two, into "a life here and a life beyond."[14] The illegitimacy of this dividing of our one life is what Buber awoke to through his soul-searching response to his encounter with Mehe.

In the 1957 foreword, Buber next contrasts this divided life of the mystic with the unifying and unified life of the dialogical person, one who is characterized as

> *bringing into unity* his whole existence as he lives it day by day, from the hours of blissful exaltation unto those of hardship and of sickness, . . . *living* this existence as unity, [affirming] *his existence as a man*, the existence into which he has been set, through conception and birth, for life and death in this unique personal form. [He] *stands* in the dual basic attitude that is destined to him as a man: *carrying* being in his person, *wishing* to complete it, and *ever again going forth* to meet worldly and above-worldly being over against him, *wishing* to be a helper to it. [He] *knows* [that which is] over against him: the great dialogue between *I* and *Thou*.[15]

The dialogical person fully embraces the circumstances within which he finds himself and in fidelity he strives and serves within these circumstances—all of which he knows as his part in his great ongoing dialogue with being. Buber ends with a statement of his sense of calling as a dialogical person by dramatically shifting to the first person: "Being true to the being in which and before which I am placed is the one thing that is needful."[16]

Again, Buber's account of his life after the course correction precipitated by Mehe merits comparison here. According to "A Conversion," Buber has let go of his early embrace of exceptional moments of ecstasy. Now possessing "nothing but the everyday out of which I am never taken," he refers to a deeper, permanent kind of oneness—a oneness that could be read as his at-oneness with the Tao: this oneness is a dwelling in the

---

14. Buber, "Dialogue," 13 (my translation).

15. Buber, "Foreword," xv–xvi (emphasis added to highlight the actions that Buber attributes to dialogical man in contrast to those actions he attributes to the mystic, page 119 above).

16. Buber, "Foreword," xvi.

concrete here and now, "where everything happens as it happens."[17] The fullness is no longer that of ecstatic experience but that of dialogue, "the fullness of each mortal hour's claim and responsibility." He concludes this account with what could be central to a Taoist outlook: "If this is religion, then it is simply *everything*, the unadorned lived All [*das schlichte gelebte All*] in its possibility of dialogue."[18] The fractured, fragmentary, fleeting oneness of *Erlebnis*-mysticism has given way to the deeper, total, abiding oneness of Being in dialogue.

Buber's strong disavowal of his earlier point of view in this foreword and his exposition of what he avows and he affirms, both here and in "A Conversion," prompt a question: What exactly in our reading of "The Teaching of the Tao" are we to set aside as elements of Buber's early *Erlebnis*-mysticism?

It is important to note that in spite of Buber's warning, "The Teaching of the Tao" is not primarily about *Erlebnis*-mysticism. The term *Erlebnis* ("lived experience") was central in "Ecstasy and Confession," the essay introducing his global anthology of mystical accounts where it appears twenty-seven times in ten pages. Here the term appears only eleven times in this thirty-page essay a year later. Therefore, we can conclude the warning Buber wrote when he was seventy-nine years old seems to be more about that earlier period of his thinking in general than about this essay on Taoism in particular.

Buber's anthology, *Talks and Parables of Chuang Tzu*, which includes "The Teaching of the Tao," was first published in 1910, then published in a second edition in 1918, and in a third edition in 1951, showing Buber's continuing commitment to his early interpretation of Taoism over the course of more than four decades. In the preface to the 1951 edition, written when Buber was in his seventies, he emphasized the importance of Taoism in his thought. There he stated this short treatise on Taoism "was originally composed . . . as an attempt to represent summarily the Taoist teaching to which I am indebted for a great deal."[19] Buber's involvement with Taoist thought included a 1924 series of lectures on the *Tao Te Ching* entitled "Talks with Martin Buber in Ascona."[20] Maurice Friedman, in his introduction to the Torchbook Edition of *Pointing the Way*, also indicated that in spite of Buber's seeming disavowal of "The Teaching of the Tao," "The Taoist *wu-wei*—the

---

17. Buber, "Dialogue," 14.
18. Buber, "Dialogue," 14 (my translation).
19. Buber, quoted in Herman, *I and Tao*, 15.
20. Eber, "Martin Buber and Taoism," 448. The lectures were given over the course of three weeks in August 1924.

action of the whole being that appears to be non-action—still informs the second part of *I and Thou*."[21]

I believe Buber wrote his 1957 foreword to differentiate between his early, all-embracing mystical phase, with its dividing of life in two, and his mature dialogical stance, in which all of life is faced as the one single reality. When Buber wrote that the earlier mystical phase was "a stage that I had to pass through before I could enter into an independent relationship with being,"[22] we can see his development took him from his early experience of moments of mystical ecstasy ("like flashes in the darkness") to a deeper sense of the oneness of the all (the authentic constancy of the "moon in a clear starlit night").[23] It is precisely "The Teaching of the Tao," written during "the mystical period" of Buber's development, that anticipates the emergence of this deeper sense of oneness Buber claims as the outcome of his great intellectual and spiritual transition.

In preparing his series of lectures on Judaism for publication in 1923, Buber wrote: "I can describe what has happened to me [from 1909 to 1923] only as a process of clarification, but not a conversion."[24] These lectures show a continuity in his thinking about the revitalization of Judaism and they also include some of the same global speculations we find in "The Teaching of the Tao." For example, Buber's essay on "The Spirit of the Orient and Judaism" (1913) makes Judaism the linchpin at the center of world cultures.[25] In it, Buber sets up an opposition between Asian thinkers and European thinkers, then places the Jew as the pivotal figure between these two opposite types. The Jew is the quintessential Asian person who can bridge the cultures of Europe and Asia. In this argument, Buber's Zionist vision makes Jerusalem the future nexus between East and West. Areas where the lectures on Judaism and the essay on Taoism overlap suggest continuities that extend across cultures as well as across the phases of Buber's thought.

Several key elements of "The Teaching of the Tao" resonate with Buber's writings elsewhere, especially his work on Hasidism and his lectures on Judaism, which he gave across the period of his transition from 1909 to 1918. They directly relate to major passages in *I and Thou* as well. Buber introduces his striking doctrine of "the teaching," which helps to make sense of his refusal to say that he himself has a teaching. The very concept

21. Friedman, "Introduction to the Torchbook Edition," ix.

22. Buber, "Foreword," xv.

23. In *I and Thou*, Buber uses these images to mark earlier and later phases in the development of a person's spiritual life: §61h. His similar use of the image of "lightning-pierced darkness" stands out in "Dialogue," 13.

24. Buber, "Preface to the 1923 Edition," 3.

25. Buber, "Spirit of the Orient and Judaism, and Judaism" 56–78.

of a teaching implies the teaching situation, for teaching is inseparable from the people involved—the teacher and the students—as well as their interaction and the process of transmission from teacher to student. These separate elements come together as facets of a single social-spiritual reality: the dialogical community.

Buber's exposure to Hasidism went back to his visits to Hasidic communities in his childhood, his scholarly work with it consumed him for two intense periods, and his primary literary output had Hasidism as its focus. Given this intense involvement, the first and most vivid examples of spiritual teaching arose for him out of the Hasidic reality of Central Europe. This Hasidic reality is the reference point behind both "The Teaching of the Tao" and *I and Thou*.

2. Buber's Concept of "The Teaching"

Buber begins "The Teaching of the Tao" with an explanation of his notion of "the teaching," a key element in his thought.[26] Most commonly, a teaching is a body of doctrines or precepts. Yet for Buber "the teaching" as the action of intuitive knowing is like a verb rather than a noun. Thus, he opens with negations, statements of what "the teaching" is not. "The teaching" as Buber defines it does not involve information as such, nor does it involve ethical prescriptions as such. Buber thus distinguishes "the teaching" from the realm of science, the cognition of the world and its contents, as well as from the realm of law or ethics, the principles of right action. To him, "the teaching" can be expressed neither as knowable contents nor as doable obligations. As with his rejection of *Erlebnis*, his purpose with his concept of "the teaching" is to set aside mediated conceptual knowledge and focus instead on the immediacy of intuition. "The teaching" is most basically the unity of the authentic life, not expressed as doctrines but embodied as the lived life of a master of spiritual life. "The teaching" is "the way." "The teaching" becomes the transmission of this "way" in a certain kind of relationship, the dialogical relationship between a spiritual master and his followers.

---

26. Shortly after the publication of the essay, Georg Simmel, his former sociology professor at the University of Berlin, acclaimed the concept in a letter to Buber: "With the concept of 'teaching' you have singled out a very important and independent category which hitherto had been mixed up with other concepts. What you communicate out of Chinese philosophy has extraordinary significance and it has the urgency of something breaking forth out of the depths, much like the theses of Meister Eckhart" (Georg Simmel to Martin Buber, 14 November, 1910, in Buber, *Briefwechsel aus sieben Jahrzehnten*, 1:287 [my translation]). This letter is not included in the English edition, *The Letters of Martin Buber*.

In "The Teaching of the Tao" Buber suggests "the teaching" is not readily graspable; instead, it involves an intuitive apperception through a spiritual process of transmission:

> The teaching contains no contents, it has only one focus, itself: the one thing that is needful. It exists beyond what is and what should be, beyond knowledge and precepts; it knows only to say one thing, the needful that is realized in the authentic life. The needful is by no means a being or accessible to knowledge; it is not discovered either on Earth or in Heaven, but rather appropriated and lived. The authentic life . . . can only be realized out of itself and is utterly nothing other than realization. Knowledge consists of the duality of reality and cognition; law consists of the duality of obligation and deed; the teaching consists of the oneness of the one thing that is needful.[27]

Buber's appeal to "realization" here connects with *Daniel* as the exposition of his "philosophy of realization" and what Buber means by "the authentic life" will become clear as we look into "the master" and "the one thing needful."

"The teaching" can not be grappled with by analysis. The naming of "underlying truth," the distinction of form and content, the subject-object split, the forming of theological concepts—these cognitive actions are all irrelevant and must be let go of in order for "the teaching" to be manifest.[28] "The teaching" does not address the what of nature (the *is* of the realm of science); nor does it address the what of obligation (the *ought* of the realm of law). Its focus is the preverbal *how* of the authentic life, which is primary and unsubsumable. The very nature of "the teaching" is extremely difficult for Western minds to grasp because we are schooled to reduce all reality to manageable cognitive elements.

Buber's lecture "The Spirit of the Orient and Judaism" (1912) corroborates what he claims about the nature of "the teaching" in "The Teaching of the Tao." "Knowledge of the nature of the world, on which the Western person who wants to master it depends, is forever subservient to the knowledge of the *way* . . . the good life, the fulfilling life."[29] "Knowledge of the nature of the world" is cognitive understanding of things, knowing the what in the realm of *I-It*. The transcendent, contrasting knowledge, that of directly and intuitively knowing the way, the how of a unified existence, is of an entirely different order. Buber sums up the nature of "the teaching" as the how of the authentic life:

---

27. Buber, "Commentary," 70–71 (my translation).
28. Buber, "Commentary," 74.
29. Buber, "Spirit of the Orient and Judaism," 61 (translation modified).

It is this that is creatively enduring in the great Asian teachings: the pristine knowledge of the meaning of authentic life, the innate certitude that "One thing above all is needed." They posit authentic life as the fundamental metaphysical principle, not derived from nor reducible to anything else; they proclaim the way. There is, so they say, no meaning and no truth for humankind anywhere except in that authentic life which unifies and liberates the world.[30]

Buber's concept of "the teaching" has key elements that carry forward into his mature thinking. First of all, it is of a piece with the human-centered approach to spirituality of his mature thought. Secondly, Buber's emphasis on the authenticity of the master, the whole person, indicates the groundedness in being of his mature thought, not the splitting of reality in two which was characteristic of his early *Erlebnis*-mysticism. The unity presented here may be close to the unity of the Vedantic monist, as in his lecture on Jakob Boehme, but it also invokes the unity of the person as the person opens up to the encounter with the ultimate Other in the ground of being.[31]

To sum up, the oneness that is intended in "the teaching"

> is not the comprehensive oneness of the world or of a body of knowledge, not the steady oneness of one God or of the spirit or of being or of anything that is thought or felt or willed things, but rather, it is the oneness of this human life and this human soul that fulfills itself in itself, the oneness of your life and your soul, you the one seized by the teaching. The authentic life is the unified life.[32]

Buber's focus on the unity of the concrete human life as "the teaching" is consistent with his existential stance, his focus on the human-centered level of existence, and it lies at the core of his understanding of the nature of the spiritual life.

---

30. Buber, "Spirit of the Orient and Judaism," 69 (translation modified).

31. Buber, "Über Jakob Boehme," 251–53. Buber introduced the concept of "the teaching" in his essay on Taoism but it also functioned as a pivotal element at the climax of *Daniel*; see *Daniel*, 135–40. Furthermore, Buber's major book on the Hebrew prophets originally had the Hebrew title *Torat Hanive'eem, The Prophetic Teaching*; see Avnon, *Martin Buber*, 66. Avnon also points out that Buber used the Hebrew word *torah* for teaching and consistently translated Torah, referring to the first five books of the Hebrew Bible, as *Weisung*, "instruction," not "law"; see Avnon, *Martin Buber*, 252n46.

32. Buber, "Commentary," 72 (my translation).

3. The Master

In "The Teaching of the Tao" Buber makes the master the central element of "the teaching" and of the dialogical community. The master's role is central because his life, the unified life, is the teaching. Thus, "the teaching has only *one* subject—itself: the one thing needful . . . that is realized in the authentic life, that is, the life of a master."[33] "The teaching" is realization, fulfillment, the unified life, the genuine life. Because "the teaching" is not a message or a body of doctrine or a set of moral precepts, it is a reality embodied in a life. It can only be passed down from one person to another when it is transmitted in the lived *I-Thou* relationship between a master, a person who has realized "the teaching," and his disciples.

Buber distinguishes between two types of oneness in people.[34] First, there are persons who through an inner process have become one. Their oneness is won as an achievement. In their move into oneness, such persons have gone beyond the conventional knowledge and ethical demands of their culture. In a seeming paradox, their life embodies both the overcoming of their spiritual heritage and their fulfilling it. They have entered into "the teaching" in such a way that their life has become the living expression of it. In simply living the life, they have elevated what was handed down to them so that it has been raised up out of mere conditional existence into the unconditional.[35]

Buber's use of particular terms for such persons helps us to see how he characterizes them. He uses some terms to characterize them in terms of what they have achieved. Thus, most frequently in this essay he refers to such a person simply as *der Vollendete*, "the completed or perfected one."[36] This is Buber's version of the Chinese *chih-jen*, "utmost man."[37] Friedman translates this term as "perfected man" while Herman translates it as "accomplished man" and Avnon translates it as "the fully realized, whole person."[38] Buber often refers to such persons as "the unified one" or person or life. Several times Buber uses the phrases "unified life" or "central human life,"[39] suggesting that

---

33. Buber, "Commentary," 70 (my translation, emphasis added).
34. Buber, "Commentary," 72.
35. Buber, "Commentary," 77.
36. "The accomplished person" [der Vollendete] is used twenty-five times (Buber, "Commentary," 75–92); *der Vollendete*, along with "the one who has stood the test" and "the proven one," is one of the titles for the zaddiks in Hasidism (Buber, *Tales of the Hasidim*, 1:1).
37. Herman, *I and Tao*, 10.
38. Avnon, *Martin Buber*, 83.
39. "The unified one" (*der Geeinte*) is used nine times (Buber, "Commentary,"

his concept is about a process rather than an objectified human entity. As those who embody the fullness of their received tradition, they are referred to as "fulfilling persons."[40] These terms are titles naming the qualities of those who have won oneness as their way of life. When such persons stand out for their role as spiritual teachers, Buber refers to them as "masters" and, because of their place in relation to those they have come to serve, they are also called "central persons"[41] in their communities.

In contrast to these persons of achieved oneness, there are "simple persons," those who have an inborn, undeveloped sense of oneness. Buber writes elsewhere of these simple persons as those who have a "naïve," innate oneness of soul and come to the master seeking guidance.[42] He defines the simple man as "the man of the original *devotio*, the man by nature at one with himself who lacks the secret knowing [of Kabbalism] as well as rabbinical knowledge, but can do without both because united he lives the united service."[43] Buber also occasionally refers to such people as the *am-haaretz*, "the people of the earth," that is, the peasant community.[44]

Regarding the persons of attained oneness, once their "attained oneness has the purity and the straightforward force of the elemental," they stand out in their society and they sense a need to seek out the simple persons, their impoverished brothers and sisters in spirit, and to speak to them in language they can hear, thereby lifting them up.[45] The simple persons who respond to the master form a circle around him and he thus becomes "the central man." The relationship between master and disciples, so constituted, is the prototype of the dialogical community.

When there is a shift from the silence of the realizing person in solitude—"the naked oneness is silent"—to engaging others and speaking to them, the life of oneness of the *Vollendete* takes expression as parable.[46]

75–92); "the unified life" (*das geeinte Leben*) is used six times (Buber, "Commentary," 72–88); "the central human life" (*das zentrale Menschenleben*) is used three times (Buber, "Commentary," 71–76); "the central person" (*der zentrale Mensch*) is used four times (Buber, "Commentary," 72–94.

40. "Fulfilling person" (*der Erfüllende*) is used five times (Buber, "Commentary," 77–94).

41. "Master" (*der Meister*) is used twice (Buber, "Commentary," 73, 81); "central person" (*der zentrale Mensch*) is used eight times (Buber, "Commentary," 72–94).

42. Buber, *Tales of the Hasidim*, 1:4–7.

43. Buber, "Supplement," 253.

44. Buber, "Beginnings," 45–48; "Foundation Stone," 60; "Symbolic and Sacramental Existence," 174.

45. Buber, "Commentary," 72–73.

46. Buber, "Commentary," 73, 78–79.

The German word *Gleichnis*, translated as "parable" in "The Teaching of the Tao," like the Hebrew word *mashal*, is much broader in meaning than the English word "parable." It refers to figurative discourse in general, including fables, apothegms, and exempla: such figures serve as vehicles of spiritual instruction and those that have a narrative component may best be referred to as "teaching stories." The term is a central element in "The Teaching of the Tao," but it also characterizes a significant portion of Buber's output, beginning with his anthologies of Hasidic stories in 1906 and 1907, and reaching a high point in the publication of *Tales of the Hasidim* in 1947.[47]

This master is the one whose life is "the teaching" because it is unified and authentic. His primary characteristic is his power as a unifier: "All that is dispersed, volatile, and fragmentary coalesces in him to oneness: his life is this oneness."[48] His power of making into one unifies all: "Chuang Tzu [says] that the accomplished person [*der Vollendete*] reconciles and brings into harmony the two primordial elements of nature, yang and yin, that divide apart the primordial oneness of existence."[49] As the central figure in the transmission of "the teaching," he "brings to 'the teaching' no new element, but rather fulfills it."[50] This fulfilling means making the living reality of the tradition visible by living it "out of the conditioned into the unconditional."[51] Buber links this transcendence with Tao: "Tao means ... that the whole sense of existence rests in the oneness of the authentic life, will only be experienced in it, that it is precisely this oneness grasped as the absolute."[52] The result is a cascade of qualities: "The accomplished man is shut into himself, all secure, unified out of Tao, unifying the world, a creating person, 'God's companion,' the companion of the universal, creative eternity."[53]

Buber exalts the master and sets him apart from the common stream of humanity: "The fulfilling person, who is constituted out of everything and yet comes from nothing, is the most unique of persons. . . . So great is his uniqueness, so unoriginal, so unprepossessing, so utterly the ultimate authenticity of humankind."[54] Yet, at the same time, the master is a human nexus through whom a spiritual heritage passes as teaching: "the

---

47. Buber discusses the nature of such narratives as he has reconstructed them in his introductions to these anthologies, most notably in his preface to *Tales of the Hasidim*, 1:xvii–xxiv.

48. Buber, "Commentary," 77.

49. Buber, "Commentary," 86.

50. Buber, "Commentary," 77.

51. Buber, "Commentary," 77.

52. Buber, "Commentary," 83 (translation modified).

53. Buber, "Commentary," 87 (translation modified).

54. Buber, "Commentary," 78.

multitude of voices transform through this human body into finality, the weak impulses of many dead are bound in him into might, he is the cleat of the teaching."[55]

The master's function is an expression of the fact that he is a locus of compassion and transmitted wholeness which overflows out of his oneness with all things: "the love of the accomplished person, after which each person can aspire, is based upon the oneness with all things."[56] As a result, those whose lives he touches are made whole: "the accomplished man does not intervene in the life of beings, he enjoins nothing upon them, but he 'helps all beings to their freedom,' he also leads them through his oneness to oneness, he makes free their being and their destiny, he redeems Tao in them."[57] And his impact is effortless. Buber quotes from chapter 57 of the *Tao Te Ching* to express these qualities in the idiom of Taoism:

> "I am without doing," says the accomplished man [*der Vollendete*],
>
> "and the people change of themselves;
>
> I love rest, and the people become upright of themselves;
>
> I am without bustle, and the people become rich of themselves;
>
> I am without desires, and the people become simple of themselves."[58]

Later, in *I and Thou*, Buber expresses similar qualities in his own idiom in a passage celebrating the compassion of the person who has taken his stance in *I-Thou*:

> To whoever stands in love and sees by means of it, people are seen as detached from their entanglement in busy-ness. Good people and evil, wise and foolish, beautiful and ugly—one after the other they become real to him as *Thou*; that is, set free, they emerge as unique beings in their over-againstness . . . and so he can be effective, helping, healing, educating, raising up, rescuing. (§19b)

Buber's prototype for the master is the *zaddik*, the charismatic spiritual leader he first witnessed in his boyhood in his visits to Hasidic villages in Central Europe with his father.[59] This early experience informed his

---

55. Buber, "Commentary," 77–78.
56. Buber, "Commentary," 91.
57. Buber, "Commentary," 92.
58. Buber, "Commentary," 93. Herman identifies Buber's *Vollendete* as Buber's equivalent for *sheng*, the Chinese word meaning "sage" (Herman, *I and Tao*, 10).
59. Buber, "My Way to Hasidism," 50–55.

sense of the *zaddik* as what the world needs, "the perfected man ... the true helper."[60] The Baal-Shem-Tov, a *zaddik* or "perfected man," had been the central figure in Buber's own spiritual awakening.[61] Over the course of more than four decades (1906–1947) Buber compiled several major collections of teaching stories based on the lives of the great Central European *zaddiks* in their communities. These collections comprise the bulk of his literary output.

A much-discussed passage in *I and Thou* is a key to understanding Buber's concept of the dialogical community (§33k).[62] This passage confirms what Buber wrote in "The Teaching of the Tao" about "the central person" in relation to his followers. "The true community arises ... through two factors: that people stand in a living mutual relation to a living center and that they also stand in a living mutual relation with each other. ... The community is constructed out of living mutual relating but the Master-builder [*Baumeister*] is its living, effecting center" (§33k). The Master-builder can be defined as the person who leads in envisioning and actualizing a cultural edifice. His role as the center of the community may at first seem indefinite: to whom or what does this passage refer? An autobiographical fragment entitled "The Zaddik" suggests the answer. There, Buber describes an Hasidic master and his followers as he remembered them from his childhood visit to their village:

> When I saw the *rebbe* striding through the rows of the waiting, I felt, "leader," and when I saw the Hasidim dance with the Torah, I felt "community." At that time there rose in me a presentiment of the fact that common reverence and common joy of soul are the foundations of genuine human community. ... Here was, debased yet uninjured, the living double kernel of humanity: genuine *community* and genuine *leadership*.[63]

When Buber introduced his major collection of Hasidic teaching stories in 1946, he turned this childhood memory into the dialogical core of the movement:

> The very foundation of hasidism [is] the life between the zaddik and his disciples which unfolds in the interaction between the quickener and the quickened. The teacher kindles the souls of his disciples and they surround him and light his life with the flame he has kindled. The disciple asks, and by his manner of

---

60. Buber, "My Way to Hasidism," 52.
61. Buber, "My Way to Hasidism," 59–69.
62. See Mendes-Flohr, *From Mysticism to Dialogue*, 121; Avnon, "'Living Center,'" 55–77.
63. Buber, "My Way to Hasidism," 53 (emphasis original).

asking unconsciously evokes a reply, which his teacher's spirit would not have produced without the stimulus of the question. ... All—each giving himself utterly—are united into an elated whole, such as can only form around an elated center, which through its very being, points to the divine center of all being.[64]

Here Buber uses the same terms as in *I and Thou* to describe the Hasidic community gathered around its master as its center. This image represents Buber's ideal of the dialogical community.

Buber wrote how he once experienced the power of the *zaddik*'s role from within when in 1910 a simple working man in Czernowitz projected the power of the *zaddik* onto him by asking for his spiritual guidance. In his dialogue with this man he glimpsed the subjective side of the *zaddik*'s role: "I caught sight in my inner experience of the zaddik's function as a leader. I, who am truly no zaddik, no one assured in God ... then experienced from within for the first time the true zaddik. Questioned about revelations and replying in revelations, I experienced [the *zaddik*] in the fundamental relation of his soul to the world: in his responsibility."[65] Here we have both Buber's denial of and his sense of identification with the *zaddik*. Grete Schaeder rightfully interprets Buber's subsequent encounter with Mehe a few years later as a "shattering experience [that] finally placed Buber within the tradition of the zaddik."[66] The *zaddik* has two roles, that of "cosmic mediator" and that of "perfect helper." Buber's own development can be seen as repeating that of the *zaddiks*: in his early life he climbed the mystic ladder, then at a crucial point he turned from the quest for spiritual attainment to serving others, "from mystical power ... to the presentness of the entire person for the sake of others."[67] Consequently, "All of Buber's thoughts on education and therapy were ... determined by the image of the zaddik."[68] Furthermore, Schaeder quotes Robert Weltsch, one of Buber's biographers, to show that Buber's identification with the role of the *zaddik* influenced the development of his philosophy of dialogue: "The origin of Buber's turning to dialogic thinking lies at least partly in his immersion in the immediacy of Hasidic speech."[69]

---

64. Buber, *Tales of the Hasidim*, 1:8–9.
65. Buber, "My Way to Hasidism," 67.
66. Schaeder, *Hebrew Humanism*, 306.
67. Schaeder, *Hebrew Humanism*, 307.
68. Schaeder, *Hebrew Humanism*, 305–6.
69. Weltsch, cited in Schaeder, *Hebrew Humanism*, 306.

At the conclusion to his autobiographical essay "My Way to Hasidism," Buber summed up his idealized image of the *zaddik* with the *zaddik* characterized as *der Vollendete*:

> The true zaddik ... is the man who hourly measures the depths of responsibility with the sounding lead of his words. He speaks—and knows that his speech is destiny. ... Men come to him, and each desires his opinion, his help. And ... *he elevates their need before he satisfies it*. Thus, he is the helper in spirit, the teacher of world-meaning, the conveyer of the divine sparks. The world needs him, the perfected man [*der Vollendete*].[70]

In this passage from 1919, Buber again affirmed the connection between the *zaddik* of Hasidism and the "perfected person," the figure he had presented earlier in "The Teaching of the Tao."

The Hasidic context provides Buber's prototype of the master, but Buber did not limit that role to the *zaddik*. Within the history of Judaism he identified several high points when individuals manifested the "unique relationship to the unconditional" of the master: Jacob, Moses, the Prophets, Jesus, the Hasidic masters.[71] In "The Teaching of the Tao," Buber widens his scope to set the role of the master in a global context. He confirmed this global breadth in his discussion of the *zaddik* in his 1921 introduction to *The Great Maggid*, where he again included discussion of the masters in Christianity and Buddhism.[72]

In "Interpreting Hasidism," written in 1963 near the end of his life, Buber confirms the global spirituality he first expressed in "The Teaching of the Tao," written in 1910. Here he again makes the case for orally transmitted teaching stories as the key to the meaning of Hasidism. He defines the teaching story, the legendary anecdote, as a brief narrated event built around "an utterance of the master ... of 'mystical teachings.'"[73] He claims such stories are at the core of spiritual transmission in Zen Buddhism, Sufism, and Hasidism.[74] The kind of mysticism he espouses "can be seen most clearly in the mode of lived realization," and thus in hagiographic narratives, anecdotes that combine an event with a master's utterance: because the master's relationship to the absolute "is so basically an existential one that no theoretical discussion can do it justice, the only suitable vehicle for

---

70. Buber, "My Way to Hasidism," 68–69 (emphasis original).

71. Buber, "Judaism and the Jews," 12; Buber, "Jewish Religiosity," 87–93; Buber, "Holy Way," 115–32; Buber, "Biblical Leadership," 119–33.

72. Buber, "Spirit and Body," 129.

73. Buber, "Interpreting Hasidism," 219, 220.

74. Buber, "Interpreting Hasidism," 220.

expressing this relationship is the anecdote that embodies the utterances of the master."[75] Accordingly, oral traditions of mysticism have a special role in the transmission of the teachings because they "attempt to preserve the living spirit of [the] teachings by retaining their connection with the situations out of which they sprang like the sparks from steel."[76]

To Buber, teaching is about the transmission of spiritual reality from master to disciple, as he makes clear in his exposition of Hasidism. The immediate reality of "the teaching" is embodied in the master. As the central person among his disciples, the master transmits the reality of "the teaching" to them, thus fulfilling its purpose. Because "the teaching" "places the unspecifiable 'How' . . . high above the codifiable 'What,'" it must always be communicated from one person to another through a life. "True to its nature as a 'How,' it is only pointed to by the word, but in its substantial truth it can only be presented through authentication."[77] The spiritual structure of the Hasidic movement "was founded upon the handing on of the kernel of the teaching from teacher to disciple . . . because in the atmosphere of the master, in the spontaneous working of his being, the inexpressible How descended swinging and creating."[78] Buber brings it home to his readers: "the teaching is a help for our concrete life—our life itself is uplifted through the speech directed to us if we listen to it. Reality calls forth reality, the reality of a person who has lived in intercourse with the reality of being in its fullness awakens the reality in us and helps us to live in intercourse with the reality of being in its fullness."[79]

In "The Teaching of the Tao," and again in "Interpreting Hasidism," Buber makes the role of the master central—and the transmission of that role comes through teaching stories, whether Taoist, Buddhist, Jewish, Christian, or Muslim. Yet there is a shift from the one to the other: in parallel with the movement from personal spiritual quest to service of others in Buber's own journey, the earlier essay emphasizes the oneness which the master realizes in his life, and the later essay emphasizes the master's role as a mediator between humanity and the sacred.

---

75. Buber, "Interpreting Hasidism," 219.
76. Buber, "Interpreting Hasidism," 220.
77. Buber, "Spirit and Body," 128.
78. Buber, "Spirit and Body," 148.
79. Buber, "Foundation Stone," 71 (translation modified).

4. The Global Historical Perspective

In "The Teaching of the Tao," Buber sets "the teaching" in a global context: "The way of the teaching [through its] pure fulfillment in a central human life . . . is to be perceived, with greater or lesser clarity, in the three manifestations of the teaching that are handed down to us in sufficient documentation."[80] He presents three masters as these manifestations: Jesus, the Buddha, and Lao Tzu. Each became the fountainhead of a major tradition. He uses the phrase "the oneness as the needful" as shorthand for the essence of the life-as-teaching of each of these masters; he contrasts this unnamable essence with the distinct cultural themes that are subject to analysis and that frame the discourse of each master:

> When we analyze each way of the teaching in content and form, we receive as the "content" not the oneness, but rather the discourse of the kingdom of Heaven and sonship to God, or the discourse of deliverance from suffering and the holy path, or the discourse of Tao and non-doing. This cannot be otherwise; for the oneness was even more than the content of Jesus or Buddha or Lao Tzu, even more than what they wanted to articulate, it was the sense and the foundation of these men. It was more than the content of their word, it was this word's life and the word itself in its oneness.[81]

Parables or teaching stories and key metaphors drew from the framing symbols of each tradition and became the vehicles of "the teaching." With this distinction between the essence of a teaching—the lived life—and its discourse, Buber affirms both the unity and the diversity of the resulting global spiritual traditions.

Thus, whether it is Jesus, the Buddha, or Lao Tzu, in each case the oneness that is the essence manifests itself through the particular foundational symbols of the master's native culture. Accordingly, in Judaism the primal message of Jesus was not about the theological concept of the oneness of God, but rather a revelation of the alikeness of being of the unified person and deity. Similarly, the teaching of Atman from the Upanishads that was taken up by the Buddha became not a metaphysical doctrine about the oneness of existence but the reality of the oneness through which the unified person confronts the world as existence, as oneness. So too, in China, the

---

80. Buber, "Commentary," 76. Buber addresses the founding of global spiritual traditions in a number of his writings: see "Spirit of the Orient and Judaism," 56–78; "Religion and Ethics," 99–107; "Judaism and Civilization," 192; "Interpreting Hasidism," 218–25.

81. Buber, "Commentary," 75.

Tao was not a metaphysical reality underlying the phenomenal world, but rather the concrete, actual path manifested in the actions of the accomplished, perfected person.[82]

I and Thou implicitly carries forward this same vision of global spirituality. There Buber refers to "towering revelations that mark the beginnings of great communities and stand at the turning points of human eras [*die Wenden der Menschenzeit*]" (§61n). Furthermore, in §36h, these revelations are the foundations of the world's great cultures. Buber does not explicitly refer to founding figures in this passage but the implication is clear, for "an originating event of encounter" requires a human respondent. He does write that it is the foundational human "response to the *Thou* . . . an act of being that is made by the spirit" that is the source of each culture. Unlike Karl Jaspers, who developed the concept of the "Axial Age" as the period from roughly 800 BCE to 200 BCE when extraordinary thinkers and sages across Eurasia arose to become founders of the world's major spiritual traditions, Buber's vision is more open-ended. He does not limit such pivotal moments to a particular time span.[83]

The role of such founders—Buber's term "master-builders," as in §33k, resonates here—is sketched in *I and Thou* very much in the terms Buber developed in "The Teaching of the Tao," yet with a difference. In *I and Thou* the emergence and the impact of the master are presented not in terms of the realization of the tao but in terms of the dialogical relationship between the eternal *Thou* and the human respondent.

> Pure effective action, action apart from arbitrary self-will, towers above the spirit of knowledge and the spirit of art. . . . From time to time the *Thou* has appeared to a person out of a deeper mystery, addressed him out of the darkness, and he answered with his life. Here the word has become life, and this life is *teaching*. . . . So this life stands before those who come after, to teach them not what is and not what ought to be, but *how* life is lived in the spirit, in the face of the *Thou*. That is, it stands ready at all times to become *Thou* for them and to open up the world of *Thou*—no:

---

82. Buber, "Commentary," 75.

83. Jaspers, *Origin and Goal*. Buber's list of foundational teachers and teachings has significant parallels to Jaspers's list of Axial movements across Asia and the Mediterranean; see Buber, "Religion and Ethics," 99–100, 103–5; "Spirit of the Orient and Judaism," 57–63; "Judaism and Civilization," 192. Within the history of the Hebrew tradition, Buber traces high points of such leadership from Abraham and Moses through the prophets to the dialogical person of the present time; see Buber, "Abraham the Seer"; *Moses*; *The Prophetic Faith*; "Biblical Leadership." The Baal-Shem, Buber's teacher through his *Testament*, stands as one, perhaps the latest, of such figures; see "Beginnings," 25.

> more than standing ready, it continually comes towards them and reaches out to touch them. (§32h, emphasis added)

Here, the exemplary life of the master was teaching during his lifetime and it continues to be teaching to posterity. A life as teaching and the "how" of life lived in the spirit continue as in "The Teaching of the Tao," yet now it is the world of the *Thou* rather than the Tao that opens up to those who come after and its in-breaking is presented as more immediate, as virtually palpable, as inviting the person of today to connect with it.

In Buber's lectures on Judaism, which come from the same period as "The Teaching of the Tao," he assigns a special role to the contribution of Judaism in the global history of spirituality. In "The Spirit of the Orient and Judaism," he at first aligns Judaism and Hinduism: when the individual "perceives himself as a battleground of prodigious contradictions, [through] the insight of the Indian and the decision of the Jew . . . the unity of being is accomplished."[84] But then he introduces universal accessibility, which Jewish teaching distinctly offers as its unique contribution to the spirituality of humankind: "Of the great spiritual systems of the East, the one destined to have a decisive effect on Western people had to be the system whose proclamation of the way of authentic life challenged every individual directly, the system that was not the privilege of the sage or the chosen but equally accessible to all . . . the Jewish teaching of decision and return."[85] With this exposition of Judaism, Buber introduces a note of urgency, the need for each individual to make a choice. He presents the contrast between those who choose and those who don't in the strongest of terms:

> The cognizance of inner duality and the immanent demand for decision—that is, of the soul's unification—divided the people into two psychologically distinct factions: one consisted of men who choose, who make decisions, who are impelled toward unconditionality and are dedicated to their goal; the other of laissez-faire men, decisionless men, men who remain indolently inert in their conditionality, and whose aim is self-aggrandizement and self-satisfaction—or, in biblical terms, men who are servants of God and men who are servants of Baal.[86]

Here Buber exalts the distinctive, existential element of Judaism—soul-uniting decision-making and the resulting lived action in one's concrete

---

84. Buber, "Spirit of the Orient and Judaism," 65.
85. Buber, "Spirit of the Orient and Judaism," 69–70 (translation modified).
86. Buber, "Spirit of the Orient and Judaism," 73.

world—as the element that elevates Judaism to its role as the bridge between the East and the West.

Buber concludes his lecture "Judaism and Mankind" by linking the exalted role of Judaism in global spirituality with the act of achieving unity:

> A Jew once said: "One thing above all is needed." With this saying he expressed Judaism's innermost soul, which knows that all meaning-contents are null and void unless they grow into a unified oneness [*Einheit*], and that in all of life this alone matters: to have such oneness. [The times when] the soul of Judaism has dwelled on the heights of such a view . . . were the great, the eternal, moments in Jewish history. At these moments Judaism was the East's apostle to mankind.[87]

5. The Core of the Teaching—"The One Thing Needful": The Unification of the Self

Buber was taken by a phrase, "One thing is necessary," which comes from the New Testament.[88] Variations of this phrase in German "*Eins ist not*," "*das Eine das Not tut*," or "*das Notwendige*," appear frequently throughout Buber's writings. Often he alludes to the phrase with other words as well.[89]

The phrase brings together three focal elements of Buber's concept of spirituality: unity, decision—unity through choosing the one priority—and responsibility or duty. Elliott Wolfson, in his exposition of the role of unity in Buber's thought, interprets the meaning of the phrase thusly: "That which is needful is the one thing, i.e., the thing that is one, that unifies."[90] For Bu-

---

87. Buber, "Judaism and Mankind," 32–33 (translation modified).

88. Luke 10:42.

89. For example, "*das eine . . . worauf es ankommt*," "The one [thing] . . . it comes down to." (§46f).

It is important to note the linguistic difference between English on the one hand and Greek, Latin, and German on the other regarding "one": its first use in English is as an adjective; thus, "thing" is often added to nominalize it. Yet the Greek word ἕν or ἑνός need take no article or noun to mean "[the] one [thing]"—both the adjective and the noun are implied in the word for "one." Plotinus, for example, consistently uses τὸ ἕν to refer to ultimate transcendent reality, which cannot be named, as "the one [thing] [which is] the unity." (In Plotinus, the article is added to emphasize the unique status of "the one.") The same is true with the Latin *unum* and the German *eins*, *Eines*, *eines* or *das Eine*. Thus the original phrase in Greek, ἑνὸς δέ ἐστιν χρεία, which literally translates to "but one is needed," while English translations add "thing" to read "but one thing is needed." This linguistic point comes into play in *I and Thou* (§36c).

90. Wolfson, "Problem of Unity," 432.

ber this unity is the focused oneness of will of the authentic life in which "the individual relates himself absolutely to the absolute." This stance is the lived life of the master.

The phrase originated in a brief New Testament teaching story about two sisters, Mary and Martha, who hosted Jesus the master in their home. Mary sat and listened to the master while Martha did the serving. When Martha asked Jesus to tell Mary to help her, he replied: "Martha, Martha, you are worried and distracted by many things; there is need of only one thing.[91] Mary has chosen the better part, which will not be taken away from her."[92]

The story sets up "the one thing needful" as the alternative to the worry and distraction that come with a focus on "many things." Here we have the one vs. the many, unity vs. multiplicity. With these alternatives, one is presented with a choice and the choice for "the one thing needful" is a deliberate choice, a choice for the good. For Buber, the act of choosing unifies the chooser. His emphasis on the unity of the person in his use of the phrase, derived from "the one," gives it his own emphasis, whereas the contrast between the one and the many was the master's point in the original story.

The other part of the phrase, "the needful" or "the necessary" carries the weight of an imperative. "The needful" here is not physical necessity, such as gravity or the causal nexus. Rather, it is "the good," the *summum bonum*, the unconditional condition which cannot be taken away because it is eternal. In this, the necessary is the essential; it is the ought of human creaturehood, the expression of what one was created to be. In this sense, to choose "the one thing needful" is to fulfill the purpose of one's existence.[93]

I believe Buber was impressed early on by Meister Eckhart's emphasis on this phrase. Buber's friend Gustav Landauer published his modern version of selected works of Eckhart as *Meister Eckharts mystische Schriften* in 1903. After Landauer's death, Buber edited the book and published it in a second edition in 1920. In Eckhart's sermon on the story, he quotes, "Only one thing is necessary" and identifies this one thing as God.[94] In Eckhart's treatise, "On Detachment," he identifies the "*unum est necessarium*," "one thing is necessary," as detachment: "Our Lord said to Martha: '*Unum est necessarium*,' which is to say, the one who would be serene and pure needs but one thing, detachment [*Abgeschiedenheit*]"—that is, detachment from

---

91. Compare *Eins aber ist not*, "but one [thing] is necessary" (Luther Bible).

92. Luke 10:38–42 (NRSV).

93. "The Good . . . reveals itself to the individual who decides with his whole being to become that which he is meant to be" (Buber, "Religion and Ethics," 103).

94. Eckhart, *Meister Eckhart: Selected Writings*, 199.

all created things to focus oneself totally on God.[95] In Buber's own writing on Hasidism he discussed such detachment in very different terms. He saw it as part of the "ever new exercise of the 'receiving power' of the zaddik," as part of *yichud*, making one or cleaving to God.[96]

Buber first used the phrase "the one thing needful" in a short early essay on the Buddha to stress the urgency of breaking through concepts in order to see the spirituality of the Buddha as a dynamic of action: "One thing is needful ... to free ourselves from the 'aesthetic,' 'philosophical,' and 'religious' ways of looking at things, from the theories and the 'isms,' and rediscover in the Buddha not an idea ... but a deed."[97] With these words, Buber picks up on renunciation, detachment, and the transcending of concepts as the necessary inner *ascesis* that opens up the phenomenon of the Buddha as a revelation—the Buddha's action *is* the revelation. The many ideas are let go of and as a result the unifying act shines forth in its absoluteness.

Late in life Buber continued to use the phrase. He even used it to conclude his disavowal of "The Teaching of the Tao": "Being true to the being in which and before which I am placed is the one thing that is needful."[98] This emphasis on fidelity within one's existential circumstances resonates with the Hasidic life as a "life in responsibility—the responsibility of the single one for the piece of the world entrusted to him."[99] Here as elsewhere the phrase expresses what Buber shares with the core of Kierkegaard's spirituality in *Fear and Trembling*. For Kierkegaard the individual has "an absolute duty to God ... in this relationship of duty the individual relates himself absolutely, as the single individual, to the absolute."[100] For Buber, as for Kierkegaard, the imperative to relate oneself absolutely to the absolute is "the one thing needful."

"The one thing needful" is thus Buber's shorthand for the Kierkegaardian duty of the individual to relate absolutely to the absolute. In his exposition of Taoism, this absolute relation is embodied in the authentic life of the unified individual, no matter what tradition that individual bears. In the context of this early treatise, an almost monistic unity is the overriding reality, whereas later that reality has become refocused toward

---

95. Eckhart, in Buber, *Meister Eckharts mystische Schriften*, 165 (my translation).

96. Buber, "Spirit and Body," 132–33.

97. Buber, quoted in Friedman, "Martin Buber's Encounter with Mysticism," 59; see Buber, "Buddha," 3–9.

98. Buber, "Foreword," xvi.

99. Buber, "Supplement," 253.

100. Kierkegaard, *Fear and Trembling*, 98; see also Kierkegaard's broader discussion, 85–108.

the wholeness of relating fully to the divine Other.[101] Buber incorporates "the one thing needful" in the account of his own transformation at the heart of *I and Thou* (§36c).[102]

In his 1946 introduction to *Tales of the Hasidim*, Buber sums up his concept of the teaching for his readers:

> To bring about the union between God and Shekinah, eternity and time . . . all that is necessary is . . . to have a soul united within itself and indivisibly directed to its divine goal. The world within which you live, just as it is and not otherwise, affords you that association with God which will redeem you and whatever divine aspect of the world you have been entrusted with. And your own character, the very qualities which make you what you are, constitutes your special approach to God, your special potential use for Him.[103]

"The one thing needful" is the unified soul directed to God. And God, the world, and the human person are the elements of this dialogue.

6. Buber's *Way*

In discussing the nature of the Tao in "The Teaching of the Tao" Buber begins where the *Tao Te Ching* begins: "The Tao that can be spoken of is not the true Tao."[104] He asserts that the Tao, like the realm of *Thou* in *I and Thou*, is not a metaphysical entity or a concept that functions to explain the world. The Western desire to make the Tao metaphysical reduces it to current Western philosophical assumptions, where over time it has been seen variously as nature, reason, or energy. Buber makes clear that this whole approach misses the radical reality of the Tao. It is none of these things; rather, it is "the imperceptible for which no image suffices, because 'in it are the images.'"[105] Yet, more pointedly, "even that which the word 'Tao' expresses is not a statement about the imperceptible. . . . Not only can no truth be stated concerning it, but it cannot be the subject of a statement at all. What can be said concerning it is neither true nor false."[106]

---

101. This shift is well presented in Huston, *Martin Buber's Journey to Presence*.
102. See the discussion of §36c in chapter 8 below, pages 199–202.
103. Buber, *Tales of the Hasidim*, 1:4.
104. Lao Tzu, *Tao Te Ching*, 1.1.
105. Buber, "Commentary," 83, quoting a phrase from Lao Tzu, *Tao Te Ching*, 21.49.
106. Buber, "Commentary," 83–84.

Yet, true to Buber's human-centered approach to all of the big questions, he asserts that the Tao can be known through its human portal, the master. Accordingly,

> In the human being the Tao can become pure unity [*reine Einheit*], as it cannot in the world, in things. The person in whom the Tao becomes pure unity is the perfected one [*der Vollendete*]. In him the Tao no longer appears but *is*. [Thus,] the Tao realizes itself [*verwirklicht sich*] in the genuine life of the perfected person. In his pure unity it emerges from appearance to direct reality. The unknowable and the unified human life, the first and the last, meet. In the perfected person the Tao returns from its world-wandering through manifestation to its self. It becomes fulfillment, becomes eternity.[107]

In the pure unity of the authentic life the unknowable Tao arises as that life. The duality of the unknowable Tao and the authentic human life, the absolute and the conditional, merge. In this there is a concentrating, a fullness, a boundlessness.

To understand the Tao one must become like the master, beginning with the implied imperative of "the one thing needful": whoever "unceasingly renews himself and just through this affirms his self in and through the transformation—which indeed is not a rigid existence [*ein starres Sein*], but rather, simply the way, Tao—he attains the eternal transformation and self-affirmation."[108] To continually put oneself in the flux of renewal is to live authentically in oneness. This is the life of transparency in Tao, for "the full manifestation of Tao [*die vollkommene Offenbarung Taos*] is . . . the one who unites the purest oneness with the most vigorous transformation."[109] Buber later related this uniting to *teshuvah*, turning, and to the *Thou*, as we shall see. Tao here is meaning: "the whole meaning of being rests in the unity of the authentic life . . . it is experienced nowhere else . . . it is precisely this unity grasped as the absolute."[110] This unity of the authentic life "grasped as the absolute" is again the working of the Kierkegaardian principle in which "the individual relates himself absolutely . . . to the absolute."

Buber presents a passage from the *Tao Te Ching* as an outline of the practice that transforms awareness as one becomes a Taoist master:

---

107. Buber, "Commentary," 87–88 (emphasis added).
108. Buber, "Commentary," 85.
109. Buber, "Commentary," 85.
110. Buber, "Commentary," 83.

> Ascend the height of self-emptying
> [*Ersteige die Höhe der Entaüßerung = kenosis*],
>
> embrace the primordial abyss of silence
> [*umfange den Urgrund der Ruhe*].
>
> The numberless beings all arise.
>
> In this I recognize their return [*Rückkehr*].
>
> When the beings come to full flower, in their unfolding each returns to its root.
>
> To have returned to the root means to rest [*ruhen*].
>
> To rest means to have fulfilled one's destiny
> [*die Bestimmung erfüllt haben*].
>
> To have fulfilled one's destiny means to be eternal.[111]

These lines from the *Tao Te Ching* outline the stages from the imperative of the spiritual quest (lines 1–2), to the phenomenology of awareness (lines 3–5), to the meaning of the transformation (lines 6–8). The practice of detachment (self-emptying, similar to Eckhart's *Abgeschiedenheit*) and its complement, embracing the abyss of silence, leads to a transformed perception of the world—all things arise and are recognized as new-old. The resulting deep perception of the realized master then resonates with eternity.

This process undergone by the Taoist to become central man parallels the process of becoming a *zaddik* in the Hasidic movement, as Buber describes it in his introduction to *The Great Maggid*.[112] Central to Buber's discussion is *yichud*, the spiritual activity of "making one" which originated in the Kabbalah.[113] Within Hasidism *yichud* means "both the unity of God and the confession of it," which to the Hasid is "a subjective-objective event, an event of meeting, it is the dynamic form of the divine unity itself."[114] Buber identifies this "making one" as the core work of the *zaddik*. By "the stripping away of bodiliness" the *zaddik* prepares "to enter into the 'condition of the nothing,' in which alone the divine renewal can take place," equipping him to do his "daily work: the thousand-fold work of 'unification,' the *yichud*."[115] This Hasidic spiritual practice of "stripping away" parallels the Taoist practice of self-emptying, just as "entering the

---

111. Lao Tzu, *Tao Te Ching*, 16.1–8, Buber's version, quoted in Buber, "Commentary," 87–88.

112. Buber, "Spirit and Body," 133–39.

113. In exoteric Jewish tradition, *yichud* refers to the traditional period of the intimate seclusion of the bride and groom immediately after the marriage ceremony.

114. Buber, "Spirit and Body," 133.

115. Buber, "Spirit and Body," 133.

condition of nothing" corresponds to the Taoist "embracing the silence." For Buber this transformation does not mean nullification of the self. The difference between the Taoist central man and the *zaddik* lies not so much in their spiritual means and goals as in the strong sense of the *zaddik*'s role as a "uniter" in the lives of the people whom he serves.

Tao to Buber is the boundless unity of the genuine human way which runs through all things. The oneness of the world which the master beholds "is simply a mirroring of his own unity, for the world is nothing foreign but rather one with the unified person."[116]

Tao is not an object of knowing but a manner of being: "it is not perceived and known, but rather possessed, lived, and acted."[117] In this sense, "the unified person experiences Tao directly. He beholds the unity in the world."[118] Examples make clear that this unity is a unity in polarity: "The oneness of the masculine and feminine elements that exist not for themselves but only for one another, the oneness of antitheses that exist not for themselves but only through one another, the oneness of things that exist not for themselves but only with one another. This oneness is the Tao in the world."[119] Here it is clear the Tao is the unity that is present along with multiplicity. As in space, so in time: the Tao that is the steady reality in continual transformation confirms itself through all moments—just as "the one" is present "in the multiplicity of things," so is the Tao in "the multiplicity of moments that follow one upon another."[120]

Buber made clear at the outset that the Tao transcends categories, including those such as being and nonbeing and life and death. Thus, the eternal Tao is also called "non-being."[121] To call it nonbeing is to suggest how elusive it is, as if from the point of view of concrete everyday reality it does not exist. Birth and death are merely one's entering and exiting the world through "the invisible gate of Heaven which is called non-being. This non-being is the dwelling place of the perfected one, the unified one who directly experiences Tao. . . . 'Heaven and Earth and I came together into existence, and I and all things are one.'"[122]

Thus, in "The Teaching of the Tao," Buber's Tao is a state of awareness, a state of being which one can enter through spiritual practices. Yet even though the Taoist process strikingly parallels the transformation of the *zaddik* in Hasidism, the emphases, the meanings, and the effects of

116. Buber, "Commentary," 86.
117. Buber, "Commentary," 84 (translation modified).
118. Buber, "Commentary," 86 (translation modified).
119. Buber, "Commentary," 84.
120. Buber, "Commentary," 85.
121. Buber, "Commentary," 85.
122. Buber, "Commentary," 85–86.

the transformations in these two traditions are different. A pervasive yet uncharacterized unity is the ultimate value for the Taoist as Buber sees it, while for the Hasid such unity is an attainment to be achieved for the sake of service to one's fellow human beings. The question arises: How does this sense of Tao relate to "the between" which becomes the crucial reality in Buber's later thought?

Buber had a profound affinity with Taoism and it continued throughout his life. In an important late lecture, Buber put the eternal *Thou* and the Chinese Tao side by side and virtually proclaimed that the way of God and the Tao were the same:

> The "way of God" is by no means to be understood as a sum of prescriptions for human conduct, but rather primarily as the way of God in and through the world. It is the true sphere of the knowledge of God since it means God's becoming visible in his action. But it is at the same time the way of salvation of men since it is the prototype for the imitation of God. Similarly, the Chinese Tao, the "path" in which the world moves, is the cosmic primal meaning. But because man conforms this his life to it and practices "imitation of the Tao," it is at the same time the perfection of the soul.[123]

In both cases, the essential issue is conforming to the presence of the transcendent and living one's life in terms of it.

Thus, "the way of God in and through the world" is the vivid presence of the Creator in the creation. Buber represents this presence elsewhere in strikingly anthropomorphic terms: much as in Genesis 3:8, "the way of God [means] that God himself walks in the person of his *Shekinah*, his 'indwelling,' through the history of the world; he takes the way, the fate of the world upon himself."[124]

The "way of God" for human beings is the "life lived in the presence of God." Buber makes clear this immediacy requires a discernment-bearing choice: God is "an elementally present spiritual reality . . . emanating from the immediacy of existence as such, which religious man steadfastly confronts and nonreligious man evades."[125] Then he uses an astonishing solar metaphor to convey a sense of "life lived in the presence of God": "God is . . . the sun of mankind. . . . The person who remains steadfast and lives in the presence of God [is] the person who breathes, walks, and bathes his self and

---

123. Buber, "Religion and Philosophy," 33.
124. Buber, "Faith of Judaism," 21.
125. Buber, "Holy Way" 109.

all things in the sun's light."[126] Yet Buber is not exclusivistic about the imperative to live "in the presence." He opens the way wide to include people of every culture in the process: "To each person the highest is open, each life has its access to reality, each nature its eternal right, from each thing a way leads to God, and each way that leads to God is *the* way."[127]

7. Conclusion

Buber did not shrink from global breadth in his quest to plumb the depths of human spirituality. "The Teaching of the Tao" shows how ambitious his reach was, from an early age. It also presents major elements of his thinking that remained as reference points, even when modified, throughout the range of his work. These elements were grounded in his experience and study of Hasidism and they give us valuable reference points for understanding his message in *I and Thou*.

As we have seen in this chapter, Buber did not compartmentalize the diverse cultural expressions of spirituality he studied. In like manner, neither should we compartmentalize Buber, dividing his earlier work from his later work. To do so would undercut the strength of his vision. It would blind us to the continuities of his work. Yet these continuities allow us to see the parts of his work in their organic relation to the whole. We have seen how some of his thinking carries forward from his early adulthood to his dialogical thinking in *I and Thou*. This approach allows us to appreciate both the earlier and the later work more fully because we see how they complement each other and how the latter fulfills the former at the same time that it lifts it to a new level.

Buber's shift from this exposition of Tao to his later view was a shift from his early vision of the monistic all-one as innate being to his enduring understanding of the all-one as task—as the imperative, the state of totality the human being is called upon to achieve. He concludes his dialogical essay "With a Monist" (1914) by making this very point: "Every true deed . . . brings, out of lived unity, unity into the world. Unity is not a property of the world but its task. To form unity out of the world is our never-ending work."[128] This "making one" is a focal point both of Buber's Taoist "perfect man" and of Hasidic life as expressed in the Hebrew term *yichud*. It is a short step from these moments to the "making one" in *I and Thou* that is the gateway to the dialogical life.

---

126. Buber, "Holy Way" 109 (translation modified).
127. Buber, "Spirit and Body," 149 (emphasis his).
128. Buber, "With a Monist," 30.

Chapter 7

Exposition of *I and Thou*—Part One

PART ONE OF *I and Thou* establishes the foundations of Buber's response to alienation, the problem he directly addresses in part two. Part one consists of three elements. First, Buber lays out his landmark distinction between *I-Thou* and *I-It* (§§1–22). Second, he presents two genealogies tracing the emergence of *I-It* (§§23–28). Third, he concludes by confronting his readers with a choice between the two alternatives, *I-Thou* and *I-It* (§§29–30). We approach the exposition of part one with a look at alienation as a distinctively modern problem, Buber's creative response to it, his development of the distinction between *I-Thou* and *I-It*, and his philosophy of dialogue.

1. The Problem of Individuation and Alienation

Buber's foundational distinction between the realm of *I-It* and the realm of *I-Thou* solves a major problem of modernity that confronted him along with many others in *fin de siècle* Europe: alienation. Laurence Silberstein singles out alienation as "the underlying problem that links together Buber's diverse intellectual activities."[1] Simply defined, alienation is the estrangement, the dislocation of the individual from others, from God, from nature, and from his or her own authentic self. In a definitive statement in his inaugural lectures at the University of Jerusalem in 1938, Buber made clear how the problem of alienation is a central issue of modern times. Buber characterized modernity as an "epoch of homelessness":

> In the history of the human spirit I distinguish between epochs of habitation and epochs of homelessness. In the former, man lives in the world as in a house, as in a home. In the latter, man lives in the world as in an open field and at times does not even

---

1. Silberstein, *Martin Buber's Social and Religious Thought*, 5.

have four pegs with which to set up a tent. In the former epochs anthropological thought exists only as a part of cosmological thought. In the latter, anthropological thought gains depth and, with it, independence.[2]

To Buber, the challenge of "homelessness," cosmic alienation, is also an opportunity, the setting for depth and autonomy in anthropological thought. In his lecture he traced the devolution of European culture to modern alienation. He prefaced this sketch of the course of things with an overarching observation: "In the ice of solitude man becomes most inexorably a question to himself, and just because the question pitilessly summons and draws into play his most secret life he becomes an experience to himself."[3] The moment of such cosmic solitude both creates the opportunity for and requires unprecedented self-probing. For Buber this condition is the ground out of which his philosophy of dialogue and the struggle over it emerges.

Alienation arose as a distinctively modern, post-Enlightenment European concern. The problem of alienation became a focus in Europe in the late nineteenth century with the emergence of modern industrial society when a number of thinkers addressed it along with its corollary, the distinctly modern problem of mass society.[4] The sociologist Georg Simmel was developing his focus on the idea of alienation around 1900, when Buber was his student at the University of Berlin. Buber's cultural-historical understanding of alienation through the work of Simmel and others became existential in his struggle with grief in response to Landauer's death. Thus, alienation became a major element of the drama which Buber lays out and addresses in *I and Thou*. Silberstein points out the "central section of *I and Thou* is devoted to a critique of the alienating forces in modern society and culture."[5] Walter Kaufmann, in accord with Paul Mendes-Flohr, confirms alienation is the dominant concern *I and Thou* addresses: "The theme of alienation is prominent [because] the aim of the book in large measure is to diagnose certain tendencies in modern society and to indicate . . . a new sense of community."[6] In his critique of modernity in *I and Thou*, Buber uses *Verfremdung*, the German word for alienation, a number of times.[7]

Buber was one among a great wave of thinkers who took up the issue of alienation, interpreting it as the underside of individuation and linking it

2. Buber, "What is Man?," 126.
3. Buber, "What is Man?," 126.
4. Homans, *Jung in Context*, 173–82.
5. Silberstein, *Martin Buber's Social* and Religious Thought, 169.
6. Kaufmann, "I and You," 38; see Kaufmann, "Introductory Essay," xxi.
7. See Buber, *I and Thou*, §37a, §43a–b, §54d.

to the culture of the European bourgeoisie. With his 1904 doctoral dissertation "On the History of the Problem of Individuation," Buber used case studies of Nicholas of Cusa (1401–1464) and Jakob Boehme (1575–1624) to interpret the development of individuation which took place as European culture evolved away from the Medieval synthesis. Like a number of others, at first he sought to resolve the problem of alienation through his global studies of what he later characterized as *Erlebnis*-mysticism. His breakthrough came over the course of time, and it first became explicit in the writing of *I and Thou*, the treatise he originally envisioned as the introduction to a magnum opus on global spirituality. With the emergence of his distinction between *I-Thou* and *I-It*, Buber placed *Erlebnis*-mysticism squarely in the *It*-world. At the same time, his distinction between *I-Thou* and *I-It* is homologous with Kant's distinction between *noumena* and *phenomena* as it was reworked by Schopenhauer.[8]

Arthur Schopenhauer was a post-Kantian philosopher whose major work, *The World as Will and Representation*, was developed over the first half of the nineteenth century. Schopenhauer elaborated Kant's original distinction between *phenomena* and *noumena*. Influenced by the early introduction of Hindu Vedanta into Europe, he linked Kant's *phenomena*, the space-time-causal nexus (Kant's "forms of understanding") with the veil of Maya (the veil of illusion) of Hindu philosophy. He tied this realm with the principle of individuation and the mind's rational mode of perception, that is, its work of dividing the world up into distinct, discrete entities so that the world is perceived as a complex of individual phenomena. Taking the *noumena*, the other side of Kant's distinction, Schopenhauer identified this as Kant's *Ding an sich*, his "thing in itself," and linked it to the will as the oneness beyond plurality, the equivalent to the Hindu phrase expressing ultimate unity, *tat tvam asi*, "that thou art," or "The oneness of the All is you."

Friedrich Nietzsche picked up Schopenhauer's distinction and reworked it as his distinction between the Apollonian and the Dionysian. He identified the Apollonian with the *principium individuationis*, by which boundaries divide individual entities and provide the basis of analytical thought. Nietzsche put forth the Dionysian as the expression of what Schopenhauer called "will" and saw it as ecstatic submergence in the greater whole, the means of release from individuality. With this formulation, Nietzsche helped to popularize the distinction that had come down from Kant by way of Schopenhauer. For each thinker, the distinction between multiplicity and unity was a means for dealing with what he saw as the problem of individuation. This distinction as a way to resolve the problem of

---

8. Mendes-Flohr, "Martin Buber's Conception of God," 241.

individuation was what Buber reworked again in his foundational formulation, his distinction between *I-Thou* and *I-It*.

To Schopenhauer, the focus on phenomena was the mode of perception that dominated in the West and this dominance meant "separation, divisiveness, hopeless finitude, and bondage to the causal nexus" of the phenomenal world.[9] Thus, Schopenhauer's exposition fit the widespread critique of alienation as one of the great symptoms of the malaise of modernity. Schopenhauer's solution was to transcend the individuation induced by the phenomenal world by means of a monistic mysticism. This analysis played out in Buber's early pursuit of *Erlebnis*-mysticism, which was derived from his synthesis of Schopenhauer's analysis and Dilthey's concept of *Erlebnis*. *I and Thou* marked Buber's breakthrough, his move beyond mystical monism in addressing the problem of alienation.

I and Thou marks the great watershed in Buber's move from monism to duality, from the pursuit of the experience of oneness to a life lived in encounter with the Other in dialogue. Buber's *It*-world fits the realm of *phenomena*, the realm of human perceptions within the spatial-temporal-causal nexus. By contrast, *I-Thou* fits the direct, holistic apperception of presence which Buber and other mystically-oriented interpreters of Kant link with the realm of *noumena*. In fact, the noumenal *Thou* can be regarded as equivalent to Kant's *Ding an sich*, the "thing in itself," which Kant posits as present but not knowable in phenomenal experience.[10] The correlation between *I-It* and the *phenomenal* realm on the one hand, and *I-Thou* and the *noumenal* realm on the other, has a ripple effect on Buber's thinking in the areas of epistemology and ontology. Buber had found a modern solution to a modern problem. Buber's breakthrough was his new resolution of the problem of individuation-alienation, this time at a deeply nuanced, existential level.

In contrast to the all-is-one of Buber's early *Erlebnis*-mysticism which was discussed in chapter 5 above,[11] the divide between self and Other becomes foundational for his mature dialogical philosophy. Buber uses *gegenüber*, nominalized as *das Gegenüber*, frequently in *I and Thou*. The German adjective *gegenüber* means literally "over against"; it is the counterpart to the self in encounter which is outside the self. As such, in its noun form it can be translated as "the Other." For Buber, the Other is an entity independent of the self and only partly known to the self. It becomes a constituent of self-identity in

---

9. Mendes-Flohr, "Martin Buber's Conception of God," 244.

10. See chapter 3, page 46, above for the discussion of "*das Du an sich*" in relation to the Kantian "*Ding an sich*."

11. Pages 107–15.

the moment of encounter when the self is open to and thus vulnerable to this otherness, for, as Buber points out, differentiation is one of the major means to self-identification. The Other is thus integral to the identity of persons as they construct themselves in relation to their Others.

Buber wrote "Distance and Relation," an important essay explaining that the difference and the distance between an *I* and a *Thou*, their otherness, is an absolute prerequisite for their dialogical encounter. This "primal setting at a distance" makes it possible for two persons to enter into relation with each other.[12] The complement to this distance is the capacity of each to enter into relation, to turn to the Other in openness and affirmation. This situation brings a double contingency into play: both the *I* and the *Thou* can independently decide whether or not to turn to the Other. When the distance is recognized and the turning to the Other is mutual, this distance becomes a "span of relation" and dialogue takes place. This mutual turning allows one person to address and confirm the Other and in turn to be addressed and confirmed by the Other in an event of genuine meeting.[13] Accordingly,

> The innermost growth of the self is . . . accomplished . . . in the relation between the one and the Other . . . pre-eminently in the mutuality of the making present of another self and in the knowledge that one is made present in his own self by the Other—together with the mutuality of acceptance, of affirmation, and confirmation. . . . It is from one person to another that the heavenly bread of self-being is passed.[14]

This relating of self and Other constitutes both self and Other in mutual consciousness. Feuerbach's ontology of that which lies between man and man as cited by Buber is not far from this: "The real I is 'only the I that stands over against a Thou and that itself is a Thou over against another I.'"[15]

2. Buber's Landmark Distinction: *I-Thou* vs. *I-It*

At the outset it is important to consider the meaning of the German word *du*, the informal second person singular pronoun, which is a key term for Buber

---

12. Buber, "Distance and Relation," 60.
13. Buber, "Distance and Relation," 69.
14. Buber, "Distance and Relation," 71 (translation modified); "Heavenly bread" evokes Hölderlin, for Buber the modern voice that best speaks return—see Hölderlin's poem, "Bread and Wine"; Buber, "What is Common to All," 109; Buber, "What is Man?," 179.
15. Feuerbach, quoted in Buber, "Afterword," 210.

and which Smith translates as "*Thou*" and Kaufmann translates as "You." In the history of the English language, "thou" has occupied the place of the German word "du." "Thou," along with "du" in German, has referred to the "you" in the intimacy of the family circle, as well as to God in the intimacy of prayer, and by extension, to intimate friends who have virtually entered the family circle. Traditionally in Germany, people outside one's family are addressed as "Sie" until they become as close as family. There is even a ceremony for the transition of a relationship when two friends move from the use of the formal "Sie" to the use of the more intimate "du" for each other. It is interesting to note from Buber's letters that he never made this transition from the formal "Sie" to the more intimate "du," even with Landauer, one of his two closest friends (although Buber's children called Landauer "Onkel Gustav").[16] By contrast the "thou" in English has become archaic or vaguely religious, thanks to its use in reference to God in the widely influential King James Version of the Bible of 1611. The word may even remind us of the antiquated and quaint locutions of the Quakers.

Well into his exposition of the realm of *Thou* as the realm of relation, Buber introduces the phrase, "the eternal *Thou*," as his circumlocution for God: "Through each event of becoming present to us, we gaze toward the fringe of the eternal *Thou*; with each we are aware of a breath of the eternal *Thou*; in each enunciation of *Thou* we address the Eternal" (§9f).[17] Mendes-Flohr points out that "eternal" is a predicate of God: "'The Eternal [One]' has been a widespread designation for God ever since Moses Mendelssohn rendered the Tetragrammaton as '*der Ewige*' ['The Eternal']."[18] Accordingly, Buber makes a connection that comes naturally in Jewish experience, for the Hebrew equivalent for the German *du*, *Thou*, is *atah*. No Jew could miss the overtones of *atah* as the word of address to God, for almost all Jewish liturgical blessings begin with the Hebrew words *Barukh atah Adonai Eloheinu*, "Blessed are *Thou*, O LORD our God." In this practice of Jewish spirituality *atah*, *Thou*, is inextricably bound with the invocation of the presence of God. Accordingly, every utterance of "thou" echoes the addressing of "the eternal *Thou*" of Jewish liturgy. Thus, it is appropriate that Buber incorporates the metaphors alluding to the *ruach Elohim*, the spirit, the breath or presence of God that originally moved

---

16. On the other hand, Buber began using "*du*" with Rosenzweig once Rosenzweig inadvertently used it of Buber in a poem celebrating their joint translation of the book of Genesis. They discussed the nuances of this shift in their subsequent correspondence. See Rosenzweig to Buber, September 29, 1925, in Buber, *Letters*, 334.

17. This phrase is used in several passages: here at §9f, as well as in §39j, §53c, §55e, and §60a.

18. Mendes-Flohr, "Martin Buber's Conception of God," 254.

over the primal waters of creation in the opening words of the Hebrew Bible (Gen 1:2) and that in Buber's vision continually moves through all of creation. Buber introduces this image by eliding it with language from the great epiphany of Isaiah, in which the prophet sees the Lord, and the *shul*, the train or edge of the divine robe, fills the temple along with the sacred fumes of the censor.[19] This early passage in *I and Thou* thus confirms his view that there is a transcendent, absolute dimension inherent in the realm of the *Thou*, all the way from the primal deep of the *tohu wa bohu* to the holy of holies in the sanctuary on the sacred mountain.

Part one of *I and Thou* begins with Buber's famous distinction between *I-Thou* and *I-It*: "To humans the world consists of two realities based on two possible attitudes [*Haltungen*] one can take. These two attitudes take expression in two primary word-pairs, *I-Thou* and *I-It*. . . . Accordingly, the human *I* is also two realities: the *I* of the primary word-pair *I-Thou* is other than the *I* of the primary word-pair *I-It*" (§1a–b, f–g). The key factor distinguishing these two realities is the attitude one takes toward what one addresses. With this distinction at the outset Buber presents an ethical choice: one can adopt one or the other of two alternative attitudes as a predominant stance in the world. In establishing this distinction, Buber is not presenting an abstract theory but a call to decision based on our existential circumstances as human beings. The pivotal nature of the choice that confronts us becomes ever clearer as Buber's exposition proceeds.

Buber continues, claiming the attitude one takes, represented with the word "speech" or expression [*Sprechen*], constitutes the *I* which "speaks": "The primary words do not express something that might exist outside of them but rather in the act of enunciation they bring about a mode of existence. For these primary words are spoken with one's being. When *Thou* is expressed, the *I* of *I-Thou* is expressed with it. When *It* is expressed, the *I* of *I-It* is expressed with it" (§2b–e). That is to say, how we address a reality determines the nature of the *I* in the act of addressing it as well as the nature of that which is addressed, for, echoing Kant's phase "*Ding an sich*," Buber states, "There is no *I* that exists in itself"—that is, "There is no *I* as such" [*Es gibt kein Ich an sich*] (§3a). The *I* is constituted in the enunciation of the attitude taken, whether the *I* of *I-It* or the *I* of *I-Thou*. Intention, expression, and being are all of one cloth: "When one expresses a primary word, one steps into the realm of that word and takes a stand there" (§3d).

"There is no *I* as such" (§3a). On the one hand, the *I* of the *It*-world is the part-self of activities and things: "I perceive something, I sense something. I imagine something. I want something. I feel something. I think

---

19. Gen 1:2; Isa 6:1.

something" (§4b). This is the world of experience (§6). On the other hand, whoever says *Thou* has turned from the realm of experiences and objects to the realm of being in its boundlessness in which the *I* is manifest as a whole self. In this position, not *having* anything, one simply stands as a whole being in relation (§5). The stance represented by the primary word *I-Thou* is the threshold for this realm of relation (§8).

Buber stresses that one's being is at stake in the choice between *I-Thou* and *I-It*: *I-Thou* is the realm of the wholeness of one's being, while *I-It* is the fractured realm of separated parts. "The primary word *I-Thou* can only be expressed with one's whole being [*mit dem ganzen Wesen*]; the primary word *I-It* can never be expressed with one's whole being" (§2f-g). The integral relation between addressing the Other as *Thou* and acting with one's whole being links to the Taoist principle of *wu-wei*, the "doing which is 'non-doing' is an activity of the whole being," as Buber articulated it in "The Teaching of the Tao."[20] The person who takes the stance of *I-Thou*, like the Taoist sage, addresses what confronts him with his whole being.[21]

The *It*-world is the world of everyday reality. It is the realm of practical life, of "getting and spending" as well as of inner and outer experiences, thought and feeling. It is fundamentally the realm of separation, of alienation. It includes conceptualizing and is riven by the subject-object split. It is the system of means and ends, of functionality. It is the world of common discourse in which everything is mediated. It is all the categories and reference points we set up and use to orient ourselves and to function in society, to identify and navigate through our circumstances, to organize and prioritize the elements that constitute our worlds. The *It*-world is amazingly comprehensive, stretching all the way from our subjective inner chatter, our stream of consciousness, to the skills and technologies by which we harness the natural and social worlds to our purposes, to the objectivity of the world as we know it through the discourses of the sciences, metaphysics, and theology.

Given that the *It*-world is so comprehensive, what remains to comprise the realm of the *Thou*? This phrasing of the question itself reflects the *It*-world as the home base from which it comes. Buber insists all of the *It*-world exists as constructs, as products of linguistic mediation, and thus as *existing only in the past*. The realm of *Thou*, by contrast, is the realm of

20. Buber, "Commentary," 91 (translation modified).

21. Buber works out implications of this stance of one's whole being in several later passages, as we shall see: §12, 14, 21, 32, 37, 39, 45, 46, 47. Buber's distinction between the *I* of *I-Thou* and the *I* of *I-It* also has its analogue in the distinction some Christian writers make between the egoic or false self system and the true self. For example, Keating, *Invitation to Love*; Finley, *Merton's Palace of Nowhere*; Bourgeault, "Gift of Life."

unmediated presence, the presence of the present, the being present to the presence. It is the direct apperception of being, the being of self and Other that is taken in in one glance. It involves radical openness to the *Thou* being addressed. It is the naked moment in which one sees or senses, decides, makes a destiny-shaping movement of the will, and takes a stance as a hitherto untested standpoint. The *I* that is constituted in this turning fully to the *Thou* is the whole person as respondent, being all he was created to be. With this description we see how radically "other" the realm of *Thou* is to the everyday, functioning *It*-world.

Buber shifts to the first person to sketch the mutuality and the totality of *I-Thou* in §14, a key passage. "The *Thou* encounters me as an event of grace—it is not to be found by seeking. . . . Yet when the *Thou* arises before me I can step into mutual relation with it" (§14a, b). "To express the basic word *Thou* in response to the Other is to act with my whole being" (§14c); "it is the distinctive act of my being" (§14a). To express oneself thusly requires one's "concentration and fusion into a unified whole" (§14c). Such wholeness expresses all of me, yet I cannot accomplish this wholeness on my own: the *I* of *I-Thou* requires a Thou because "I become *I* as I address the Other as Thou" (§14c). This "direct relation" is at once both "receptive and active, a being chosen and a choosing" (§14b). Any such action of the whole being appears to approach passivity because with it, all partial actions seem to be suspended, as they are grounded in their finite concreteness. Buber sums up: "All real living is encounter [*Begegnung*]" (§14d).[22]

Resemblances between *Thou* in the direct encounter as Buber describes it here and the working of Tao in his treatise on the Tao must not be overlooked. We do not experience either *Thou* or Tao:

> Tao . . . like the rising and falling of notes in music, "it belongs to the playing." We cannot discern it in any particular being. If we look for it in heaven or on earth, in space and in time, it is not there; yet heaven and earth, space and time are founded in it alone. And if we look for it in the "mystery of the nature of God," neither is it there, yet God is founded in it alone. Nevertheless, "it can be found through the seeking": in the unified life—there it is not perceived and known, but rather realized, lived, expressed in action.[23]

Neither *Thou* nor Tao is to be found by seeking in the *It*-world, yet in each case it is present in the unified life that wholly responds to it.

---

22. Buber's exposition in this section strongly echoes the Taoist discussion of *wu-wei*, which was introduced in ch. 6 above, page 129.

23. Buber, "Commentary," 84 (my translation).

3. *I-Thou* in the Three Spheres of Existence

In §9, Buber introduces three spheres of existence that he uses as a framework for his analysis throughout the book: first, life with nature, which is below the threshold of language; second, the interhuman world, which is the home of language, where we can give and receive the *Thou* among fellow humans; and third, the sphere of creativity, the reality of "forms of the spirit," above ordinary language.[24] In each of these spheres, whether nature, the interhuman world, or the sphere of creativity, one can treat the Other either as an *It* or as a *Thou*. Buber explains how this works in each sphere in the sections that follow (§§10–12, 19).

First, Buber discusses nature as a sphere of relation. He uses the example of a tree: one can contemplate a tree as an object; but one can also step into relation with it as *Thou*.[25] Buber uses further examples in part three—a cat (§52a–c) or a fragment of mica[26]—to show how entities in the natural world can become *Thou*. "When will and grace come together I can ... be drawn into a relation to the tree as I contemplate it; then the tree is no longer an *It*. The power of exclusiveness has seized me" (§10h). The intention of the person is joined by grace and the person becomes a participant in the *I-Thou* relation, being drawn into it and seized by it. Later in part one, he sums up the possibilities of relating in this realm of nature as instances of gratuitous mutuality facilitated by our open receptivity to creatures:

> Let the meaning of the impact ... of the creature and our contemplation of it remain a mystery. Believe in the artless magic of life, in service to the All, and the meaning of that awaiting, that attentive gaze, that "craning of the neck" of the creatures will come to you. Any word would falsify; but look, beings live all around you and toward whichever of them you approach you come upon Being (§19c).

Second, Buber discusses *I-it* and *I-Thou* in the interpersonal sphere. When one person addresses another as *Thou*, one is enacting the relation expressed in Kant's second categorical imperative: "Act in such a way that you treat humanity, whether in your own person or in the person of any

---

24. Buber returns to this formulation almost verbatim and develops it further near the conclusion of the book in §55.
25. Buber, *I and Thou*, §10, and referred back to in §19c, §24e, and §39a; see also "Postscript," 124–26; Buber discusses similar tree examples in *Daniel*, 54, and "Man and His Image-Work," 157–58.
26. Buber, *I and Thou*, §52g; see also Buber, *Daniel*, 140.

Other, never merely as a means to an end, but always . . . as an end."[27] Accordingly, to address another person as *Thou* is to treat the Other no longer merely as a point in the time-space continuum: the Other becomes at once exclusive, singular, whole, and boundless. As *Thou* the Other is exclusive in that the unmediated encounter lies beyond any realm of comparison: the Other is taken for what he is in himself as a unique creation. As *Thou* the Other is also singular or unique; his concrete particulars are not transcended for some "spiritual essence"; rather, they are taken together so the Other is openly received in his concrete-spiritual totality. Furthermore, the Other is whole: just as one must do violence to tear apart the unity of a melody into its individual notes, or a poem into its individual words, or a statue into its component planes—so the *Thou* is a unity until we abstract from the Other his individual features. Finally, the Other is boundless: he fills the orb of sky; for in the moment of encounter everything lives in the light of his countenance (§11b).

In the interhuman world, to address the Other as *Thou* is to open oneself to the unmediated presence of the Other. In §19, Buber teaches several things about this interhuman sphere of *I-Thou* relating. This turning to the Other is an act of compassionate love that is not about feelings. Rather, it exists as "the between." It involves a distinctive way of seeing the Other as *Thou*. Because this love is the "taking responsibility by an *I* for a *Thou*," it is salutary. Therefore, it includes an exclusiveness of focus in relating to each person who arises before one. We now consider each of these elements in turn.

Buber begins by stating what this *I-Thou* love is not: it is not a feeling. He uses the example of Jesus in the Gospels, whose feeling for the possessed man (Luke 8:26–51) is of a different kind than his feeling for the beloved disciple (John 13:22), yet in both cases his love as compassion are one and the same. To paraphrase Buber, feelings can accompany love but they do not constitute it. One "has" feelings, whereas love simply takes place. Feelings may dwell in a person but the person dwells within love.

Therefore this *I-Thou* love is not internal or subjective, part of the inner psyche of the individual. Rather, it is constituted as "the between," a category that for Buber is distinctive to the ontology of human existence. Buber states this emphatically: "This is no metaphor, but the actual truth: love does not adhere to the *I* as if the *Thou* were merely its 'contents,' its possessed object; but love is *between I* and *Thou*. Whoever does not know this, know this with his very being, does not know love" (§19b).[28] In the years after writing *I and Thou*, Buber followed up on this insight, making "the between" the key

---

27. Kant, *Groundwork*, 36.
28. Buber's emphasis.

element of his philosophy of dialogue. In his inaugural lectures at the Hebrew University in 1938, he made it the centerpiece of his ontology of the human: he presented "the between" as "what is peculiarly characteristic of the human world" to the point that "man is made man by it." There he defined "the between" as "one being turning to another as another, as this particular being, in order to communicate with it in a sphere which is common to them but which reaches out beyond the special sphere of each."[29]

Buber shows that the between is the dynamic central element in a number of interactions: "In a real conversation . . . a real lesson . . . a real embrace . . . a real duel . . . what is essential . . . takes place between the participants in the most precise sense . . . in a dimension which is accessible only to them both."[30] He characterizes the between as a "remainder" in any authentically spontaneous encounter: "If I and another come up against one another, 'happen' to one another . . . there is a remainder somewhere where the souls end and the world has not yet begun, and this remainder is what is essential."[31] The between is the hidden, dynamic element of dialogue:

> In the most powerful moments of dialogue, where in truth "deep calls unto deep," it becomes unmistakably clear that it is not the wand of the individual or the social but of a third which draws the circle around round the happening. On the far side of the subjective, on this side of the objective, on the narrow ridge, where *I* and *Thou* meet, there is the realm of "between."[32]

Buber sketches how when we take the position which enables us to see others as *Thou*, our perception of them is transformed. As people of all kinds—good and evil, wise and foolish, beautiful and ugly—pass before the eye, they are "set free to emerge as unique beings in their over-againstness." Regarded through the lens of love, "one after the other they become real . . . as *Thou*" (§19b).

At the end of *I and Thou*, Buber goes so far as to make *the between* the linchpin of human destiny: "The theophany comes ever *nearer*, nearer to the sphere *between beings*, comes nearer to the realm that is hidden in our midst, in the between [*im Dazwischen*]" (§61w).[33]

In *Two Types of Faith*, a later work, Buber interprets the command to love one's neighbor in the Torah (Lev 19:18) with language that parallels

---

29. Buber, "What is Man?," 203.
30. Buber, "What is Man?," 203–4.
31. Buber, "What is Man?," 204.
32. Buber, "What is Man?," 204.
33. Buber's emphasis.

that of his sketch of human diversity in §19b. To Buber, the Hebrew word translated "neighbor," *re'ah*, literally "the one near by, the near," means

> one to whom I stand in an immediate and reciprocal relationship, and this through any kind of situation in life, through community of place, through common nationality, through community of work, through community of effort, especially also through friendship. . . . "Love thy *re'ah*" means: be lovingly disposed towards men with whom you have to do at any time in the course of your life.[34]

Because this love is "the taking responsibility by an *I* for a *Thou*," it is salutary. Thus, the person who takes the Other as *Thou*, living in the interhuman world, takes responsibility for the Other—"and so can be effective, helping, healing, educating, raising up, rescuing" the Other (§19b). Thus, each and every person who arises along our path in the course of a lifetime become our neighbor, our opportunity for service.

The difference between this love in the *I-Thou* relation and the compassion characteristic of the Taoist sage is that the latter "is based upon the sage's oneness with all things."[35] Accordingly, the sage's love "is wholly free and unlimited, does not depend on the demeanor of the Other, and knows no alternatives; this is unconditioned love."[36] A person who practices such love "stands in community with all."[37] By contrast, the love of the one who addresses the Other as *Thou* is based not on some sort of totalization of unity but on the otherness of the Other in tension with the shared common ground of being. In "Distance and Relation" Buber elaborates on the complex nature of the tension between the duality and the oneness in relation: on the one hand, a person "can accomplish the act of relation in the acknowledgement of the fundamental actuality of the distance"; on the other hand, "in moments and forms of grace, unity can arise from the extreme tension of the contradiction as the overcoming of it."[38] Like the walking stick that once connected Buber to an oak tree in the twilight at the end of a hike, "the between" [*das Inzwischen*] at once both divides and unites the *I* and the *Thou*.[39] In §11, Buber makes it clear there is a sacredness in engaging another as *Thou*: it is a universally holy act, like prayer and sacrifice, that nurtures the living. Like prayer or sacrifice, the *Thou* is not in time and space but rather

---

34. Buber, *Two Types of Faith*, 69–70.
35. Buber, "Commentary," 91–92.
36. Buber, "Commentary," 92.
37. Buber, "Commentary," 95.
38. Buber, "Distance and Relation," 64.
39. Buber, "Author's Preface," 47.

space and time are within the *Thou*. As long as the sky of the *Thou* spans over me, the winds of causality are held at bay and the whirlpool of fate is stayed. One's stance in the sacredness of such relating, with its depth and truth, is the cradle of real human life. That is, to address another as *Thou* is to enter a reality that is the great alternative to the *It*-world.

The third realm of *Thou* is the sphere of creativity, whether in the arts, in the life of the mind, or in the shaping of one's life (§§12, 19a). As in his other discussions of creativity, Buber here uses the creation of visual art as the paradigm for his analysis and merely hints at other modes of creation.[40] He was very attuned to the visual and verbal arts and pursued the study of them when he was a university student. To Buber the arts have their origin in a *Gestalt*, a form that confronts the individual with the urge to become a work, a product of one's creativity. This *Gestalt* is no mere product of the soul but rather something that arises to confront the soul with its call for the soul's actualizing-creating power. It calls forth the whole being: if the person follows through and addresses the emerging *Gestalt* with his whole being, then the actualizing power emerges and the work arises.

As with any *I-Thou* encounter, the creative act involves both a sacrifice and a risk (§12b). Infinite possibility is surrendered on the altar of creation for a specific, concrete expression of a *Gestalt*: everything else that up to the moment played in the imagination must be relinquished—nothing of it may penetrate into the work. This narrowing of focus is the Other's demand for exclusivity. The risk lies in the fact that the Other, the *Gestalt*, can only be addressed with one's whole being: whoever gives himself to it dare not hold back any of himself. Unlike nature or fellow humans, the act of creating does not allow that I retreat into the comfort of the *It*-world: it commands. If I do not serve the compulsion to create properly, either it breaks down or it breaks me. I can neither experience nor describe the *Gestalt* that confronts me; I can only actualize it (§12c). And yet I see it in its radiance as that which confronts me—I see it more clearly than all the clarity of the world of experience, not as an inner image, but as a presence. Considered objectively, the *Gestalt* is not "there"—yet what could be more present than it? I stand in an actual relation to it: it affects me as I affect it.

Thus, for Buber, to make is to create, to invent is to find, to give shape is to discover. To the extent that I actualize the creative *Gestalt*, I disclose it. In the act of creating I bring the *Gestalt* across—into the *It*-world. The work then becomes a thing among things but it *can* confront its receptive beholder as the embodiment of the *Gestalt* (§12). Rivka Horwitz links this

---

40. See Buber, "Distance and Relation," 59–71, and Buber, "Man and His Image-Work," 149–65.

work with the *Gestalt* that confronts one in the theophany recounted in Job 4:12–21, which Buber translates in part as:

> One stands, I do not perceive his appearance,
>
> as a *Gestalt* confronting my eyes;
>
> what I hear is silence and voice.[41]

The *Gestalt* is visible, yet not visible; audible, yet not audible—until I bring it forth into the light of day: "The unmediated relation includes one's influence on the Other. The artist's act of creation is the occurrence in which the *Gestalt* becomes the work of art. The Other fulfills itself through the encounter: through the encounter it enters the world of things where it then endlessly has its impact, always as an *It* but also endlessly becoming *Thou*, inspiring and blessing. It "embodies itself": its body emerges from the flow of the spaceless and timeless presence onto the shore of existence" (§19a).

Buber's discussion of the three spheres of existence here enables us to see how the *I-Thou* encounter is manifested across the whole spectrum of existence. The interhuman world is the primary sphere, but the *I-Thou* encounter is equally real, though manifested differently in the natural world and in the realm of creativity.

4. A Double Genealogy of *I-Thou* and *I-It*

Once Buber has presented *I-Thou* and *I-It* and laid out their differences and their qualities, he concludes his exposition of the nature of *I-Thou* and *I-It* in part one with a two-part genealogy that reconstructs their origins, first at the broad anthropological level (§§23–27) and then at the level of individual development (§§27–30). Such a philosophical genealogy is a kind of argument about a present human condition through an imaginatively reconstructed history. The accuracy of the reconstructed story is not the point of the genealogy. Rather, the focus is on the conclusions the genealogist intends to draw from it. Buber's fundamental conclusions here are two: first, that the *I-Thou* is an inherent, primal human reality, and second, the opposition of *I-Thou* and *I-It* is a universal phenomenon across history.

Buber's double genealogy here was likely inspired by Friedrich Nietzsche's *Genealogy of Morals*. Nietzsche wrote of his method that his

---

41. Job 4:16 (my translation); see the Buber-Rosenzweig translation, cited in Horwitz, *Buber's Way*, 65n22. See the discussion of this verse in connection with Buber's concept of revelation in chapter 9, page 259.

antiquarian work was the exploration of his "genealogical hypothesis."[42] Nietzsche, like Buber, was concerned about modern bourgeois values, which he characterized in the figure of "the ultramodern milksop who no longer bites."[43] Nietzsche's purpose was a rhetorical one: he described his intended reader in terms of this scenario:

> Whoever sticks with it and learns how to ask questions will have the same experience that I had: a vast new panorama will open up before him; strange and vertiginous possibilities will invade him; every variety of suspicion, distrust, fear will come to the surface; his belief in ethics of any kind will begin to be shaken. Finally, he will be forced to listen to a new claim ... a critique of all moral values.[44]

Similarly, Buber's purpose in constructing his genealogies here is to challenge bourgeois assumptions regarding the priority of the *I-It* world of alienation and to lead people to question it deeply enough that they will think more seriously about the nature of the *I-Thou* relation as a step toward reclaiming it.

Like Nietzsche, Buber reconstructs the origins and development of a current-day actuality as part of his argument about its essential nature. For both Buber and Nietzsche the reconstructions make visible elements of their respective phenomena that might otherwise be ignored. These are elements that challenge modern assumptions. Each thinker would expose them as being significantly more pernicious than is commonly assumed. In each case, the analysis leads to the writer's exalting a value that otherwise would be lost to the modern mentality. Nevertheless, Buber's post-romantic assumptions and his cosmic-mythological claims have a more idealistic basis than do Nietzsche's *a priori* foundations.

Through interpretive paraphrase and commentary we will now trace the developments in each of Buber's two genealogies. Buber's sketch of anthropological origins, like that of Rousseau in his *Discourse on the Origins of Inequality*, is predicated on vast speculations, as his introductory "one may conjecture" [*man darf vermuten*] suggests.[45] Buber further suggests his approach is symbolic, not empirical or fact-based, when he writes that our knowledge of primal peoples opens only brief glimpses into the development of the primary words *I-Thou* and *I-It*. Furthermore, he acknowledges

---

42. Nietzsche, *Birth of Tragedy*, 152.
43. Nietzsche, *Birth of Tragedy*, 156.
44. Nietzsche, *Birth of Tragedy*, 154–55.
45. Rousseau, *Discourse on the Origins of Inequality*; Buber, *I and Thou*, §23d.

that primal peoples still alive in modern times are no more than analogues of the original primal humanity of the distant past (§27a).

Buber begins by imagining the world of primal peoples is built out of a narrow circle of presence-intensive actions. Their world is reflected in their languages, which he claims consist largely of sentence-words (§23b). Such people live in a holistic world in which each person is embedded, standing out in the texture of experience like little more than a bas relief. This existence is a primal stage of "genuine original unity, lived relation" (§23b). With these words Buber gives a hint that the primal human state of being was a living "two-and-one," for the "genuine original unity," the oneness, was at the same time "lived relating," the polarity of *I* and *Thou* (§23b).

Thus, to Buber, *I-Thou* is foundational in human development: "In the beginning is relation" (§23a).[46] Standing like an incipit, these first words of his genealogical account seem to echo the first words of Genesis and perhaps also those of the Gospel of John and of Goethe's Faust. With this claim, Buber grounds humanity in *I-Thou* as its primal reality. The relational process, the living sense of the Other and living with the Other, is the source of the first elementary, spirit-stirring impressions and bodily stimulations of "natural humanity."

To Buber, *I-Thou* antedates any *I*. In the beginning the *I* is enclosed within the primal relational event. By its nature there are two partners in this relational event, the human person and the Other, both present in their full actuality. Yet, inasmuch as in this event the world is a duality, the duality of *I* and *Thou*, the person senses in it a cosmic subjectivity [*eine kosmische Pathetik*] of the *I*, without becoming inwardly aware of the *I* as such (§24c). Buber identifies the elemental relational process (the primal *I-Thou*) with kinetic or bodily stimulation and links it to the mysterious power which "natural peoples" call *mana* (a dynamic element of Polynesian culture much discussed by early-twentieth-century anthropologists). To Buber it was traces of this power that remained when the stimulus-image later gave way to the object-image. He speculates that the sense of this power which the Polynesians named *mana* opened the way to Brahman in India and to *dynamis* and *charis* in Mediterranean spiritualities (§23e).

Buber uses the moon to illustrate the first stage of the evolutionary process. To begin with, its regular appearance merely affected the body with a kinetic stimulus image. From this repeated effect early people gradually differentiated a sense of the moon as the agent of this effect. In this differentiation the bodily impact of the stimulus-image was transformed into

---

46. Buber, *I and Thou*, §23a; Gen 1:1: "In the beginning God created the heavens and the earth"; John 1:1: "In the beginning was the word"; Goethe, *Faust*, lines 1224–37: "In the beginning was the deed."

an object-image. An *It* that could be experienced emerged out of a *Thou* that up to this point was merely undergone. Then over time the body began to recognize itself and to differentiate itself from its environs, to perceive its unique singularity. Yet at this stage of bodily differentiation, the body endured solely as coexistence and therefore it could not yet take on the character of implied "*I*-ness" (§24d).

At some point, given the differentiation of the body from its environs, the *I* emerged, first as the *I* of relation. "The I emerges with the force of an element in the splitting of primal experience, when the vital primal expressions *I-affecting-Thou* and *Thou-affecting-I* have been reified and hypostatized" (§23f). Once the *I* of relation emerged and stood out in its separateness, it mysteriously etherealized while taking on a distinct functionality: it fused with the body in its separation from its environs as the awakening of the sense of *I*-ness within it. "The *I-It* is now made possible as a result of this recognition, this differentiation and detachment of the *I*" (§24a). Only at this point did the conscious *I*-act, the first element of the primal *I-It*, of *I*-oriented experience, arise: the *I* that emerged asserted itself as the bearer of perceptions, and its environment as its object (§24e). From this point on, a statement such as "I see the tree" no longer declared a relation between the human-*I* and the tree-*Thou* but now stated the perception of the tree-object through the newly emergent human *I*-consciousness. Through this shift, the *I* erected the barrier that separates subject and object. With this, the primary *I-It*, the word of separation, had been spoken (§24e). This emergence of *I-It* is as far as Buber goes in constructing his account of the anthropological origins of *I-Thou* and *I-It*.

Taken as a whole, this genealogical construction reveals some of Buber's cardinal assumptions. First, he assumes the wholeness and unity of primal humanity in its life of primal relationality, the *I-Thou* reality, was the natural, original state of human existence. Second, he also assumes the cosmic dimension is the framework for human development. He sums up this genealogical account with his emphasis on this dimension when he writes that in the history of consciousness, "cosmic being manifests itself as human becoming" because "spirit contains nature," not the other way around (§25b). That is, to Buber, nature is a manifestation of spirit in contrast to the modern empiricist view that inverts this to see spirit as an epiphenomenon of the material causal nexus, mere imaginary constructions that humans indulge in in the face of concrete material reality. Third, the opposition of *I-Thou* and *I-It* emerged from the primal *I-Thou* in the development of human consciousness. This opposition has had many names across the ages and cultures, but in its nameless truth it is universally inherent across human history. It lies at the core of human existence.

Buber concludes the first part of his genealogy on a note of hope. The relational life of primal humanity becomes a promise to us: while the modern "ethereal concern over faceless numbers" leads only to nothingness, the alternative, the reality of life in its cosmic setting, opens a path to God (§26c). According to Buber's studies of Taoism, Hasidism, and primal Christianity, it is the masters at the founding of these traditions who point the way to such renewal, to a new stage of this life of wholeness in relation, as we have seen in chapter 6.

In the next sections (§§27–28) Buber recapitulates his genealogy by tracing the course of individual development, which he claims offers a more complete understanding of the nature of the emergence of *I-It* from *I-Thou*. Here he reaffirms his earlier statement from §25a that "in the beginning is the relation" (§27e), but he now provides more cosmic claims for it. The course of individual development as he constructs it here becomes his argument that "the spiritual reality of the primary expressions arises naturally— first the *I-Thou* out of the natural bond and then the *I-It* out of the natural process of separation" (§27b).

Buber writes that the course of development which he traces can only be understood when the analysis is grounded in its "cosmic and meta-cosmic origins" (§27g). Drawing on the theory of the Great Mother of Johann Bachofen current at the time, Buber states that individual existence begins in the womb of the "Great Mother" (§27d). Birth is a step in the individual's gradual detachment from the cosmic bond with the Great Mother, the movement "out of the undifferentiated, formless primal world," from which a person relinquishes the natural bond as he or she enters into the spiritual bond which is relation (§27d). This shift takes place as the person develops bodily into a mature human being (§27g).

To Buber, "The prenatal life of the child is a purely natural bond . . . so cosmic that it seems like the incomplete deciphering of a primal inscription" (§27c). He quotes a traditional Jewish maxim to characterize this primal cosmic bond: "In the mother's body one knows the universe; at birth it is forgotten" (§27c).[47] Yet the prenatal cosmic sense "remains in us as the secret image of desire. This . . . longing [*Sehnsucht*] is the spirit of the postpartum being as it pursues the cosmic bond of the true *Thou*" (§27c).

Following Buber's narrative account, at birth the cosmic bond of prenatal existence is carried forth into life as "the *a priori* of relation, the inborn *Thou*" (§27e). As birth is a major step in the process of letting go of the Great Mother, it is also the beginning of the person's responsibility to create the form of his world as his means of establishing himself in creation. The inborn *Thou*

---

47. Derived from the Talmud: Niddah 30b:18–23.

carries the cosmic relation forward as gift and promise, underlying the strivings imposed upon the infant by post-partum existence. The developing child must "draw out [relation] and make it into actuality for himself. By observing, listening, touching, forming he finds his world" (§27d). The creation reveals its form as the developing person encounters each of its immediate elements as *Thou*. In this process the creation arises to meet the one who is actively reaching out to it. In the reciprocal power of relating, the flash and counterflash of encounter, the strenuous action of the developing person entices, is a reaching out, an engaging with its surroundings until they become the familiar elements of its world (§27d–e).

To Buber "the primal value of striving toward relation" manifests itself from birth. He presents examples of the infant's grasping, observing, discovering the *Gestalt* of the teddy bear or the carpet, even responding to the simmering kettle in the kitchen, as "interacting with a living, imparting Other." This continual working with the environment is a striving that manifests "the instinct to make everything into a *Thou* . . . to relate to everything" (§27e). This urge toward relation comes to fruition in the encounter, the infant's wordless saying *Thou* to each Other as it arises.

The development of the child's soul is bound up with its longing for the *Thou* and the fulfillments and disappointments of this longing. In its first instinct to make contact, the child moves toward reciprocity and tenderness. Then the instinct to create, also determined by the inborn *Thou*, emerges in the child's personifying and conversing with elements of its world. This work largely takes the form of play (§27g).

As with the genealogical sketch of humanity as a whole, here also the maturing body "as bearer of [the soul's] perceptions and executor of its impulses" begins to stand out from its environs, at first "simply in the next-to-each-other of self-orienting, not in the absolute severance of the *I* from its object" (§28b; see §24d).

"The person becomes *I* through the *Thou*" (§28a). This passage explains Buber's original claim, "I become *I* as I address the Other as *Thou*" (§14c). As the Other comes and then disappears and relational events solidify and then disperse, the *Thou* of relation fades away again and again while at the same time the developing person becomes increasingly conscious of the unvarying partner in these encounters, the *I*. For some time this *I* awareness is there only in the texture of the relational event, yet it becomes "increasingly perceptible as that which reaches out to the *Thou* and yet is not it. It breaks out ever more strongly, until all at once the bond is burst and the *I* detaches itself and becomes autonomous. For a moment it confronts itself as if it were confronting a *Thou*. Then all at once it takes possession of itself and from this point forward it stands in relation to this new self-awareness (§28a).

The maturing body eventually stands out as *I* in the absolute severance of the *I* from its objects (§28b).

Once *I*-awareness has reached this new level, the *I-It* begins to come together. At this point the *Thou* of relation that has continually faded away becomes an *It* to the *I*, an object of detached perception and experience. The *Thou* has become an *It*, standing in reserve as it were, until it arises again as a *Thou* in a new relational event.

The detached *I* that emerges with *I*-awareness is different from the *I* of *I-Thou*. It has shriveled down from its holistic fullness in *I-Thou* to the scope of a functional pinpoint, an experiencing and using subject, addressing everything as an "it-for-itself." It empowers itself in its autonomy and joins itself to things to form the second primal expression, the *I-It*. "The individual who has become '*I*-ness,' the one who says *I-It*, places himself before things but does not stand over against them in the flow of mutual action" (§28b). The individual now objectifies and isolates and arranges things in his vision, devoid of any sense of the cosmic dimension, the dimension possible only through relation.

At last the individual has fully arrived in the *It*-world where he can construct the whole realm of things to be experienced and exploited. Now for the first time he constructs things out of their qualities, "qualities belonging to the relational events of the remembered *Thou* which he retains in his memory: he now *has* experiences. Using the powers of imagination, the person "completes the powerful germ found in the *Thou*, combining all qualities to disclose 'substance.'" With this process, the individual "places things in a spatial, temporal, thematic framework" so "each thing receives its place, its function, its measure, its contingent nature" in the *It*-world (§28b).

With the emergence of the *I*'s work of constructing the *It*-world, Buber's genealogy stands complete, except for his goal, the seed of which he has planted near the outset of the story. As the developing individual detaches over time from the womb of the Great Mother, first through physical birth and then through the birth of the *I* of *I-It*, he acquires the potential to gradually replace that "natural bond that he is losing with a spiritual bond which is relation" (§27d). In the course of his development, the individual's pursuit of "the cosmic bond of the true *Thou*" is based on the continuing reality of his "inborn *Thou*, the *a priori* of relation" (§27e). The individual moves away from his bond with "the Other that originally is grasped, taken up in exclusivity, and can be addressed with the primary *Thou*" in the course of his development. Yet because of his inborn *Thou*, he can reclaim it through a conscious process as a mature human being. This reclaiming is a replacing of the original natural bond with a conscious spiritual bond. This replacing is the state that, "in spite of being beset by all kinds of ills, is the full flowering of nature" (§27c).

In the last several paragraphs we have traced Buber's genealogy of the development of the individual. We now turn to consider the import of this genealogy. First of all, the polemical nature of Buber's analysis stands out. At different points in the course of his genealogical narrative he pushes back against modernizing materialistic and rationalistic interpretations of individual development. For example, in his exposition of the newborn's longing for relation, Buber opposes those materialists like Freud who take this longing as a wish to return to the womb. As he puts it, such materialists take the human spirit to be "a parasite of nature," which they imagine thus because they "confuse the spirit with their own intellect" (§27c). With the reference to their "confusion," Buber's tone regarding these materialists takes on a mocking edge. Again, when Buber writes of the infant's hands reaching out, he states: "One may call this animalistic but this does not advance any understanding of it" (§27e). Later, he attacks scientific reductionism when he writes that the understanding of the child's play, which to him can only be advanced in its cosmic-metacosmic context of origins, "is compromised by every attempt to reduce it to spheres narrower than these" (§27g). What is at stake here for Buber is his fundamental assumption that *I-Thou* is the primal and therefore innate human reality. Such a view is nonsense to the materialist.

Buber's second version of the genealogy of *I-It* at the level of individual development builds on the cardinal assumptions he presented in his first, anthropological version. Now the Great Mother is used as a figure for the person's cosmic bond in its prenatal and perinatal existence: Buber features the inborn *Thou* as the neonate's inherent longing for relation. The *I*'s emergence, detachment from its matrix, and rise to domination correspond to the development of the *It*-world, the realm of separation. This is the reality that is intensified to the point of alienation in the modern world. As with the anthropological version of his genealogy, Buber again offers hope, this time in the form of a spiritual trajectory. The *I* of *I-It* is merely the middle of the story, for when the person lets go of the original cosmic bond, the inborn *Thou*, the *Sehnsucht*, the longing for relation figured as the inborn *Thou* remained central. In adult life it continues, pushing toward the person's reclaiming the original cosmic bond by developing a conscious spiritual bond. Thus, the conclusion to Buber's double genealogy prefigures the pattern of departure and return which becomes central in part two of *I and Thou*.

Buber completes the frame of his dual genealogy of the *It*-world with a pause, a recollection of the realm of *Thou*, the reality that gives coherence to his reconstructions. In a moving and poetic passage, he calls us back to the *Thou* moments. He invokes them as

> moments of silent depth in which we see the world order as Presence. In such moments a note is heard in its very flight, for which the ordered world is its indecipherable score. Such moments are immortal, yet the most fleeting of all. No substance can be creamed off from them, yet their power penetrates the Creation as well as human knowing. Streams of their power penetrate the ordered world and irradiate it again and again (§28d).

This invocation of the visionary *I-Thou* moments in the cosmic context resonates with the temporary elevated state described by Plotinus[48] and the musical metaphor echoes the sense of Tao, which "belongs to the playing."[49] Such visionary moments are as evanescent as a single note in a symphonic score. Yet they are at the same time immortal and the source of strength that gives us coherence in the *It*-world. Buber's evocation of these moments is a signpost pointing a way forward into the realm of the *Thou*.

5. Either/Or

Buber concludes part one by drawing together his exposition of the differences between the realm of *I-Thou* and the world of *I-It*. Then he presents each of these states as an implicit either/or and he invites his readers to choose between them.

Buber frames his dual genealogy with a claim that echoes throughout *I and Thou*: "This is the exalted melancholy of our fate—that each *Thou* in our world must become an *It*" (§22a).[50] Buber stresses this is not a one-way process, for "the *It* is a chrysalis while the *Thou* is a butterfly" (§22c). Buber's point is every *It* is a latent *Thou* and every *Thou* is a living *It*, every *Thou* is like a flaming coal that can fade to the ash of *It*, but can just as quickly be kindled back to fire by a gust of the spirit. According to Buber, these transformations are marked by the one great boundary that runs through all of human life, the hiatus between the *I-Thou* and the *I-It*, between the realm of Presence [*Gegenwart*] and the realm of objects [*Gegenstand*] (§16).

On the one hand, the *Thou* is exclusively present in our primal direct relations until it fades to an object among objects and is assigned its measure and boundaries. In genuine contemplation, a natural being reveals itself to

---

48. Plotinus, *Enneads*, 4.8.1.
49. "Chuang Tzu," alluded to in Buber, "Commentary," 84.
50. This sentence is repeated three times: in §25a, §32b, and §52e.

me in the mystery of reciprocity only until it again becomes describable, analyzable, classifiable, a point at which manifold systems intersect. Similarly, in addressing a person as *Thou*, I take in the person in his uniqueness, present and touchable but devoid of qualities, until I let the person once again become a he or a she, an aggregate of qualities, a quantum without a shape, an object at hand, and a datum of experience. In this *It*-mode I can abstract from the person the color of her hair, the tone of her voice, the grace of her manner. But with all this abstraction, I am in the realm of the language of objects and I catch only the edges of actual life (§22).

On the other hand, the shift back from *It* to the unmediated relation to the *Thou* is a shift from individualized particularity to wholeness, from dream to manifestation. Every possible mediating element becomes an impediment. When the encounter takes place, every means has dissolved away (§15). In the face of the unmediated relation, mediation has become irrelevant. The actual, fulfilled present exists only to the extent that presence-encounter-relation exists. Only to the extent that the *Thou* becomes present does presence arise. Between the *I* and its *Thou* there is no conceptualizing, no instrumentality, no prior intention, no prior knowledge, no imagining of possibilities. Memory itself is transformed in the shift to *Thou*. Between the *I* and the *Thou* there is no agenda, no desire, no prior expectation or assumption: longing itself is transformed as it is fulfilled.

Presence seems fleeting and transient, yet it is ultimately what establishes itself and endures. By contrast, objects are not duration but they are mental constructs, stagnancy, place-holding, fractioning, reification, aloofness, relationlessness, and lack of presence. True beings are lived reality which are always in the present; objects exist only in the past (§17). The *I* of *I-It*, surrounded by a multiplicity of "contents," has only a past, no present. By the time we conceptualize something, it is already removed from the immediacy of the present. Therefore, to the extent that one lets himself take things as sufficient for life because he can experience and use them, one lives in the past. Such moments of living are without presence. Furthermore, one has nothing but objects, and objects consist of having been.

Buber concludes this part of his exposition with an admonitory warning about the conceptual realm (§18). At the outset, he makes the nature of the *I-Thou* clear: "I speak of nothing other than the actual human being, of you and me, of our life and our world—not of an I-in-itself [*ein Ich an sich*] and not of a Being-in-itself [*ein Sein an sich*]" (§18a). Then he argues there is no "third thing" in the realm of ideas that can circumvent the opposition between *I-Thou* and *I-It*.

Buber suggests that some people who make themselves at home with experiencing and using the world of things construct for themselves a realm of ideas to use as their means of escaping from their intimations of nothingness. They are idealists who busy themselves constructing an alternative to materialism. They weave an *Ersatz* alternative to a part of the *It*-world. They wish to escape the materialistic-naturalistic reality of the causal nexus by constructing an edifice of ideas, hoping thereby to create an alternative to the objectified *It*-world. In doing so, they use the same mental materials out of which they had made the furnishings of the *It*-world to begin with. Approaching these constructions, they put aside the ugly garments of everyday existence, drape themselves in pure linen, and comfort themselves with visions of primal being or of what should be, in which their lived life has no part. In "Dialogue," an essay that has been regarded as the companion piece to *I and Thou*, Buber specifies this. Among the *Ersatz* alternatives to the "ever anew" of *I-Thou* there arises the "once for all" congealed in the metaphysical speculations of the gnostics, the ethical hair-splitting of the halachists, and the creedal formulations of the dogmatists.[51]

To go about proclaiming such ideas as a reality might make people feel good. Yet the *It*-humanity they imagine, postulate, and propagate has nothing in common with the embodied humanity which addresses fellow humans as *Thou*. The most noble of these fictions is a fetish; the most exalted fictional sentiment is a burden. Such ideas are no more enthroned above our heads than resident in them; they wander among us and accost us. At this point Buber scorns those who leave the primary word unspoken: wretched are those who merely name concepts, who mouth the discourse of *I-Thou* without entering into its reality (§18).

As we approach the end of part one, Buber confronts us with a decision: addressing his reader as *Thou*, he lays down a challenge: "It is up to you [*es liegt an dir*] to what extent the immeasurable becomes reality for you" (§29c). First, he recaps the distinction between *I-It* and *I-Thou* that he laid out at the beginning. He then uses irony by voicing the mindset of the modern person. His last word brings us up short, as the following contrast indicates.

When a person takes up the *I-It* attitude, he *perceives* what exists in his surroundings, things, and events with their qualities arrayed in space and time in the ordered and detached world of perceptions. The density and duration of this realm make it a fairly reliable setting that sustains human life. "It is always there, next to your skin, even huddled in your soul. Yet it remains as your object, primally alien, both outside and within you" (§29b). Buber explains the character of this *It*-world at some length as the "ordered and detached world" (§29b).

---

51. Buber, "Dialogue," 12, 18.

The alternative is the *I-Thou* attitude with which one "encounters being and becoming as his Other . . . what is there opens itself to one in events and what happens affects one as Being" (§29c). The Other becomes a presence, and it bears cosmic import. "It is up to you how much of the immeasurable [in the encounter] becomes reality to you" (§29c). Each *I-Thou* encounter confirms one's solidarity with the world. The *Thou*

> comes to bring you forth . . . . It is not outside you, it stirs in your depths . . . yet beware of the urge to stow it away as your possession—for then you will make it vanish. It is your present; only while you have it do you have the present. . . . Between you and it there is mutual giving: you say *Thou* to it and give yourself to it, it says *Thou* to you and gives itself to you. You cannot make yourself understood with others concerning it, you are alone with it. But it teaches you to encounter others, and to stand your ground in such encounters. (§29c)

The realm of *Thou* lacks the density and duration of the *It*-world; it is too intimate to be discussed. Thus, our tendency as denizens of the *It*-world is always to grasp it in spite of its fleetingness, to "make it into an object for oneself—at which point it vanishes once again." Yet its reality, its confirming our solidarity with the world of creation, its affecting us as Being, this ontological affirmation leads us "to the *Thou* in which the lines of relations though parallel converge"; these affirmations of Being point beyond to the Source of being, giving us a glimpse of eternity (§29c).

Finally, Buber uses a sketch of *I-Thou* from an ironic *It*-oriented perspective to address the tension created by the crisis of alienation, itself provoked by the mushrooming of the *It*-world, the distinctive by-product of modernity. This ironic *It*-world perspective leads to Buber's critique of modernity in part two of *I and Thou*.

Here at the climax of part one, in his most sustained ironic passage in the book, Buber vividly portrays the strangeness of the realm of *Thou* as it appears to denizens of the *It*-world. Here, he takes on the voice of those at home in the *It*-world, those who see it as self-contained and complete: "The privileges of the *It*-world . . . move one to regard the *It*-world as the world he has to live in, and in which it is comfortable to live, the world which presents him with all kinds of stimulations and excitements, activities and knowledge" (§30e). From this perspective, the realm of *Thou* looks outright dangerous, as Buber continues: "In this solid and congenial narrative [of the *It*-world], the *Thou*-moments seem to be odd lyric-dramatic episodes, with their own seductive magic, but dangerous in pulling us to extremes, dissolving the well-tried coherence of things, leaving more doubts than answers, shaking our certainty—that is, uncanny, dispensable moments" (§30e).

Buber's point is, to the *It*-minded, the realm of *Thou* can be seen as uncomfortable, unnecessary, and threatening. This recoil of the *It*-minded, who place themselves squarely in the concrete, everyday world of *It*, recalls a parallel in Plotinus where the philosopher points out how the realm of the One looks to those who are at home in the finite, material world of the many: "The mind reaching toward the formless finds itself incompetent to grasp where nothing bounds it or to take impression where the impinging reality is diffuse; in sheer dread of holding to nothingness, it slips away. The state is painful; often it seeks relief by retreating from all this vagueness to the region of sense, there to rest as on solid ground . . . ."[52] In either case, what may lie beyond the commonsense material world is taken as dangerous by many, especially, as Buber emphasizes, in the modern era where the *It*-world is preeminent.

Buber ends part one with a final, climactic point, appealing to the reader as *Thou*: "And in all of the seriousness of truth, *Thou*: without *It* a human being cannot live. But whoever lives by *It* alone is not human" (§30g). Kaufmann, who himself translates Buber's German *du* with "listen," marks this vocative use of *Thou* as an idiomatic German expression of intimacy sometimes brought in to intensify the pointedness of one's address to a lover or a close friend.[53] Here at the conclusion of part one Buber urgently and intimately exhorts his readers to take very seriously the distinction and its implications—and to choose the *Thou*.

---

52. Plotinus, *Enneads*, 6.9.3.
53. Kaufmann, *I and Thou*, 85n5.

Chapter 8

Exposition of *I and Thou*—Part Two

BUBER USES A DISTINCTIVE form of exposition in part two. The argument does not advance in a linear fashion. Rather, the treatment of the material is worked out as a form of counterpoint. Like the movement back and forth between two voices in a Bach fugue, the exposition swings between the world of *I-It* and the world of *I-Thou*. The whole is thus keyed to the fundamental claim made near the beginning and repeated a number of times throughout the book: "This is the exalted melancholy of our condition, that every *Thou* in our world must become an *It*."[1] Like a Bach fugue, the play between the two states of being is contrapuntal and punctuated by the transitional movement of turning.

As an example of this contrapuntal play, the back-and-forth between discussion of the *I-Thou*-oriented free person and the *I-It*-oriented, self-willed person runs across four sections at the heart of part two (§§36–39). Along the way Buber modulates from the individual level to the social level, making broad cultural observations as he contrasts "times of healthy life" with "times of sickness" (§36f–g). He also contrasts the foundational moment of any given culture in the *I-Thou* moment and its decline as it wanders away into the state of *I-It* (§36h–j). Then he returns to the individual level. He portrays the free person, shifts to the contrasting characteristics of the self-willed person, returns to the free person, and builds to a climax, presenting the self-willed person and despair as an opening to the present possibility of turning (§37d–e).

In my interpretation of Buber's message in part two, I will construct an historical-thematic reading of the text. Buber's vision of history provides the framework within which he leads the reader down to the present

---

1. Buber, *I and Thou*, §22a; "exhalted melancholy" here might recall Pascal's "*grandeur et misère de l'homme*"; Buber repeats this assertion in one form or another throughout *I and Thou*: §25a, §32b, §36d, §48a, §52d, and §61b.

moment and the possibility of transformation that this moment offers. He places the concrete world within a pattern of cosmic phases; to him our current phase, that of modernity, lies at the bottom of a cosmic cycle. There are three strands to Buber's exposition in part two: first, he presents the historical descent of culture into the *It*-world; second, he presents the extreme cosmic and personal alienation of modernity; and third, he presents the modern period as an alembic, a crucible of transformation, and he shows how we can find a path through and beyond the extremity of this nadir in the cycle. Thus, he provides a path one can take to emerge from the modern crisis of alienation into a life of relation, a life with *Thou*. Accordingly, in this exposition we will keep Buber's rhetorical purpose in part two in mind: to graphically show the complex intermingling of *I-Thou* and *I-It* in the course of human life, revealing the pull and the impact of the *It*-world as it exists alongside the countervailing call of a *Thou* to an *I*, realized in a life of authenticity in dialogue.

With these historical moments, the metanarrative of *I and Thou* presents the archetypal paradigm of human existence as a journey of departure and return. If we mark the major moments of this narrative pattern, we can trace how they unfold in *I and Thou*. As laid out in part one, the story begins with the primal birthright of primitive humanity or the newborn child, "the inborn *Thou*" [*das eingeborene Du*] (§§27–28). Then in part two, Buber sketches human history as a kind of wandering, a progressive movement away from the inborn *Thou* and a descent ever more deeply into the *It*-world. When we reach modern times, the individual is now a wayfarer deeply mired in the world of *It*, but he still has the potential for return through transformation: he can turn himself around and learn to relate to the eternal *Thou*. Buber makes the historical moment of modernity a crisis of opportunity, then he outlines the steps of such a return. Finally, he describes the life of the one who has reclaimed the *Thou* and lives in relation. Thus, Buber's core distinction between *I-Thou* and *I-It* serves as the broad framework for this entire journey.

1. History as Cosmic Gyre

Part two continues Buber's sketch of the evolution of the *It*-world begun in part one and lays out the consequences of its expansion over the course of history. Ever since our condition, "that every *Thou* in our world must become an *It*" (§22a), first arose in the primal history of the race (§25a–b), history has been marked by the steady growth of the *It*-world (§31a).

Primitive cultures begin with "a small world of objects" (§31b). This rudimentary *It*-world, as it is absorbed or developed over time, leads to the flourishing of a culture. As a result, "the *It*-world of each culture becomes more extensive than that of its predecessor in a process that can be clearly discerned in history" (§31b). This expansion of the *It*-world takes place in the realms of material knowledge, social differentiation, and technical achievement. The individual's basic connection with the *It*-world includes both "*experiencing*, which continually reconstitutes the world, and *using*, which leads to its manifold purpose, the sustaining, easing, and equipping of human life" (§31c, emphasis added).

Buber points out a fundamental inverse relationship in this process: as the realm of *It* expands in the course of history, the realm of *Thou* correspondingly diminishes. As the world of *It* takes over each culture, often through the historical influence of prior cultures, the world of objects becomes ever more extensive. The powers to experience and to use things—the *It*-world of functionality—continually develop from generation to generation, leading to the extremity of the modern era, "the sickness of our age which is like that of no other" (§36i).

The expansion of the *It*-world to dominance becomes the great obstacle to living in relation: "the development of the abilities to experience and to use comes about primarily through a decrease in the power to relate" (§31d). Thus, the primary word of separation, *I-It*, becomes an *Ersatz* "shelter" for humans both in the "outer" realm of social institutions and in the "inner" realm of subjective feelings (§33c–i). The split between these two realms is itself a symptom of the dominance of *I-It*.

So far, Buber's vision of history suggests a course of relentless decline. Yet this is not the case, for the degeneration into the *It*-world through history finds its counterpart in a process of renewal, which completes the pattern of history as a spiral or cosmic gyre. The elements of this pattern of history stand out clearly if we integrate §36h with §61l–w from the culmination of *I and Thou*. In §61, Buber posits "two primary metacosmic movements of the world" in the history of the divine-human relation: cosmic movement away from the primal source ("expansion into its own being" [*Ausbreitung in das Eigensein*]) and cosmic movement toward the primal source [*Urgrund*] ("turning to connection" [*Umkehr zur Verbundenheit*]) (§61l). Movement away from the primal source is movement into autonomy, into the *It*-world. The contrasting movement toward the primal source is summed up in the act of "turning" (postbiblical Hebrew, *teshuvah*), turning to relating to the *Thou*, which we will examine in detail shortly.

Buber uses the lifecycle of the butterfly as a metaphor for the cyclical pattern these opposing movements take through time: "In turning, the Word is born on earth; in expansion, the Word becomes a chrysalis by taking the form of religion; in renewed turning it gives birth to itself again with new wings" (§61l). Here again, turning is the dynamic element. To paraphrase this pregnant sentence, the birth or advent of the word on earth is the moment of divine disclosure and presence in human life. When this moment of divine disclosure becomes embodied in the forms of religious thought, practice, and institutions, it enters a kind of dormancy and becomes enclosed as if in a cocoon. Renewed turning releases the dormant essence from its trappings, allowing its emergence into renewed life full of power and beauty.

In part two and part three of *I and Thou*, Buber describes three kinds of world-historical moments that constitute this gyre pattern, and he implies a fourth. Each of these four moments, which we may identify serially as periods of breakthrough, fidelity, straying, and crisis, has a distinctive character in the overall cosmic pattern.[2]

First are the times of breakthrough, of an "originating relational event" when "the substantiating [*wesende*] Word manifests itself" and "the bonding between the *I* and the world renews itself" (§36h; §61v). As "an originating event of encounter" in which there is "an immediate response to the *Thou* at its source," it is "an act of being [*Wesensakt*] of the spirit" (§36h). Such moments become the foundations of the great world cultures. "The mighty revelations which the religions invoke . . . stand at the beginnings of great communities and at the turning-points of the ages" (§61n). In each of these turning points, the revelation comes through a master, a spiritual founder who initiates a new cycle: revelation "comes to him and seizes his whole elemental being in all its suchness and coalesces with it" (§61n).[3]

Second are times of fidelity, when "the effective [*wirkende*] Word holds sway and the concord between *I* and the world is maintained" (§61v). During these times, every great culture that has been founded on such a moment of breakthrough develops from it:

> An originating relational event . . . strengthened by the similarly directed power of succeeding generations, creates in the spirit a distinctive conception of the cosmos: only through it does the cosmos of humankind become possible again and again—only through this act can humankind, with confidence of soul and a distinctive vision of the cosmos again and again build dwelling places for God and humans and fill oscillating

---

2. Douglas Oakman points out that this fourfold historical pattern goes back to the Deuteronomic vision of history.

3. Avnon shows how, for Buber, Moses best fits the paradigm of the "originator," *Martin Buber*, 167–70. Buber delineates his concepts of revelation, the master, and the teaching in clear terms in §36h, discussed along with §32h in chapter 6 above, pages 135–36.

time with new hymns and songs and bring human community into form. (§36h)[4]

In the next sentence Buber states the conditionality upon which this phase depends: "But [the human being] is free and consequently creative only so long as he possesses, in *acting* and *receiving* in his own life, that act of the being—so long as he himself continues to enter into relation" (§36h, emphasis added).

Third are times of straying, those times when "the Word becomes taken as common currency [*geltend*]," that is, reduced to empty phrases. During such times, "loss of reality [*Entwirklichung*], alienation between *I* and the world, and the growth of fate come to full term" (§61v). Buber elaborates what he means by "the growth of fate":

> *When* a culture ceases to be centered in the living and continually renewed relational process, then it hardens into the *It*-world, into which the ardent deeds of solitary spirits break through from time to time like eruptions. From then on the flow of causality, which before had been unable to disturb the spiritual framework of the cosmos, rises up to become an oppressive, stifling fate. Wise and masterful destiny, which, as long as it resonated with the fullness of meaning of the cosmos, held sway over all causality, has fallen into a sense-contradicting demonism subject to the rule of causality. (§36h)

This passage describes the cultural shift from a cosmos of living dialogue to a mechanical *It*-world in which meaning and destiny have been reduced to the senseless play of the causal nexus. Buber places modernity in this phase of straying, even as some elements of the present era are approaching the phase that follows it. Much of part two of *I and Thou* focuses on Buber's critical analysis of modernity—its growing alienation, the loss of reality, the oppressive power of the causal nexus, and the recasting of destiny as fate. We will closely examine the elements of this analysis in the pages ahead.

Such departures from the relational phase bring about the fourth, or crisis, moment at the bottom of the cycle. This is the time of greatest uncertainty and it is characterized by dissolution. It is the time of the degradation of a culture, leading to "the great shudder, the holding of the breath in the dark, and the preparing silence" (§61v; see §43a–c). This is the great hiatus in the cycle—the time between the end of one revolution of the cycle and the emergence of the next, which will come about with a renewed in-breaking

---

4. Buber makes clear at different points in *I and Thou* that at these high moments of history the cosmos becomes spiritually apprehended as the home, the dwelling place of humanity: §36h, 55i, 61i, and 61v.

of relation. This is the time of the loss and renewal of humanity, a kind of cultural death and rebirth. In this phase history is shifting to another turn in the cosmic spiral: another breakthrough event will take place at the crucial culminating moment in this phase, "maturing at the time when the true element of the human spirit, suppressed and buried, comes to a hidden readiness so urgent and so tense that it awaits only a touch from the One who will touch it in order to break forth" (§61o).

At the point when destiny is thus degraded into fate caught in the net of causality, the "storming desire for salvation" from its grip can only be realized when

> it is stilled by one who teaches escape from the cycle of births [such as the Buddha] or by one who takes the souls that have fallen to alien powers and rescues them into the freedom of the children of God [such as Jesus]. Such an achievement arises out of a new event of encounter which is the process of assuming substantial being, that is, out of a new destiny-determining response of a person to his *Thou*. In the outworking of this central act of being, a culture can . . . be renewed. (§36h)

Just as such renewal came about across the cultures during the Axial Period, as Buber alludes to it here, so it can happen again now at the twilight of the modern era.

The spiral of history, therefore, moves round and round between times of healthy life grounded in the relational event and times of sickness through straying from it into alienation (§36h). This vision of history informs the whole of Buber's argument. To sum up Buber's vision, history is not a circle or a straight line but a cosmic gyre, a giant spiral which he identifies as "the way": "Every coil of this way leads us at once into both deeper corruption and more fundamental turning. . . . In each new eon fate becomes more overwhelming, turning more shattering" (§61w). Yet "history is a mysterious convergence": in each arc of this turning the Theophany comes nearer. *I and Thou* concludes with this Jewish vision of history's omega point, put in Buber's terms: the last turn of the gyre will be the messianic one, the disclosure of the kingdom as the realm that lies *between* beings and which now lies hidden in our midst (§61w). In the present era of crisis, this hidden "between" of relational reality stands available to individuals who undertake the arduous process of turning, and it is this possibility to which Buber calls his readers.

2. Modernity, the Era of Profound Alienation, as Nadir

To Buber, the modern era stands out as a period of straying from relational reality, a time "in which the loss of reality [*Entwirklichung*], alienation between *I* and the world, and the growth of fate come to full term" (§61v). Because the modern era is an especially low moment in the cycles of history—"the sickness of our age is like that of no other" (§36i)—Buber's analysis consists of a substantial critique of modernity. At the core of this critique is the problem of alienation, "modern man's palpable condition of lack of relation" (§59a). This alienation, this lack of relatedness or estrangement—whether between *I* and the eternal *Thou*, between *I* and nature, between *I* and others, or between *I* and the self—entails fragmentation, the loss of true being. It is the dominant characteristic of the *It*-world, which has reached its full flood in our era.

Walter Kaufmann has commented that "the immense popularity of *I and Thou* during the sixties was due largely to the fact that the second of its three parts deals at length with alienation and suggests that ours is a sick age."[5] Alienation is a broad term that changes in meaning from one thinker to the next. Buber's concept of alienation and his critique of modernity in terms of this concept have their antecedents in the thought of Hegel and Feuerbach. Hegel had linked alienation with the subject-object split, while Feuerbach tied it with the lack of relation between persons which leads to the estrangement of the individual from his true being. Buber picks up both of these threads. When he introduces the problem of alienation as "the reduction of the human power of relating" (§33a), he immediately identifies *I-It*, "the primal word of separation," as "that which holds the *I* and the *It* apart from each other" (§33c). Likewise, echoing Feuerbach's concept, Buber writes of the ontological emptiness of the autonomous self: "The more one is dominated by the *Eigenwesen*, the deeper the *I* deteriorates into unreality" (§39t).

To Buber, alienation takes place on several levels. His analysis focuses on three of these levels: modern homelessness in the universe or cosmic alienation; the modern scientistic-materialistic dogma that all reality is reducible to the causal nexus, which is essentially alienation from nature; and the modern embracing of the subjective life as a retreat from objectivity, which is self-alienation. We now consider his critique at each of these three levels.

---

5. Kaufmann, "Introductory Essay," xxi.

Cosmic homelessness

To Buber the culturally shared image of the cosmos as the home within which mankind dwells is an outgrowth of the primacy of the *I-Thou* relation in a society. He presents this connection between relating and dwelling as the ideal from which modernity has fallen:

> Every great culture rests on an original relational event, on a response to the *Thou* made as its source, on an act of being [*Wesensakt*] of the spirit. This act creates in the spirit a distinctive conception of the cosmos—only through this act . . . can humankind, with confidence of soul and a distinctive vision of the cosmos, again and again build dwelling places for God and humans and fill oscillating time with new hymns and songs, and bring human community into form. (§36h)

Again, at the end of *I and Thou*, Buber elaborates on this image of the integration of culture and cosmos:

> Only with the anchoring of time in the relation-oriented life of salvation and the anchoring of space in the community unified around its center does a human cosmos arise and remain around the invisible altar, grasped in the spirit out of the cosmic material of the eon. . . . [Again and again through such relating,] the universe becomes our home with its sacred hearth upon which we offer sacrifice . . . [and] all gates are unified into one great portal opening into actualized life. (§§61i, 55i, 55k)

But, as Buber writes in "What is Man?," such "epochs of habitation" give way to "epochs of homelessness. In the former, man lives in the world as in a house, as in a home. In the latter, man lives in the world as in an open field and at times does not even have four pegs with which to set up a tent."[6] The modern period is one of the most severe of the epochs of cosmic homelessness, as he states in his analysis of the problem of modernity: "When a culture ceases to be centered in the living and continually renewed relational process . . . the cosmic home which was constructed around its altar, the spiritually apprehended cosmos collapses [and] it hardens into the *It*-world" (§§36h, 61r). This loss and decline is "the sickness of our age" (§36i).

Buber's historical sketch in "What is Man?" traces the evolution of the image of the cosmos as home in Plato, Augustine, and Dante, to its decline from Pascal to Kant to Heidegger, to the abstract cosmology of the *It*-world

---

6. Buber, "What is Man?," 126.

of Einstein in which "the universe can still be thought, but it can no longer be imagined; the person who thinks it no longer really lives in it."[7] Modern alienation's cosmic dimension is thus captured in the image of cosmic homelessness, the condition of the modern imagination characterized by his image of the world as "an open field" in which we "do not even have four pegs with which to set up a tent."[8]

To Buber, the modern condition is "characterized by the union of cosmic and social homelessness" in which the modern person feels "exposed by nature—as an unwanted child is exposed—and at the same time isolated in the midst of the tumultuous human world."[9]

Buber shows the starkness of cosmic homelessness, and with it the erosion of community, by throwing it into contrast with his ideal of the true community built around relating: "The true community arises . . . through these two factors: that people stand in a living mutual relation to a living center and that they also stand in a living mutual relation with each other. . . . The community is constructed out of living mutual relating but the Master-builder [*Baumeister*] is the living, effecting center" (§33k).[10] Buber's comments late in life confirm the consistency of this vision:

> Community is founded on the immediacy of relation. . . . All genuine community consists of men who have a common, immediate relation to a living center, and just by virtue of this common center have an immediate relation to one another. In the midst of the Hasidic community stands the *zaddik*, whose function it is to help the Hasidim, as persons and as a totality, to authenticate their relation to God in the hallowing of life and just from this starting point to live as brothers with one another.[11]

Buber's metaphor of the "living, effecting center, the Master-builder," around which people take their stand in mutual relating, is the eternal *Thou*, or the embodiment of the eternal *Thou* as the *zaddik* or master at the heart of the spiritual community. His metaphor of the center echoes Plotinus's use of the same metaphor to point to the human community in

---

7. Buber, "What is Man?," 133.
8. Buber, "What is Man?," 126.
9. Buber, "What is Man?," 200.
10. This passage was introduced in chapter 6 above, page 130. Mendes-Flohr refers to this statement as Buber's credo. See *From Mysticism to Dialogue*, 122. Furthermore, Mendes-Flohr reads *I and Thou* as, among other things, "a grammar for the reconstruction of *Gemeinschaft* [community]" (*From Mysticism to Dialogue*, 10). See Avnon, "'Living Center,'" 61–63, 73, on the role of the Master-builder in constructing community.
11. Buber, "Interrogation of Martin Buber," 68.

relation to the Transcendent One: "A circle turns not upon some external but on its own centre, the point to which it owes its rise. The soul's movement will be about its source; to this it will hold, poised intent towards that unity to which all souls should move . . ."[12] Plotinus continues with proliferating metaphors, envisioning the community as a choir which sings facing its center as a conductor:

> [When] we reach towards the *One*, it is we that become present. We are always before it, but we do not always look: thus a choir, singing set in due order about the conductor, may turn away from that centre to which all should attend; let it but face aright and it sings with beauty, present effectively. We are ever before the *One*—cut off is utter dissolution; we can no longer be—but we do not always attend: when we look our Term is attained; this is rest; this is the end of singing ill; effectively before Him, we lift a choral song full of God.[13]

Buber thus makes his critique of modern alienation at the cosmic level, summed up by the image of homelessness, by tracing the decline from the primal sense of the universe as the dwelling place of mankind to a setting of human existence characterized by indifferent natural forces. The latter is taken up by moderns as the matrix of cause and effect, which Buber identifies as the dominant dogma of modernity.

The dogma of the causal nexus

At the core of the problem of alienation is the modern dogma of process [*das Dogma des Ablaufs*], the belief that the causal nexus is the mechanism of everything that happens (§36j). "Causality [*Ursächlichkeit*] has unlimited reign in the *It*-world" and it encompasses both "every 'physical' event that can be perceived by the senses" as well as "every 'psychical' event existing or discovered in self-experience" (§36a). In both cases, events are perceived to have reality only insofar as they constitute links in the chain of causality. Common causality has mushroomed "to become threatening and oppressive fate" (§36h).

---

12. Plotinus, *Enneads*, 6.9.8.

13. Plotinus, *Enneads*, 6.9.8. Following the Greek, το ἑν, *to hen*, in the original, I have replaced McKenna's "the Supreme" in this passage with "the One." Note that Buber's metaphor of the Center/Master-builder here has its correspondences in Plotinus's use of the metaphor of the Creator-Poet (3.2.17) or Choragos behind the human drama in (1.6.7).

Buber argues this dogma has become more and more pervasive in modern thought, the result of its extension from being an axiom of scientific thinking to functioning as the dominant modern cosmology:

> The quasi-biological and quasi-historical thought of to-day, however different the aims of each, have worked together to establish a more tenacious and oppressive belief in fate than has ever before existed. . . . Whether it is the "law of life" of a universal struggle in which all must take part or renounce life, or the "law of the soul" which completely builds up the psychical person from innate habitual instincts, or the "social law" of an irresistible social process to which will and consciousness may only be accompaniments, or the "cultural law" of an unchangeably uniform coming and going of historical structures—whatever form it takes, it always means that humankind is set in the frame of an inescapable happening that he cannot, or can only in his frenzy, resist. (§36j, Smith translation modified)

This dogma thus appears to have enclosed us in a vacuum bell of causality from which there can be no escape.

One response to this fatalistic outlook is to mistakenly embrace it as a kind of liberation: "Those who are overcome by the world of *It* are bound to imagine that the dogma of immutable process is a truth that clears a way through the rampant profusion of things—even as in very truth this dogma leads them ever deeper into enslavement in the *It*-world" (§36l).

The ideology of science falsely promises that we humans can liberate ourselves through the advancement of our scientific knowledge. Buber completely inverts this view: he points to *I-Thou* relating, a reality completely other than the causal nexus of the *It*-world, as the means of our liberation. Yet before we can consider this alternative there is a third level of modern alienation Buber considers to be a particular sinister aspect of the modern predicament: that is "the turn inward."

The turn inward

The modern dogma that reduces the physical world to the causal nexus has precipitated a second, more universal response, a turn inward to focus on the inner, subjective life of the individual and to exalt the life of feelings as an escape from the suffocating *It*-world of the causal nexus. Through this turn inward, the individual "takes his stand in the shelter of the primary word of separation" in an unconscious attempt to "hold off the *I* and the *It* from each other" (§33c). With this turn inward, the individual divides life into two separate realms, that of public institutions and that of private feelings, as if this split would protect the realm of *I* from the realm of *It*. This splitting as a fundamental structure of modernity uniquely distinguishes modern man as "psychological man" (§32h). Buber shows how this focus on inner feelings psychologizes human reality, making it self-contained, and thereby undercuts the power of interpersonal relating (§49a–b).

The embracing of subjective life, the turn inward, reduces reality to the inner experience of the individual, which Buber calls "the psychologizing of the world."[14] This reduction of reality by internalizing it eliminates otherness—all is taken as inner experience: *Erlebnis* becomes the only reality. Solipsism reigns supreme.

With sardonic wit Buber exposes the self-indulgent *cul de sac* of modernity's signature inwardness in short order: "If, as a modern person, you have learned to be deeply preoccupied with your own feelings, despair at their unreality will not easily lead you into a better way—for despair itself is also an interesting feeling" (§33j). Wallowing in such subjectivity, the counterpart to the "bell jar" of the causal nexus, has become a pervasive modern phenomenon.

Moreover, Buber makes clear how this modern turn inward throws the soul into a labyrinth of subjectivity, a profound imbroglio of self-contradiction:

> When one does not work out and actualize the inborn *Thou* in what he encounters, then it turns inward. It develops on the unnatural, impossible object, the *I*; that is, it develops where there is no place at all for it to develop. Thus, a kind of confrontation arises within the self, and this cannot be relation, or presence, or flowing exchange, but only self-contradiction. Some may try to interpret this as a relationship, perhaps one that is religious, in order to extricate themselves from the horror of their inner doppelgänger; but they are bound to discover again and again the will-o'-the-wisp in any such explanation. Here an unfulfilled life has taken flight to a lunatic illusion of fulfillment; now it gropes around in mad corridors while losing itself ever more profoundly. (§42b)[15]

Buber strongly warns that this modern turn inward includes internalizing the *I-Thou* relationship, thereby obliterating "the between." This loss is especially destructive: "All [such] modern attempts to recast the primal reality of dialogue as . . . a process that is contained within the

---

14. Buber, "On the Psychologizing of the World," 144–52.
15. On self-contradiction, see §40d, §41e, and §42.

self-sufficient interior life of the individual are futile: they take their place in the abysmal history of the annihilation of reality [*Entwirklichung*]" (§50e). Such subjectivism, like the objectification of the external world, is another abyss of modern alienation.

To sum up, Buber's analysis of modern alienation equally exposes the bleakness of both its objective and subjective sides. He argues that neither objective, public institutions nor the private inner realm of feelings "has access to real life. Institutions produce no public life, and feelings produce no personal life" (§33i). Both sides in this split are based on a reductionism that drains the life out of human reality. Buber explains how "the common life of modern man [has] by necessity sunk down into the *It-* world" (§35a). In such a condition, "modern work and modern possession [have] wiped out almost every trace of over-againstness, of meaningful relation" (§35a). The advanced institutions that are products of modernity such as the means of production, the capitalist economic system, the state, even religious institutions, themselves are constructions coming from, expressing, and reinforcing the limits of the *It*-world (§§33–35). "The experiencing and using *I* that prevails" in these institutions that function as the apparatus of civilization, whether of the leaders or the led, takes the *Thou* of relating as a threat to their modern order and efficiency (§35a).

3. Individualism: The Individualist [*Eigenwesen*] Versus the Person

A major focus of Buber's critique of modernity is his critique of individualism. Individualism germinated as a mark of modernity when John Locke formulated the idea of the individual as a basic social unit in the late seventeenth century. Soon it was forged into the emerging bourgeois ideology as one of its major elements, becoming the foundation for the modern ideals of individual liberties and individual rights. Individualism puts the individual human subject at the center of the liberal ideology grounded in Enlightenment ideals, ideals that came to political expression in the twin American-French revolutions. Since then, the ideology of individualism has prevailed as a central element of modernity.

Buber critiques individualism in part two of *I and Thou* by extensively developing his distinction between the two major modes of human existence, those constituted by the difference between *I-It* and *I-Thou* (§§35–42). He makes clear at the beginning of *I and Thou* that there are two different "*I*'s in each human being and he repeats the exact words of this claim here: "The *I* of the primary word *I-Thou* is a different *I* from the *I* of the primary word *I-It* (§§1g, 39c). On the one hand, there is the individualist [*das Eigenwesen*], the "self-willed man," who is oriented to the *It*-world; on the other hand, there is the person [*die Person*], the free person, who is oriented to the *Thou* (§37d-e). Buber makes clear in his exposition that for any given instance this distinction is orienting, not absolute:

> No one is pure person and no one is pure individuality [*Eigenwesen*]; none is wholly real, and none wholly unreal. Everyone lives in the twofold I. But there are some so delimited by personhood that they may be called persons, and some so delimited by individuality that they may be called individualists. True history works itself out in the struggle between the one and the other. (§39s)

Buber alludes to the Hebrew Scriptures when he calls the word "*I*" "the true shibboleth of mankind" (§§40b, 41e). The Gileadites pronounced the Hebrew word for stream *shibboleth*, while the Ephraimites pronounced it *sibboleth*. Thus, the army of Gilead used this difference to discern Ephraimite imposters in their midst during the tribal war recounted in the book of Judges (chs. 11–12). In the same way, Buber argues, the use of the word "*I*" can be used to discern whether one is speaking from the "*I*" of *I-It* or from the "*I*" of *I-Thou*, each of which has its own distinct character.

The individualist [*der Eigenwesen*]

Buber coined the term *Eigenwesen* for the character of the *I* on the *I-it* side of the distinction. He formed this term by combining the self-reflexive "*eigen*," meaning "one's own," with the noun "*Wesen*," meaning "being," "creature," or "entity." Thus, the *Eigenwesen* is the autonomous self. *Eigenwesen* corresponds closely to Max Stirner's *der Einzige* which is the focus of his book *Der Einzige und sein Eigentum* that Buber comments on in his essay on Kierkegaard, "The Question to the Single One."[16] Philip Wheelwright translates Buber's *Eigenwesen* as "the solitary one" and "the isolated one."[17] Buber uses *Eigenwesen* extensively (fourteen times) in §39. In a footnote to his translation of *I and Thou*, Kaufmann renders Buber's term as "literally own-being or self-being," and yet he translates it as "ego."[18] Kaufmann's use of "ego" for *Eigenwesen* can be distracting because it evokes Freudian categories that are foreign to Buber's thinking. In a letter to Smith, cited

---

16. Buber, "Question to the Single One," 41; see Wood 81, note 31.
17. Wheelwright, "Buber's Philosophical Anthropology," 76.
18. Kaufmann, *I and Thou*, 111n7.

in Kaufmann, Buber wrote that he was concerned about Smith's use of the word "individuality" for *Eigenwesen* and stated, "*Eigenwesen* . . . refers to a man's relation to himself."[19] Thus, Buber emphasized that his neologism should convey the quality of self-enclosure or autonomy, the exact characteristic that his exposition develops. Even Buber's introduction of the term in *I and Thou* reinforces the self-reflexivity of its meaning: "The *I* of the primary word *I-It* makes its appearance as individuality [*Eigenwesen*] and becomes conscious of itself as a subject (of experiencing and using)" (§39d). So, with the *caveat* from Buber's letter in mind, I will use both "individualist," following Smith, and the original German term *Eigenwesen* interchangeably to discuss Buber's analysis here.

Buber bears down on the negative qualities of the *I* of *I-It* in §39, where he establishes its opposition to the *I* of *I-Thou* by going back and forth between the two. Earlier in *I and Thou* Buber pointed out that the *I* of the primal expression *I-It* is a shriveled counterpart to the fullness of the *I* of *I-Thou*: "The *I* emerges changed, shriveled out of its substantial fullness to a functional pinpoint, an experiencing and exploiting subject addressing all as an *It*-for-itself" (§28b). Later in *I and Thou* Buber uses *der Selbstbehauptungstrieb*, "the drive to self-assertion" to name the motivational force behind the *I* of *I-It* (§46g).[20] Near the end of the book he adds the phrase "bending over backwards" [*Zurückbiegung*] to characterize the grotesque posture of those who become self-absorbed because they habituate themselves to the *I* of the *I-It* stance (§61j–k, aa). Simply put, the *I* of *I-It* manifests itself as autonomous individuality [*Eigenwesen*]. Buber characterizes it as self-differentiation, self-construction, and self-appropriation.

Concerning self-differentiation, the individualist becomes conscious of himself as an experiencing subject through differentiating himself from the rest of the *It*-world, the not-self (§39f). This setting oneself apart, this distancing, becomes one's habitual or "natural state." Yet in this act of dividing reality into self and not-self, and assuming the stance of the self separated from the not-self, the *I* of *I-It* distances itself from true being [*Sein*] (§39n). It has set itself on the path of alienation. Elsewhere Buber makes clear this self-differentiating *I* is the *I* of the *ego cogito* that Descartes made the foundation of his philosophy.[21]

Regarding self-construction, for the individualist, the Socratic "know thyself" means "know thy distinguishing qualities [*Sosein*]" (§39n). The

---

19. Kaufmann, *I and Thou*, 112n7.

20. This expression invites comparison with the Sanskrit *ahamkara*, "I-making," in the *Bhagavad Gita*. See chapter 9, page 222 below.

21. Buber, "Religion and Philosophy," 39–40.

individualist identifies himself as being such-and-such and nothing else. In this "setting himself off from others, the individualist distances himself from Being" (§39n):

> The individualist feasts on the fiction of its special being which it has constructed for itself, for to "know" itself means primarily to produce a powerful, worthy self-appearance [*Selbsterscheinung*], one capable of ever more thorough self-deception and, through its contemplation and veneration of its own false image, to produce for itself an illusory knowledge of its own [*eigener*] being-that-way (§39o).

In this inner action the individualist constructs and feasts on the unique self-qualities that he has made up for himself. His self-image consists of an illusory construct that he contemplates and venerates as an idol based on what he perceives as his unique "being-that-way."

Self-appropriation becomes part of the dynamics of the individualist as well: the individualist's self-awareness is that of the self as the subject whose aim is to experience and to use things in the world of objects. Its narcissistic focus is on its sense of possession: "My kind, my race, my creativity, my genius" (§39p). It plays the role of the consumer, consuming "life" by experiencing and using things. Buber characterizes this kind of living as a kind of dying that lasts a lifetime (§39i). The individualist seeks to appropriate as much of experience and as many things as it can. Its desire for *Erlebnis* is a major focus of Buber's critique, as we have seen in chapter 5. The ideology of individualism fits hand in glove with that of consumerism, yet acquisitiveness is a self-defeating illusion:

> It knows itself as subject: this subject may appropriate [*sich zu eigen machen*] as much as it wants to as its own, yet it will never gain any substance by this: it remains a functional point in a schema, that which experiences, that which uses, and nothing more. None of its extensive and manifold qualities and none of its passionate "individuality" can help it to gain substance. (§39q)

This *I* is consumed by its own desire to substantiate itself, to reify itself through what it "possesses."

Buber's analysis characterizes the individualist as the "*willkürliche Mensch*," that is, the arbitrary, the capricious, or self-willed individual. We might call this figure the will-dominated subject. In a long paragraph Buber sketches his character and its dynamics (§37e). Such an individual focuses on using or exploiting his circumstances. Yet he is reduced to being defined by his instincts and the objects in his environment. "The feeling of his arrogance is fulfilled in the arbitrariness of his self-will." He lacks the higher will of the free person but exerts his little, arbitrary self-will as if it were that higher will. He continually intervenes in the events around him in order to shape their outcomes. His motivations are framed by questions such as, "Why shouldn't I help out destiny? Why not apply the available means which such a purpose requires?" He can only presume that all human motivations, even those of the free human being, are so framed. In his unbelieving core he "can perceive nothing but unbelief and self-will," the basis for his purposes and his means to achieve them. Caught up in his own arrogance, such a person lives "without sacrifice and without grace, without meeting and without presentness, in a mediated, self-purposed world—it cannot be otherwise and this is his doom" (§37e Smith). He senses the emptiness of this façade, thus he practices self-deception: he exerts "the best of his intelligence to avoiding or even disguising true self-reflection." Kaufmann points out that this paragraph shows strong echoes of Kierkegaard's analysis in *The Sickness unto Death*.[22]

Buber emphasizes that the *Eigenwesen*, the *I* of *I-It*, exists on a slippery slope of self-deception. Under the tyranny of the rampantly growing *It*-world, "The *I*, more and more powerless, dreams on and on that it is in charge" (§35b). Buber uses an item of folklore to convey the growing domination of the individual by the *It*-world. His actual German word is *Alp*, comparable to "elf," which refers to a spiritual entity from German folk tradition that comes to the sleeping individual, takes advantage of the relaxation of the will to have its way with the body, and steals the soul.[23] "When the individual allows the *I-It* to prevail, the relentlessly expanding *It*-world overwhelms him and drains him of the reality of his own *I* [*entwirklicht sich ihm das eigne Ich*] until the Alp over him and the ghost [of the self] within him whisper to each other the confession of their mutual doom" (§34).[24] Thus, the modern dogma of process, the causal nexus, merges with the false sense of self and the individual is swallowed up in the world of *It*.

Buber presents Napoleon as an example of this demonic distortion of the individualist. Napoleon was the modern dictator who reduced his subjects to denizens of the *It*-world (§41). Advanced technology allowed the dictator to extend his power to exploit a greater mass of humanity than ever

---

22. Kaufmann, *I and Thou*, 110n5. Buber's characterization here directly parallels that of Kierkegaard's aesthetic stage, that of the romantic soul, as he presents it in the "Dipsalmata" and "The Diary of a Seducer" in the first volume of *Either/Or*. See Perkins, "Buber and Kierkegaard," 275–78.

23. Smith and Kaufmann both use the somewhat inaccurate "incubus" to translate Buber's *Alp*.

24. See Buber, *I and Thou*, §33i.

before. At the same time, the dictator's project of domination and his own subjectivity were reduced to further components of the *It*-world. Drawing from Napoleon's reconstructed journal, Buber shows the end-point of this reduction: "I am the clock which exists and does not know itself" (§41d).[25] These words show the dictator at a loss when he tried to articulate a sense of self: he himself was reduced to a mechanism in the eyes of his subjects and in his own eyes—possessing only the arbitrary authority of a clock.

Even the great masters of the realm of *Thou* in human history, whom we will examine more closely later, are distorted by those of us working from within the modern *I-It* mentality. These masters, specifically Socrates, Goethe, and Jesus (§40f–i), who lived prototypical lives of "pure effective action" (§32h), are misused by those of us who come after them. As modern people fully equipped with information, we amply mix admiration, even idolatry, with psychology in response to these lives (§32h). With this vision of modernity's tools of distortion, Buber lays a great burden upon us, the inhabitants of the modern era, to be authentic interpreters of the past masters.

To Buber, the *It*-world is not evil in itself. It becomes evil when we presume it autonomously to *have* being. "The *I-It* does not inherently come from evil—just as matter does not inherently come from evil; the *I-It* comes from evil, as does matter, when it arrogates to itself the power of being" (§34). Buber's interpretation of Genesis 4:6–7 sheds some light on this distinction. The potential for evil is there; it is up to the person to overpower it by taking a stand against it.[26] The *It*-world dominates those who let it have mastery, overwhelming them and even robbing them of their authentic *I*. Yet the *It*-world must yield to the one who calls it what it truly is—"the partitioning and alienation of that out of whose fullness, streaming close at hand, every earthly *Thou* arises to meet us" (§37a).

The person

The *I* of *I-It* has its counterpart in the *I* of *I-Thou*. Whereas the *I* of *I-It* loses itself in illusion, the *I* of *I-Thou* manifests itself as fully realized humanity. For the *I* of *I-Thou*, the counterpart to the *Eigenwesen*, Buber uses the German word "*die Person*," "the person." This term corresponds to the key Danish term Kierkegaard used to mark off "the single one" from the crowd, *den enkelte*. Buber renders it into German as *der Einzelne* in his essay on

---

25. Buber is quoting from Napoleon, *Corsican*, 480.
26. Buber articulates this point in *Good and Evil*, 86–89.

Kierkegaard, and Wheelwright renders it into English as "the single one," "the focused one," or "focused singularity."[27]

In Buber's analysis, the person is characterized by his openness to relation, his participation with the Other, and his reality as grounded in being. The person becomes conscious of himself simply as having subjectivity or subjective capacity, not as a subject over against objects, and he does this through entering into relation [*Beziehung*] with other persons. This reality, this finding solidarity with the Other through dialogical connecting, confirms him and his natural mode of being. As Buber has put it elsewhere using a commensal metaphor, "It is from one [human being] to another that the heavenly bread of self-being is passed."[28]

For the person, the Socratic "know thyself" means "know thyself as being." Unlike the individualist who says "I am such and such," the person looks upon himself and simply affirms "I am." "The person becomes conscious of himself as participating in being, as being-with, and therefore as a being" (§39n). The aim of the person, the one who has taken his stance in relation, is "relation's own being," that is, contact with the *Thou*. Unlike the individualist, whose existence is a kind of death-in-life, the person finds that "through contact with each *Thou*, a breath of the eternal life stirs us" (§39j).

The *I-Thou* relation means participating or sharing in a reality that is greater than the individual *I* and this participation gives the *I* its meaning:

> Whoever stands in relation participates in a reality, that is, in being [*Sein*], which is neither merely part of him nor merely lies outside him. All reality is an action in which I participate without being able to appropriate it for myself [*mir eignen*].... The more direct the interaction with the *Thou*, the more complete the participation. The *I* is real in virtue of its participating in reality. The fuller its participation, the more real the *I* becomes. (§39k–l)

Here Buber carries forward his earlier focus on realization, as in *Daniel*, as a major element of his dialogical philosophy.[29]

Buber makes clear the *I* of *I-Thou* is radically distinct from the *Eigenwesen* not because of self-denial or the renunciation of a part of one's person but because of the stance of this *I*. The nonappropriating openness of the person "does not mean that the person in any way 'gives up' his being

---

27. Buber, "Question to the Single One," 40–82; Philip Wheelwright, "Buber's Philosophical Anthropology," 75; Eller's discussion of the nuances of Kierkegaard's *den enkelte* and Buber's translation of it as *der Einzelne* is worth consulting: *Kierkegaard and Radical Discipleship*, 103–13.

28. Buber, "Distance and Relation," 71.

29. Buber, *Daniel*, 66–78, 92–96.

such-and-such, his being different. Rather, this 'being such' is no longer his point of departure; rather, it is simply there, the necessary and meaningful setting of his being in the world" (§390).

This sketch of Buber's *Eigenwesen*, the *I* of *I-It*, and of his "person," the *I* of *I-Thou*, is brief and abstracted from the concreteness of lived experience. However, by beginning to orient us to the outworking of Buber's foundational distinction between *I-It* and *I-Thou*, it serves as a point of departure for the dynamic process at play when a particular human being grapples with his choices in his concrete historical and existential context. To see how this works out in practice, we return to modernity as our context and to the choices with which it confronts us.

4. Existence on the Cusp of *Teshuvah*

Buber presents the deepening entanglement of the modern era in the *It*-world as the road to destruction. Yet, in true dialogical fashion, he shows there is the possibility of return at every step along the path of this decline. The individual who identifies with the *I* of the *It*-world has fallen prey to its seductions; yet, at the same time, he finds himself both attracted to and threatened by the realm of the *Thou*. In this twilight state, the individual can develop double vision: he can begin to see both the cost of his being bound up in the *It*-world and the potential of his entering into relation. In part two of *I and Thou* Buber repeatedly emphasizes this duality of decline and potential. At the same time, Buber's exposition echoes Kierkegaard's treatise on despair entitled *The Sickness unto Death*, that originally explored the links between despair and the loss of selfhood, on the one hand, and between despair and spiritual renewal on the other.[30]

To Buber, modernity, the nadir of the cosmic-historical spiral, is an era of great darkness. Like Kierkegaard, Buber deconstructs the illusions that come with the assertion of the autonomous self. Kierkegaard wrote, "The self is its own master, absolutely its own master, so-called: and precisely this is its despair, but also what it regards as its pleasure and delight. On close examination, however, it is easy to see that this absolute ruler is a king without a country, actually ruling over nothing."[31] Buber echoes Kierkegaard: "In such times the person within the human being and within humanity leads a subterranean, hidden, and as it were voided [*ungültig*] existence" (§39t). With the dominance of the *It*-world, the person, the link to the inborn *Thou*, is discounted as not valid. Yet modern human beings are not merely being

30. Kierkegaard, *Sickness unto Death*, 32, 26.
31. Kierkegaard, *Sickness unto Death*, 69.

sucked into a black hole. The *I* of *I-It* has atrophied but not disappeared completely: this condition contains the seed of hope.

The modern dogma of process and the modern belief in fate seem to exclude the possibility of renewal (§36j–k). Today these elements of modern ideology so blind the individual that, even though "perhaps underneath, deep down in the unloved knowing in the depths within, he really intuits the direction of turning that leads through sacrifice. Yet he rejects this knowledge" (§43a). There is still hope—through despair. Reflection on the massive falling away from the *I-Thou* that is a central characteristic of modernity, and reflection at the personal level on the gap between the de-realized *I* of *I-It* and the real *I* of *I-Thou*, can allow one to sink down into such despair: "Letting oneself sink down and into the rooting soil called despair [*Verzweiflung*], the soil out of which both self-destruction and rebirth arise, *could* be the beginning of turning" (§37f). In other words, such despair in the current crisis confronts each one of us with a destiny-determining choice (§37f). Kierkegaard's comment on repentance, his counterpart to Buber's *teshuvah*, again finds its echo in these words of Buber's. Kierkegaard wrote, "If repentance is to arise, there must first be effective despair, radical despair, so that the life of the spirit can break through from the ground upward."[32] Similarly, Buber grounds the true self in relatedness to the eternal *Thou*. Kierkegaard wrote: "In the relationship to God . . . devotion is the self and . . . in the giving of oneself the self is gained."[33]

The self of the individual submerged in the *It*-world and thereby bereft of the true *I* is an illusion constructed by means of self-deception. Yet no matter how deeply one sinks down into this illusory existence, there is always the potential for change: "The individual feasts on the fiction of its special being which it has constructed for itself . . . . Yet real self-knowledge would lead it to self-obliteration—or to rebirth" (§39o). One constructs an "authoritative apparent self," the *I* that dreams it is in charge, but this construct is extremely precarious and unstable, to the point of collapse—or breakthrough to renewal.

From the illusory perspective of the *It*-world, the *Thou* that is the catalyst for the flourishing of the true, authentic *I* is often regarded as a dangerous, threatening illusion: from the point of view of the *I* of *I-It*, "*Thou*-moments seem to be odd lyric-dramatic episodes with their own seductive magic, but dangerous in pulling us to extremes, dissolving the well-tried coherence of things, leaving more doubts than satisfaction behind them,

---

32. Kierkegaard, *Sickness unto Death*, 59; compare this with Buber on despair in *Daniel*, 133–34: "Despair . . . is the highest of God's messengers: it trains us into spirits that can create and decide."

33. Kierkegaard, *Sickness unto Death*, 50n.

shattering security—in short, uncanny, dispensable moments" (§30e). This characterization of the view held by the person immersed in the *It*-world remarkably parallels that of Plotinus regarding those who pull back from approaching The One: "The mind reaching towards the formless finds itself incompetent to grasp where nothing bounds it or to take impression where the impinging reality is diffuse; in sheer dread of holding to nothingness, it slips away.... It seeks relief by retreating from all this vagueness to the region of sense, there to rest as on solid ground."[34]

From the perspective of the *It*-world, the individual continues to think and operate in terms of the causal nexus, to imagine "predictions from objectivity" and "the dogma of immutable process... clear a way through the rampant profusion of things—even as in very truth this dogma leads him ever more deeply into enslavement in the *It*-world" (§36l). Here Buber reasserts this is not the whole of the modern individualist's reality: "But again the world of *Thou* is still not closed to him. He can still go out to it with his concentrated being and with newly arisen power to enter into relation, he can find his inner freedom" (§36l).

Buber presents this concentrating as the assertion of moral will, the taking of an authoritative stance *vis à vis* the *It* as Alp. This is the opening that can lead to the breakthrough: "One gains power over the Alp by addressing it by its real name" (§37a). This naming of the Alp applies to the *It*-world as a whole: "The *It*-world which up to now has dwarfed the individual's puny strength with its uncanny power, must yield to anyone who recognizes its true nature: particularization and alienation from the *Thou*" (§37a). This confronting of the *It* for what it truly is enables receptivity to the eternal *Thou*, "that out of whose fullness, streaming close at hand, every earthly *Thou* arises to meet us—that which at times appeared great and terrible like the Mother Goddess yet always had a maternal air" (§37a). With this allusion to the Mother Goddess (see §27c–d), Buber reminds readers of our primal link to *Thou* before birth and during infancy as the "inborn *Thou*" (§27e-g). It is this *Thou* that still remains close at hand and is actualized in this process.

5. Crisis: *Teshuvah*—Reversal/Turning

The downward path of the *Eigenwesen* has led to possession, despair, denial, and destruction—but it can also lead to the "most definitive revelation, whose serene strength changes the face of the world: turning" (§36j). Here

---

34. Plotinus, *Enneads* 6.9.3.

Buber invokes the centerpiece of his argument, the dynamic transformation that he develops from the Hebrew concept, *teshuvah*.

The postbiblical Hebrew word *teshuvah*, nominalized from the biblical root word *šûb*, means "turn," "return," or "reversal." Originally, the Hebrew prophets used the imperative form of *šûb* to call for an about-face, a turning to God, from previous conduct, a transformative act initiating "a new relation to God that embraces all spheres of life and claims the will."[35] This is a turning to God with all one's being, the giving up of a wrong attitude to God as a step toward a right standing before God as "the one thing needful." Thus, *teshuvah* is a "turning aside from everything that is ungodly, a trust in God in rejection of all human help and all false gods, and the unconditional recognition of God's will in one's conduct."[36]

Buber uses the noun *Kehre*, the German equivalent of *teshuvah*, and its verb forms (*kehren, umkehren*) in this biblical sense in *I and Thou* as the pivotal action in the archetypal arc of return. He posits "reflexion" or "bending back on oneself" [*Zurückbiegung* and *Rückgebogen*]—literally "bending over backwards," meaning turning one's experience inward, psychologizing, also known as *incurvatus in se*—as the opposite of this turning or "going out" to the Other as *Thou*, moving toward encounter.

Elsewhere Buber makes clear that *teshuvah* is the pivotal event: "Turning stands at the center of the Jewish conception of the way of man."[37] *Teshuvah* as turning originally meant the kinetic turning of the body and by extension came to mean a change of course of the whole person. To Buber, *teshuvah* means to turn one's whole being to the Other as *Thou*. This act of turning to *Thou* is the core religious act in Judaism and in all religion, for "the relation of an *I* to a *Thou*" is "the way in which the unmistakably religious of all ages have understood their religion."[38] Buber points out that *teshuvah* was the core of the message of Jesus, which the Greek *metanoeo* and the English "repent" wrongly reduce to a psychological phenomenon. Buber corrects the Greek in the Gospels to show Jesus' teaching was founded not on *metanoiete* but on *shuvu*: "Turn ye! for the Kingdom of God is at the hand of man" (Matt 4:17, Buber's translation).[39]

---

35. Würthwein, "Repentance and Conversion," 4:980–89; see Petuchowski, "Concept of 'Teshuvah,'" 175–85, and Fabry, *šûb*, 461–522; examples of the call to "turn" in the prophets include Hos 6:1 and Jer 4:1.

36. Fabry, *šûb*, 461.

37. Buber, "Way of Man," 164.

38. Buber, "Religion and Modern Thinking," 79.

39. Buber, "Faith of Judaism," 21. *Shuvu*, the imperative form of the verb *šûb*, is used in the Salkinson-Ginzberg Hebrew New Testament. See Matt 4:17, Salkinson-Ginzburg translation.

For modern people, the act of turning is not easy: "the further a person has strayed in dissevered existence, the more difficult the venture and the more fundamental the turning" (§46g). As we have seen, when one is mastered by the *Eigenwesen*, the person part of the human being "leads a hidden, subterranean and, as it were, voided existence—until it is called out to and awakened" (§39t). The dormant *I* of *I-Thou* must be awakened and can only be awakened by the call—"the essential relation cannot be learned, it can only be awakened."[40]

To turn at this crucial moment is to break through to renewal: "Turning is the *re*-recognition [*das Wiedererkennen*] of the Center and the act of addressing oneself again to it. In this act of one's being, the submerged relational power of the person arises again, the wave that carries all the spheres of relation swells to overflowing and gives new life to our world" (§54d). The act described here has two aspects: cognitive recognition and conative, deliberate reorientation. The object of this awareness and intention is "the Center," a key symbol of the One, the Supreme, the Source of all, terms which Buber shares with Plotinus.[41]

This turning involves a breaking off from the *I* of *I-It* to a wholly different mode of being in the world:

> Whoever is dominated by the idol that he wishes to acquire, to have, and to hold—possessed by his desire to possess—has no other way to God than turning [*Umkehr*], which is a change not only of the goal but also of the nature of one's action. The man who is possessed is healed not by redirecting his state of possession to God but rather by being awakened to and nurtured in the bonds of relation. (§58b)

Thus, turning is not simply a shift from one object to another, even if the second object is called God, but rather a radical change in one's mode of being, from part-using to whole-relating. A crucial element of the healing process, turning as the process of making whole, is sacrifice, letting go of what one possesses. In this letting go, "the one thing it all hinges on becomes visible, utter openness to Presence" [*die Gegenwart*] (§46f).

The following chart shows the elements that come together in the action of *teshuvah* as Buber discusses it. *Teshuvah* is a renewal or transformation that is fundamental for a life of faith.

---

40. Buber, "Religion and Ethics," 103.

41. For striking examples of the use of these terms in Plotinus, see *Enneads*, 6.9.8, 6.9.10.

EXPOSITION OF *I AND THOU*—PART TWO

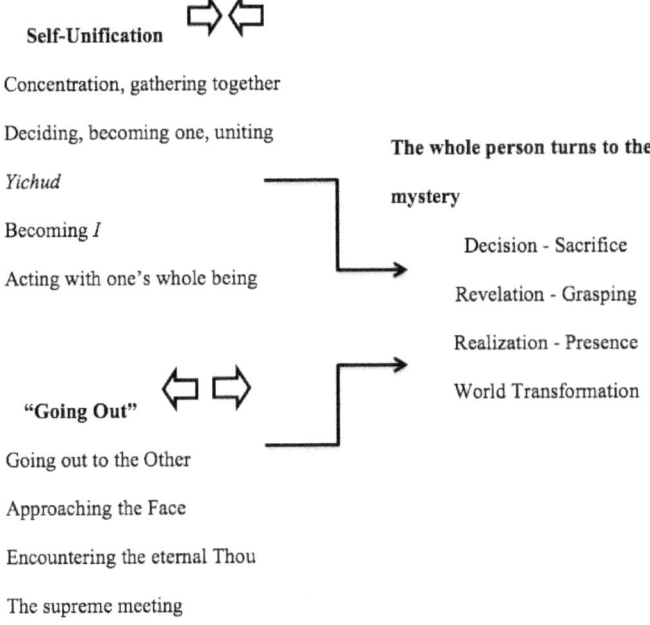

Elements of *Teshuvah* according to *I and Thou*

In a dialogical move at the heart of his exposition of the dynamics of turning, Buber inserts the voice of the interlocutor. In a series of four questions the interlocutor struggles to understand how turning is possible in the face of man's domination by the *It*-world (§37b). The interlocutor's verbs ask: How can one muster the strength, be raised up, gather himself together, become aware?

Buber's answer is rooted in one of the foundational claims at the outset of *I and Thou*. "*I-Thou* can be spoken only with one's whole being." Furthermore, the *I* and the *Thou* arise together in a single action: "My gathering myself together and uniting into a whole being can never take place through my effort alone, nor can it take place without me. I become through my relation to the *Thou*: I become *I* as I say *Thou*" (§14c). This emergence of the *I* of *I-Thou* is premised on a simple central axiom: "All real living is encounter [*Begegnung*]" (§14d). We see this real living as the duality of *I* and *Thou* when Buber equates reality with mutual action—action in the Presence:

> Reality [*Wirklichkeit*] exists only in action [*Wirken*], its power and depth in the power and depth of action. "Inner" reality, too, exists only if there is mutual interaction [*Wechselwirkung*]. The most powerful and deepest reality exists when everything enters

into action, the whole person without reservation and the all-embracing God—the unified *I* and the boundless *Thou*. (§50o)

Given this foundation, we turn to two key passages that discuss the emergence of the soul as a unity (§§50h, 50p). Buber defines this unification in these terms: "The [soul's] powers gather themselves into a core, everything that would pull them apart is overcome, and the being stands alone in itself and exults" (§50h). In this coming together of the soul, it is the whole person that is involved, not just some abstract entity: "the instincts are not too impure, the sensuous is not too peripheral, the emotions are not too fleeting—everything must be integrated into a single power. This is no abstracted 'self' but the whole unbounded [*ungeschmälerten*] person. Such concentration aims at, and is, reality" (§50p).

Buber emphasizes that this becoming one of the soul, this concentration together of its powers, is the decisive moment for a person (§§50h, 50p), for now he is in a position to make a crucial choice: he can settle for simply savoring this inner state of unity—or taking it as his point of departure, he can go out to encounter: "Gathered together in unity, the person can now go out to the full encounter with the mystery and with wholeness. But he can also savor the bliss of this unification of his being and, without taking up the supreme duty, let himself fall back into the scattering of his being" (§50h). The great divide that Buber presents for the crucial choice here is the great divide that emerged in the course of his own intellectual development. It is the divide between his early focus on mystical unity as an end in itself and his later sense of vocation, his task of bringing unification, *yichud*, into the world.

Buber makes clear that God speaks to each person in that person's circumstances and that the person's response to God consists in the choices he makes in relation to these circumstances: "God speaks to man in the things and beings that He sends him in life; man answers through his actions in relation to just these things and beings."[42] This dialogical relation between the person and the eternal *Thou* is thus inseparable from the person's relation to the multiplex world in which he finds himself.

Buber uses "going out" as a metaphor for putting oneself at risk, that is, taking on one's vulnerability as one exercises responsibility in response to the divine imperative—the presence of *Thou*—implicit in one's circumstances. Every step in our life involves decision—"Everything on our path is decision, whether expressly intended, dimly intuited, or wholly mysterious"—but

---

42. Buber, "Spinoza," 94; for similar formulations, see also Buber, "Prejudices of Youth," 51, and "Religion and Philosophy," 39.

deciding "in the inmost being" whether to go out at this point "is the primal mystery, the crux of our destiny" (§50h).

The standing of the person who steps into relation by deciding to go out to the *Thou* in his life in the world may seem ambiguous to observers. This is because when the *Thou* confronts me and I step into direct relation with it, the involvement of my whole being includes a depth that goes beyond mere overt action: "The relation means being chosen and choosing, receptivity and action in one, as an action of the whole being which means the suspension of all partial actions; consequently all sense of action based on the particular limits of the *It*-world is bound to appear as passivity" (§46d). This standing in relation directly evokes *wu-wei*, the "actionless action" of the one whose standing is in the Tao, as we have seen in chapter 6 above.[43] Buber elaborates such living as preparation for the life of encounter—and then takes it to a new level:

> This is the activity of the person who has become a whole being, activity that has been termed "doing nothing": nothing separate or partial stirs in him anymore; thus he makes no intervention in the world. The whole person, united in his wholeness and at rest in his wholeness, is effective—he has become an effective whole. To have achieved steadiness in this state of being is to be able to go out to the supreme meeting. (§46e)

Life in the spirit involves developing this dialectical openness as an ongoing habit, "the continually renewed movement of one's being towards concentration and going out" (§61f).

Three key passages at the center of *I and Thou* help to show how the elements of *teshuvah* work together (§§36c, 36e, and 36j). We begin a close look at each of these passages by noting the first is presented in the first person, as if it is an account of Buber's own act of *teshuvah*. This makes it more intimate and more compelling because it functions as the account of a witness to a spiritual encounter.

First-person testimony

In the first of these passages the beginning paragraph opens with the narrator's assessment of his stance, his self-situating as the willful or capricious *I* of *I-It* (the *Eigenwesen*, which is equivalent to Kierkegaard's aesthetic individual). This stance before seemingly limitless choices, the intertwining of capricious will and fathomless potential, opens as an abyss before the yet-to-be

---

43. Page 129.

actualized individual. "The flammable tinder of all my powers of will boundlessly seething within, all my possibilities revolving around me as potential, these two intertwined as if inseparable, glimpses of powers pulling at me from all directions, the All as my temptation" (§36c).

Then a new level of *I*-awareness before the *Thou* comes about in the decision-cum-action, the grasping—the doing which is knowing. This response to the *Thou* with the whole being is a taking up of the one thing— "the one thing needful"—which the present moment presents as the One Task intended for me. Both hands are thrust into the fire: the whole person immerses himself as action into his cosmic circumstances (the Heraclitean flux) which purifies, as Buber points out elsewhere: "Whatever is to be learned about the hidden relationship of metal and dross cannot be recognized from the outside; it will be disclosed only to him who throws himself into the testing fire."[44] ". . . and—I, born in an instant, with both hands deep in the fire, where *the one thing* which is meant for me lies hidden—my action, grasped: now!" (§36c, emphasis added). With this action, the abyss of infinite capricious choices drops away, a sense of the center emerges, and the centered life arises: "Immediately the threat of the abyss is banished; no longer the centerless many plays upon me in the shimmering simultaneity of its claims" (§36c).

Realization begins now—with the person's clarity about the continuing choice between the life-task, the continual relating to the Absolute, the One thing, and the old way of delusion in a sea of capricious choices. The definitive exercise of the will in *teshuvah* is the breakthrough to realization [*Verwirklichung*], making real, that Buber had explored in depth in his 1913 book, *Daniel: Dialogues on Realization*.[45] "Rather, now, only two paths stand side by side before me: the other and *the one* [*das Eine*], the delusion and the charge laid upon me. At this point realization [*Verwirklichung*] begins in me" (§36c, emphasis added).

The decisive taking of one's life task includes reworking the material of lesser motivations in order to incorporate them into the greater whole of the life task. In a discussion of Hasidic spirituality Buber expanded on the dynamics of incorporating one's passions and character structure into one's emerging work as a lifelong effort[46]:

> For having decided does not mean undertaking the one thing while leaving the other lying there a lifeless hulk, clogging my

---

44. Buber, "Holy Way," 108.

45. Buber, *Daniel*, 69–72.

46. Buber, "Beginnings," 54–55, and "Way of Man," 142, expand on the dynamics of this decisive moment.

soul layer upon layer. Only the person who incorporates all the power of the other in his doing *the one thing* [needful], who in the realizing [*Wirklichwerden*] of the chosen allows the unadulterated passion of the unchosen in, who "serves God with the evil impulse," decides the event. (§36c, emphasis added)

This central passage lays out the moment of turning as a transformation, a shift from the *I* of *I-It* to the *I* of *I-Thou*. Here potential gives way to action in the sacrificial grasping or taking hold which is the decision to act in accord with "that which one is meant to be." In this moment, the Absolute "reveals itself to the one who decides with his whole being to become that which he is meant to be."[47] Thus, the *I* of *I-Thou*, the realizing self, is reborn. The endless potentials of the *It*-world fall away as the person chooses relating with the *Thou*, and he has met the course of his destiny. Two images stand out in this process: "fire" and "the one." The image of hands in the fire seems counterintuitive, but it follows from the notion of the flammable will, which has now burst into flame in the act of turning. In an early account of the teaching of the Hasidim, Buber equates fire with devotion: "*Hitlahavut* is 'the inflaming,' the ardor of ecstasy. It is the goblet of grace and the eternal key. [This ecstasy] catches fire again and again from precisely the most regular, most uniform events."[48] Also: "The divine is a fire that melts again the human ore, but what is produced is not of the nature of fire."[49] This act of turning is not gratuitous: it is the act uniquely appointed for the emerging person as a uniquely created creature in singular circumstances. This act is what Buber gives special status to; it is "the one thing needful." The phrase "the one [thing]" reverberates all the way through the passage through the nominalization of the German article "*eine*":

"*the one thing* . . . which is meant for me—my action

"*the one* . . . the charge laid upon me

"undertaking *the one*

"doing *the one thing* . . . realizing the chosen." (§36c, emphasis added)

The "one thing needful" is the deed held out to the person as his defining act, the act which marks his destiny. It is the redemptive analogue to what Jorge Luis Borges calls the single defining moment of a life: "Everyone is defined forever in a single instant of their lives, a moment in which a man

---

47. Buber, "Religion and Ethics," 103.
48. Buber, "Life of the Hasidim," 74–75.
49. Buber, "Fragments on Revelation," 114.

encounters his self for always."⁵⁰ So too, using different metaphors, Kierkegaard presents this moment of coming into relation with the Absolute as the supreme moment of identity formation:

> When around one everything has become silent, solemn as a clear, starlit night, when the soul comes to be alone in the whole world, then before one there appears, not an extraordinary human being, but the eternal power itself, then the heavens open, and the I chooses itself or, more correctly, receives itself. Then the personality receives the accolade of knighthood that ennobles it for an eternity.⁵¹

"The All," or infinite potential, pulls at one, both from within as the *I* of *I-It* ("all my powers of will boundlessly seething within") and from without as the *It* of *I-It* (all the possibilities presented by my circumstances). Grace breaks through in a split second as at once both sacrifice ("both hands deep in the fire") and emerging destiny ("the one thing . . . which is meant for me"), both a letting go and a taking hold in the Presence.

The pilgrim

In a second remarkable passage Buber takes another approach in his exposition of *teshuvah*. He shows how turning, as an act of choosing transcendent freedom in the Presence, discloses one's self-defining deed and thereby one's destiny: "Destiny and freedom are linked to each other as if with solemn vows. Only the one who actualizes [*verwirklicht*] freedom encounters destiny" (§36e). He then uses the first-person pronoun to show the dynamic core of this turning: "In my discovery of the deed that intends me, in this setting into motion of my freedom, the mystery reveals itself to me" (§36e). In my radical openness to the Absolute, to the presence of the eternal *Thou*, three realities happen at once. First, I discover "the deed that intends me." That is, I gain a sense of my vocation. Second, this moment is an awakening or inaugural event: it is a "setting into motion of my freedom." And third, it is the moment of vision when "the mystery reveals itself to me," when I gain holistic understanding: the presence of the Creator, my destined identity, and the work before me all converge in single awareness.

Buber then recapitulates, using esoteric language to represent *teshuvah* as a pilgrim's ritual approach to the sacred Presence, the Face of God. To begin with, the person who is turning must face the unknown: "He believes there

---

50. Borges, "Divine Comedy," 19.
51. Kierkegaard, *Either/Or*, 2:177.

is a defining purpose, a telos [*Bestimmung*] for him: it awaits him, he must go out to it. And yet he knows not where it lies; what he does know is that he must go out to it with the whole of his being" (§37d).[52]

To do this, he must forget the realm of causality, put aside all that he has, and step naked before the Face—and in the unknown depths of this encounter make his pivotal life decision: "The one who forgets all causality and decides out of the depths, who detaches himself from goods and garments and steps naked before the Face: destiny gazes upon this free being as the counter-image of his freedom" (§36e). The pilgrim lets go of causality as his realm of motivations, which frees him to make decisions on a different basis altogether. This letting go includes divesting himself of all attachments until only the bare, vulnerable *I* alone comes before the Presence. The pilgrim's action here is at once the apophatic gesture of letting go of all that he has and the full self-abandonment—*Gelassenheit*—of the leap of faith. This is *zerizut*; it is Kierkegaard's "absolute relating to the Absolute" discussed in chapter 6.[53]

Buber's language here strikingly echoes that of a passage where Plotinus, borrowing from the language of the mystery religions, uses the ritual of stripping oneself bare and approaching the presence as his version of the move toward transcendence: "To attain the Good, we must ascend to the highest state, fixing our gaze thereon and laying aside the garments we donned when descending here below; just as, in the Mysteries, those who are admitted to penetrate into the inner recesses of the sanctuary, after having purified themselves, lay aside every garment and advance stark naked."[54] Just as Plotinus borrowed the language of initiation of the ancient Greek mystery religion to express the pursuit of the Platonic vision of the good, so Buber adapts that same language to turning, the move from the *It*-world to full openness to the divine Presence. In each case, the stripping away of the nontranscendent—whether laying aside actual clothing or, metaphorically speaking, the physical world, as for the mysteries and for Plotinus, or, in Buber's case, detaching oneself from one's self-understanding as a denizen of the *It*-world—is preparation for entry into the presence

---

52. Smith and Kaufmann use "destiny" here for Buber's *Bestimmung* just as they use "destiny" for Buber's *Schicksal* in §36. *Bestimmung*, from the root word *Stimme*, "voice," suggests "calling" or vocation, thus the personal quality of the relation between the eternal *Thou* and the human *I*. The call is to become what one was created to be. This fits with Buber's claim in "Religion and Ethics." See page 138 above.

53. Kierkegaard's "absolutely relating to the Absolute" is discussed on pages 100, 139–41 above.

54. Plotinus, cited in Osborne, *Ramana Maharshi*, xi; it calls to mind the Sanskrit phrase, *atmanam vidhi*, "Know thyself and be free."

of the transcendent. For Plotinus, this is the vision of the One. For Buber, it is the Presence of the eternal *Thou* in dialogue.[55]

This imagery evokes the archetypal process of death and rebirth. With Buber's "going out" to the Presence in the depths, which Plotinus refers to as the inner recesses of the sanctuary cave, by stripping down all that one has, one reduces oneself to total vulnerability before the Creator. That is a death, yet at the same time an opening up to a new life, a rebirth. The destiny that gazes upon the person at this moment is his heightened sense of the life he was created to fulfill. Elsewhere Buber uses this same pattern of death and rebirth more explicitly to trace the process each person must traverse to come to God:

> [For each of us there is] that decisive hour of personal existence when we had to forget everything we imagined we knew of God, when we dared to keep nothing handed down or learned or self-contrived, no shred of knowledge, and were plunged into the night. When we climb out of it into the new life and there begin to receive the signs . . . there arises for us with a single identity the Lord of the voice, the One.[56]

Buber then sketches the effects of this transformation on the person who is turning: "Destiny is not his limitation, but his fulfillment; freedom and destiny enfold each other to form meaning. And in this meaning destiny, with eyes only a moment before so severe but now filled with light, gazes as if radiating grace itself from within" (§36e).

Turning as a spontaneous response to the eternal *Thou*, a giving up or letting go and an opening of oneself in total vulnerability before the Present Creator, becomes a moment of awareness which Buber represents as the "gaze" of destiny. As the moment of defining purpose for the person, it is the moment of vision. That destiny "gazes" at the person in this moment instead of the reverse, the person gazing at his destiny, underscores that the person's awareness in this moment is a kind of self-conscious awareness. In this moment he is the subject, in his bareness and fullness, of the all-powerful, determining Other. This otherness is the irradiating reality of graciousness. In this moment the certainty of being as a created entity transcends the uncertainty of the subject's radical contingency. The person sees a way to be what he was created to be.

The "gaze" of destiny is transformed from harsh fate to illuminating promise by the encounter, as are the person's memories and desires (§15a).

---

55. The Hasidic and Taoist stripping away we have observed in chapter 6, pages 142–43, provide further analogues for this process.

56. Buber, "Dialogue," 14–15.

The directness of the encounter transforms the whole person: "A person does not emerge from the moment of the supreme encounter as the same being he was when he entered into it" (§60a).

Buber goes on to make clear that at the heart of this process the person sacrifices his little, arbitrary, unfree will that is controlled by things and instincts, the self-will of the individualist; he relinquishes this to the higher will and thereby "shifts from defined to destined being" (§37d). He has "offered up his little will to God and encounters Him in the great will" (§49g).[57] Henceforth, the free human being is no longer ruled by his own finite purposes. Rather, "he has only *the one thing*, his continual resolve to proceed toward his destiny. He has fixed on this resolve and he will renew it at each fork in the path" (§37e, emphasis added). Accordingly, he "would sooner believe that he was not really alive than believe that the decision of his higher will was not sufficient for the way ahead and needed to be propped up by some finite means" (§37e).

The person's destiny is the larger reality that comes into play in *teshuvah*, for in presenting oneself without reservation to the *Thou* as the Absolute, a number of things happen at once: I set into motion/actualize my freedom by relinquishing my little will to the greater will; in my encounter with the imperative of my being I discover the deed that intends me; the mystery reveals itself to me as I see the coming together of my being with the Absolute. I also learn the mystery includes my not doing the deed as I intended to do it: "but also in that I cannot carry out the deed as I intended it—in this resistance, too, the mystery reveals itself to me" (§36e). In this my intentions have become subsumed in the course of the evolving actuality of the life which the eternal *Thou* gives me.

The overthrow

In a compelling third passage a few pages later, Buber delineates the radical nature of the breakthrough announced in §36i. He shows the scope of the hiatus between the dogmatic blindness of moderns who are swamped in the *It*-world and the iconoclastic power of the one who is breaking free from it through turning. Notice how Buber emphasizes the opposition through his repetition of the opposing terms "dogma" and "turning":

> *The dogma* of the causal nexus leaves no room for freedom, none for its most real revelation of all, whose calm strength changes the face of the world—*turning*. This *dogma* does not know the

---

57. See the discussion of Buber on gnosticizing in chapter 5 above, page 114.

human being who through *turning* overcomes the universal struggle, through *turning* tears to pieces the fabric of customary motives, through *turning* breaks the spell of his class status, and through *turning* stirs up, rejuvenates, and transforms the secure constructs of history. In its board game, *the dogma* of the causal nexus allows you only one choice: to follow the rules or to drop out. Yet the person who is *turning* overthrows the pieces on the board. *The dogma* freely allows you to play out its contingencies with your life and "to remain free" in your soul; but the person who is *turning* regards this "freedom" as the most humiliating servitude. (§36j, emphasis added)

If we single out the agent and the process of this breaking out from the blindness of modern ideology, we get a deeper sense of the nature and dynamics of turning: it is freedom, expressed as the "most real revelation of all, whose calm strength changes the face of the world." Buber uses a series of verbs here to show turning as this transforming action: the turning person "transcends the universal struggle, tears to pieces the web of habitual instincts, breaks the spell of his class status, and stirs up, rejuvenates, and transforms the secure constructs of history." In these actions the one who is turning "overthrows the pieces" of the board game which the dogma of process would force upon us. Buber's use of the board game as a metaphor for the *It*-world recalls Heraclitus: "Time is a toddler moving pieces on a game board; overpowering, he overthrows kings at a whim."[58] The one who is turning overthrows the false dualism that opposes the causal nexus of modern empiricism to "inner freedom" of self-enclosing subjectivity by recognizing this dualism as a devil's bargain which simply tightens the bonds of "the most humiliating servitude" (§36j).

Buber's images for *teshuvah*—the hands thrust into the fire, the pilgrim's stripping, the overthrow of the board game—like his concept of revelation in §61, build on the foundational event of his own spiritual life, his spontaneous spiritual initiation at the age of twenty-six.[59] There the event of *teshuvah* from the human side is focused on *zerizut*, intentness, readiness, openness for the supreme encounter. We see this same spirit in the descriptions of *teshuvah* here at the heart of *I and Thou*, whether it is the devotee's readiness to plunge both hands into the fire (§36c), the pilgrim's act of stripping down on the way to the Presence (§36e), or the turning person's quickness to overturn the game board, the causal nexus of the *It*-world

---

58. Heraclitus of Ephesus, *Cosmic Fragments*, #52.
59. Discussed in chapter 2 above, pages 18–26.

(§36j). From the human sense of the divine side of the encounter, its essence is revelation as Presence, as call to action.

Sacrifice is at the center of this dynamic of transformation. The one thing that is meant for me, my destiny, is *hidden* until I grasp it in the act of thrusting my hands in the fire, the act of self-offering. The instant of sacrifice is the instant of transforming encounter, the moment of receiving one's divine commission. The flames mark both the energy of the universe (as in Heraclitus) and the transformation from the *I* of *I-It* to the *I* of *I-Thou*, as in the call of the prophet Moses at the burning bush in the desert in Exodus 3, and again in the call of Isaiah, touched by the burning coal in the temple in Isaiah 6.

Teshuvah takes place as this sacrifice. The free person's defining purpose awaits him: "He must go to meet it, yet he does not know where it is to be found; he simply knows that he must go out to it with his whole being" (§37d). This going out is a letting go: "He must sacrifice his little, unfree will, the one that is controlled by things and drives, to his great will, the one which moves away from being defined toward finding its destiny" (§37d). In a key passage on prayer and sacrifice, Buber links the two as the dual primordial act of worship (§49f). Prayer and sacrifice together "place themselves 'before the Face' in the fullness of the sacred primal word that signifies reciprocity: they speak the *Thou*, and then they hear" (§49h): "The one who prays pours himself out in unrestrained dependence, and knows that he has—in an incomprehensible way—an effect upon God, even though obtaining nothing from God: when he no longer desires anything for himself, he sees his effect [*Wirkung*] burning in its highest flames" (§49g). This "no longer desiring anything for oneself" is the letting go of sacrifice. With this letting go, God moves. Such prayer and sacrifice become the systole and diastole of living before the Presence. "So too the one who makes sacrifice . . . The upright servant of former times, who believed that God yearned for the scent of his burnt offering . . . knew that we can and ought to give to God. And this is also known by the one who offers up his little will to God and meets Him in the great will. 'Thy will be done,' he says, and says no more" (§49g).

This dual action of prayer-sacrifice places one in the supreme encounter, the fire of self-and-world transformation, the kindling of the flame of ardor for God, *hitlahavut*, through the extinguishing of the flame of desire.[60] This joint action means "no longer desiring anything" but instead offering up one's "little will to God and *meeting* Him in the great will" (§49g, emphasis added). The wayfarer is now poised to meet God in the world—in every encounter life in the world presents to him. He has begun the return

---

60. Buber, "Life of the Hasidim," 74–82.

to full relatedness. "A person does not emerge from the moment of the supreme encounter as the same being he was when he entered into it" (§60a). Transformation has taken place. This dynamic recalls Kierkegaard's "self as sacrifice": "In the relationship to God ... devotion is the self and in the giving of oneself the self is gained."[61]

6. Process: Swinging between *Thou* and the *It*-World

Teshuvah, turning, the supreme moment in the recovery of the *I-Thou* relation, does not make the presence of the *Thou* permanent or secure in anyone's life. Buber repeats this warning several times in considering the nature of human existence: "This is the exalted melancholy of our condition, that every *Thou* in our world must become an *It*" (§§22a, 32b, 52d). Yet in Buber's exposition of the naturalness of the shift from the *Thou* of presence to the *It* of objectification, he shows the shift back to *Thou* is always potential and imminent, whether in the sphere of knowledge, of creative expression, or of action: "Again and again that which has the status of object *may* blaze up into Presence" (§32c, emphasis added). The one who has "turned" to face fully the *Thou*, thereby embarking on the path of the spiritual wayfarer, is not oppressed by the causal nexus of the *It*-world because "he knows that his mortal life by its very nature swings between *Thou* and *It*" (§36d). This swinging becomes the hallmark of the wayfarer's life. He moves back and forth between the threshold, the holy realm of *Thou*, where "the spirit kindles itself ever anew," and the impoverished *It*-world where it is his task to let this spark from beyond be proven true in action (§36d). This swinging, the character-defining struggle between *person* and *Eigenwesen*, is the balance scale upon which the true hidden history works itself out (§39s).[62]

The life of freedom

In an extended passage (§37d–e) Buber sketches the characteristics of the ideally free person who, much like the *zaddik* or perfect person, is the counterpart to those who are bounded by the limits of the *It*-world.[63] These charac-

---

61. Kierkegaard, *Sickness unto Death*, 50n.

62. "Hidden history," a pivotal element in Buber's view of history as dialogue, is discussed in "In the Midst of History," 78–82. See also Buber, "Autobiographical Fragments," 19. Avnon, *Martin Buber*, has used this concept to structure his interpretation of Buber's thought.

63. Friedman points out that the language describing the free man here is "the direct

teristics stand out in Buber's verbs. The free person is the one who repeatedly *decides* to step out into his destiny. He simply "*knows* he must go out to it with his whole being." He *knows* "what comes will only come about when he *decides* on that which he has the power to will." He *sacrifices* "his little, unfree will . . . to the great will, which turns him from being predetermined toward finding his destined purpose. . . . He *hearkens* to what is emerging, to the way of Being in the world . . . in order *to actualize it* . . . through his human spirit and human action, through his human life and human death" (§37d, emphasis added). He *acts*; he *realizes*; he *encounters*—and in so doing, he becomes aware of and confirms his destined purpose.

When a person breaks through in the decisive act of *teshuvah*, he is ready to take up a life of vulnerable, uncertain freedom, a life journey continually ventured in fidelity to his destiny "on the narrow ridge" of continual decision. Buber articulated the nature of this life autobiographically years later: "My standpoint [is] the 'narrow ridge'[: I do] not rest on the broad upland of a system that includes a series of unquestionable statements about the absolute, but on a narrow rocky ridge between the abysses where there is no certainty of expressible knowledge but only the certainty of encountering that which is hidden, the Enduring."[64] Like the mountaineer, Buber the wayfarer forsakes the comfort and familiarity of conceptual constructions for the bare elements, the heady, risky venture into the precarious unknown where the only certainty one can count on is that of encounter itself.

> The free person does not have a purpose here [in the concreteness of lived existence] while fetching the means for it from there [the transcendent realm of *Thou*]: he has only "the one thing" [*das eine*], his repeated decision and resolve to proceed toward his destined purpose [*Bestimmung*]. Having forged this resolve repeatedly at every fork in the path, he will continually renew it. He would sooner believe that he was not alive than that the decision of the great will is insufficient and needs to be propped up by any form of mediation. He believes; that is, he encounters. (§37e)

The decision made at the breakthrough, his original act of turning, plays itself out in the lived life, one of his destined purpose [*Bestimmung*] working itself out by renewed affirmation at every fork in the path. His awareness along the way is vitalized by trust in the "great will," the higher will. For this journey, "the one thing needful" [*das eine*] is alignment with, and continual

---

application in almost the same words" of Buber's characterization of *der Vollendete* in "The Teaching of the Tao" ("Martin Buber and Asia," 419).

64. Buber, "What is Man?," 184.

openness to, the unmediated "great will" by itself [*nur . . . hier*], without props or urgency or any machinations on the part of the wayfarer [*die Mittel . . . da*]. In short, the breathtaking stance of openness to the venture is the wayfarer's continual resolve.

Buber elaborates on the disposition that marks this life lived in openness to one's unknowable evolving circumstances and his unfolding destiny. The one who lives this life is open to the *Thou* in the present while he steps forth toward his unknown *telos*: "It awaits him; he must go out to it, yet he does not know where it is to be found. He simply knows that he must go out to it with his whole being" (§37d). This stepping out into the unknown involves continual sacrifice of all other priorities to the one thing needful, the call of destiny: he must continually "sacrifice his little will, unfree because it is controlled by things and instincts, to the great will which turns him . . . toward finding his destined purpose" (§37d).

This stance involves an effort of hearkening to discern the co-being of the emerging self and the way, or Tao [*Er lauscht dem aus sich Werdenden, dem Weg des Wesens in der Welt*], as the means of giving birth to this destiny:

> He neither merely grasps at the situation nor does he simply allow things to happen: he hearkens to what is emerging, to the way of Being in the world, not to be carried along by it but to actualize it as it needs and wills to be actualized by him through his human spirit and human deed, his human life and human death. In this stance, "he believes" means "he encounters" [*begegnet*]. (§37d)

The wayfarer on this path neither asserts himself from the position of autonomy nor passively submits to the course of events. Rather, like the Taoist perfect man, with his whole being he attends to the emerging signs of the situation and acts decisively in dialogical relation to it. Assuming this dialogical stance *is* the act of faith. This stance, because it is that of the whole person, may appear to others as passivity, like *wu-wei*, but it is actually that of utmost decisiveness.

The wayfarer learns to live a life of openness in the interplay between relating to the *Thou* and existence in the *It*-world:

> The one to whom freedom is assured . . . knows that his mortal life is by its very nature a swinging between *Thou* and *It*, and he senses the meaning of this. It suffices him to be able to cross again and again the threshold of the holy place wherein he is not able to remain. Indeed, having to leave it again and again is for him an intimate part of the meaning and destiny of this life.

> There, on the threshold, the response, the spirit, kindles itself ever new within him; here, in an unholy and needy country, this spark is to be proven in action. What here [in the *It*-world] is called necessity cannot frighten him, for there [in the realm of *Thou*], he has recognized the true necessity, namely, destiny [*Schicksal*]. (§36d)

The threshold, the liminal place or narrow ridge of relating, is one pole in this dialectical life that is fulfilled in service at the other pole, the world of mundane existence. Thus, the wayfarer lives in two realms: that of the sacredness of relating and that of mundane existence, analogous to what Augustine called "the region of unlikeness" [*regione dissimilitudinis*].[65]

The presence of the *Thou* continually moves over the world of *It* "like the spirit upon the face of the waters" (§35c).[66] The one thing needful is balance, for the person who obeys the spirit lives with this duality: he "knows himself incapable of fully actualizing the *Thou*, yet daily puts its reality to the proof in the *It*-world, in accordance with what is right and fitting for the day, defining—discovering—the boundary between *Thou* and *It* anew each day" (§35c). Buber uses "the presence of spirit" to show the communal impact of one's bringing the *Thou* into the workings of the *It*-world:

> Only from the presence of spirit can meaning and joy stream into all of his work, reverence and the strength to sacrifice into all of his possessions—filling them not to the brim but to the extent needed; only from its presence can everything that is worked and possessed, while remaining attached to the *It*-world, nevertheless be transfigured into what confronts us—the manifesting of the *Thou*. There is no back-behind-it; there is, even in the moment of deepest need, indeed only in that moment, a previously unimagined beyond-it. (§35c)

This is not machination but transcendent breakthrough. Through the wayfarer's continuing access to *Thou*, human work and human possession are infused with meaning and joy, awe and sacrificial power—not overwhelmingly but sufficiently for the day—so the things of the *It*-world that are worked and possessed are transfigured into the manifestation of the *Thou*. Through this dialectical life, in the very moment of deepest need, there is a hitherto-undreamt-of movement forward and outward.

---

65. Augustine, *Confessions*, 7.10.16.
66. With this phrase, Buber deliberately echoes Gen 1:2.

The process of becoming

As we have seen, the life-changing event of "stepping before the Face" frees and empowers one to make a new kind of destiny-shaping decision. This event opens one to a life lived by continually stepping into the intimate presence of *Thou*, which evolves into an assured sense of the synergy of one's freedom and that of Being. As Buber writes elsewhere, "The Good . . . reveals itself to the individual who decides with his whole being to become that which he is meant to be."[67] In accord with *I and Thou*, this should be seen as an ongoing process, not a singular event:

> The person who is not confined to the *It*-world is free to step again and again into the realm of relation [*Beziehung*]. Here *I* and *Thou* stand freely over against each other in a reciprocity that is not involved with or even tainted by any causality; here one is established at once both in his freedom and in that of Being. Only the one who knows relation and the presence of *Thou* is empowered to decide. The one who decides is free because he has stepped before the Face. (§36b)

The process of transformation that begins with *teshuvah*, the radical turning to relation, moves the self from the illusory subjectivity of self-willed existence to its grounding as a participant in Being. The one who takes a stand in relation takes part in Being, which is neither merely within nor merely external to the self. The actuality in which the self can take part is *happening* [*Wirken*], the spiritual process of actualizing which the *I* cannot appropriate but can only take part in (§39k). The more completely the *I* participates in the actuality of Being, the more actual it becomes.

Buber lays out the dynamic link between the life in relationship with *Thou* and the realization of the real self: "The purpose of relation [*Beziehung*] is the relation itself, that is, contact with the *Thou*. For through contact with each *Thou* a breath of the eternal life stirs us" (§39j). *Beziehung* is openness to the *Inzwischen*, the between, the ontological reality that is completely other than what is in the *It*-world. Because *Beziehung* means relation with the *Thou*, our openness to any and every level of being is theophany, is movement of the spirit, is the dialogical act of speaking to the eternal *Thou*.

Participation [*Teilnahme*] in reality is the mode of existence of one who takes his stance in *Beziehung*, as opposed to the self-appropriating stance of self in the *It*-world:

---

67. Buber, "Religion and Ethics," 103.

> The one who takes his stand in relation participates [*nimmt teil*] in a reality [*Wirklichkeit*], that is, in a Being [*Sein*] that neither merely belongs to him nor merely lies outside him. All reality is an activity [*Wirken*] in which I participate without being able to appropriate it for myself. Where there is no participation, there is no reality. Where there is self-appropriation, there is no reality. (§39k)

The ontology of the authentic self in the primal *I-Thou* is of a different order than the existence of the illusory self which is constructed from the stance of the *I* in the *It*-world. "The more direct and unmediated the contact with the *Thou*, the more complete the participation. The *I* is real in virtue of its participating in reality. The more complete its participation, the more real the *I* becomes" (§39k–l).

The process of swinging back and forth between *Thou* and *It*, which is part of the structure of human existence, is a dynamic element in the process of spiritual development. Direct, unmediated contact with the *Thou* in this swinging opens up the participation that makes the *I*—the *I* of *I-Thou*—real in authentic subjectivity:

> Yet the *I* that steps out of the relational event into separation and the self-awareness of separation does not lose its reality. Its participating remains buried within, preserved as a living potentiality.... "The seed [of God] remains in him."[68] This is the realm of subjectivity in which the *I* is aware at once both of its bond in connection and of its separateness. Authentic subjectivity can only be understood dynamically, as the swinging of the *I* in its lonely truth. This is the place where the desire for ever higher, more unconditional relation and for full participation in Being arises and is heightened. In subjectivity the spiritual substance of the person comes to maturity. The person becomes conscious of himself as participating in Being, as being-with, and thus as being. (§39m–n)

The *I* of *I-Thou* is the subjectivity of relatedness, of intersubjective life. This subjectivity consists of a single awareness of the double reality of both connection and separation which the *I* of *I-It* lacks.[69]

In this way Buber lays out the life of the wayfarer as a realizing of the ontological reality of the *I* of *I-Thou* while living in the dialectical process of moving back and forth between *Thou* and the *It*-world. In this life, the *I* of

---

68. Buber is quoting from 1 John 3:9.
69. See Buber, "Distance and Relation," 63–64.

I-Thou is constituted as relational, as with the *Thou* in the *Dazwischen*, the "between," as event.[70]

Fullness

In a passage near the end of *I and Thou*, Buber employs the image of the rising moon on a clear, starlit night to characterize the life in which relating to *Thou* has become a practice to the point that it has formed one's character:

> Pure relation can be raised to constancy in space and time only by becoming embodied in the whole stuff of life. It cannot be preserved [*bewahrt*], but only proven true [*bewährt*] in action, it can only be done, only put into one's life. One can do justice to the relation with God in which he has come to participate only by actualizing God anew in the world each day according to his powers and to the measure of that day. This is the only authentic assurance of continuity. (§61h)

Daily renewal, proving true "ever anew," is the means of moving toward constancy, of "developing into a fullness of reality." In this practice, "even though human life neither can nor ought to overcome the *It*-relation, it becomes so permeated with relation that relation wins in it a streaming, penetrating constancy . . . . like the rising moon on a clear, starlit night" (§61h). Thus, the dialectic of the wayfarer's life is steadied in the supreme relationship by the series of daily encounters provided in the mundane actuality of everyday life. A life practice of such openness to *Thou*, not the futile attempts to capture some byproduct of the encounter, leads to the steadiness of realization and of the *I* of *I-Thou*.

7. Crisis: The Reader Must Decide

Buber concludes part two by presenting the reader with a nightmare scenario (§43). In the sections leading to this vision Buber has sketched characteristics of Socrates, Goethe, and Jesus as masters who made the authentic choice and lived in the fullness of *Thou*-relating (§40f-h). Then he has sketched the contrast, the characteristics of Napoleon as a modern figure who became swallowed up by the *It*-world (§41b-e). Now he presents the scenario: the moment when a solitary person—perhaps Buber at

---

70. Buber elaborated on "the between" as a follow-up to *I and Thou* and expressed it most succinctly and powerfully at the conclusion of "What is Man?," 202–5. See also Buber, "Replies to My Critics," 706–7.

a crisis in his life or the modern everyman?—"shudders at the alienation between the *I* and the world" (§43a). This scenario lays out the modern predicament in graphic terms.

In the anguish of a tormented night, the person finds himself as in a nightmare at the edge of an abyss: "the bulwarks [of the order of everyday life] have fallen and the abysses shriek." This is the moment when he urgently casts about until he gets a glimmer of hope: "the sense comes over him that something might be done about it." Again, as at the end of part one, Buber uses "you" (*Du*) explicitly to bring the reader into this moment of extreme soul-searching: "As when *you* lie in the worst midnight hour, tormented by a waking dream . . . and *you* realize in the midst of *your* anguish . . . " (§43a, emphasis added). This moment becomes the moment of wild hope: "and you realize . . . life is still ongoing, I must simply work my way back through to it—but how, how?" (§43a).

This is the moment that becomes an opening: the person opens to the depths and touches the potential for direction, for turning, for deliverance: "And perhaps, deep down in the unvalued knowing of the depths within, he truly knows the direction, the direction of turning that leads by way of sacrifice" (§43a). Yet sometimes the person tragically misses his chance—he lets the opportunity for authenticity slip by: "But he discards this knowing" because, given the modern values to which he has become acculturated, "the 'mystical' does not stand up to the electric sun" of modern technology (§43a). With this, he makes a fatal, tragic swerve and he is left once again with the false dichotomy of "world as subject" and "world as object." Through this inner sequence, his sense of the alienation of *I* and world has simply deepened, as the rest of the scenario makes clear in haunting, concrete terms.

Because the person has sidestepped his path to rescue, he is reduced to two modern sets of possibilities, two sets of images of reality. The first set reduces all reality to the object-universe: all that is has become *It*. The second set images all reality as a construction of the soul: all that is has become *I*. Both alternatives have the same overarching title: "One and all." Buber takes this phrase from the Greek philosopher Heraclitus: ἓν καὶ ἐξ ἑνὸς πάντα ("One and out of one all").[71] In either case the endpoint is a thoroughgoing oneness, a oneness marked by the complete absence of the dialogical Other. On the one hand, the universe is the *It*-world, the causal nexus where the individual is merely an insignificant cog in the cosmic process, destined for obliteration. On the other hand, the *I* may seem completely safe because the world can do absolutely nothing to it when it is not part of an open relation but is simply self-identity—yet this is solipsism,

---

71. Heraclitus of Ephesus, *Cosmic Fragments*, #B50.

the ultimate end point of the modern path, the shudder at the static, dead reality of total self-encapsulation.

Having presented flashes of relating and laid out the means of hope through *teshuvah*, even the life of fullness, in the course of part two, Buber brings it to a climax with this intense vision of horror. He has taken the reader to the abyss. Having provided the alternative to the abyss and the urgent yet necessary struggle towards it in the pages of part two, he now confronts us, telling us in so many words that the modern mentality is heading us toward disaster. He has brought us to the point of crisis where, like Ortega's shipwrecked mariner, we must sink in despair or find a radical, difficult way out—the way of *teshuvah*. Ortega's image expresses the gravity of this predicament:

> To live is to feel oneself lost—he who accepts this has already begun to find himself, to be on firm ground. Instinctively, as do the shipwrecked, he will look around for something to which to cling, and that tragic, ruthless glance, absolutely sincere, because it is a question of his salvation, will cause him to bring order into the chaos of his life. These are the only genuine ideas: the ideas of the shipwrecked. All the rest is rhetoric, posturing, farce.[72]

Buber signals one way out: one can pivot beyond this abyss by turning. Yet the path of *teshuvah*, should one choose to embark upon it, is no easy course. Buber offers no assurances and no comfort in the face of its tasks. Elsewhere he writes,

> It is a cruelly hazardous enterprise, this becoming whole. . . . Everything in the nature of inclinations, of indolence, of habits, of fondness for possibilities which has been swashbuckling within us, must be overcome, and overcome, not by elimination, by suppression. . . . Rather must all these mobile or static forces, seized by the soul's rapture, plunge of their own accord, as it were, into the mightiness of decision and dissolve within it.[73]

We conclude this exposition of part two of *I and Thou* by recalling the broad cosmic-historical picture Buber sketched for us at the very center of part two, where he traced the course leading to *teshuvah* as an invisible thread running through the cosmic cycles:

> Through the rise and fall of cultures runs a nameless way [*Weg*]. This is no way of progress or development but a spiral descent through the spiritual underworld—at the same time an ascent

---

72. Ortega y Gasset, *Revolt of the Masses*, 157.
73. Buber, *Good and Evil*, 129.

> to the innermost, most refined, most convoluted vortex one can name; here there is no way to go further and no way to go back but only the option of an unprecedented turning—the breakthrough. Will we have to go this way to the end, to the trial of ultimate darkness? (§36i)

The nameless way, like the Tao, is invisible but always there throughout human existence. Yet it is not subject to human effort ("progress") or to human evolution ("development"). It is paradoxical. The descent which is also an ascent echoes Heraclitus: "The way up and the way down are one and the same."[74] It is a vortex into which one seems to fall, as into a giant crevasse. Yet the point of greatest need, of the impasse, the bottom—this is where turning can take place. At this point the only possibility is that of radical, complete turning, unthinkable because it is unprecedented.

Buber uses the word "breakthrough" for this moment, echoing Meister Eckhart. Eckhart had originally coined the German term *Durchbruch*, "breakthrough."[75] Matthew Fox comments: "Eckhart warns us, it takes courage to break through: 'Only those who have dared to let go can dare to reenter.'"[76] Buber then poses a rhetorical question to highlight the danger and uncertainty one must face in the depths of this path: "Will we have to go this way to the end, to the trial of ultimate darkness?" Of course we must if we choose it—it is the nature of radical totality, of breakthrough. For the climax that opens out to renewal, Buber then concludes by quoting two lines from Hölderlin that capture the essence of the spiritual crisis:

> But where danger lies,
>
> The rescuing arises as well. (§36i)[77]

Yes, the depths of spiritual crisis are a strange mix of peril and hope, of letting go and grasping hold, of transformation as death and rebirth.

With *teshuvah*, everything is at stake. It is no wonder that in the companion essay to *I and Thou* Buber charts this breakthrough very much in terms of the archetypal pattern of death and rebirth:

> [In] that decisive hour of personal existence . . . we had to forget everything we imagined we knew of God . . . we dared to keep nothing handed down or learned or self-contrived, no shred of

---

74. Heraclitus of Ephesus, *Cosmic Fragments*, #60.
75. Eckhart, *Breakthrough*, 218.
76. Fox, "Introduction," 49.
77. Buber is quoting from Hölderlin, "Patmos," 3–4 (my translation). The two opening lines leading to these set an important context: "The God is near / But hard to take hold of" (my translation).

> knowledge, and were plunged into the night. When we rise out of it into the new life and there begin to receive the signs, what can we know of that which—of him who gives them to us? Only what we experience from time to time from the signs themselves . . . out of the givers of signs, the speakers of the words in lived life, out of the moment Gods there arises for us with a single identity the Lord of the voice, the One.[78]

The plunge down into darkness, a kind of death, is followed by a rebirth, a rising to new life in dialogical reality, the receiving of signs pointing to "the Lord of the voice."

Thus, Buber ends part two by raising the stakes for the choice which he presented at the conclusion of part one (§30); he leaves us with a nightmare image which calls for a clear decision. We can plow unabated into disaster and destruction. Or we can risk all in response to the call of the *Thou* and awaken to a life of dialogue.

---

78. Buber, "Dialogue," 14–15.

Chapter 9

Exposition of *I and Thou*—Part Three

PART THREE OF *I and Thou* presents the eternal *Thou* as the completion and fulfillment of dialogical reality. It develops in a fugue-like pattern as it moves back and forth between presenting the *I-Thou* of human-divine encounter and presenting the *I-It* of reduction to human self-sufficiency. Accordingly, part three opens with a presentation of the eternal *Thou*; then shifts to critiques of modern European doctrines of dependency, specifically those of Friedrich Schleiermacher and Rudolf Otto; and considers Hindu, Christian, and Buddhist traditions of mystical absorption in the transcendent divine as obstacles to dialogically relating to the eternal *Thou*. Then it returns to discussion of the three realms of existence—first introduced in part one (§§9–12)—as they stand in the light of the eternal *Thou*. It corrects misconceptions of dialogical existence spawned by Max Scheler's comments on idols and Søren Kierkegaard's swerve away from creation. Then it moves back to identifying the moment of supreme encounter with Buber's concept of revelation. Part three concludes by describing the ever-intensifying cycles of the divine-human dialogue as it modulates throughout time between divine-human encounter and rigidification into religious systems. This exposition of the cosmic-historical cycles leads to the climax of the book, the image of the single event in which human turning *is* divine redemption.

1. Finite *Thou* and Eternal *Thou*: Presence as "The One Thing Needful"

The first several sections of part three (§§44–48) lay out how the *I-Thou* relation is grounded in the eternal *Thou*, for whenever one person addresses another as *Thou*, one has opened to a glimpse of the eternal *Thou*. Buber uses a geometrical metaphor to emphasize this point: the straight lines of relating which mark the immediate connection between the *I* and any and every

Thou all converge like radii at the center of the circle, the eternal *Thou*. The inborn *Thou* is realized to a degree in each relation while at the same time it is fulfilled only in its relating to the eternal *Thou*.

At the outset Buber establishes the core theme of part three by directly grounding the question of God in dialogical reality. "God is the Being directly and immediately and lastingly over against us, who rightfully can only be addressed but not expressed" (§48c). With these words Buber sums up his key distinction between the radical existential stance of the person before the Presence—the dialogical core—and the language people use to talk about God. Because the eternal *Thou* cannot ever become an *It*, the eternal *Thou* is fundamentally knowable only as relational and never objectifiable. Because Buber focuses only on the human side of the divine-human relationship, he speaks only of the eternal *Thou* as known within it. He makes this clear in summary comments: "I am absolutely not capable nor even disposed to teach this or that about God." He goes on to say his work is anthropological in that he can only discuss the human experience of faith. As such, he bears witness to the human side of "that meeting in which all meetings with others are grounded."[1] Accordingly, he presents the eternal *Thou* as the name of God is presented in Jewish tradition. The name revealed to Moses in the great founding theophany of Hebrew religion (Exod 3:14, discussed in §60d) is never spoken—in the Hebrew Scriptures it is the one word written without vowel points—but always referred to indirectly by the substitute word *Adonai*, "LORD," or in Hasidic tradition as "the Name." Similarly, Buber refers to the eternal *Thou* using circumlocutions. He never objectifies God or directly names divine attributes. Significantly, Buber also treats the eternal *Thou* very much like the eternal Tao is presented in the *Tao Te Ching*:

> The tao which can be expressed in words is not the eternal Tao;
>
> the name which can be uttered is not its eternal name.
>
> Without a name, it is the Beginning of Heaven and Earth;
>
> with a name, it is the Mother of all things.[2]

Both the *Tao Te Ching* and Buber specify that the naming of qualities reduces the unnamable to an *It*. Accordingly, Buber dismisses all theological talk, "talk about God's being and works," as always and unavoidably mistaken because it presumes to treat the eternal *Thou*, which cannot become an *It*, as an *It*. Buber repeatedly points out that in every religious tradition there is a

---

1. Buber, "Replies to My Critics," 690–91.
2. Lao Tzu, *Sayings of Lao Tzu*, chapter 1, 19.

natural human tendency to reduce the eternal *Thou* to an *It*. Thus, although "humans have addressed their eternal *Thou* using many different names," (§45a) those hallowed names have been completely misused, becoming the most burdened of all human words. Yet, in spite of this very degradation, he believes these names are the most imperishable and indispensable of human words.[3] The one truth, in spite of all the illusory talk, is all people who have ever addressed God have intended God as God is (§45b). For whoever pronounces the word "God" and really intends *Thou* addresses the true *Thou* of his life, no matter what illusion about the deity he may hold. This includes those who abhor the name and believe themselves to be godless: when they address the *Thou* of their life with their whole devoted being, by this stance they are addressing God (§45c). The relation is the core of the reality; in contrast, concepts such as theism or atheism disclose no spiritual reality, for they are merely abstract concepts. Within this line of thinking, Buber implicitly expands the meaning of Kierkegaard's dictum, "Truth is subjectivity." Kierkegaard explains this dictum in explicit terms: "An objective uncertainty held fast in an appropriation-process of the most passionate inwardness is the truth, the highest truth attainable for an existing individual."[4] This thinking relates to the *zaddik*'s focus on the passion of the whole heart as spirituality.[5]

Buber next explicates the limits to the dynamics of the *I-Thou* encounter. In our encounter with another person we know only the course of our own lives and the moment of that encounter. Regarding the course of the other person's life, we know only the part of it that is present in the encounter. To imagine anything of the other person beyond the encounter is to go beyond *I* and *Thou*, to think in terms of *It* (§46a–c).

Grace, the gift of a moment of mutual presence, glorious because at once both beautiful and sacred, comes to us gratuitously. Our part in the coming of grace is our choice and resolve to be fully open: "Grace pertains to us to the extent that we go out to it and await its presence" (§46c). In Buber's words, this "going out" is our opening ourselves toward encounter and our awaiting it in the receptive stance which he calls "waiting" (§46c). He uses the word *harren*, "to await with hopeful expectation," which Smith unfortunately translates here as "persist." *Harren* is equivalent to the Hebrew *qavah*, "to wait, expect, look for, hope," a key word in the Hebrew Bible for the stance of those who are faithful before God. In §60, Buber quotes one of its definitive instances in Isaiah 40:31, as we shall see. Because grace is a

---

3. See Buber's dialogue with an unidentified scholar, recounted in "Prelude," 6–9.
4. Kierkegaard, *Concluding Unscientific Postscript*, 182.
5. Buber, "Life of the Hasidim," 74–122.

gratuitous gift, we cannot make it our object; we can only receive it when it comes to us. Our responsibility is solely for our own stance: our task is continually to open up to the grace of encounter, to go out to its unforeseeable presence and impact.

As the counterpart of grace, the activity of the person who functions as a whole being is called "non-doing" [*Nichttun*]. In "The Teaching of the Tao," Buber wrote of "non-doing" as *wu-wei*, "actionless action," the activity of the "completed man," the master or central figure.[6] To achieve stability in this state of being is to ready oneself for going out to the supreme meeting. For this, one need only do away with the spell or illusion of separation. Yet to do away with this separation, no precept can express "the one thing needful," for no precept can capture the primally simple reality of encounter or the existential reality of going out to it. All advice and methods are "grounded in the *It*-world and can not take you one step, *the* step, beyond it" (§46f). In terms of precepts, "going out" is unteachable. One can only hint at it through the negative way, through naming what it is not, until "the one thing needful," complete acceptance of the present, stands out for what it is. Yet, as Buber writes elsewhere, this "going out" can be awakened.[7]

This breakthrough, the difficult venture of elemental turning, does not entail obliterating the *I*, as mystical treatises too often claim. The *I* is indispensable in every relation, including the highest, where the *I* of *I* and *Thou* is again required. What it does require is giving up the false drive of self-assertion [*der falsche Selbstbehauptungstrieb*] (§46g). To give this up is to let go of self-making, the *I* we construct as the *I* of *I-It*. This is the *ahaṃkara*, the "I-making" false self which is presented as the obstacle to real living in the *Bhagavad Gita*: "The one deluded by egotism [*ahaṃkara*, "I-making"] thinks 'I am the doer.'"[8] To let go of this *I*, one must let go of all compulsions to hold onto or possess things, to reify and appropriate to oneself a moment of experience. For Buber, such a relinquishment means becoming the *I* of relation, finding one's stance in the face of "the unreliable, evanescent, ephemeral, unfathomable, perilous realm of relation" (§46g). To become at home with the *I* of *I-Thou* is to find one's true center, to achieve stability in one's state as a whole being—elsewhere referred to as achieving the constancy of the rising full moon in the starlit sky (§61h). This is the courage-filled counterpart to the fearfulness and recoil of the *I* of *I-It*, the *I* to which "moments of the *Thou*" appeared strange and threatening (§30e).

---

6. Buber, "Commentary," 88–92.
7. Buber, "Religion and Ethics," 103.
8. *Bhagavad Gita* 3.27.

Buber elaborates in §47, contrasting the relation to any given finite *Thou* with the relation to the eternal *Thou*. Here he uses several names for the latter—"the absolute relation," "the pure relation," "the perfect, complete relation" (§47b; the "unconditional relation" in §40i)—as he sketches its distinctive character. Each relation to a finite being is exclusive. The *Thou* of the finite Other is set free and stands forth, unique and over-against us. This *Thou* fills the heavens in the sense that everything else appears to live in its light (§11b). Yet when this finite *Thou* becomes an *It*, we pit it against the world; thereby we hold onto *It* and shut out the world (§47a). By contrast, the crucial point of God-relating is at once simple and difficult because it is total and absolute. To relate to the eternal *Thou*, to step into the absolute relation, is to let go of concern with things and beings, with earth and heaven as such, because all is included and gathered up in this absolute relation. To step into the pure relation does not mean to turn away from everything but rather to see everything in the eternal *Thou*, not renouncing the world but placing it in relation to its Ground. Whoever sees the world as "in God" stands in God's presence. This dynamic moment is the essence of realizing that Buber elaborates on in a powerful summative statement: "To exclude nothing, to leave nothing behind—everything, to apprehend all of the world with the [eternal] *Thou*, giving the world its rightful place and its truth—putting nothing alongside God but taking all in God—this is completed, fulfilled relating [*vollkommne Beziehung*]" (§47b).[9] When we go out in this way to our *Thou* with our whole being, bringing all of the being of the world to this *Thou*, we find the One who cannot be sought (§47c). Yet this finding is not a *terminus*—it is open-ended; it involves a continual "straining forward" or *epektasis*.[10]

In spite of Buber's disavowal of theological discourse, he uses it to lay out the antinomies that help to make sense of what he says—and what he says he cannot say—about approaching God in divine-human dialogue. Thus, he asserts "God is at once both 'the wholly Other' and the wholly same, the wholly present; God is at once both the *mysterium tremendum* that appears from beyond and overwhelms and also the mystery of the self-evident, closer to me than my *I*" (§47d). Accordingly, to explore conditional being as if it stood apart from God is to come to the indissoluble; to deny conditional being as if God alone really mattered is to stand before nothing; but to hallow this life of conditional being, to receive it all from God and to give it all back to God, is to meet the living God (§47e).

---

9. *Vollkommne* here echoes Buber's reference to the *zaddik* as *der vollkommene Mensch* in "My Way to Hasidism." See page 21 above.

10. *Epektasis* is not Buber's term; it is a strong parallel that is mentioned in Phil 3:13 and developed by Gregory of Nyssa in *Life of Moses*. See Buber, "The Way of Man," 150.

Buber concludes this section by presenting the path of spiritual home-coming. Our inborn sense of *Thou* suffuses our relation with every particular *Thou* so that we carry this sense forward—beyond the disappointment each time a *Thou* fades to *It*—toward more fully realizing the eternal *Thou*. Our path becomes one of striving in which "every relational event becomes a viewing station that opens up a glimpse into *the* fulfilling event" (§48a, emphasis added). Progress along this path toward and with the Ultimate, with anticipatory partaking and yet not fully partaking along the way, takes place in the spirit of "waiting," of alertness, self-surrender, and tangency [*Gelassenheit*, echoing Eckhart] in relation to all things, which is a form of service. Along this path a person's heart is not turned away from things; rather, everything now meets us in the One. In this coming to, the way unfolds as a continual process while the person lives in and with the Center (§48a). Both the mediated and the unmediated converge in this life of realization: "It is a finding without seeking, a discovering of that which is the most primordial, of the origin. One's sense of *Thou* cannot be satiated until one finds the infinite *Thou*, yet it has had the *Thou* present to it from the beginning; the Presence had simply to become wholly real to him out of the reality of the hallowed life of the world" (§48b). In this life the Absolute is God, the ineffable yet dialogical Presence: "God is the being that is directly, most immediately and lastingly over against us, who may properly only be addressed, not expressed" (§48c). Thus, Buber concludes, having shown how "it all comes down to the one thing—utter openness to Presence" (§46f).

2. Critique: *I-Thou* vs. Creaturely Dependency

In the next few sections (§§49–51) Buber situates the dialogical relation with the eternal *Thou* by critiquing what he sees as excesses on one side or the other of the *I-Thou* relation. He begins with modern German instances which in his view overemphasize the *I* side of the *I-Thou* relation by focusing on religious feeling. Then, in §50, the longest section in *I and Thou*, he turns to consider two great masters in the history of the human spirit, Jesus and the Buddha, as they have been interpreted in their ensuing traditions. To Buber these traditions skew the *I-Thou* relation by reducing it to the *Thou* side of the relation.

In §49, Buber considers Friedrich Schleiermacher's concept of faith as "the feeling of dependence" and Rudolf Otto's more recent expression of faith as "creaturely feeling" (§49a). In both cases, the focus on feeling becomes a focus on an intrapsychic reality; in this way it has pulled spiritual life away from the "between" of *I* and *Thou* to the inner life of the experiencing subject. To Buber, the problem with faith as feeling stands out even more clearly than the problem with love as feeling, which, as we have seen, he addressed in a strong paragraph near the beginning of *I and Thou* (§19b, discussed in ch. 7 above[11]).

Buber completes his critique of the one-sidedness of religion as feeling by claiming there is mutual giving and receiving on both sides in the human-divine dialogue, and continual creation as an ongoing action is the divine part of this dialogue, complementing the human actions of prayer and sacrifice (§49d–h).

First, having critiqued the overemphasis on the subjective side of the relation, Buber addresses the reader to acknowledge the reality of subjective feeling as part of the *I-Thou* relation in personal terms: "Yes, in the pure relation you have felt yourself completely dependent such as you cannot feel in any other—and completely free, too, as never and nowhere else; both creaturely and creating. In this state you sense neither one more than the other and neither limited by the other but rather both boundlessly and together" (§49d). Here Buber celebrates feeling as *part* of faith within the human-divine relation, much as he earlier acknowledged feeling as part but not the whole of love (§19b).

Buber elaborates on the expansive feelings that can accompany the absolute relation by relating them to the realm of creation, where the human being senses himself as both creature and creator, as a reflection of the Creator. "Creation—it happens to us, it burns itself into us, recasts us; we tremble and become faint, we submit. Creation—we take part in it, we encounter the Creator, offer ourselves to him as helpers and companions" (§49f). Here Buber uses one of his primary theological images, that of God as Creator, and he sees creation and one's current status in it as revelation. In the language of Buber's paragraph, the *I-Thou* relation is realized through the creation as the human being manifests the image of the Creator in his own creativity. This echoes the passage in the testament of the Baal-Shem-Tov that was pivotal in Buber's own spiritual initiation: "he is hallowed . . . and is worthy to create and is become like the Holy One, blessed be He, when He created His world."[12]

Buber concludes his comments on the human side of the relation with the eternal *Thou* by reflecting on the dialogical dimension implicit in the universal practices of prayer and sacrifice. These are the two great vehicles of the spirit that course through the cultures and ages. "Unlike

---

11. Pages 156–58.
12. Buber, "My Way to Hasidism," 59; see pages 20–21 above.

magic, which tries to have its effects and works its arts in the void without stepping into relation with God, prayer and sacrifice place themselves 'before the Face' in the fulfillment of the sacred expression of *Thou*, which means an exchange between *I* and *Thou*: those who perform these actions say *Thou* and then they listen" (§49h).[13]

The power of prayer and sacrifice lies in their dialogical nature. This power goes far beyond a mere sense of dependence, making both of these practices bearers of the relation, and thereby giving the relation itself its reality.

3. Critique: *I-Thou* vs. Christian Mystical Absorption

Buber moves from his critique of religion as dependency to his critique of its opposite: religion as mystical absorption or immersion. Here "descent into the Self" for divine-human union is regarded as the core religious act. Buber distinguishes two major forms of this unitive mysticism, the Western unification of the human and the divine and the Eastern realization of the identity of the human and the divine. "Both assert a state that is beyond *I* and *Thou*": the one "causes the span of relation to disappear at its consummation, the other treats the span of relation as an illusion to be overcome" (§50a). Each statement refers to "the great sayings of identification" at the heart of the world's mystical literature. Buber invokes the great master-teachers of spirituality to make his point: Jesus as the fountainhead of a major Western spiritual tradition and the Buddha as the zenith of a major Eastern spiritual tradition.

Buber begins by pointing out the statement attributed to Jesus in the Gospel of John, "I and the Father are one" (John 10:30), which is used as a reference point for the idea of the unity of the human and the divine in Western mystical discourse. According to Buber, this saying arose out of the myth-sized life of the person of Jesus, where in the Johannine theological tradition Jesus' life was related to the concept of incarnation. Over time this notion of incarnation became transformed until it emerged as the eternal process of the birthing of God in the human soul as Meister Eckhart, the Medieval mystical theologian, conceived of it.[14] Buber makes clear this trajectory of mystical thought is based on a serious misreading of the Gospel of John that to him does not anywhere entail mystical union but stands rather as "the Gospel of pure relation" (§50e). Thus, to Buber, the statement "I and the Father are one"

---

13. Buber expands his claim that prayer is dialogical in "God and the Spirit of Man," 126.

14. Eckhart, *Meister Eckhart: Modern Translation*, 95–102.

is not about ontological or mystical unity or identity but rather a unity of will or purpose in the *I-Thou* relation. Buber reads this statement not as a claim of union but rather as the core of relationality and therefore as the paradigm for the relation of every human *I* to the eternal *Thou*:

> The Father and the son, alike in being—we may even say God and humanity, alike in being—are the indissolubly real Two, the two bearers of the primal relation, which from God to man is termed sending and imperative, from man to God attentive looking and listening, and between the two is termed knowing and loving. In this relation the son, although the Father dwells and works in him, defers to the "greater" and prays to him. (§50e)

With these words Buber reinterprets the traditional christological content, specifically the metaphorical language of Father and son, rereading it anthropologically as the generic expression of every divine-human relation. With this interpretive move as his starting point, he celebrates the Gospel of John as "the Gospel of pure relation."

At the same time, Buber respects Eckhart while demarcating the limits of the mysticism of unification, which he critiques with words very similar to those of his explanatory note decades later in his foreword to *Pointing the Way*.[15] In both places Buber critiques the divide between the exalted state of mystical oneness and the lowly state of everyday life to which the mystic returns after his or her peak experience. Here Buber poses a series of rhetorical questions: When a person emerges from an experience of ecstasy, "is he not then bound to find that Being is split in two, with one part of it abandoned to hopelessness? . . . what does all this 'enjoyment of God' benefit a life that is rent in two? . . . what does [such ecstasy] have to do with me, the one who still has to live on earth?" (§50i). High points of ecstasy do not lead to ultimate unity; rather, they make our dividedness more radical and more starkly painful. Buber concludes this argument by invoking a global outlook and appealing to the spiritual masters: it is because of such splitting that "the great masters of the spiritual life"—such as Lao Tzu, the Buddha, Jesus, and the Baal-Shem-Tov—"have renounced the blisses of ecstatic 'union'" (§50i).

Buber interprets the experience of ecstatic union in relation to the dialogical ground at the center of his vision by relating it to two kinds of events "in which duality is no longer experienced" (§50g). The first such event is the act of self-unification, "the lived actuality of the becoming one of the soul" (§50p). This unification is not dialogical; it takes place within the individual. Buber describes it as a concentrating that comes with making a

---

15. Buber, "Foreword," xv–xvi, discussed above in chapter 6, pages 118–22.

destiny-determining decision: "One pulls one's powers together into a core and every thing that tends to pull it in different directions is overcome" (§50h). This effort is not about denying the actuality of the person or about exalting or detaching some part of the person, as in the doctrines of absorption. Rather, the intentionality of self-unification is the drive toward the wholeness of the undiminished human being (§50p). Buber quotes Paracelsus to express the ecstatic quality of this moment of self-unification: "One's being stands alone in itself and rejoices in its exaltation" (§50h).[16] This achievement of unity becomes the defining moment for a person because in it the person makes a fateful decision. On the one hand, taking this moment as a step of preparation, the person, gathered into unity, "can finally go out to the fully achieved encounter in its mystery and wholeness" (§50h). Or, on the other hand, taking the moment as an end in itself, the person "can simply enjoy the bliss to the full and, without taking up the supreme duty, fall back into the scattered being of everyday living" (§50h). Buber then broadens the import of this crucial moment by highlighting the existential reality that undergirds this and every moment: "Everything on our way is decision, whether intended, dimly intuited, or wholly mysterious" (§50h).

The second kind of event in which duality is no longer experienced has to do with "the unfathomable nature of the relational act itself" (§50i). Buber quotes a sentence from Eckhart that expresses the ecstasy of union, "One and one united, there bareness shines into bareness,"[17] and interprets these words to be saying that in this experience, "*I* and *Thou* are absorbed: humanity, which until now stood over against the godhead, is merged into it—glorification, deification, and solitariness have appeared" (§50i). Yet to Buber the ecstasy of union expressed in Eckhart's words was no actual or metaphysical union. Buber uses the long-standing analogy between spiritual ecstasy and sexual-erotic ecstasy which goes back to the Song of Songs to explain the real dynamics of this experience. Thus, when lovers are

> enraptured by the miracle of the sexual embrace . . . in the passion of fulfilling Eros . . . their knowledge of *I* and *Thou* founders on the feeling of a unity that does not and cannot in actuality exist. . . . The relation itself in its vital unity is felt so intensely that its counterparts seem to fade away before it [and] the *I* and the *Thou*, between which it is established, are [temporarily] forgotten. (§50j)

To Buber this blurring of *I* and *Thou* in the erotic embrace comes as an element of the intensity of passion. This reality is to be understood as similar

---

16. Paracelsus, *Die große Wundarznei*, 315.
17. Eckhart, *Meister Eckharts mystische*, 183.

to the individual's sense of oneness and it is to be understood as the way experience is perceived as indistinct at the edge of Being, just as sight blurs at the edge of the visual field. Again, as before, he concludes his exposition by pulling readers back from this edge or margin through his making a broader claim regarding the nature of the hallowing of everyday life: "But greater for us than all the webs of enigma on the margin of Being is the central reality of the everyday hour on earth, with a gleam of sunlight on a maple branch and a sense of the eternal *Thou*" (§50j). "The everyday hour" can be at once the perception of nature's glory and of the presence of the eternal *Thou*. For Buber once again, the primal choice is and ought to be for Presence in dialogue.

4. Critique: *I-Thou* vs. Hindu Mystical Absorption

Buber next turns to the Eastern ideal of the realization of the identity of the human and the divine, expressed in the claim "that All-being and self-being are the same." An implication of this identity is what concerns Buber because "therefore no saying of *Thou* would ever yield ultimate reality" (§50k). Buber uses a story about enlightenment from the Upanishads to explain the nature of the Hindu doctrine of Advaita, nondualism. According to the story, Indra, the prince of the gods, becomes the disciple of Prajapati, the creative spirit, to learn how to find and know the Self. After a century of spiritual discipline under Prajapati, Indra is finally given the freeing insight: "If one rests in deep, dreamless sleep—this is the Self, the Immortal, the Assured, the All-being" (§50l).[18] In the words of the Upanishad, Indra the student responds, calling this representation of enlightenment a negative thing, which confirms Buber's point: "In such a state one knows nothing either of himself, 'I am this,' or of others, 'These are beings.' He has fallen into annihilation. I see no value in this" (§50k).[19] Prajapati the teacher agrees. For his purposes, Buber leaves the story here but in the text of the Upanishad it continues, bringing home the point that Buber challenges. Prajapati overcomes Indra's hesitancy—similar to the spiritual hesitancy we have seen in §30 and in Plotinus—drawing Indra into five more years of discipleship, which lead to his final enlightenment, his identity with Brahman. Here we see how Buber is selective in his interpretation of the mysticism in the Upanishads.

18. Buber, quoting from the Chhandogya Upanishad 8.11.1, *Upanishads*, 4.386—note that Buber substitutes the German "*Allwesen*," "All-being," for the original word in the Sanskrit text, *Brahman*, which refers to the Hindu ultimate reality as a deity.

19. Buber, quoting from the Chhandogya Upanishad 8.11.1, *Upanishads*, 4.386.

Buber continues his argument. In this life we cannot know if or how this Advaita doctrine is true, but the one thing we do know is this: the doctrine has nothing in common with the Jewish idea that lived reality can be made sacred, for it reduces lived reality to the realm of illusory appearances, which in Hindu metaphysics is *maya*, the net of illusions. Taking a stance in stark contrast to Advaita, Buber affirms the alternative for himself and those who share his path: "But *we* are resolved to nurture the sacred value of our reality, that which is gifted to us for this life . . . as sacred" (§50n, emphasis added). One might ask: Is this, Buber's version of the Adamic task, the stewardship of creation, not comparable to the *bodhisattva* ideal of universal compassion as expressed in Mahayana Buddhism?

Buber continues, developing what he means by "lived reality" [*gelebte Wirklichkeit*]:

> In lived reality there is no unity of Being. Reality in its power and depths consists only of effective action. By extension, "inner" reality exists only in relational interaction. The power and depth of reality arise when one's all is thrown into this interaction—the whole human being, nothing held back, and God the all-encompassing—the united *I* and the boundless *Thou*. (§50o)

At first glance it might seem like the "effective action" of this passage contradicts the "not-doing" that is consonant with the Taoist *wu-wei*. Yet effective action is exactly this "not-doing" because it expresses the whole person in full response to the *Thou*. This mode of existence appears to be "not-doing" or passivity precisely because it is the only partially visible unified self, not the ego, that is in motion here.

To Buber, the action of uniting the self and going out to God is the human task. The becoming one of the soul, its concentration into unity, does not divide the person into higher and lower parts, as it seems to in the Hindu ideal, which sets the self apart as it seeks the "pure," the real, the eternal, and discards everything else. On the contrary, our task is to unite the whole human being: the raw instincts, the seemingly superficial senses, the fleeting emotions. The whole undiminished person aims at and *is* reality. This task is ongoing, never complete: "Unification of the soul is never final."[20] To Buber, the "pure Subject" of Hindu absorption brings spiritual discourse to "the most exalted heights of *It*-language," yet ultimately this discourse is about what is experienced, about *Erlebnis*; it is not lived reality (§50p–q).

---

20. Buber, "Way of Man," 150.

5. Critique: *I-Thou* vs. Buddhist Mystical Absorption

As an extension of this analysis, in the next paragraph Buber turns to consider the Buddha, whom he immediately identifies as "the fulfilled one" [*der Vollendete*], a key term he used throughout his discussion of the masters in "The Teaching of the Tao." Buber notes how the "noble silence" of the Buddha, his refusal to make assertions regarding the nature of unity or regarding the question of existence after death, avoids "the antitheses of the *It*-world." Buber follows the Buddha, whom he calls a "true teacher," up to a point. Like all true teachers, the Buddha refuses to impart opinions; rather, his focus is to teach "the way," what Buber in a neologism calls "the life of wholeness" [*das Heilsleben*], the life of treading the sacred way. Both Buber and the Buddha know that in the mystery of lived reality neither being nor nonbeing but rather the coexistence of being and not-being holds sway. There Buber and the Buddha are at one: for both, "To stand undivided over against the undivided mystery is the primal condition of wholeness" (§50r). Furthermore, the Buddha denies the nihilism of "fools," insisting humans can tread the way, which, together with Buber, he grounds in "the Unborn, Unoriginated, Uncreated, Unformed."[21] Elsewhere Buber again quotes from this Buddhist text to acknowledge the Buddha as a great master of the spiritual life: "The Buddha, the 'Awakened One,' . . . knows a genuinely divine, an 'Unborn, Unoriginated, Uncreated.' He knows it only in this wholly negative designation, and he refuses to make any assertions about it. Yet he stands related to it with his whole being. Here is neither proclamation nor worship of a deity, yet unmistakable religious reality."[22]

At this point, in faithfulness to the truth of his encounter with the Buddha, Buber identifies the differences between dialogical life and the teaching of the Buddha (§50s). The Buddha's goal, "the cessation of suffering" through release from the cycle of births, is expressed in Buddhism as an accomplishment in these terms: "Henceforth there is no return."[23] To Buber, the possibility of such "return," reincarnation, is beyond human knowledge; however, for Buber, unlike the Buddha, if there were such a return, "we would not seek to escape it but rather earnestly desire in each embodied existence [*krasse Dasein*] to express both the eternal changing *I* and the eternal unchanging *Thou*" (§50u). Like the teaching of his Western spiritual counterparts, the Buddha's teaching clearly leads to the goal of the unification of the soul,

---

21. Buber, *I and Thou*, §50r, quoting from *Nibbāna Sutta* in the Pali Canon.
22. Buber, "Religion and Philosophy," 27–28.
23. Buber, *I and Thou*, §50u, quoting from *Iti-Vuttaka Sutta* in the Pali Canon.

which includes the necessary transcending of the "thicket of opinions."[24] Yet when, according to a late Mahayana tradition, the Buddha goes on to teach transcending "the illusion of forms,"[25] he seems to disregard what for Buber is indispensable, the real world of bodily reality that is reliable because it is real. To Buber this denial of the concrete reality of the physical world is anti-dialogical because it undercuts the span linking *I* and *Thou*, the divide between Creator and creature: "Thus, [the Buddha] does not lead the unified being further toward that supreme expression of *Thou* that unification opens up to him. Rather, his innermost decision seems to go directly to the suspension of the power to say *Thou*" (§50v).

Buber concludes his interpretation of the Buddha in relation to his dialogical vision by observing that "the Buddha knows the saying of *Thou* to other human beings—his vastly superior yet deep, unmediated interaction with his disciples shows this—but he does not teach it" because the simple concrete over-againstness of being to being is alien to the universal, transcendent compassion in which "all that has become is held boundlessly in the breast."[26] Buber concludes his interpretive comments on the Buddha by acknowledging that in the depths of his silence the Buddha knows the saying of *Thou* to the primal source "based on a substantial relational event"; yet regarding this relational knowing, the Buddha once again preserves silence before his followers (§50w).

Buber next sums up his critique of unitive mysticism: "All doctrines of absorption are based on the colossal delusion that takes place when the human spirit bends back on itself [*Zurückbiegung*] . . . making the world and God into functions of the soul within the individual," whereas in truth spirit exists from the individual person outward—between the person and that which is beyond the person. Because the turn inward "necessarily shuts out the world and God," it denies relating as the meaning of spirit (§50y). It is important to note that, for Buber, "the human spirit bending back on itself," *Zurückbiegung*, is the reduction of the Other, whether the world or God or another person, to a function of the soul. This is a psychologizing, whether traditional or modern, of *Beziehung*, relating to the Other. In human existence there is always a tension between the reality of *Beziehung* and the longing for absorption: "The relation of an *I* to a *Thou* [is] the way in which the unmistakably religious of all ages have

---

24. Buber, *I and Thou*, §50v, quoting from the *Sabbasava Sutta* in the Pali Canon.

25. Here Buber is quoting a phrase from the *Surangama Sutra*—this is the one Buddhist source which Buber quotes in *I and Thou* that is not in the Pali Canon; it is a postcanonical text from later Chinese Buddhist esotericism.

26. Buber, *I and Thou*, §50w, quoting from *Karaniya Metta Sutta* in the Pali Canon.

understood their religion, even if they longed most intensely to let their *I* be mystically absorbed into that *Thou*."[27]

Buber then quotes and critiques a saying attributed to the Buddha as the epitome of this bending backward, this absorption of reality into the soul. He uses the Buddha's statement to build to his dialectical climax: "Within this my fathom-high, sensation-afflicted ascetic's body there is the world, the arising of the world, and the cessation of the world—and the way that leads to the cessation of the world."[28] Buber makes a clear distinction between one's sense of self and the being of the world, then shows how they are interdependent yet bound up with each other in a dialogical relation. To him the arising and the cessation of the world occur neither within nor outside the person. They are a "continual happening which both correlates with and is dependent on me, my life, my decision, my work, and my service" (§50dd). This continual happening is embedded in creation, revelation, and redemption as Buber understands them, as we shall see.

At this point, Buber again presents the alternatives—the turn inward versus the turn to engagement with the world—and calls for his readers to believe in the world, engage with it, give themselves to it, love it, embrace it: "All depends on how I allow my stance toward the world to develop." Those who merely "experience" their attitude live in their heads; whatever happens within them,

> they do not even ripple the skin of the world. . . . Only those who believe in the world engage with the world itself and, giving themselves to it, they cannot remain godless. Let us love the actual world, the world that will never let itself be extinguished, that which is simply actual in all of its horror—let us dare to embrace it with the arms of our spirit—and our hands will touch the hands that sustain it. (§50dd)

Elsewhere Buber wrote of his own love for the world:

> Bound to the world, receiving and acting, man stands directly before God—not "man" rather, but this particular man, you, I. This very teaching of man's being bound with the world in the sight of God, the reply of Hasidism to Spinoza, was the one element through which Hasidism so overpoweringly entered into my life. I early had a premonition, indeed, no matter how I rejected it, that I was inescapably destined to love the world.[29]

---

27. Buber, "Religion and Modern," 79.
28. Buber, *I and Thou*, §50z, quoting from *Rohitassa Sutta* in the Pali Canon.
29. Buber, "Spinoza," 99.

"I know nothing of a world or a 'worldly life' that can separate a person from God" (§50ee). Buber links such conceptions that separate the world from God with alienation and the reduction of things to the *It*-world. He then reasserts the core of dialogical spirituality, "the one thing needful," which is the continually unifying life: "Whoever actually goes out to encounter the world, goes out to God. Self-gathering into unity and going out, both in authenticity, the one-and-the-other, which is the One, is the needful" (§50ee).

Thus, in his critique of unitive mysticism, the doctrines of absorption, Buber acknowledges what they achieve as far as they go, the unification of the self. Yet he criticizes them for not advocating the second step in the two-step spiritual process: the going outward in embracing the world. Together, the two moments constitute the spiritual wholeness Buber testifies to, "the one thing needful." In spite of the practices of some of their followers, both Jesus and the Buddha embody this twofold wholeness. Buber's critique here is motivated by his sense of the need to reinstate the primacy of the dialogical in the face of the persistent human tendency toward the unitive.

Buber follows up his critiques of mystical absorption by reasserting the primacy of "lived reality" which he introduced at the end of his critique of Hinduism (§50o–p). He considers the "religious" situation of the human being, one's being there in the Presence, in terms of its essential and unresolvable contradictions, and asserts the only way to address these contradictions is to live them (§51a–b). They must be lived, only lived, and always again, ever new, unforeseeably, unanticipatedly, unadvisedly lived. Buber shows that Kant's conceptual resolution of the antinomy of freedom and necessity, for example, is conceptual but cannot be relegated to mere thought worlds: "I must live in the actuality of my standing-before-God where 'I have been given over' and 'It depends on me' are both true at the same time. I cannot use a theological construct to resolve this; I must take it upon myself to live both in one, and in this being lived, they are one" (§51b).

6. *I-Thou* and the Three Spheres of the Created Order

Following upon this critique of the doctrines of absorption, the next five sections (§§52–56) continue to develop the contrast between the finite *I-Thou* and the divine-human encounter. Buber now relates the levels of the *I-Thou* encounter within the order of creation to the encounter between the human *I* and the eternal *Thou*. In the first five paragraphs of §55, Buber essentially repeats §9 to remind readers of the distinction of the three spheres of the created order which he first presented there.³⁰ He now builds on that analysis in these sections. The first sphere is "life with nature," where the relation approaches the threshold of language (§55b). This realm includes animals, plants, and minerals. The second sphere is the interhuman realm in which relation takes expression in language between persons (§55c). The third sphere is life with spiritual-intellectual entities in which relation is beyond language yet creates language to express it—as image or metaphor (§55d). This third sphere, the sphere of creativity, includes the mental, spiritual, and aesthetic realms.³¹ The one Presence streams through all three spheres; it transcends each yet is immanent to all (§55f).

Buber's division of the order of things into domains is based on their relation to language, "the word," which has special meaning in his thought, going back to the primal divine act of speech as constituting the ontology of creation: elsewhere Buber points out the Hasidic axiom that "the whole world is only a word out of the mouth of God."³² The parallel between Buber's analysis of spheres or domains and the great chain of being stands out. Buber's concept of the divine act of creation, a fundament of his thought, functions as the dividing line or gulf that sets off the Creator, the eternal *Thou*, as radically different from mutable creatures. On the one side of this great divide is the transcendent Creator, which Buber sometimes refers to as "the metacosmic"; on the other side is "the cosmic," "the world," "the All" (§§27g, 54e, and 61l). This divide is central for Buber and he makes it central by referring to Meister Eckhart, "the greatest of all . . . Christian mystics and scholastics," in his discussion of modern thought: "Eckhart [places] above the *esse est Deus* ["Being is God"], as the higher truth, the sentence, '*Est enim (Deus) super esse et ens*. ["There is one (God) above existence and being"]'"³³

The traditional "chain of being" or *scala naturae* is hierarchical, with God at the top, inert matter at the bottom, and humanity in the middle.³⁴ Buber does not refer explicitly to this schema and he clearly differentiates his thought from that of the Platonic tradition, which turns the chain of being into a multiple-level hierarchy of value. By contrast, Buber's hierarchy

---

30. That first presentation of the three spheres is discussed in chapter 7 above, pages 155–60.

31. The importance of this third sphere to Buber is grounded in his intensive, lifelong involvement with the arts, which had been a focus of his university studies.

32. Buber, "My Way to Hasidism," 49.

33. Buber, "Religion and Modern Thinking," 73–74, quoting from Eckhart's Latin sermon on Rom 8:18–23. Eckhart, *Meister Eckhart: Selected Treatises and Sermons*, 192–95.

34. See Lovejoy, *Great Chain of Being*.

of value, *I-Thou* vs. *I-It*, runs athwart this aspect of the traditional concept of the great chain of being. Yet both place humanity in the middle of the order of things and see mankind as a partaker in both higher and lower realms. Elsewhere Buber relates this "double nature of humanity" to our twofold reality as dialogical beings:

> The double nature of humanity, as the being that is both brought forth from "below" and sent from "above," results in the duality of his basic characteristics.... As a being who is sent, the person exists over against the existing being before which he is placed. As a being who is brought forth, he finds himself beside all existing beings in the world, beside which he is set. The first of these categories has its living reality in the relation *I-Thou*, the second has its reality in the relation *I-It*.[35]

The sphere of life with nature

Buber invokes experiences with his cat to reflect on the nature of the dialectical relation between humans and animals. For him the animal's power of looking is a kind of speaking. Its eyes convey the mystery of becoming. As language, the gaze of the cat expresses its creaturely stirring between the simple being-there of plants and the spirit's cosmic venture which is human existence. Buber calls the mystery so expressed in the cat's gaze "the stammering of nature at the first touch of spirit" (§52a).

Buber characterizes his meeting the gaze of his cat as a brief dialogical encounter. The mutual gaze is in part something that domesticated animals have received from humans. The cat's gaze is dialogical—"language"—in that for this moment of contact it conveys amazement and questioning in response to "the streaming human gaze in the total reality of its power to relate" (§52b). The quality that stands out in these encounters is their evanescence: "For the interval of a glance, the world of *Thou* had shone out from the depths; now it has already died back into the *It*-world" (§52c). The encounter came and went so suddenly that it left Buber questioning: "Had the burden of the *It*-world really been removed from the animal and from me for the interval of a glance?" (§52d). Buber's reflection on his encounter with the animal realm here, similar to his encounters with a horse as a young man,[36] left him with a sense of the mystery of the dialogue which lies below the threshold of language.

---

35. Buber, "God and the Spirit of Man," 127 (translation modified).
36. Buber, "Autobiographical Fragments," 10.

Buber's reflections on the gaze of animals lead him to exclamations in response to the relative fragility of breaking through to *Thou*: "How powerful is the continuum of the *It*-world and how delicate the manifestations of the *Thou*! There is so much that can never break through the crust of thinghood!" (§52e–f).

This difficulty and the evanescence of breaking through to *Thou* leads him to recall an earlier moment in which self-awareness came to him as a result of taking up and gazing at a piece of mica during a hike. In dialogical fashion he breaks off his exposition to directly address the piece of stone in these words: "Oh shiny piece, which upon gazing at you I once first understood that *I* is not something within me—with you nevertheless I was merely bound up within myself; only in me, not between me and you, it then took place" (§52f). Mica, the gleaming semitransparent mineral, becomes the counterpart to the *I* in Buber's act of gazing at it. His apostrophe to it shows the two sides of self-awareness, remembered first as the occasion of his negative discovery of what the *I* is not—because it is constituted in part by "the between" in the encounter. But he also knows that, as experience, his encounter with the mica was a matter of his self-involvement and that this discovery in itself took place solely within him. Upon reflection, precipitated by his examination of the mica, his awareness, like the mica, manifested its translucent layers.

In a passage at the climax of *Daniel*, Buber had earlier given a more extensive account of this same encounter with the mica. This earlier account expands on it:

> I walked on the road one dim morning, saw a piece of mica lying there, picked it up, and looked at it for a long time. The day was no longer dim: so much light was caught by the stone. And suddenly, as I looked away, I realized that while looking at it I had known nothing of "object" and "subject"; as I looked, the piece of mica and "I" had been one; as I looked, I had tasted unity. I looked at it again, but unity did not return. Then something flamed up inside me as if I were about to create. I closed my eyes, I concentrated my strength, I entered into an association with my object, I raised the piece of mica into the realm of that which has being. And then . . . only then did I feel: *I*; only then was *I*. He that had looked had not yet been *I*; only this, this unified being [*dieses Verbundene*] bore the name like a crown. Now I felt about this former unity as a marble image might feel about the block from which it has been carved: it was the undifferentiated, while *I* was the unification.[37]

---

37. Buber, *Daniel*, 148–52, translated in Kaufmann, *I and Thou*, 146n9; compare

To paraphrase this crucial passage, at first he looked at the mica and, losing all sense of subject and object, felt a sense of oneness with it. Then he looked away and reflected. This reflection yielded an awareness of this oneness he had experienced. When he returned his gaze to the mica, the unity did not return. At this point an inner striving, a "flaming up inside"—that is, the feeling of an emerging act of creating—prompted him to close his eyes and with an intense effort of self-concentration to raise that piece of mica "into the realm of that which has being," into its reality as *Thou*. In this moment of knowing the mica as *Thou*, he knew himself as *I*. This knowing was affirming and empowering: he "bore it like a crown." At this point in his exposition, he alluded to the analogy of the uncarved log, a central metaphorical figure in the *Tao Te Ching*,[38] which for him becomes carved into a marble image, perhaps recalling the image of the human life task in Plotinus as well.[39] Buber took up self-differentiation as the *I* of *I-Thou* from "unity" as the move from uncarved log to image. The process of transformation from the uncarved log to the image parallels the move in this moment of encounter with the mica and in his lived experience from undifferentiated primal unity to the emergence of the person in dialogue.

This comparison of the two passages allows us to see how Buber refers to a definitive experience of nature at two different moments about ten years apart. The reference in *I and Thou* condenses the earlier account to make a simple point about the ephemeral character of human *I-Thou* encounters with nature. The account in *Daniel*, on the other hand, expands to present the relationship between the encounter and the constitution of the *I* of *I-Thou* by means of that encounter.

Similarly, in §10, Buber writes in the first person to use his relating to a tree as his example of the reality of *I-Thou* in the natural realm. He first describes his taking the tree as an *It* (§10b–g), then he describes being drawn into an *I-Thou* relation to the tree as he attentively contemplates it so "will and grace are joined" and he is "seized by the power of exclusiveness" and all of the tree's qualities are united into the event of encounter (§10h–k). He then declares that with nature, as with interhuman intercourse, "the meaning of the relation is reciprocity": "What I encounter is neither the soul of a tree nor a dryad, but the tree itself" (§10l–m). Again, as with the encounter with the mica, Buber described an encounter with a tree in *Daniel*. There Daniel invited his interlocutor to contemplate a particular tree, a stone

---

Kierkegaard, *Either/Or*, 2:181.

38. *Pu*, "the uncarved log," in Lao Tzu, *Tao Te Ching,*, 28.12.
39. Plotinus, *Enneads,* 1.6.9.

pine.[40] Daniel described the act of objectifying the tree as *It*, then he urged a transforming move—toward unity, toward the tree as the archetypal "tree of eternal life." His directions to his companion in the dialogue give a sense of the process of shifting from the tree as *It* to the tree as *Thou*:

> Now seek to draw near to this stone pine itself . . . with all your directed power, receive the tree, surrender yourself to it . . . in the transformation your direction is with you, and through it you experience the tree so that you attain in it to the unity. For it draws you back into yourself; the transformation clears away like a fog; and around your direction a being forms itself, the tree, so that you experience its unity, the unity. Already it is transplanted out of the earth of space into the earth of the soul, already it tells its secret to your heart, already you perceive the mystery of the real.[41]

Here the unity of the person comes with a fleeting uniting with the tree as *Thou*, as was the case with the mica. Buber's preface to *Daniel* had focused on an oak tree and his contact with it by means of his walking stick as an image of genuine dialogue.[42] In a late essay, Buber used another encounter, this one with a linden tree, to argue that that encounter completes the reality of Kant's *Ding an sich*: "Of *x* we know what Kant points out to us as the thing in itself, namely, that it is. Kant would say: 'And nothing more,' but we who live today must add: 'And that the existent meets us.'"[43]

Buber continues in *I and Thou* by contrasting the fragility, the ephemeral nature, of human contact with entities in nature, those below the threshold of human language, with the immutability of the eternal *Thou* who is always over against the human person. Right away he highlights the contingent nature of the human side of the divine-human relation. In this "one all-embracing relation," potential and actual being are the same. By its nature the eternal *Thou* never ceases to be *Thou* for us. In the contingency, the contradictions, the fickleness of lived experience, one knows God, yet also knows "distance from God and the anguish of the aridity in the troubled heart." Yet in the midst of this chaos the person never knows "the loss of the Presence" because "it is only we who are not always there" (§52g). With this, he echoes the Augustinian axiom that marks the wandering soul, "You were with me, but I was not with you."[44] This contrast

40. Buber, *Daniel*, 54.
41. Buber, *Daniel*, 54.
42. Buber, *Daniel*, 47.
43. Buber, "Man and His Image-Work," 157.
44. Augustine, *Confessions*, 10.37.

between the constant divine Presence and the human turning away was summed up in his observation that if we think that we hear nothing in the ongoing divine-human dialogue, it is because "long ago we ourselves have put wax in our own ears."[45]

Buber cites Dante to show how poetry makes exceptional use of language by using the third-person form, *colui* in Italian, as a dialogical reference to the eternal *Thou*. Thus, the poet's references to Beatrice (love for whom transformed his spiritual life, in his prose work, *La Vita Nuova*), show the back and forth between *Thou* and *It* characteristic of a human relationship. Yet for Dante's exalted visionary references to the eternal *Thou* he uses *Colui*, "That One," in a figurative sense thirty-four times in the first canto of the *Paradiso*—for example, "The glory of *that One* who moves all / Pervades the universe . . . ."[46] Buber argues that poetry by its more formal nature—the constraints of poetic form and voice—requires this circumlocution, this use of the third person, as a metaphoric reference to God, whereas the intimacy, potential, and openness of *Thou* would be more appropriate in prose or prayer.

In §53, Buber explains implications of the difference between a person's actual relations in the created order and a person's relation with God, the perfect, pure relation. Relations between creatures are exclusive and subject to the in-breaking of the Other, whereas the relation with God is at once both exclusive and all-inclusive. Similarly, relations between creatures involve mutual recognition across differences although each only imperfectly knows the other, while with God one's "limited knowing opens out into a boundlessly being known" (§53b). Finally, creaturely relations involve a swaying back and forth between the chrysalis state of becoming and the butterfly state of being, while God, the eternal *Thou*, is unchanging because God is unconditioned: it is we who bring the eternal *Thou* into the *It*-world and its discourse and this is our continual human task.

In the next section Buber focuses on the relation with the eternal *Thou* as the alternative to the space-time continuum of the *It*-world. Once again he invokes the powerful metaphor of the center: the eternal *Thou* becomes the center where all the lines of creaturely *I-Thou* relations intersect. The "pure relation" between *I* and the eternal *Thou* opens up a distinct mode of existence. We are no longer "given up to alienation from the world and the de-realization of the *I*" (§54d). The act of *teshuvah*, turning oneself again to the center and rerecognizing it, is an "act of being." It allows our "submerged power of relation to arise anew as the wave which causes all

---

45. Buber, "Postscript," 137 (translation modified).
46. Dante, *Paradiso*, 1.1 (translation mine, emphasis added).

the spheres of relation to crest in living streams and renew the world." By it the isolated moments of all our relations bind together into "the continuity of the world of *Thou*" (§54d). The vision culminates in speculation on the Tao-like primal duality of relation that runs through "timeless creation" as the primal mystery (§54e).

The reality of relation, whether below, at, or above the verbal, consists of all acts of relation through which any given thing becomes present to us, and in each case we move toward, address, and are encompassed by the eternal *Thou*, the one radiant Presence linking all things and radiating through them (§55a–f).

At any level, we humans can extract the finite *Thou* from Presence, reducing our life with nature to "the physical world," our interpersonal life to "society," our spiritual-aesthetic life to "the noetic"—yet this reduction, a kind of reification, deflates the meaning of each and removes their transparency, reducing them to functions and flattening them into dull surfaces. This reduction makes them dull and empty even when we dress them up by using exalted terms such as "cosmos," "*eros*," or "*logos*." Yet we truly have cosmos, *eros*, or *logos* only when we relate to them as *Thou*: "There is Cosmos for us when the universe becomes our home, with a holy hearth where we offer sacrifice; there is Eros for us when others become for us images of the eternal and community with them is revealed; there is Logos for us when we address the mystery with work in the service of the spirit" (§55i).

Whether transverbal as "the inviting silence of the spirit," verbal as "the loving speech of persons," or subverbal as "the eloquent muteness of the creature," "all are portals leading into the presence of the Word." The word here is the plenitude of meaning in the relation between the *I* and the eternal *Thou*. When this, the perfect encounter, takes place, the spheres of relation are all "united into one great portal of real life and we no longer know through which we have entered" (§55j–k).

The sphere of life with other people

Buber next focuses on the interhuman sphere as "a main portal into whose all-inclusive opening the side portals lead" (§56b). In our life with other persons "language is completed in enunciation and reply . . . the moments of relation are bound together by the medium of speech in which they are immersed" (§56a). The full human reality of *I* and *Thou*, "the reality that cannot be lost," consists of the reciprocity of "beholding and being beheld, knowing and being known, loving and being loved" (§56a).

Buber turns without comment to conflated lines from the book of Genesis to provide exalted poetic imagery that expresses the meaning and implications of the interhuman *I* and *Thou*. At the climax of his exposition of the interhuman realm as the central portal to the reality of *Thou*, Buber drops in a simple unattributed quotation full of symbolism: "When a man is intimate with his wife, the longing [*Sehnsucht*] of the eternal hills wafts over them" (§56c). This sentence conflates two phrases from the book of Genesis: "The man knew Eve his wife . . ."[47] and lines from the deathbed blessing attributed to the patriarch Jacob:

> The blessings of your father surpassed
>
> The blessings of the eternal hills,
>
> The longing for the heights of the world order [*olam*].[48]

Elsewhere Buber comments on *yada*, the Hebrew word meaning "to know": "In the sentence: 'Adam knew his wife Eve,' the relationship of being to being is meant in which the real knowing of *I* and *Thou* takes place, which is unlike that of subject to object. This knowing lays the foundation for the religious world view."[49] Thus, using poetic images from Genesis, Buber directly links the knowing between Adam and Eve with the eternal *Thou*, the breath of the spirit, expressed as longing, wafting from on high. The interhuman *I* and *Thou* merges with the *I* of mortals and the eternal *Thou*. In a later section of *I and Thou*, Buber puts this idea more prosaically: "Whoever loves a woman, bringing her life to presence in his own, the *Thou* of her eyes affords him a glimpse of the radiance of the eternal *Thou*" (§58c).

Buber's reflections climax by connecting the interhuman *I* and *Thou* with the human-divine *I* and *Thou*: "one's relation with another human being is the real analogy [*Gleichnis*] of the relation with God" (§56d). This statement of the nexus of these two levels of *I* and *Thou* resonates as his central insight: "My most essential concern" came to be "the close connection of the relation to God with the relation to one's fellow human being."[50] Similarly, years later he repeated his emphasis on this connection: "The *I-Thou* relation to God and the *I-Thou* relation to one's fellow human being are at bottom related to each other."[51] Buber concludes with the observation that both the interhuman and the human-divine relation allow "genuine address to receive

---

47. Gen 4:1 (my translation); see the Buber-Rosenzweig translation.
48. Gen 49:26 (my translation); see the Buber-Rosenzweig translation.
49. Buber, "Philosophical and Religious World View," 130.
50. Buber, "Postscript," 123–24.
51. Buber, "Interrogation of Martin Buber," 99.

genuine response." The difference is "in God's response, everything, the universe [*alles, das All*] reveals itself as language" (§56d). The universe began as language—"the whole world is only a word out of the mouth of God."[52]—and here it reaches its fullness as language. Language has widened out to be much more than human words; it has been expanded to be the all-inclusive verbal and nonverbal expression of love.

> The one real God . . . is the goal and origin of all being. . . . God in all concreteness as speaker, the creation as speech: God's call into nothing and the answer of things through their coming into existence, the speech of creation enduring in the life of all creation, the life of each creature as dialogue, the world as word—to proclaim this Israel existed. It taught, it showed that the real God is the God who can be addressed because he is the God who addresses. . . . He is therefore both the boundless and nameless as well as the father who teaches His children to address Him. . . . God speaks to man in the things and beings that He sends him in life; man answers through his action in relation to just these things and beings.[53]

Here, a person's concrete, finite existence is the arena and locus of the divine-human encounter. All of the portals come together as dialogical speech, the expression of meaning. All is relational: the Creator, creation, we humans in our response and responsibility.

The sphere of creativity

Buber next alludes to the third realm, the third portal, our life with spiritual-intellectual entities—the "noetic" world, the realm of validity—which, although beyond speech, spawns human speech (§55d). Picking up on his earlier discussions of this realm (§§12, 19a, 32e–h), he links it to the *Logos* and to form [*Gestalt*[54]] and makes clear it is present for human beings when they address the mystery of existence dialogically through their exercise of form-creating imagination in creative work and service (§55i–j): "Form arises from one's encounter with the Other in the world."[55] Elsewhere he

52. Buber, "My Way to Hasidism," 49.

53. Buber, "Spinoza," 91–94.

54. The German word *Gestalt*, a key term of Buber's, can be translated "form," "figure," "pattern," or "image"; such an entity is an object of perception that has a meaning greater than the sum of its parts. The word has entered into the English language and so I keep it in translation.

55. Buber, "Postscript," 129 (my translation).

discusses the central role of artistic creativity in the creation of relational space, of cosmos as "home."[56]

The artist—whether the medium be the plastic arts, the performance arts, or the verbal arts—creates the work of art through the encounter with the Other in the world, the fundamental event of perception elevated to vision. All perception is intent on figure [*Gestalt*]. Yet, through the artist, seeing, which he calls "the first world formation," is transformed into vision, "the second figuration which is in still far higher measure . . . a personal one, and thus immeasurably manifold."[57] Artistic imagination is "discovery through figuration."[58] Consequently, "art is the realm of 'the between' which has become a form."[59]

Thus, to Buber the realm of creativity is dialogical at its core. He uses painting as an example: "Each great painter is a discoverer . . . of a view of the world in which a certain manner of seeing manifests itself that is peculiar to this painter. This [view] is a reality of relation, the product of a meeting."[60] He continues:

> When we regard the arts together, we mark that the decisive event that engenders the work of art is not the perception of a being but the vital contact with that being, an ever-renewed vital contact with it which the experience of the senses only fits in as a factor. One cannot say of this contact that it is reflected or displayed in the work: waves proceed from it that are converted in production, powers are put in motion by it through whose transformation the work arises. The artist does not hold a fragment of being up to the light: he receives from his contact with being and brings forth what has never before existed.[61]

In this way human creativity is, in its essence, dialogical. It produces meaning-bearing forms of expression.

Along with knowledge, love, and faith, art is one of the potencies by which humankind "transcends the natural and establishes the human as a unique realm of being," a bulwark against alienation.[62] The "prepersonal individual" operates in the *It*-world of "using and getting," while one who

---

56. Buber, "Man and His Image-Work," 149–65; see also "Productivity and Existence," 5–10.

57. Buber, "Man and His Image-Work," 159.

58. Buber, "Man and His Image-Work," 161.

59. Buber, "Man and His Image-Work," 165.

60. Buber, "Bergson's Concept," 84.

61. Buber, "Bergson's Concept," 84.

62. Buber, "Man and His Image-Work," 163.

has become a person is dissatisfied with this realm and longs for the perfection of relation. The artist longs "to experience and realize his relation to the substratum of sense things through figuration in the vision and in the work." The artist "does not portray the form, does not really remould it [but] drives the form into its perfection in its fully figured reality, and the whole visual or acoustic field becomes refashioned ever anew."[63] By extension, full appreciation of the artist's work is the recipient's reactivating of the *I-Thou* of the creative moment, the moment of presence. Here Buber, along with his romantic precursors, sees the creative process and receptivity to it rather than the created product as the core reality of the aesthetic realm.

7. *I and Thou*: The Role of Solitude

In §57, the interlocutor questions the role of solitude as a portal in relating to God, quoting the Mystical Prayer of Symeon the New Theologian of Byzantium, "Come Solitary One, to this solitary, for as you see I am all alone" (§57a).[64] This prayer seems to echo Plotinus's "flight of the alone to the Alone."[65] Buber begins his reply to the interlocutor by acknowledging a certain ascesis: he says it is always necessary to detach oneself from experiencing and using things, that is, absorption in the *It*-world, in order to achieve any act of relation. Yet he fine-tunes this distinction when he distinguishes between those who are attached to particular things by the desire to use them and those who are bonded with things simply because they live in terms of the power of making present. Only the latter are ready for God because they bring forth their naked human reality to encounter the divine reality.

Solitude is necessary as a space of purification to prepare for entering the Holy of Holies, for it allows us to practice introspection, to probe ourselves for our unavoidable failings, and thereby it serves as a tool that allows us to prove ourselves true. Again Buber poses an either/or, for one can use solitude as the occasion to test oneself and master oneself for what is to come. Alternatively, one can use solitude as a fortress within which to withdraw from things and simply enjoy one's own soul in internalized dialogue. This is a fall of the spirit into spirituality as an end in itself. This path leads to the ultimate abyss where under a delusion one imagines he converses with God within. Yet, as surely as God surrounds us and indwells

63. Buber, "Man and His Image-Work," 164.

64. Buber included the entire prayer in his anthology of world mysticism, *Ecstatic Confessions*, 36–42.

65. Plotinus, *Ennead*s, 6.9.11. Corrigan interprets the meaning of this phrase as focused intimacy, not self-absorbed mysticism. See Corrigan, *Reading Plotinus*, 166.

us, we never "have" God: we truly speak with God only when our inner chatter dies away to silence.[66]

Elsewhere Buber alludes again to Symeon the New Theologian where he affirms the positive side, the importance of solitude as an element of one's relation to God: "I regard it as unqualifiedly legitimate when a man again and again, in an hour of religious fervor, adoring and praying, enters into a direct, 'world-free' relation to God; and my heart understands as well the Byzantine composer of hymns who speaks as 'the alone to the Alone,' as also that Hasidic rabbi who, feeling himself a stranger on earth, asks God, who is also, indeed, a stranger on earth, to grant him, just for that reason, his friendship."[67]

8. Critiques: *I-Thou* vs. Scheler on Idols and *I-Thou* vs. Kierkegaard on "The Single One"

As part of his "clearing the decks," his apophatic method of ruling out everything marking the less-than-ultimate embrace of the Presence, Buber addresses the distinction between God and idols presented by Max Scheler in his book, *On the Eternal in Man* (§58). To Scheler every person necessarily holds something as an absolute value and thus as God. Once we see that what we hold to be absolute is a finite entity, we will naturally turn from that to the infinite beyond it, the infinite God. In response, Buber argues that in this method of analysis God becomes reduced to an object alongside other objects, all of which are in the *It*-world. To substitute the true object for the false object even when we use "God" as the label for the "true" object is to substitute one *It* for another and to miss the relational point.

One's relating to any given thing that occupies the throne of supreme value in one's life, thereby suppressing the Eternal, is always about using, possessing, savoring as an end in itself. It is this preoccupation with the impenetrable *It*-world that blocks out one's vision of God. Buber gives two examples of those who are bound by their commitment to the *It*-world: those taken with nationalism and those taken with possessions. Alluding to the Sermon on the Mount (Matt 6:24), Buber challenges the very idea of possession: "Can the servant of Mammon say *Thou* to his money? And how can he even know where to start with God if he does not understand how to say *Thou*? He cannot serve two masters—not even one after the other; he

---

66. Compare §32b: "Only silence before the *Thou* . . . silent waiting . . . permits one to take one's stand with it in the reserve where the spirit is not manifest, but *is*" (emphasis added).

67. Buber, "Interrogation of Martin Buber," 86.

must first learn to serve in a different way" (§58c). This learning to serve "in a different way" is making the breakthrough from *I-It* to *I-Thou*, the breakthrough which cannot be taught.

The *Thou*-saying relation continually reopens us to the vision of God. The only way for those "possessed by possession" to return to God is *teshuvah*, a change not merely of one's goal but also of one's stance. This change requires much more than merely redirecting one's possessiveness; it requires being awakened and becoming raised up in relatedness. Buber gives two examples of those who successfully turn to God in this radical way: the lover who lives with the beloved as *Thou* and the one who serves a people, "glowing in boundless destiny." In each case giving oneself is one's act of addressing God (§58c).

Buber uses stern language to bring home his point: the person who keeps himself in the mode of possessing and simply switches from calling on entities that are demonically distorted for him to calling on the name of God is a blasphemer—the idol may have crashed behind the altar but any such altar is a desecrated place and can only hold unholy sacrifices. Buber concludes by taking up the "woe" form of declamation that goes all the way back through the prophets to Amos: "Woe to the possessed who think that they possess God!" (§58d).

In §58, Buber, in dialogical fashion, addresses Scheler's modernistic psychologizing, a form of encapsulating the *I*. He thereby transcends it by using it to throw the *I-Thou* relation with the eternal *Thou* into relief. Similarly, in §59, Buber addresses Kierkegaard's modernistic internalizing of spirituality. In this instance, Buber opposes what he sees as Kierkegaard's Marcionite tendency to denigrate the created order by his extreme emphasis on inwardness. Kierkegaard sums this up in his concepts of "religious man" and the "single, isolated, detached person before God" (§59b, Kierkegaard's technical terms). Buber contrasts this "single one" with the person who takes his stand in the creation in continuing dialogue with the Creator.

Kierkegaard characterizes the religious individual as the one who has no need for the world or for beings in the world because he has his absolute relation with God. With Buber's sketch of this figure and his reply, he foreshadows the deeper dialogical response to Kierkegaard that he later undertook as "The Question to the Single One" in 1936. Buber introduces Kierkegaard's opposition between the individual and the crowd by identifying Kierkegaard's crowd as a modern social construct that is part of the alienated *It*-world. To this Buber opposes his notion of community, the social reality that arises through the same power that is at work in the relation between the individual person and God. Buber uses the metaphor of rivers pouring into the sea to explain the interplay of human community and the divine-human relation. The divine-human relation is "the universal relation into which all the rivers pour, yet without exhausting their waters" (§59a). Buber may have drawn this metaphor from Plotinus, who wrote: "Imagine a fountainhead that has no source outside itself; it gives itself to all the rivers, yet is never exhausted by what they take, but remains always integrally as it was,"[68] or from Jeremiah, who wrote: "My people . . . abandoned me, the source of living water, in order to dig pits for themselves, flawed pits which do not hold water."[69] Yet ultimately to divide life into a juxtaposition of God and the *It*-world is to reduce God to an *It* as well: to pray simply to ease one's burdens is to let words fall into the ear of the void. The "atheist" who "out of the night and yearning cries out to the Nameless from his garret window" is more godly than this.[70]

Buber traces Kierkegaard's categories: "ethical" man is caught up in the tension between "is" and "ought" in the actual world. Kierkegaard's contrasting category, "religious" man, has gone on to side with God in the tension between God and the world. In Buber's reading of Kierkegaard this means an exclusive focus on God in which the person has surrendered his own will so "every 'ought' is dissolved in unconditional Being and the world as such has lost its validity" (§59b). The person simply performs the "nothingness" of action. Kierkegaard's "nothingness" of action is a void; this is something very different from the "non-action" or *wu-wei* which Buber values. Thus, we see how in Buber's view Kierkegaard's emphasis on inwardness undercuts the reality of the creation.

Buber concludes his response to Kierkegaard here by presenting his alternative vision, his vision of "hallowing this life." In true dialogical response to his predecessor, he rises to some of the most exalted images in *I and Thou*. He first invokes one of his central spiritual concepts, "stepping before the Face" (§59b), which he introduced in his exposition of "the supreme encounter" at the heart of *I and Thou*. There the person "puts aside all that he has, and steps naked before the Face" (§36e). Here again Buber uses *Angesicht* ("face," "countenance"), following the Hebrew *panim*, which is used in the Bible as a metaphor for the divine countenance, the grace- and favor-bestowing Presence.

To step before the Face is to enter into the fullness of the Presence in everything: "the world becomes wholly present and illuminated by eternity and the person can say *Thou* to the Being of all beings in one word. Here there is no more tension between the world and God but only the One

---

68. Plotinus, *Enneads*, 3.8.10.
69. Jer 2:13 (my translation); see the Buber-Rosenzweig translation.
70. Compare the parallel passage at §45c.

Reality [*die Eine Wirklichkeit*]" (§59b). The calm strength of such turning "changes the face of the earth" (§36j); this life is later called "life face to face with God in the One Reality" (§61q). In this stance, a person knows the eternal *Thou* in the world and the world in the eternal *Thou*. This unification of God and world is the task of hallowing to which humankind is called. Buber characterizes this life in clear terms: the person before the Face is not, as Kierkegaard seems to say, "freed from responsibility—he has simply exchanged the anguish of the finite, the exploration of effects, for the momentum of the infinite"; he has taken up "the power of loving responsibility for the whole unexplorable world-process"; he has found his "deep involvement with the world in the face of God" (§59b). The course of such a person's life will be "to practice decision in the depths of spontaneity, serene decision ever again for right action—until he dies" (§59b). In contrast with Kierkegaard's "solitary one," Buber's "person before the Face" takes action not as a negation but as "purposive, commissioned, needed, and belonging to Creation" (§59b). This action does not impose itself on the world but rather "grows from it as if it were non-action," *wu-wei* (§59b).

9. *I-Thou*: The Dialogical Nature of Revelation

Buber brings his exposition of spirituality to a climax in §60. Here he recalls his earlier introduction of *teshuvah*, "turning" or "returning," in his core presentation of the supreme encounter at the center of *I and Thou* (§36c). He now combines it with "stepping before the Face" with which he has just concluded his response to Kierkegaard. This "moment of supreme encounter" is the moment of theophany or revelation and Buber alludes to three biblical theophanies in the course of his discussion—that to Elijah in the "voice of whispering silence" in the cave (1 Kgs 19:11–18), that to Jacob in his wrestling with the stranger by the brook (Gen 32:24–30), and that to Moses in the burning bush on the mountainside (Exod 3:1—4:17). The whole section can be read as a commentary on the moment of transformation that Buber himself underwent as his spiritual initiation at the age of twenty-six in the spiritual encounter that was evoked by the testament of the Baal-Shem-Tov (discussed in ch. 2).

Section 60 is framed by the dialogical pattern of question-and-answer. It begins with the question, "What is the eternal primal phenomenon, present in the here and now, which we call revelation?" (§60a). The question presents revelation as timeless, yet "here and now," a primal phenomenon that is continually present. Then Buber explains the nature of revelation and concludes with an iteration of the same words, "This is the eternal revelation that is present here and now" (§60d). In between he presents his understanding of the nature of revelation. At the outset he equates revelation with "the being-act of pure relation," "the moment of supreme encounter" (§60a). Then he underscores that a person who emerges from that moment is not the same as he was when he entered it. In other words, because it is a dialogical moment, the moment of supreme encounter transforms the person:

> The person who emerges from the being-act of pure relation has now in his being a something more, something that has increased in him, of which he did not know before and whose origin he cannot rightly identify.... we receive what we did not have before, and we receive it in such a way that *we know it has been given to us.* (§60a, my emphasis)

That is to say, "the being-act of pure relation," the *I-Thou* encounter with the eternal *Thou*, precipitates a change of being of the human *I*, the development of something new and more. This development involves both the act of receiving something and a new knowing that that something has been given. Yet what that something is and what its origin is remain hidden in mystery.

Here Buber refers to lines from the prophet Isaiah to illuminate the nature of the encounter as dialogue: "Those who wait for God"—those who fully open themselves to the divine Presence—"exchange vital powers"—receive in exchange a new strength. That is, those who put themselves in the Presence participate in reciprocity with God.[71] Buber then delineates the nature of what it is that a person receives in the supreme encounter. Building on these lines from Isaiah, he specifies that what is transmitted is "a Presence, a Presence as strength" (§60b). Contrary to the common assumption that revelation is the imparting of content-knowledge, he insists that this transmission involves no "content" (§60b). He next explains each of three elements of the transmission.

First, there is "binding in relation," "the whole fullness of actual reciprocity, of being taken up, of being bound up in relation" (§60b). The person cannot explain how this binding comes about and he finds out it makes life harder—because it is heavier with meaning.[72] This being "taken up" and "being bound" [*Verbundensein*] is used three times in this sentence, implicitly invoking the *Akedah*, the patriarch Abraham's binding of his son Isaac for sacrifice, which stands out in Jewish tradition as the archetypal moment of

---

71. Isa 40:31 (my translation); see the Buber-Rosenzweig translation.
72. See Buber, "Jewish Religiosity," 92.

sacrifice and revelation. In it Abraham and Isaac offer their all and in exchange they receive a bounty of renewed life and blessing from God.[73]

Second, the revelation provides the ineffable confirmation of the meaning: "Meaning is assured. Nothing, nothing can any more be meaningless. The question of the meaning of life is no longer there. But if it were there, it would not have to be answered" (§60b). With this deep, intuited affirmation, the human being *knows*—to the point that the question of meaning itself fades away. The person is not able to articulate it, to express it in concepts or images. It is "a meaning that one cannot translate"[74]—and yet it is more deeply certain to him than the perceptions of his own senses.

Third, Buber uses question-and-answer to introduce the element of divine intentionality into the relation: "What does the at once revealed and concealed meaning intend with us, desire from us? Not to be explained . . . it simply wills to be enacted by us" (§60b). "Meaning . . . enacted . . .": the noetic takes expression as the kinetic; that is, revelation is the expression of transcendent meaning in human action. To allude to the archetypal moments of revelation of Elijah and Moses and Jacob mentioned above, the "whispering voice of silence" kindles the recipient like the burning bush and takes expression in the torque of the wrestling body. Thus, the meaning of the encounter carries the intentionality of confirmation, of being put to the proof, into our this-worldly action. The recipient becomes the witness, the means through which the meaning intends to be borne into the world. There is a radical Kierkegaardian dimension to this intentionality. Unlike the notion of the universally valid tablets of the law raised up over everyone's head, the meaning of revelation is such that it can only be proven true by each person in his acting "in the *singleness* of his being and in the *singleness* of his life" (§60b). Thus, meaning manifested by one's acting in the world is "the strength that the human being receives" in the encounter-as-revelation.[75] "Singleness" [*Einzigkeit*], meaning uniqueness or oneness, underscoring the reality of the "lived concrete" as a single, singular, unified reality, is repeated for emphasis.

No predetermined behavior can lead us to the supreme encounter—"The one thing needful is acceptance of the Presence" (§60b, repeating §46f). We enter into the encounter having nothing but *Thou* on our lips and this stance continues in a deeper sense beyond the moment of the encounter.

> The mystery—that before which we live, in which we live, out of and into which we live—always remains what it was. It has

---

73. Gen 22:1–19; Buber uses the image of binding and sacrifice again in §61i, this time adding the image of a cosmic altar.

74. Buber, "Religion as Presence," 115.

75. Buber, "Religion as Presence," 116 (emphasis added).

> simply become present to us and with its presence has made itself known to us as wholeness [*Heil*]. We have "known" it, but we have no knowledge of it that reduces or softens its mysteriousness.... We cannot go to others with what we have received and say, "This is what must be known; this is what must be done." We can only go forth and confirm its truth in our action. It is not that we "should"—we simply can—we simply must. (§60c)

The sense of mystery always remains at the core of human existence and of every encounter. Yet, in the moment of supreme encounter, our sense of ourselves in relation to the eternal *Thou* is transformed.

Buber concludes by returning to the terms with which he began this reflection on "the eternally present revelation," stamping it with iterations of his personal credo: "I know of no revelation, I believe in none that is not the same in its primal phenomena as this" (§60d). God does not name himself or define himself to human beings. Here Buber translates the Tetragrammaton, the Hebrew name of God revealed to Moses in the great theophany at the burning bush in Exodus 3:14—Hebrew ʼeh·yeh ʼă·šer ʼeh·yeh, often translated as "I AM WHO I AM"—to make his point: "I am present such as I am present" [*ich bin da als der ich da bin*].[76] Buber's term "the eternal *Thou*" carries the power of this founding Hebrew revelation of God as dialogical into the rest of Buber's discourse. Buber continues with a culminating progression of seemingly tautological affirmations: "The Revealing One is the Revealing One. Being is present, nothing more. The eternal fountainhead of strength streams forth, the eternal touch of presence awaits, the eternal voice sounds forth, nothing more" (§60d).

Elsewhere Buber used the language of smelting as metaphors to distinguish between revelation itself and what proceeds from it: "The divine is a fire that melts again the human ore, but what is produced is not of the nature of the fire."[77] Here the divine fire transforms the human substance in the encounter. This encounter itself is totally hidden away in mystery. Thus, there is a gap between the encounter and what the person takes away from it: the fire is neither the ore nor the transformed, refined metal. The person comes away from the encounter with signs of transformation that point toward the fire. The human mind "experiences the unconditional as that great something that is counterposed against it, as the *Thou* as such. By creating symbols, the mind comprehends what is in itself incomprehensible."[78] There is an irreducible gap between the encounter and the mental equipment of

---

76. See Buber, *Moses*, 51–55 for Buber's full discussion of this primal revelation.
77. Buber, "Fragments on Revelation," 114.
78. Buber, "Herut," 150.

the one who undergoes it. Thus, the symbols the person finds to "speak" of the encounter with the divine both hide or cover it over and yet also point back to it. Therefore, we cannot distinguish between the human and the divine element in any given representation of the encounter. As a result, we continually live in the paradoxical tension of faith: "There is no security against the necessity of living in fear and trembling; there is nothing else than the certainty that we live in the revelation."[79] Yet "we win the foundation for an at once faithful and critical attitude" when we continually take up the "task of opening ourselves as we are, as a whole and a unity, to the continual revelation that can make all, all things and all events, in history and in our lives, into its signs."[80] Accordingly, history is "the plunge bath in which genuine authority must ever again purify itself, seek to free itself from the slag of the human which has become perceptible as such . . . through self-refining."[81] That is, within each new circumstance, we must turn from the interpretive response to the fire itself.

In sum, the Eternal is eternally present, yet known as Presence by humans in "openings," in exalted moments of surrender to dialogue between the human and the divine. Such encounters direct the recipients' life actions because they have given them a new footing, a new sense of agency and intensity in the world. These characteristics recall Buber's own sense during his moment of supreme encounter, his spiritual initiation (as discussed in ch. 2). According to his description of that encounter, he sensed himself as the Hasidic soul. He received a new awareness, grasping the *imago Dei* in himself "as action, as becoming, as task." He sensed it as "primal reality," opening itself to him then and there. He then understood in a new way, perceiving this new awareness as a "summons to proclaim it to the world."[82]

Buber repeatedly worked to show the continuity between the great theophanies of the biblical narrative and the less dramatic experiences of encounter that people undergo in modern times. He explored this link in a lecture on the Hebrew Scriptures entitled "People Today and the Jewish Bible" (1926). In that lecture Buber emphasized the otherness of the eternal *Thou* by discarding the use of psychologies of the unconscious to explain the nature of revelation. For him, the Presence, the manifestation of the divine Other as dialogical reality, is what links Buber's own spiritual initiation both with modern people and with the classic biblical accounts of revelation.

---

79. Buber, "Fragments on Revelation," 114.

80. Buber, "Fragments on Revelation," 114.

81. Buber, "Fragments on Revelation," 114–15; as we have seen, this self-refining or straining forward, *epektasis*, was developed by Gregory of Nyssa, *Life of Moses*; see page 223 above.

82. Buber, "My Way to Hasidism," 58.

"Sometimes we have a small experience that because it is of the same kind as the great experiences can provide access to them."[83] Then he repeats the central dynamic of his exposition in §60a: "It happens that we unexpectedly notice a perception in us that was missing just a moment before, and whose origin nothing can enable us to trace."[84] Quoting from Nietsche's *Ecce Homo* here as he does in §60a, he expands his description to emphasize the otherness of the divine Other in the dialogical moment of revelation and links it to all revelations, great and small:

> What has happened to me was precisely otherness, was being taken hold of by something other. Nietzsche puts it with great fidelity: "we take and do not ask who it is that gives." I, however, think that what matters above all is to take with precisely the knowledge that *someone is giving*. Those who take what is given to them and do not experience the giver's giving do not really receive, and the gift becomes a theft. If we do experience the giving, however, we know by experience that revelation exists. And we set off on the path on which our life and the world's life will make themselves known by signs—on the path, that is, that leads in. On that path we will have the great experiences that are analogous to these small ones.[85]

Buber linked what he called such small, quiet moments of revelation together with the great, classical ones by characterizing the recipient in the process of revelation: "For people today, natural events are the bearers of revelation, and revelation happens where the witness of the event who has endured the event experiences its revelatory content and lets himself be told what the voice speaking in the event wished to say to him, to the witness, to his manner of being, his life, his sense of obligation."[86] The recipient is the one who "endures" or undergoes the event, "lets himself be told what . . . the event wished to say to him," and becomes shaped by it in "his manner of being, his life, his sense of obligation." In this process, the recipient is transformed from being a witness *of* revelation into bearing witness *to* it. Buber had earlier linked the greater and lesser revelations in his lectures on "Religion as Presence": "The revelations that the religions invoke . . . the forceful revelations in contrast to those quiet ones that occur here and now and at all times everywhere . . . are nothing else than the eternal revelation. It is not

---

83. Buber, "People Today," 11 (translation modified).
84. Buber, "People Today," 11 (translation modified).
85. Buber, "People Today," 10–11.
86. Buber, "People Today," 10.

the voice that is different, but the hearer and the moment."[87] In all of the moments of revelation, whether great or small, the purpose remains the same: the transformation of the recipient and thereby the world in the dialogical encounter between the human person and the eternal *Thou*.

10. *I-Thou* vs. *I-It* as the Dynamic Factor in the History of Religions

Buber begins the final section of *I and Thou* by reasserting the mystery of the eternal *Thou* in a series of apophatic statements, negations of the qualities people typically associate with God. These negations are necessary because the eternal *Thou* cannot be reduced to an *It* (§61a). Any attempt at measurement, or even to claim that it is measureless, categories such as bounded and boundless, qualities such as aseity or omniscience, experiences, concepts—all are irrelevant to the eternal *Thou*. Like the Tao, it can be found neither in nor beyond the world. Even to say "I believe that it exists" is to miss the point. All we have is the bare, unadorned *Thou*, the eternally Nameless Being.[88]

Buber next addresses the human side of the divine-human encounter (§61b). In spite of this fundamental irreducible reality of the *Thou*, it is our nature as human beings to continually reduce the eternal *Thou* to an entity in our *It*-world, to a thing to make the *Thou* manageable. As a result there is a continual fundamental tension between the reality of the eternal *Thou* and our human reality. This tension is expressed in history as a spiral path that swings back and forth between movement toward and movement away from the living God. We previously encountered this description of history as a "cosmic gyre" in chapter 8 above.[89] We move toward the eternal *Thou* when the Presence and the power are received in revelation and away from the eternal *Thou* when we subtly shift from the Presence to the forms of the Presence, when we reduce our focus on it to its contents, to symbolic objects and concepts or practices. This cycle of dissolution and renewed breakthrough to Presence is the course of the human way through time.

Once Buber establishes these framing concepts, in dialogical fashion, he raises a question, the answer to which concludes *I and Thou*. He asks, "How is it that the Presence and the power we humans receive in revelation become changed into 'content,' . . . formed into the articulated body of knowledge and the prescribed behavior of the religions?" (§61c). The

---

87. Buber, "Religion as Presence," 125.
88. Buber, "People Today," 4.
89. Pages 174–78.

answer comes in two parts, the "outer psychic layer"—the individual human being considered apart from his historical context—and the "inner factual layer"—the primal phenomenon of religion in historical context. The former is discussed in the next seven paragraphs (§61e–k) and the latter in the final thirteen paragraphs (§61l–w).

The outer psychic layer: the individual human being

Buber first traces the historical process of human straying from the immediacy of the divine-human encounter (§61e–g). In the divine-human encounter the ineffable confirmation of meaning comes as a grace to humans. It is a natural human desire to extend this confirmation across time, to own it as something at hand that can provide security in every moment of life. As a result, people turn God into an object of belief. "At first belief... completes the acts of relation but gradually it replaces [the person's] continually renewed being-movement towards concentration and going out to the relation with the calm reassurance of a believed-in *It*" (§61f). That is, the authentic trust that is maintained in spite of all by the one who, struggling, knows both distance from and nearness to God, gives way to the inauthentic "secure certainty" of the one who presumes to be a beneficiary of divine protection, "since he believes that there is One who will not let anything happen to him" (§61f). Similarly, the life-structure of pure relation is not enough to satisfy the thirst for extension in space, representation in community, which leads to making God into a cult object. The cult at first completes the unmediated saying of *Thou* in living prayer, linking it with the senses, but then gradually replaces it. Eventually one's act of being in relating to the eternal *Thou* without rules gives way to the structured worship and the established precepts of organized religion.

Next Buber affirms the alternative to such straying, the path to the genuine fulfillment of human desire in relation (§61h–j). The only means of raising pure relation to constancy is to embody it in the very fabric of one's human life. Relating cannot be stored up but only continually put to the proof in action, repeatedly poured out into living it in holy insecurity. A person honors the relation to God in which he has participated only when he realizes God anew each day, according to his power and the measure of that day (§61h). The pure relation is fulfilled when the beings of daily encounter are raised up to become *Thou*. When, as a result, a human life is penetrated by such relating, it takes on a radiant constancy. With this constancy the moments of supreme encounter become more than mere flashes in the darkness—they take on a steady presence like that of the rising moon on a clear, starlit night (§61h). Similarly, constancy in space comes about when the radial lines of relation extend from each person to the eternal *Thou* as their center. The common relation with the center completes the circle and undergirds authentic existence in community. When time and space are so bound in relation, in a relation-oriented life of wholeness, in a community unified by a common center, a human cosmos arises around the invisible altar, grasped in the spirit out of the cosmic stuff of the eon.

At this point Buber lays down a caveat about the pitfalls of spirituality which apply both to those who are God-obsessed and to those who are self-absorbed (§61j). The encounter with God comes upon a person for one purpose: that the person may confirm meaning in the world:

> All revelation is summons and sending. Yet again and again, instead of making the revelation real in the world, the recipient turns back to be absorbed in the Revealer. Such a person no longer stands over against God, for he has reduced God to an *It* and himself to God-talk. Like the person bent on self-realization (who may very well be the same God-obsessed soul), instead of letting the gift take its full effect, he wants to reflect on the Giver (or the experience)—and misses both. (§61j)

The one who goes forth in response to the sending has God continually before him, whether he is aware of the Presence or not (§61k). The deeper the fulfilling, the stronger and steadier God's nearness. Such a person cannot directly concern himself with God but he can continually converse with God. In the irony of false appearances, the God-obsessed, in spite of their apparent turning to the primal source, actually belong to the world's movement of turning away from it; by contrast, the apparent turning away of the one who simply goes to fulfill his mission is actually an expression of the world's movement toward God.

The inner factual layer: the cosmic-historical gyre

Buber's reflections widen to cosmic scope in the final paragraphs as he brings *I and Thou* to completion (§61l–w). He presents two meta-cosmic movements, expansion away into self-being and *teshuvah*, return to relation with the eternal *Thou*. The history of the human relation to God traces the blending and separating, the struggle and coming to terms of these two tendencies in a pattern of oscillation which Buber represents with the image of the chrysalis and the butterfly: in returning, the word is born on earth; in moving away, it takes on a chrysalis form as religion; then again in return it goes out to the *Thou*, giving birth to itself again with new wings (§61l).

Buber then repeats what he has asserted elsewhere concerning revelations.[90] "The powerful revelations which stand as the origins of great communities and thus function as the turning-points ushering in new eras are nothing other than the eternal revelation" (§61n). As early as in "The Teaching of the Tao," Buber identified Lao Tzu, the Buddha, and Jesus as spiritual founders who brought about such new spiritual eras. The powerful revelations that came to these masters, as to the prophets of Israel and to the *zaddik*s of Hasidism, are of the same quality as the numberless quiet revelations that will never become visible on the great stage of human history. In each case, revelation is an eternal reality, taking place at all times and everywhere.

Buber repeatedly works to present the relationship between the divine and the human in revelation. As an *I-Thou* moment, revelation is always a blend of the divine impetus and the power of the human person (§61p). The *I-Thou* encounter between God and the human recipient is itself the revelation. Buber uses strong verbs to describe a great revelation as transformation and to name its by-product, a new *Gestalt*: "the revelation *breaks forth*, *seizes* the whole of the elemental human stuff, *melts* it *down*, and thereby *produces* a new *Gestalt*, a new *Gestalt* of God in the world" (§61o, emphasis added). The breaking forth is the event of revelation, the encounter. The event transforms the recipient by seizing him as a whole being and melting down his substance. What comes forth as a product of this encounter as revelation is the recipient's production of a *Gestalt*, "a new *Gestalt* of God in the world" (§61o). Buber emphasizes this product by repeating the expression "a new *Gestalt*."

Like the gap between the mystic and his message in Buber's early essay "Ecstasy and Confession" (1909), there is an immeasurable gap between the actual encounter and that which the recipient takes away from it to share with his community. That by-product has been smelted in the person of the recipient and thus bears the marks of his humanity. Buber here and subsequently uses the word *Gestalt* (figure, image, or symbol) or word (message, meaning) for this by-product of the encounter. Whether the visual *Gestalt* or the auditory word, Buber uses the one or the other as a synecdoche for the human construct that the recipient brings away from the divine-human encounter. *Teshuvah*, turning, allows one to interpret the *Gestalt* or word afresh as a culturally transmitted window or

---

90. Especially §32h and §36h, discussed in chapters 6 and 8 above, pages 135–36 and 176–80.

opening into the original divine-human encounter. Word, auditory event, as a term for the product of revelation, involves "voice." Each voice has a distinguishing timbre, marking the unique concrete presence of its agent. In Walter Ong's analysis of the phenomenology of sensory experience, he points out that sound demarcates immediate present action in a way that sight does not.[91] Buber makes hearing the "voice" of revelation the goal of the reading of the Hebrew Bible that comes about for the reader through *teshuvah*: "There is no other going back but the turning around that turns us about our own axis until we reach, not an earlier stretch of our path, but the path on which we can hear the voice!"[92]

Buber focuses on the role of the recipient in the revelatory event. The divine-human encounter as revelation impacts its recipient as transformation: "Revelation does not pour into the world through its recipient as through a funnel: it comes upon him, it seizes his whole being in all of its suchness, and fuses with it" (§61n). Here Buber dismisses the analogy of the funnel or microphone, where the revelation would be some "thing" that merely passes through its recipient as a passive vessel and emerges into the world as divine contents. The smelting metaphor here, as elsewhere,[93] indicates the radical nature of the blending action. The impact of the encounter between the human and the divine is an amalgam of the two; its by-product is a *Gestalt* or image.

Buber's translation of the revelation to Eliphaz in the book of Job illuminates the blending of and the difference between the elements in the divine-human encounter as he sees it: "One stands, I do not perceive his appearance, as a *Gestalt* confronting my eyes; what I hear is silence and voice."[94] The eternal *Thou* is present to the human *I* in the theophanic encounter both as visible form and invisible presence, both as silence and voice. The Presence itself, the *Thou*, is neither visible nor audible, yet, through the faculties of the human *I*, it takes on both form and voice. At the moment of unification, of the recipient's unconditionally offering his will to the Unconditional, the human being perceives the Presence and in this act of apperception forms an image. The image, like the burning bush in the great initial theophany to Moses,[95] is an element in the world

---

91. Ong, "World as View," 634–47.
92. Buber, "People Today," 21.
93. Pages 252 and 261.
94. Job 4:16 (my translation); see the Buber-Rosenzweig translation. See Buber, "Religion as Presence," 65; Kaufmann, *I and Thou*, 60–61; §12c.
95. Exod 3:1–6.

of human perception, yet at the same time it is shot through, irradiated by the invisible Presence.

Buber shifts to an anatomical metaphor to clarify the role of the human recipient, who in all of his "suchness" bears the revelation into human reality: "The person who is the 'mouth' is just this and not a loudspeaker, not an instrument, but an organ, an organ that sounds forth according to its own nature, and this sounding forth means *modifying* [the revelation]" (§61n, emphasis original). The recipient as "mouth" changes the revelation: he embodies it in his own bodily life. That is, the revelation takes on the qualities of his own natural voice. The lived reality of the recipient embodies both the human and the divine elements. Thus, both the revelation and the cultural milieu of the recipient become transformed in his life-expression as the recipient.

Buber points out the cultural-historical aspect of this blending of human and divine elements: "In the course of history, in the evolution of human substance, continually new realms of the world and of the spirit are raised up to form, called to divine form. Continually new realms become the place of theophany" (§61p). The examples he presented in "The Teaching of the Tao" show this embodied cultural element in specific terms: with Lao Tzu in the Chinese context we have the teaching of the Tao, with the Buddha in the Indian context we have the teaching of release [*Erlösung*], and with Jesus among the prophets in the Hebrew context we have the teaching of the kingdom of God.[96]

In "Herut: On Youth and Religion" Buber confirms the cultural evolution of revelations: "The founders of new religions . . . stand in fact within the continuity of their people's creation of symbols and images. . . . All religious founding, all genuine personal religion is merely the discovery and raising up of an ancient treasure, the unveiling and freeing of a folk-religion that has grown beneath the surface."[97] Yet at the same time, and in keeping with his claim for progressive revelation (§61p), there is creative change as the symbols, working as receptacles of theophany, evolve from age to age: "In mankind's great ages, the Divine, in invisible becoming, outgrows old symbolisms and blossoms forth in new ones."[98] He traces the ongoing evolution of human symbols for God as he sees it:

> The symbol becomes ever more internalized, moves ever closer to the heart, and is ever more deeply submerged in life itself. . . .
> It is not God who changes, only theophany—the manifestation

---

96. Buber, "Commentary," 75–80.
97. Buber, "Herut," 155–56.
98. Buber, "Herut," 150.

of the Divine in man's symbol-creating mind—until no symbol is adequate any longer, and none is needed; and life itself, in the miracle of man's being with man, becomes a symbol—until God is truly present when one man clasps the hand of another.[99]

This evolution is a kind of apophatic process across the course of history.

Buber grounds the human perception of God in the twofold spiritual-material reality of traditional Jewish anthropology: "Although we earthbound creatures never behold God apart from the world but simply behold the world in God, nevertheless through the gaze of the spirit we continually construct God's *Gestalt*" (§61p). Humans cannot see God; we see the world in its beauty and power as "in" God; yet through its gaze the human spirit continually constructs and reconstructs the divine *Gestalt*. This continual activity of imagining the divine in an image or *Gestalt* is part of our nature which in itself is neither good nor evil. Yet a danger arises when we take one of these our images of God for God *se ipsum*, or for the revelation of God.

"The one who is sent forth by the revelation carries an image of God in his eyes, in the eyes of his spirit, in the real visual power of the spirit. The spirit responds [to the eternal *Thou*] through its image-bestowing gaze" (§61p). The recipients of revelation, whether the revelation is great or small, imagine. The spirit of the one sent forth by the revelation responds to the divine *Thou* through its image-forming gaze: "It is not in the brain that divine images originate, but in the eye, in the undiluted human being's faculty of vision which is touched by a ray of the Divine. . . . Divine images originate . . . on that plane of man's being which is open to that which is other than man, though it can reflect it only in human terms."[100] It is this gaze and the image or *Gestalt* of God that it forms that is the human response to the divine *Thou* and that the recipient carries into his life in community. Because the *Gestalt* is the human response to the encounter with the divine, it points to the divine element while being totally human. Using Buber's smelting analogy, the divine fire transforms the ore, the human material, and the refined metal, the human image-forming response, is all the community has access to.

The *Gestalt* is the product that comes out of the smelting process which is revelation; it becomes "a new *Gestalt* of God in the world" (§61o). "Accordingly, in the repeated transforming of the elemental human material in the course of history, ever new realms of the world of the spirit are raised up to *Gestalt*, called to divine *Gestalt*. Ever new spheres become the locus of

---

99. Buber, "Herut," 150–51.
100. Buber, "Preface to the 1923 Edition," 7.

theophany" (§61p). That is, in revelation, the ancient treasure continually finds new forms of expression.

Again, in "Herut," Buber expresses the same skein of issues he takes up here in concluding *I and Thou*. There the dialogical "between" of *I* and *Thou* in the divine-human encounter is the dynamic reality: it is the "primary reality . . . constituted by the Unconditional's effect upon the human mind, which, sustained by the forces of his own vision, unflinchingly faces the Supreme Power."[101] The dialogical encounter between the human *I* and the eternal *Thou* is the revelation: the human mind "experiences the Unconditional as that great something that is counterposed against it, as the *Thou* as such."[102] Here, as in §61p, the human response to the intensity of the divine Presence in this encounter is image-bestowing: "By creating symbols, the mind comprehends what is incomprehensible; thus in symbol and adage, the illimitable God reveals himself to the human mind, which gathers the flowing universal currents into the receptacle of an affirmation."[103] Here too we have the coming together of the human and the divine that is the dialogical encounter. In this encounter the incomprehensible *Thou* gains form through the response of the relating *I*. The resulting symbol or word is what the receptive mind creatively gathers or constitutes as the receptacle or vessel of meaning; the symbol becomes the affirmation of the Presence. Thus, *Gestalt* and word, "forms which the Unconditional itself initiates within the human mind,"[104] function as tools or instruments bearing the mark of the *I-Thou* relation.

In "Herut," Buber also shows how the encounter between the human *I* and the eternal *Thou* involves both receptive and active elements on the human side: "The Unconditional affects a person when he lets his whole being be gripped by it, be utterly shaken and transformed by it, and when he responds to it with his whole being: with his mind, by perceiving the symbols of the Divine; with his soul, by his love of the All; with his will, by his standing the test of active life."[105] These words express the inner reality of *teshuvah*, the totality and unity of the person who turns in surrender to the eternal *Thou*. In terms of receptivity, "he lets his whole being be gripped by it, be utterly shaken and transformed by it." On the active side, he responds with his whole being. Buber's words echo the great commandment of Deuteronomy 6—in dialogical fashion, the Mosaic discourse bids

---

101. Buber, "Herut," 150.
102. Buber, "Herut," 150.
103. Buber, "Herut," 150.
104. Buber, "Herut," 150 (translation modified).
105. Buber, "Herut," 153.

all who hear the great proclamation, the *shema*, "He our God, He [is] One," to "therefore love Him your God, with all your heart, with all your soul, with all your might."[106] So Buber: with the mind, one loves God through the symbols that point to him; with the soul, one loves "the All," both the Creator and the creation; with the will, one [107]"stands the test of active life," affirming the reality of the divine Presence in the concreteness of everyday life, thereby hallowing this world.

Because a *Gestalt* is an amalgam of *Thou* and *It*, the *Gestalt* can be reduced to use as an object in doctrine and ritual, yet because it always carries a kernel of relation that lives on like an ember beneath the ashes, at any point it can also be rekindled as a vessel of Presence through the power of relating that it signifies (§61q). Thus, the function of the *Gestalt* as a vessel is only one side of the twofold pattern, the path [*Bahn*] toward God and the counter-path away from God, which constitutes human history (§61u).

Buber outlines a historical pattern of movement from breakthrough to suppression to renewed breakthrough as the eternal and eternally present word, the expression of revelation, courses through time. To begin with, in the maturing of an age, the suppressed and buried authentic element of the human spirit comes to such a subterranean urgency and tension of readiness that a mere touch of the One who will touch it causes it to break forth anew. The revelation which then becomes manifest seizes the whole ready element in its readiness, recasts it, and forms a *Gestalt*, a new form of God in the world. The word at the fountainhead of such an age has manifested its essence as revelation. It appears as substance-bearing and through it the bond between the *I* and the world is renewed.

In the ensuing era, when the tradition that springs from it is alive and growing and the word is effective in the life of its forms and it rules, the accord between the *I* and the world is sustained. But later, in an age of decline, the expansion of religious tradition suppresses return, removing the *Gestalt* from encounter with the divine. Then the countenance goes out of the *Gestalt* as if extinguished: its lips grow cold, its hands hang down, God knows it no more, and the universal dwelling place built around its altar, the human cosmos, collapses. As part of the destruction of their reality, the people who live through this process are oblivious to it (§61r). In this way the word is reduced to mere common currency and the tradition has lost its vital relation to the eternal *Thou*. Derealization and alienation between *I* and world become the norm. Fatalism comes to full term—and all is suspended in the

---

106. Deut 6:4–5 (my translation); see the Buber-Rosenzweig translation.
107. Buber, "Herut," 153 (translation modified).

great hiatus, the preparing silence that is readiness for a new outbreaking of the spirit (§61s–v).

To Buber prayer serves as the bellwether of "the path or counter-path of the eternally present Word in history" (§61u). For this, Buber distinguishes between true prayer and degenerate prayer. In a late essay Buber defines the essence of true prayer: it is "that speech of man to God which, whatever else is asked, ultimately asks for the manifestation of the divine Presence, for this Presence's becoming dialogically perceivable. The single presupposition of a genuine state of prayer is thus the readiness of the whole person for this Presence, simply turned-towardness, unreserved spontaneity."[108] As an act of dialogue between the human *I* and the divine *Thou*, true prayer unites and purifies belief and cult by bringing them into living relation with the eternal *Thou*. When true prayer is alive in a religion, it attests to its true life. When prayer degenerates to less-than-real dialogue with the divine *Thou*, this is a sign that religion has degenerated. Prayer degenerates when the power to relate becomes more and more buried under objectification—and it becomes ever more difficult to say *Thou* to the Eternal with one's whole, undivided being (61q). Yet true prayer remains as the power of relating, the seed fire that can flame up into Presence. Whenever *Thou* is said with the whole being as prayer, one breaks out of false security once again into the venture of the infinite.

With the modern subject-object split the subjectivism side reduces God to the soul, which is a false setting free, while the objectivism side reduces God to an object, a false nailing down of the divine reality. Either God as soul or God as object can become the goal of an *Ersatz* quest, a deviation from the way of reality, the narrow ridge of holy insecurity. By contrast, life before the Face is life in the one reality. The person who goes out to this life before the Face avoids both such "subjectivism" and such "objectivism," choosing and living with reality over appearances (§61q). In every age there are those who at some point "must break out of the false security of objectified religion into the venture of the infinite"—they know they must emerge from "beneath the temple dome which has been constructed over the community and go forth under open skies," like Abraham before them, "to live in the ultimate solitude. . . . Their impulse [is toward] life before the Face, life in the One Reality, and the person who continually goes out to this relating determines to live in true being, the way of reality, thereby saving himself from illusory objectivity before it has destroyed his own truth" (§61q).

I and Thou concludes with an allusion to Buber's sustained critique of modernity as it sketches his exalted vision of history, history as the way

---

108. Buber, "God and the Spirit of Man," 126 (translation modified).

[*Bahn*] of redemption.[109] The way of history is no circle. As fate becomes more oppressive with each new eon, turning becomes more dramatic: the theophany comes ever closer, it approaches in the realm between beings, it approaches as the kingdom hidden in the center, in "the between." History is the mystery of coming: even as corruption becomes ever more pervasive, the turning becomes ever more fundamental. Yet the transformation which for us is turning, *teshuvah*—from God's side—this is the advancing course of redemption (§61w).

11. Conclusion

I and Thou is a manifesto of the dialogical that embodies the dialogical. Like a piece of mica, the book is a fragment that contains many layers. And like that piece of mica, its reader can hold it up for scrutiny, close his or her eyes, and sense the self on the threshold of true dialogue.[110]

I and Thou presents an essentially Hebraic vision, the vision of an epic *agon*, the great human struggle between the pull of the *It*-world and the call to life in dialogue that runs through human history.

This struggle is also a key to the layout of the book, illuminating the nature of our twofold human reality in part one, lying at the base of things in the critique of modernity in part two, and creeping into the core of human spirituality in part three. The realm of *I-It* entices us again and again with the persistence of the pull of gravity. The *It*-world is like the role of water for the swimmer. Water is the swimmer's obstacle, but it also is the means of the swimmer's propulsion. The good swimmer is adept at managing both of these functions and thereby moving through the water toward a goal. Similarly, the person who seriously enters the life of dialogue learns to take his or her lapses into the *It*-world as points of departure for further advance in the life of dialogue.

---

109. According to Friedman, while Ronald Gregor Smith was translating *I and Thou* into English, Buber wrote Smith that he used the word "*die Bahn* in *I and Thou* with Lao Tzu's Tao in mind" (*Martin Buber's Life and Work*, 1:431). Yet Smith translated *Bahn* as "way" in §36h and as "course" in §61u and §61w.

110. Buber's encounter with a piece of mica is discussed above in this chapter, pages 237–238.

Chapter 10

The Open Challenge

THIS BOOK HAS BEEN about approaching Buber anew in a new generation, now after almost a century since he originally penned *I and Thou*. As we look at where this exploration has taken us, it can be summed up in three moments: locating Buber in his time and ours, taking in his central message of dialogical presence, and hearing his prophetic voice.

1. Locating Buber's Timely Task

Buber is hard to pin down as a philosopher, a theological thinker, a spiritual master for the simple reason that his thinking takes us to the most elusive, most evanescent of places: "the between." A crucial element of Buber's dialogical philosophy, "the between" is the climactic focus of his inaugural anthropological lectures at the Hebrew University in 1938. For Buber "the between" is the realm "on the narrow ridge where *I* and *Thou* meet."[1] It can be used as a rich metaphor for our understanding of Buber's life and work. If we consider "the between" as a temporal metaphor, it points to transition, change, contingency, the moment of encounter in the flux of time. It is "the flight of the note" within the movement which is the larger symphony, the universal process (§28d). We have examined several moments of encounter in Buber's life and times and the tensions inherent within them. Here we briefly highlight three broader cultural moments that form the backdrop within which his dialogical vision evolved: Buber's sense of the *galut*, "exile," condition of the Jewish people, his stance between tradition and modernity, and his concept of the position of Judaism as the gateway between Eastern and Western cultures.

---

1. Buber, "What is Man?," 204.

If we turn to Buber's own words from a series of annual lectures to a Zionist student group in Prague from 1909 to 1912 for guidance, we can begin to locate him between the condition of *galut*-alienation and that of *shalom*-homecoming. *Galut* is the Hebrew term for the dispersion forced upon the Jews by the Roman army in 70 CE. This event penetrated down to the very foundations of Jewish existence. It has a world-historical impact: "This event split Judaism's history in two, in a manner that probably never happened before or since to any other people."[2] It also had a decisive cultural-spiritual impact on the development of Judaism: in this violent moment "its absolute and its relative life [were] sundered"[3] and the Jews became an "uprooted people." Their forced removal from their homeland in Israel created their unique position in the world, and their ongoing condition as a people became defined by perpetual exile. Buber reflected deeply on this condition as early as his student years when he participated in the Zionist movement that was developing at that time. Early on he wrote of *galut* as the condition of uprooted Judaism, of degradation, decline, and uncertainty, which threw the people into "the unspeakable torment of everyday living, the longest and most painful martyrdom ever suffered by any people on earth."[4]

In an essay at the turn of the century, he wrote of the need for Jewish cultural and spiritual renewal in terms of *galut*: "We want to free ourselves from the bonds of *galut*. . . . we need more than anything else to cleanse ourselves from the inner *galut*."[5] At that time he compared the need for Jewish renewal to that of the Italians of the early Renaissance, calling fellow Jews "to connect with the great *Urzeit* [primal time] of our people . . . to grasp the hands of our forefathers across the eons."[6] This theme of *galut*-decline and the need for spiritual renewal lay at the heart of his own spiritual initiation a few years later. According to his own account, when he first was awakened to the spirit of Hasidism, "the primally Jewish came over me, flowering to newly conscious expression in the darkness of *exile*."[7] With these words Buber explicitly made *galut* the context of his own spiritual awakening.

Galut continued to be a defining theme for Buber after that awakening. In Prague in 1910, he referred to the nearly two millennia since the expulsion from Israel as "the Age of Exile" which "expelled us from the

2. Buber, "Spirit of the Orient and Judaism," 71.
3. Buber, "Renewal of Judaism," 53.
4. Buber, "Judaism and Mankind," 30.
5. Buber, "Land of the Jews," 207.
6. Buber, "Land of the Jews," 207.
7. Buber, "My Way to Hasidism," 59 (emphasis added).

very core of our existence" and called upon his audience to choose between being *galut* Jews and being primal Jews [*Urjuden*].[8] Where the *galut* Jew suffers from the marginalization, the watering down of the heritage, and the loss of identity that come with the condition of exile, the primal Jew plumbs to the depths to find, reclaim, and celebrate the wellsprings of the ancient heritage that he shares with his own people going back to biblical times. Throughout his life Buber continued to characterize *galut* as a distortion of Judaism and to call for renewal through a return to the wholeness at the heart of the Jewish heritage.

By 1909, Buber wrote at length about *galut* as the condition of exile that separates the Jew from his homeland, his native language, and his native way of life, thus functioning as the condition that fundamentally divides the Jewish soul.[9] He pointed out that in exile, a person's innermost identity stands perpetually at odds with his situation. In this hiatus the individual person himself becomes divided.[10] Such an individual has the distinctive task to become aware of the circumstantial and inner tension and to decide how to live in the face of it. Given Buber's intense awareness of the *galut* condition, it is no coincidence that Deutero-Isaiah, who underwent the Babylonian *galut* of biblical times, had a central place in Buber's thinking. Aharon Shoishar, a friend of Buber's in Jerusalem, claimed Buber "sometimes considered Isaiah his best friend."[11] It is clear from Buber's analysis of *galut* and his call for renewal that for him "homecoming" or renewal can take place as a transformative event within the condition of physical *galut*. For Buber, the returning, renewal, and reclaiming evoked by his long, hard look at *galut* motivated and shaped his lifelong projects to articulate the dialogical and to make Hasidism and the Hebrew Scriptures accessible to modern people.

A second "between" that helps to locate Buber in retrospect is his position between tradition and modernity. Buber was clear about where he stood in this regard and articulated this stance. In a retrospective essay written in 1957, titled "Hasidism and Modern Man," Buber placed himself squarely between the origins of the Hasidic movement in the life of the Baal-Shem-Tov (1700–1760) and the present of his own lifetime. He explicitly stated the ontological breadth of his dialogical vision: that "the claim of existence itself" led him to see "human life as the possibility of a

---

8. Buber, "Judaism and Mankind," 29, 31.
9. Buber, "Judaism and the Jews," 16–21.
10. Buber, "Judaism and the Jews," 18.
11. Quoted in Friedman, *Martin Buber's Life and Work*, 2:269.

dialogue with being." Then he linked his own dialogue with being to the Hasidic way of life he had so deeply studied, for it

> was involved in a mysterious manner in the task that had claimed me. I could not become a Hasid. It would have been an impermissible masquerading had I taken on the Hasidic manner of life—I who had a wholly other relation to Jewish tradition.... It was necessary to take into my own existence as much as I actually could of what had been truly exemplified for me there, of the realization of that dialogue with being.[12]

It was clear to Buber that he was no clone of the original *zaddik*s: he followed in the path of his grandfather as a post-Enlightenment interpreter of his heritage. Thus, in his decades of work on Hasidic texts Buber saw himself as a mediator between the *zaddiks* of the pre-Enlightenment Hasidic movement of the eighteenth century and the people of modern Western culture. Even more so, in his decades of translating the Hebrew Scriptures into German, he saw himself as mediating between the ancient roots of his tradition and modern Western sensibilities. These two life-projects can be taken as two strands in his overall task to bring enduring core values of the past to present-day humanity. In *I and Thou* this mediating of past and present manifests itself in his critique of modernity for allowing the realm of I-It to mushroom and to dominate modern life, and in his call to *teshuvah*, to the turning that can open us anew to the realm of *Thou*.

When Buber wrote in 1957 of his project to acquaint the West with Hasidism, he claimed it was the core of Hasidism itself which motivated him to testify to that "great reality of faith" which its narratives conveyed to him: "There was something that commanded me, yes, which even took hold of me as an instrument at its disposal .... It was something that hid itself in Hasidism and would, or rather should, go out into the world. To help it do this I was not unsuited."[13] That something was the spiritual kernel of Hasidism which was hidden beneath its unrefined cultural husk. This testimonial statement recalls Buber's account of his spiritual awakening in which "the primally Jewish opened up to" him [*das Urjüdisches ging mir da auf*] in his envisioning of "man's being created in the image of God as deed, as becoming, as task."[14] That is, when he envisioned the image of "the perfect man,"[15] in that moment he "became aware of the summons to proclaim it to

---

12. Buber, "Hasidism and Modern Man," 24.
13. Buber, "Hasidism and Modern Man," 22.
14. Buber, "My Way to Hasidism," 59.
15. *Der vollkommene Mensch*—"the fully realized, whole person" (Avnon, *Martin Buber*, 83).

the world."[16] Accordingly, it became his task to make that which was hidden, "the kernel of this [Hasidic] life," visible through his portrayal of it as "at once reality and teaching" in his retelling of the "legendary anecdotes," the teaching stories of the Hasidic tradition.[17]

A third "between" that helps to locate Buber's thought is his position between East and West. In his fourth annual lecture in Prague in 1912, he identified all Asian spiritual traditions as having a single spiritual core, one that came to full articulation in the Axial Period.[18] He characterized this common spirituality by contrasting it with the orientation of the European cultural complex that came later:[19] through an extensive discussion Buber developed his claim that the sensory European type ultimately found its apotheosis in the drive toward form, whereas the contrasting kinetic Asian type exalted process over form.[20] Buber then identified Judaism as a manifestation of process-orientation, the Asian side of this typology—even if Judaism was "the smallest and youngest" of its strands.[21] Although he put Judaism within the Asian orbit, he acknowledged that it "settled along the spatial divide between Orient and Occident and [blossomed] forth at the temporal divide between the flowering of the Orient and the flowering of the Occident."[22] He then baldly asserted: "All that I have said about the Oriental is especially true of the Jew."[23]

To Buber, European cultures have from their beginnings lacked the spiritual depth of Asia: "None of the great religious teachings originated in the Occident."[24] The West merely "received and reworked what the Orient had to offer."[25] Europe's spiritual geniuses have merely "received, supported, proclaimed" the teachings of Asia—"and even the greatest of them, Eckhart, is but a late emissary of the oriental master."[26] He then pointed out what has been missing from within the cultures of Europe:

16. Buber, "My Way to Hasidism," 59.

17. Buber, "Hasidism and Modern Man," 25–27. It is worth noting that "kernel" and "husk" were used in a similar way by Rudolf Bultmann in his *New Testament and Theology* at about this time to characterize his project of "demythologizing" biblical stories to make their import more accessible to modern people.

18. Buber, "Spirit of the Orient and Judaism," 56–57.

19. Buber, "Spirit of the Orient and Judaism," 57.

20. Buber, "Spirit of the Orient and Judaism," 57–62.

21. Buber, "Spirit of the Orient and Judaism," 62–63.

22. Buber, "Spirit of the Orient and Judaism," 63.

23. Buber, "Spirit of the Orient and Judaism," 64.

24. Buber, "Spirit of the Orient and Judaism," 68.

25. Buber, "Spirit of the Orient and Judaism," 68.

26. Buber, "Spirit of the Orient and Judaism," 68.

> What is it that Europe lacks, of which it is forever in need and which it can never generate out of its own resources? . . . What it lacks is the pristine knowledge of the meaning of authentic life, the innate certitude that "One thing above all is needed." It is this that is creatively enduring in the great Oriental teachings, and in them alone.[27]

That is, Europe lacks what Asia has provided—the teaching of "the one thing needful," the global theonomous imperative.

Here Buber confirmed what he had claimed in his Prague lecture three years earlier regarding Judaism's pivotal role, that of bringing Eastern spirituality to the unenlightened West: in "the great Jews" of biblical times "the great idea of Asia became exemplary for the Occident—the Asia of boundlessness and of holy unity, the Asia of Lao Tsu and of Buddha, which is the Asia of Moses and of the Isaiahs, of Jesus and of Paul."[28] "In the great, the eternal moments of Jewish history . . . Judaism was the Orient's apostle to mankind."[29]

Buber concluded the body of his lecture on the spirit of the Orient and Judaism with the warning that the present time is "the era of the Asiatic crisis": Asia is losing its great spiritual traditions in the seemingly unstoppable process of Westernization. He then called for "a searching of our souls, a turning inward, a return," and presented the Jewish people, the people exiled from Western Asia to the post-Roman Mediterranean and to Europe, as the means of that renewal: "For this world-historical mission, Europe has at its disposal a mediating people that has acquired all the wisdom and all the skills of the Occident without losing its original Oriental character, a people called to link Orient and Occident in fruitful reciprocity, just as it is perhaps called to fuse the spirit of the East and the West in a new teaching."[30]

In the final words of his lecture, Buber echoed and extended Deutero-Isaiah's eschatological vision, that of Jerusalem as the holy city on the sacred mountain mediating the spiritual intercourse of the human race. According to the great concluding vision of Isaiah,

> In order that all tribes and tongues come and see my glory,
>
> I will establish a sign among them . . .
>
> Then let all of your brethren come home from all the nations . . .

---

27. Buber, "Spirit of the Orient and Judaism," 68–69.
28. Buber, "Judaism and Mankind," 29.
29. Buber, "Judaism and Mankind," 33.
30. Buber, "Spirit of the Orient and Judaism," 78.

Here to the mountain of my holiness, to Jerusalem!³¹

Buber's concluding words carry this great Isaianic theme forward: "Jerusalem still is—and today more than ever—what it was considered to be in antiquity: the gateway of the nations. Here is the timeless passageway between Orient and Occident.... Today Jerusalem is the gateway of the nations in an even more profound, broader, more threatening and more promising sense than before."³²

Lest the views expressed in Buber's speech of 1912 be dismissed as early speculations that were superseded by the later development of his thinking, we should consider an essay of 1951 that reasserts this very vision of Asian spirituality and of Judaism's distinctive pivotal role in the global development of that spirituality. In "Religion and Ethics" Buber wrote, "Twice in the history of mankind . . . there has been an attempt to bind the radical distinction between good and evil to the Absolute."³³ The first of these attempts was the spread of a teaching consisting of "a universal continuity of meaning" across China, India, Iran, and Greece. Buber concluded that all these versions of the teaching "complete one another as if they stood together in one book."³⁴ When this broad dissemination of the teaching of transcendent values across Asia began to erode through the emergence of skepticism, it was completed and superseded by a second great expression of transcendent values: the birth and development of Hebrew religion.³⁵ The impetus of this second historical phenomenon "extends into our own time."³⁶ Again, in his late summative essay, "Interpreting Hasidism," Buber made a similar claim: "The central truth of Judaism and Hasidism . . . has its origin in the immovable central existence of values that in the history of the human spirit and in the uniqueness of every great religion has again and again given rise to those basic attitudes concerning the authentic way of man."³⁷

These elements of Buber's cultural position—in exile, between tradition and modernity, and between Eastern and Western cultures, each in its own way implying the past of origins, the present of the modern condition, and the future of eschatological hope—are the great cultural-historical realities that provide the dramatic setting for his dialogical vision and message, to which we now turn.

31. Isa 66:18–20 (my translation); see the Buber-Rosenzweig translation.
32. Buber, "Spirit of the Orient and Judaism," 78.
33. Buber, "Religion and Ethics," 99.
34. Buber, "Religion and Ethics," 100.
35. Buber, "Religion and Ethics," 103.
36. Buber, "Religion and Ethics," 108.
37. Buber, "Interpreting Hasidism," 221.

2. Focusing on Buber's Message: The Dialogical Core

For Buber the core of spirituality is the continual encounter between the human being in his lived experience and the eternal *Thou*. The eternal *Thou* is met when the person, with his whole being and within the present totality of his circumstances, chooses openness to, affirms an absolute commitment to, the eternal *Thou* as the Absolute, the one priority. This dialogical core extends out to the whole of life and to all of being.

The *sine qua non* for this dialogical core is the otherness of the *Thou*. In a passage where Buber critiques Carl Jung's concept of the psyche as an all-inclusive totality, he uses explicit language to explain the absolute distinction between the self and the Other that is necessary in order for *I-Thou* relating to take place. He stresses the reality of the contact between oneself and the Other: "The actual Other who meets me meets me in such a way that my soul comes in contact with his as with something that it is not and that it cannot become. My soul does not and cannot include the Other, and yet can nonetheless approach the Other in this most real contact."[38] The completion or unification of the self which Buber describes as a blissful sense of oneness is not to be confused with one's encounter with the Other: "This Other . . . is and remains over against the self, no matter what completeness the self may attain, as the Other."[39] The self as a unity may seem to incorporate the "otherness" of the unconscious, even to internalize the "otherness" of the world. Yet one's conscious awareness, as ideas or images, merely contains and possesses these contents of awareness as *It*-objects. This self-contained material is actually internal and not the Other of the *I-Thou* encounter. "So the self, even if it has integrated all of its unconscious elements, remains this single self, confined within itself. All beings existing over against me who become 'included' in my self are possessed by [my self] in this inclusion as an *It*."[40] Only when the Other is fully accepted and received in its radical otherness can one truly relate to it as *Thou*: "Only then when, having become aware of the unincludable otherness of a being, I renounce all claim to incorporating it in any way within me or making it a part of my soul, does it truly become *Thou* for me. This holds good for God as for man."[41]

---

38. Buber, "Religion and Modern Thinking," 88.
39. Buber, "Religion and Modern Thinking," 88–89.
40. Buber, "Religion and Modern Thinking," 89.
41. Buber, "Religion and Modern Thinking," 89.

Furthermore, in his essay "Distance and Relation," Buber lays out a twofold movement that structures human life.[42] This twofold movement consists of a dialectical relationship between "a primal setting at a distance" on the one hand, and "an entering into relation" on the other. As a first step the human being constructs a world out of the "unsteady conglomeration" of things as an edifice within which to live.[43] "From the meeting of natural being with man . . . the new and enduring arises, that which comprehends and infinitely transcends the realm" of animal existence.[44] One's synthesis of the "unsteady conglomeration" of things into "world" allows one to perceive the unity of being. Further, the perception of the unity of the world is reciprocal with the perception of the unity of the self: "The single being [of the self] has received the character of wholeness and the unity which are perceived in it from the wholeness and unity perceived in the world."[45]

Given this structuring of being itself and his own being, the person can take the second step—to turn and enter into relation with it: "He who turns to the world and looking upon it steps into relation with it . . . from then on he is able to grasp being as a wholeness and a unity."[46]

The first act of constructing "world," the "setting at a distance," creates the condition or span that is necessary in order to turn, that is, to step into relation with the Other as the Other and to make the realization that comes with this act: "Only the view of what is over against me in the world in its full presence, with which I have set myself, present in my whole person, in relation—only this view gives me the world truly as whole and one."[47] The act of seeing the world as a whole "in its full presence" in juxtaposition with oneself, "present in my whole person," as one steps into relation allows one the sense of wholeness and oneness. Thus are *I* and *Thou* both fully present, presence to presence. The human "setting at a distance" allows the person to "accomplish the act of relation in the acknowledgement of the fundamental actuality of this distance."[48] Such moments are what we might call authentic moments of "the-two-and-the-one." Only in such moments of turning "*can unity arise from the extreme tension of the contradiction as the overcoming of it.*"[49] Thus, when a person perceives the wholeness of "world" as Other in juxtaposition

---

42. Buber, "Distance and Relation," 59–71.
43. Buber, "Distance and Relation," 61.
44. Buber, "Distance and Relation," 61.
45. Buber, "Distance and Relation," 63.
46. Buber, "Distance and Relation," 63.
47. Buber, "Distance and Relation," 63.
48. Buber, "Distance and Relation," 64.
49. Buber, "Distance and Relation," 64 (emphasis added).

to the wholeness of "self," unity arises as the momentary overcoming of the tension between self and Other. This is the *I-Thou* moment.

In approaching such moments of the-two-and-the-one there is always the danger of over-identification with the Other, as Buber has pointedly reminded us: "The relation of an *I* to a *Thou* [is] the way in which the unmistakably religious of all ages have understood their religion even if they longed most intensely to let their *I* be mystically absorbed into that *Thou*."[50] The intense longing to be mystically absorbed into the *Thou* and the resistance to this longing is an essential tension of *I-Thou* relating. The issue is one of balance: the two do not ever become one, nor do they separate into mutual isolation; the task is ever and again the act of turning toward the-two-and-the-one.

To Buber one further element is crucial for such authentic moments of dialogue to take place: they must be grounded in "lived concreteness." His major exposition of lived concreteness is in a major essay of his mature period, "Religion and Philosophy." Lived concreteness [*das erlebte Konkret*] is the radical at-handedness of the moment-by-moment flux of individual human existence. For him, this lived concreteness is the necessary condition within which dialogue between persons takes place. It is also "*the* meeting place between the human and the divine."[51]

When Buber emphasizes the radical contingency of this reality, he implies its transcendence: "The actually lived concrete is the 'moment' in its unforeseeableness and its irrecoverableness, in its undivertible character of happening but once, in its decisiveness, in its secret dialogue between that which happens and that which is willed, between fate and action, address and answer."[52] The immediacy of the lived concrete is the locus of transcendence, at once both at the interhuman level and in relation to the eternal *Thou*. This linking of interhuman and human-divine dialogue is a foundational insight that undergirds all of Buber's work. In the 1957 postscript to *I and Thou* he wrote, "My most essential concern [has been] the close connection of the relation to God with the relation to one's fellow man."[53] He reaffirmed this claim in his dialogue in *Philosophical Interrogations* some years later: one basic insight had guided his life's work—"that the *I-Thou* relation to God and the *I-Thou* relation to one's fellow man are at bottom related to each other."[54] Openness to the Other, whether human or divine, is formative: it

50. Buber, "Religion and Modern Thinking," 79.
51. Buber, "Religion and Philosophy," 35 (emphasis added).
52. Buber, "Religion and Philosophy," 35.
53. Buber, "Postscript," 123–24.
54. Buber, "Interrogation of Martin Buber," 99.

shapes one's destiny because it is a matter of the whole person risking the unprecedented in the totality of his circumstances.

Buber points to lived concreteness as the essential underlying factor in the history of human religions, for in his view the history of religion is the history of a continual "struggle for the protection of lived concreteness": "The religious essence in every religion . . . is the certainty that the meaning of existence is open and accessible in the actually lived concrete, *not above the struggle with reality but in it.* . . . Meaning is to be experienced in living action and suffering itself, in the unreduced immediacy of the moment."[55] In this essay Buber sums up his lifelong stance opposing the tendency toward abstractions, which is the characteristic of the philosophical project from its beginnings in ancient Greece to the present. The immediacy of "the actual lived concrete" in the individual's ongoing struggle with reality, in one's experience of living action and in one's suffering itself—this is the locus of the meaning of existence. One attains ultimate meaning when one "stands firm, without holding back or reservation, before the whole might of reality and answers it in a living way." Such unreserved standing firm in answer to reality is one's full participation in dialogical existence. Accordingly, the person who takes this stance "is ready to confirm with his life the meaning which he has attained."[56]

The dialogical core—the otherness of the Other, the mutual openness of authentic dialogical encounter, the radical immediacy of the lived concrete—this makes presence possible. Buber puts all of these elements together in a passage near the end of his essay on distance and relation, where he sketches the being-forming dynamic of mutuality in presence:

> The inmost growth of the self is not accomplished . . . in man's relation to himself, but in the relation between the one and the Other, between [persons], that is, preeminently in the mutuality of the making present—in the making present of another self and in the knowledge that one is made present in his own self by another—together with the mutuality of acceptance, of affirmation and confirmation. . . . It is from one [person] to another that the heavenly bread of self-being is passed.[57]

In such dialogical moments, one's becoming present and one's becoming known by the presence of the Other in mutual acceptance, affirmation, and confirmation are truly transformative.

---

55. Buber, "Religion and Philosophy," 35 (emphasis added).
56. Buber, "Religion and Philosophy," 35.
57. Buber, "Distance and Relation," 71.

3. Hearing Buber's Prophetic Call

Buber was clear about his lifelong task: "I have been concerned from first to last with restoring immediacy to the relation between man and God, with helping to end 'the eclipse of God.'"[58] Accordingly, I take Buber to be a prophetic voice for our time, both in his critique of the abyss of modernity and in his call to the recovery of presence. It is up to us as his twenty-first-century readers to respond to this voice by taking in his central message and turning back to presence.

Throughout his life work Buber aligned himself with the prophets. It is easy to see why: dialogue is the nature of the prophetic phenomenon. The prophetic voice sounds forth between heaven and earth, mediating between the transcendent eternal *Thou* and the concreteness of earthbound, mundane life. The prophetic message is a warning and a summons; it points out the dire consequences of the present secular course of action and it presents its hearers with an alternative path, opening up a choice, the choice for them to move towards the authenticity of presence. The unfinished, open-ended nature of this prophetic mediation is the essence of dialogue; it is illustrated by the paradigmatic story of the prophet Jonah. Jonah's warning to the people of Nineveh was not fulfilled—to the chagrin of the prophet—because his audience's genuine dialogical response changed the course of events away from what the prophet had warned was to come. Buber asserts this very point: the prophet's message sets "the audience to whom the words are addressed before the choice and decision, directly or indirectly. The future is not something already fixed in this present hour; it is dependent upon the real decision, that is to say, the decision in which the person takes part in this hour."[59] The message is dialogical, a call inviting a response. Our response to the call as its receivers is our part in an open-ended dialogue, a part that contributes in shaping the historical process as it moves it forward.

Buber once sketched a historical sequence of spiritual leaders from the beginning to the present time. At each stage, the form of leadership was what best fit the lived concrete of that historical-cultural moment and the uniqueness of the person within his or her unprecedented historical situation.[60] Buber discerned a series of basic types "according to the difference in the successive situations, the great stages . . . in the dialogue between God and the people."[61] This sequence of prototypical figures in "the way of God through

---

58. Buber, "Interpreting Hasidism," 224.

59. Buber, *Prophetic Faith*, 2–3; see also Buber, "Dialogue between Heaven and Earth," 219.

60. Buber, "Biblical Leadership," 119, 127.

61. Buber, "Biblical Leadership," 127.

mankind" moved from the ancient patriarchs and the classical prophets all the way to the present moment, in which Buber represents today's spiritual leader as "the dialogical person," the person who in our time "commits his whole being to God's dialogue with the world, and who stands firm throughout this dialogue."[62] Thus, today's spiritual leader, the dialogical person, is a participant in a heritage that extends across time from the biblical prophets to the present moment. Buber became just such a leader.

In a foreword to his one novel, written late in his life, Buber wrote poignantly of the unique challenge posed for spiritual seekers by the present historical moment and suggested his role in helping them deal with this challenge:

> In this hour of history the crucial thing is not to possess a fixed doctrine, but rather to recognize eternal reality and out of its depths to be able to face the reality of the present. No way can be pointed to in this desert night. One's purpose must be to help [people] of today to stand fast, with their soul in readiness, until the dawn breaks and a path becomes visible where none suspected it.[63]

Here he characterizes "this hour of history," the modern period, as "this desert night," a dark wilderness which seems directionless and lacks sustenance. Under these conditions there is one thing needful: "to recognize eternal reality," that which transcends the *It*-world, "and out of its depths to be able to face the reality of the present." Buber is calling us to learn to recognize what is unchanging, the eternal *Thou*, and therewith to find the means to stand up, to withstand what confronts us in our circumstances in the modern world. Because we live in a transitional period of waiting until daybreak and "no way can be pointed to" under the conditions of our modern crisis, the task of the one who would help, the servant—in this instance, Buber—is reduced to helping the people of our time "to stand fast with their soul in readiness, until the dawn breaks and a path becomes visible where none suspected it." To "stand fast," or stand firm, is to maintain one's soul with resoluteness in anticipation of that which cannot be anticipated—until daybreak reveals it. This is to live in the eschatological tension of unimagining hope. The spiritual stance of "standing fast with the soul in readiness" recalls the alacrity to which the Baal-Shem-Tov testified and which was a central dynamic in Buber's own spiritual initiation. As we have seen, Buber's role in helping people to take that stance was his prophetic calling.

---

62. Buber, "Biblical Leadership," 131–32.
63. Buber, "Foreword to the New Edition," xiii.

Fitting with the darkness of the desert night, Buber elsewhere used the metaphor of eclipse to characterize the decline and loss of the *I-Thou* relation. To him "the eclipse of God" was a more accurate way than Nietzsche's "death of God" to characterize modern secularism, untethered from all values. For Buber, modern times present a particular challenge to the dialogical relation between the human person and the eternal *Thou*, one in which the *I-It* has grown to such gigantic proportions that it has blocked out the *I-Thou* relation. Yet for Buber this modern condition is wholly a result of human change; by 1957 he used an auditory metaphor for this change: we moderns are no longer receptive to the voice of the eternal *Thou* because "we have put wax in our ears."[64] Again, this condition, like that of an eclipse, is not permanent. Buber's prophetic voice calls us to go beyond it.

We see Buber's prophetic voice in one of its most powerful manifestations in his lecture "People Today and the Jewish Bible."[65] There he raised an issue: What is the bridge that links the person of today and the biblical message?[66] He makes clear that part of the problem is the nature of revelation: the prophet's message is by its nature a kind of "stammering," a piece of dialogical discourse that is broken off, fragmentary, impossible to enunciate:[67] "The messenger who is seized by the divine word can only speak it forth by means of human words: as such, he can only express from what and whence mankind is to be redeemed but not for what purpose and to what end."[68] The divine word is the ineffable "word" of the Creator's intention and presence; the messenger's words are the transposition of that meaning into the limited linguistic tools of the messenger's mind and historical-cultural moment.[69]

Equally, the problem lies in the spiritual alienation of modern secular culture. Thus, it is extremely difficult—"the most difficult [task] of all"—to bridge the abyss between the ancient revelation of redemption and persons of today who are shaped by modern secular culture. Yet Buber is a prophetic voice—he steps in to be that bridge. Unavoidably, the knowing he calls us to

---

64. Buber, "Postscript," 137.
65. Buber, "People Today," 4–21.
66. Buber, "People Today," 13.
67. Buber, "People Today," 13. Buber marked the prophetic message as a stammering, whether it was Moses, (*Moses*, 48); the Baal-Shem-Tov, (*Legend of the Baal-Shem*, 10); or the prophetic voices arising in the present time, "Hope for this Hour," 229.
68. Buber, "People Today," 13 (my translation).
69. This gap between the intention/presence of the transcendent, eternal *Thou* and the concrete circumstances of the prophet's moment of utterance is a recurrent distinction in Buber's work.

is a matter of inner transformation. Buber points out the means, the perilous path one must take to move into this way of knowing: this transformation

> is the most difficult of all. . . . And yet, here there is a way in, a dark and silent path which cannot be revealed in any other way than if one has the audacity to remind his interlocutors of their darkest and most silent hours. I mean the hours at the lowest depth when one finds oneself upon the trembling trap door which can open up under one in the next instant—it is totally uncanny that it has not yet fallen through into corruption, insanity, immediate "suicide"; at this point something touches *you* [*du*] like a hand, it reaches out to *you* [*du*], intends to be grasped*—*ach*—it takes terrible courage to grasp it and to let oneself be raised up by it out of the darkness! [In this moment] redemption takes place—if we rightly experience that which gives itself to be experienced: that our Redeemer lives**, the one who wills to save us, but [this can happen solely] through our *acceptance* of his redemption *in the turning about* of our being. Way in, I said. All of this is still not a standing in biblical reality. But it is the way into it and the beginning.[70]

In this passage Buber speaks as a prophet, revealing the *how* of authentic response. In our potential dialogue with God, the *turning about* of our entire being *as acceptance* of the divine gift is the inmost intimacy of the divine-human between. Note how, as Buber points to this crucial moment of our innermost experience, he moves into addressing his audience as *Du*, *Thou*. Then at the crux of turning he utters "*ach*," the untranslatable German-language interjection which here is an instance of the stammering he has described as an intrinsic element of prophetic discourse.

The lecture builds until Buber ends it with all the intensity of the prophetic voice: he emphatically asserts the distinction between the idolatry of merely bowing down before a written text and the authenticity of the unified life in fully responding to it and being shaped by it:

> It is not a matter of "turning back to the Bible." It is about once again taking up the authentically biblical, unified life with our whole time-bound being: [bringing] the whole weight of our modern complexity of soul, [and making] the fathomless substance of this historical hour present to it without any omissions. It is about standing firm in a dialogically responsible way,

---

70. Buber, "People Today," 13 (my translation); italics added to emphasize Buber's use of "*du*," "*Thou*," "*ach*"; biblical echoes: * Ps 73:23–24, ** Job 19:25.

facing our present-day situation in the openness of faith that is true to the biblical vision.[71]

Buber invites his audience to join him, to stand with him as the bridge between heaven and earth. He continues:

> Are we referring to a book? No—we mean the voice. Are we saying that one should learn to read it? No—we mean that one should learn to listen to it. There is no other way back but that of turning, a turning that rotates us on our own axis, not to an earlier place on our path, but a being led to the path on which the voice can be heard! We want to go straight through to spokenness, to the [present] being-spoken of the word.[72]

This prophetic call to true dialogue, our living, full, transforming encounter, can come about via our authentic confrontation with the text.

As we have seen, Buber himself suggested a dynamic relationship between text and voice. In his postscript to *I and Thou* he warned of the limits of the dialogical in the transmission of spiritual truth when he invoked "the melancholy of the holy men who repeatedly offered the great gift in vain."[73] But he also offered us the possibility of receiving the gift in dialogue with the prophets, the spiritual masters.[74] In such a practice, the written word evokes the spoken word, which in turn can evoke the preverbal reality of the master's vision in the life of the reader. He traced this development from written word to spoken word to life-vision when he wrote, "Spirit become word, spirit become form—[spirit] does not germinate and grow in the human world without being sown, but arises from the human world's meetings [*Begegnungen*] with the Other."[75] Spirit, the wholeness of one's spiritual life that is deeper than the medium of verbal expression, takes root through what is sown, by what is transmitted when one encounters the wisdom of a master through the medium of the master's words.

I and Thou marks the emergence of Buber's mature dialogical philosophy. As the pivotal expression of Buber's life task, it carries traces of his development through the struggles, anguish, and suffering that led to this breakthrough. It also points forward to his long years of work completing his studies of Hasidism and his project of translating the Hebrew Bible. *I and Thou* is thus a beacon, shining light on Buber's lifelong calling—and ours.

---

71. Buber, "People Today," 21 (my translation).
72. Buber, "People Today," 21 (my translation).
73. Buber, "Postscript," 131.
74. This was discussed in chapter 2, page 16 above.
75. Buber, "Postscript," 129.

In 1957, Buber wrote a postscript to the book as a moment in the dialogue with his readers that its publication thirty-four years earlier had initiated. In this postscript he sketched the emergence of *I and Thou* in relation to his own inner process. He began by tracing his own steps to and beyond its creation. The whole process started with a lifelong vision, "a vision which had come to me again and again since my youth."[76] When this vision "reached steady clarity," it "was so manifestly suprapersonal in its nature that I at once knew I had to bear witness to it." This need to bear witness to the vision "was impelled by an inward necessity." The verbal expression of the vision came later: "Some time after, I was given the right words as well and could write the book."[77] He then explains how the decades following the creation of the book became a time of clarifying and explaining and filling out the vision in a series of subsequent essays.[78]

As prophecy, the three parts of *I and Thou* trace the open-ended story of the primal dialogical relation, its loss, and its possible recovery. Buber's pivotal testament at the center of his lifetime of work, *I and Thou* opens up his prophetic "no" and his prophetic "yes" to his modern readers about our time and our task. It became the foundation and the frame for his subsequent work.

4. Conclusion

The message of *I and Thou* in its broadest context is a critique and a corrective of the malaise of modernity. Yet the purpose of its prophetic call is to keep a sharp focus on each successive present moment as a moment of immanent response to the eternal *Thou* in the immediacy of the unprecedented present historical-personal moment. In our present historical moment of deepening crisis—the rise of a chaotic new populism as a pushback against globalism, the muscle-flexing of new global strongmen, the economic-ecological crisis—we, like Elijah, can find ourselves facing the world and the eternal *Thou*, finding temporary shelter at the entrance to the cave, as the world comes unhinged at the stormy blast, the firestorm, and the earthquake. At this moment in our history *I and Thou* shows how "the voice of sheer silence" can speak to us once again in dialogical encounter. The ancient prophet's cave, the temporary refuge, can open up to us "the *Urim* and *Tummim*[79] of our innermost heart," "the cave of the

---

76. Buber, "Postscript," 123.
77. Buber, "Postscript," 123 (translation modified).
78. Buber, "Postscript," 123–24.
79. In the Hebrew Bible the *urim* and *thummim* were elements of the priestly

heart," as the place where God and the authentic self as the *I* of *I-Thou* meet and our next steps become clear to us.[80]

As we have seen, Buber's own struggle and the emergence of his dialogical vision led to the sharpening of focus to which he calls us, the focus that comes with the acuity of the prophet's dedicated, surrendered vision. To look for a sign is to open oneself to seeing the authenticating signature of the Creator in the unfolding events of one's time on the historical stage. This will enable each one of us to take action at this moment in the unfolding course of events. Buber is clear about signs and the power of decision in response to them.

To reopen *I and Thou* at the present moment in history, a century after it became his breakthrough testament and his manifesto of the philosophy of dialogue, is to see it from a new angle. We are not at a different historical moment within the ongoing crisis of human struggle, the current phase of the broad experiment, the project of modernity, of which the book is both a part and a challenge.

The book is strong medicine—both a critique of the modern period and a call to a deeper humanity that underlies both past and present times. It offers at once an analysis of the modern predicament and a way to transcend it. Part one lays out the foundational distinction between *I-Thou* and *I-It* and sketches the process that led to the current crisis. Part two presents the contest between *I-Thou* and *I-It* that runs through the history of humankind and takes us into the struggle we must undergo if we are to take the path beyond our modern engulfment in the *It*-world. Part three marks some signposts in our recent spiritual history, thereby clearing the way toward a life of authenticity. That life, envisioned as a life of continual dialogical response to the eternal *Thou* in the face of each new moment, is the promise Buber holds out to each of us if we but turn in openness and surrender to reach out and grasp it.

---

breastplate used to discern the divine will. See Exod 28:30 and above, page 6.

80. Buber, "Holy Way," 137.

Appendix 1

Chart: The Three Global Traditions in "The Teaching of the Tao" (Chapter 6)

BUBER'S CLAIM: THE UNIFICATION of the self is the one thing needful for the transforming insight which is the encounter with the Absolute. Put in dialogical terms—to become *I* and to say *Thou* to the eternal *Thou* happen together: they are a single spiritual gesture. This insight, first expressed as the core message in "The Teaching of the Tao" in 1910, underlies the philosophy of dialogue articulated in *I and Thou*: "Becoming *I*, I say *Thou*" (§14c). How Buber relates this insight to global spiritual movements is made clear when we place his words analyzing major spiritual founders in "The Teaching of the Tao" side by side, as this chart shows.[1]

The Jewish/Ur-Christian teaching of the kingdom of God (Jesus)	The Indian teaching of release (Buddha)	The Chinese Tao-teaching of the tao (Lao Tzu)
"content"—the talk of the kingdom of heaven and sonship (75)	"content"—the talk of deliverance from suffering and the holy path (75)	"content"—the talk of Tao and nondoing (75)
Primal Christianity [*Urchristentum*] was not about the oneness of God, but rather the identitfication of the unified person with God; here too, the existing being is . . . only there for the sake of the needful. (75)	For Buddha it is totally obvious that . . . it is absolutely not essential to concern oneself with the nature or existence of God. (75)[2]	[In] the Tao-teaching . . . all that is said of the "way" of the world points to the way of the accomplished person, and maintains in it its confirmation and fulfillment. (75)

1. Parenthetical references identify pages in the version of Buber's essay titled "Afterword" (my translations).

2. Buber continues this passage with a short gloss on classical Hinduism: "Even in

285

The Jewish/Ur-Christian teaching of the kingdom of God (Jesus)	The Indian teaching of release (Buddha)	The Chinese Tao-teaching of the tao (Lao Tzu)
	Buddha overcomes Vedic learning with the dissolution of the "view" that does not belong to the accomplished person on the "way," and Brahmanic law with the abolition of castes in the monastic order. (76–77)	Lao Tzu overcomes official wisdom through the teaching of "non-being" and official virtue through the teaching of "non-doing." (77)
For Jesus the witness [of his unified life] was . . . consummated through his death, the unique absolute to which mankind must surrender. (78)	Next to [Jesus] stands Buddha. (78)	Lao Tzu's life presents itself the least because his life, the concealed life, was just that of his teaching. (78)
The discourse [of Jesus] is fully in parables. (79)	The discourse [of Buddha] is fully in parables. (79)	The discourse of Lao Tzu is a discourse in images. (79)
In the teaching of Jesus the parable is the immediate word of fulfillment found in him as the central person. (80)	In the teaching of Buddha the parable is the immediate word of fulfillment found in him as the central person. (80)	The parable in the Tao teaching is . . . the poetry of one to whom the teaching has already been delivered in its fulfillment. (80)
The teaching of Jesus . . . becomes dialectic . . . if the messenger who (never immediately) takes it over from the hands of the fulfilling person is an impetuous propagator like Paul. (94)	The teaching of Buddha . . . becomes precepts . . . if the messenger who (never immediately) takes it over from the hands of the fulfilling person is an organizer like Asoka. (94)	The teaching of the tao . . . becomes poetry . . . if the messenger who (never immediately) takes it over from the hands of the fulfilling person is a poet like Zhuangzi. (95)

the Upanishads the significance of the teaching of the Atman [is] that what one calls being is nothing other than the oneness of the self and that consequently the unified person encounters the world as being, as oneness, as one's self." (75)

Appendix 2

Buddhist Texts Quoted in *I and Thou* (Chapter 9)

EIGHT OF THE NINE passages of Buddhist scripture that Buber quotes come from the *Sutta Pitaka* in the Pali Canon, the standard collection of Theravada Buddhist scriptures. The *Sutta Pitaka* consists of more than 10,000 *suttas* (discourses), teachings attributed to the Buddha. The seventh quotation listed below comes from a later esoteric Chinese work, the *Surangama Sutra*.

Buddhist quotation (Smith)	Text source
1. [§50c] "It is not possible to lay hold of a Self and a Self-appertaining in truth and in reality."	*Majjhima Nikāya, Sutta* 22, *Alagaddupama Sutta*: The Snake Simile, verse 25. Translated by Nyanaponika Thera, 2006 [MN 22 PTS: M i 130] http://www.accesstoinsight.org/tipitaka/mn/mn.022.nypo.html
2. [§50r] "If, O monk, the opinion dominates that soul and body are one in being, there is no life of salvation; if, O monk, the opinion dominates that the soul is one and the body another, then too there is no life of salvation."	*Samyutta Nikāya*, Part 2 *Nidāna Vagga*, 12 *Nidāna Samyutta, Sutta* 35 *Kaḷara-Khattiya Vagga, Sutta* 35. Translated by Bhikkhu Bodhi, 2000 [SN 2.12.4.35] http://obo.genaud.net/a/dhamma-vinaya/wp/sn/02_nv/sn02.12.035.bodh.wp.htm
3. [§50r] "There is, O Monks, an Unborn, neither become nor created nor formed."	*Khuddaka Nikāya, Udāna* 8.3, *Nibbāna Sutta*: Unbinding (3) Translated by Thanissaro Bhikkhu, 2012 [Ud 8.3 PTS: Ud 80] http://www.accesstoinsight.org/tipitaka/kn/ud/ud.8.03.than.html

APPENDIX 2: BUDDHIST TEXTS QUOTED IN *I AND THOU*

Buddhist quotation (Smith)	Text source
4. [§50u] "cessation of pain"	*Samyutta Nikāya* 56.11 [V:420] [The Third Noble Truth, First Sermon, Deer Park, Benares], Dhammacakkappavattana Sutta: Setting the Wheel of Dhamma in Motion, translated by Thanissaro Bhikkhu, 1993 [SN 56.11 PTS: S v 420] http://www.accesstoinsight.org/tipitaka/sn/sn56/sn56.011.than.html
5. [§50u] "Henceforth there is no return"	*Khuddaka Nikāya, Itivuttaka* §1: The Group of Ones. Translated by Thanissaro Bhikkhu, 2001 [KN Iti 1–27 PTS: Iti 1–19] http://www.accesstoinsight.org/tipitaka/kn/iti/iti.1.001-027.than.html
6. [§50v] The "thicket of opinions"	*Majjhima Nikāya* 2.1; 72. *Sabbasava Sutta*, translated by Thanissaro Bhikku, 1997 [MN 2 PTS: M i 6] http://www.accesstoinsight.org/tipitaka/mn/mn.002.than.html
7. [§50v] The "illusion of forms"	A reference to one of the 5 skandhas of clinging, see the *Surangama Sutra* (in Chan, Mahayana Buddhist tradition) http://www.buddhisttexts.org/uploads/6/3/1/6331706/surangama_new_translation.pdf
8. [§50w] [Buddhist] love where "all that has become is illimitably comprised in the breast."	*Khuddaka Nikāya, Sutta-Nipata* 1.8 143–52 *Karaniya Metta Sutta*: Loving-Kindness, translated by Nanamoli Thera, 1995. [SN 1.8 PTS: Sn 143-152] http://www.accesstoinsight.org/tipitaka/kn/snp/snp.1.08.nymo.html
9. [§50z] "Friend," says the Buddha, "I proclaim that in this my fathom-high ascetic's body, affected with sensations, there dwells the world and the beginning of the world and the extinction of the world and the way that leads to the extinction of the world."	*Samyutta Nikāya* 2.26 Rohitassa, translated by Bhikkhu Nanananda, 2007. [SN 2.26] http://www.accesstoinsight.org/lib/authors/nanananda/wheel183.html#fnt-26

Appendix 3

I and Thou Expresses a Hebraic Vision

THE VISION THAT *I and Thou* presents is essentially a Hebraic vision, the vision of an epic *agon*, the great human struggle that runs through human history. This struggle is between the call to *I-Thou* and the pull away from *I-Thou* into the *It*-world. It is what Buber sees as the hidden spiritual history of the human race.

Yet, as we have seen, some interpreters of *I and Thou* have raised the question about the degree to which it is a Jewish work. At first reading and in keeping with Buber's original concept of the project of which *I and Thou* was to be the general introduction, it can be regarded as a general work along the lines of its predecessor in Buber's output, *Daniel: Dialogues on Realization*. *I and Thou* does not make many direct allusions to Judaism or the vocabulary of Judaism or even to the Hebrew Bible. In fact, its religious allusions draw from global religious traditions: from the Upanishads (§50k), classical Taoism (§§46–48), Buddhism (§50), and Christianity (§§19, 40, 50), to Zulu and Fuegian idioms and Mana in primal cultures (§23).

However, a close look reveals the profoundly Jewish grounding and vision of the book. Buber's major concepts lie at the heart of the Jewish biblical-theological tradition: "the eternal *Thou*" (twenty-one times) as his key term for God, "the Face" as a reference to the presence of God based on its prominence as a metaphor in the Hebrew Bible, "turning" (§36i–j) as the central dynamism of Buber's spirituality is his direct translation of the postbiblical Hebrew term *teshuvah*. Buber makes many allusions to biblical images: the spirit on the waters at creation (§§9f, 39j, 55e), Jacob wrestling with the angel, the breath of babes (§60a). He references the Mosaic tablet of the law (§60b), the holy of holies (§57c), Jewish sacrifices (§49g–h), Jewish prayer (§49g–h), the theophanies to Moses (§60d) and to Isaiah (§§9f, 55e). He incorporates the stories and images of early Christianity—which he claims as a Jewish movement, marking it as a high point in the history of Judaism.¹ He appropriates Jesus' claim "there is one thing needful" as his own and alludes to it more than five times throughout the book. He alludes to the *golem* (§33i), the *Akedah* (§61i), Yiddish lore (§27c), and Hasidic spirituality (§36c) as elements of postbiblical Jewish culture. Thus, because Buber resolutely refused to abandon his own "confessional stance" as a Jew,² his breakthrough book and the vision it expresses are profoundly Jewish. At the same time, his allusions to elements of global culture—both Europe and Asia are amply represented throughout the book—confirm the breadth of his vision as well.

In the years leading up to writing *I and Thou*, Buber immersed himself in his studies of Hasidism. Buber's untranslated Hasidic study, *Der grosse Maggid und seine Nachfolge*, was the book he wrote immediately preceding *I and Thou*. Furthermore, Buber's lectures on Judaism, given over the course of the decade before he wrote *I and Thou*, as well as his lecture series "Religion as Presence," delivered at the Frankfurt Lehrhaus immediately before he finalized it, provide a skeleton key to the concerns and spiritual dynamics it expresses. A further indication of the Jewishness of Buber's vision as expressed in *I and Thou* comes from his own life-project, his discovery and recovery of what is primally Hebrew, as he recoiled from his secularized Jewish upbringing and his immersion in secular Austrian-German academic life. His two intense periods of Hasidic study (1904–1908 and 1919–1921) punctuate this recovery.

One of the focal points in Buber's effort to recover the "primally Hebrew" was his continual effort to set Hebrew-Jewish language and ways of thinking in contrast with Greco-European cultural concepts. The essay entitled "Biblical Humanism" stands out as a manifesto of this project.³ In it Hebrew humanism parallels Renaissance humanism, which has been conceived of as a return to the classic texts of Europe in an attempt to recover the fullness of classical humanity. By contrast, Buber's Hebrew humanism focuses on the fashioning of Hebrew humanity through a return to and a recovery of "the language and writings of classical Israel."⁴ To Buber, the turn to dialogue with the Absolute is the narrow way of this recovery: "Only that man is a Hebrew

---

1. For Buber's interpretation of what he calls "early, original Christianity," see "Judaism and Mankind," 32–33; "Renewal of Judaism," 45–48; "Jewish Religiosity," 92; and *Two Types of Faith*, 24–35.

2. For Buber's comment on taking this "confessional stance," see "Hasidism and Modern Man," 42.

3. Two other essays limning this opposition stand out as well: "Spirit of the Orient and Judaism" and "Religion and Ethics," which works out some of the broader implications of this distinction.

4. Buber, "Biblical Humanism," 211.

APPENDIX 3: *I AND THOU* EXPRESSES A HEBRAIC VISION

man who lets himself be addressed by the voice that speaks to him in the Hebrew Bible and who responds to it with his life."[5]

Through this relating dialogically with the eternal *Thou* as voiced in the text of the Hebrew Bible, the transformation takes place: "the reality of language becomes operative in a person's spirit. The truth of language [proves] itself in the person's existence."[6] In this way, this concrete transformation can "follow upon a rebirth of the normative primal forces" of Hebraic reality. Here "the building blocks for the structure of personality [are] produced from the depths of language."[7]

Buber contrasts the biblical word with the word of Greek antiquity. On the one hand,

> The word of Greek antiquity is detached and formally perfected. It is removed from the block of actual spokenness, sculpted with the artful chisel of thought, rhetoric, and poetry—removed to the realm of form. It would be considered crude and useless—barbarian—were it to retain any immediacy. It is valid only when it becomes pure form.[8]

By contrast, the biblical word "is present in its full biblical force only when it has retained the immediacy of spokenness. It is essential . . . that a psalm is outcry and not poem, that a prophetic speech is appeal and not properly formal elocution."[9] This is why, in the biblical word,

> the humanized voice of God, resounding in human idiom and captured in human letters, [can] speak not *before* us, as does a character in the role of a god in the epiphanies or Greek tragedy, but *to* us. . . . Untransfigured and unsubdued, the biblical word preserves the dialogical character of living reality.[10]

Buber points out that the ideal in the Greek cultural realm "might be called the Apollonian."[11] "The power of giving shape is set above the world. The highest faculty of the human spirit is the formative one: it wants to *form* the person as perfectly as possible; it wants to *form* the polis as perfectly as possible."[12] In the Hebrew thought world, by contrast, the primal power of

---

5. Buber, "Biblical Humanism," 212–13.
6. Buber, "Biblical Humanism," 213 (translation modified).
7. Buber, "Biblical Humanism," 218.
8. Buber, "Biblical Humanism," 214.
9. Buber, "Biblical Humanism," 214.
10. Buber, "Biblical Humanism," 214–15 (emphasis his).
11. Buber, "Biblical Humanism," 215, quoting Konrad Burdach.
12. Buber, "Biblical Humanism," 215–16.

language as an event in mutuality grounds biblical humanism in a dialogical core. Unlike the Greek idea, "Its intent is not the person who is shut up within himself, but the open one; not the form, but the relation; not mastery of the secret, but immediacy in facing it; not the thinker and master of the word, but its listener and executor, its worshipper and proclaimer."[13] In response to the biblical word, its hearers fulfill it: "The word is fulfilled ... not in a perfected form," as with the Greek idea, "but in a proof of self" of the hearer:

> Biblical humanism cannot, as does its Western counterpart, raise the individual above the problems of the moment; it seeks instead to train him to stand fast in them, to prove himself in them. This stormy night, these shafts of lightning flashing down, this threat of destruction—do not escape from them into a world of logos, of perfected form! Stand fast, hear the word in the thunder, obey, respond! This terrifying world is the world of God. It lays claim upon you. Prove yourself in it as a man of God![14]

Buber's distinction between the Greek perfection of form and the Hebrew spontaneity, directness, and mutuality of dialogue explains major qualities of *I and Thou* as a text: the division into sections which function as "breathing units of thought;" the use of the interlocutor's voice at key points in the development of the discourse; the back-and-forth between the vagaries of *I-It* and the fullness of *I-Thou* as the exposition moves from section to section—these all stand out as such dialogical elements.

---

13. Buber, "Biblical Humanism," 216.
14. Buber, "Biblical Humanism," 216.

Bibliography

Augustine of Hippo. *Confessions*. Books 1-8. Edited and translated by Carolyn J.-B. Hammond. Loeb Classical Library. Harvard University Press: Cambridge, MA, 2014.
Avnon, Dan. "The 'Living Center' of Martin Buber's Political Theory." *Political Theory* 21.1 (February 1993) 55–77.
———. *Martin Buber: The Hidden Dialogue*. Lanham, MD: Rowman & Littlefield, 1998.
Ba'al Shem Tov. *Tzava'at HaRivash: The Testament of Rabbi Israel Baal Shem Tov*. Edited by Dov Baer. Translated by Jacob Immanuel Schochet. New York: Kehot, 1998.
Bachofen, Johann Jacob. *Myth, Religion, and Mother Right*. Princeton: Princeton University Press, 1992.
The Bhagavad-Gita. Translated by R. C. Zaehner. London: Oxford University Press, 1969.
Bloom, Harold. "Introduction." In *On the Bible: Eighteen Studies by Martin Buber*, edited by Nahum N. Glatzer, ix–xxxii. Syracuse, NY: Syracuse University Press, 2000.
Borges, Jorge Luis. "The Divine Comedy." In *Seven Nights*, rev. ed., translated by Eliot Weinberger, 6–24. New York: New Directions, 1984.
Bourgeault, Cynthia. "The Gift of Life: The Unified Solitude of the Desert Fathers." *Parabola* 14.2 (Summer 1989) 27–35.
Breslauer, S. Daniel. *The Chrysalis of Religion: A Guide to the Jewishness of Buber's "I and Thou."* Nashville: Abingdon, 1980.
Buber, Martin. "Abraham the Seer." (1939) In *On the Bible: Eighteen Studies*, edited by Nahum N. Glatzer, translated by Sophie Meyer, 22–43. New York: Schocken, 1968.
———. "Afterword." (1957) In *I and Thou*, translated by Walter Kaufmann, 169–82. New York: Scribner's, 1970.
———. "Afterword: The History of the Dialogical Principle." (1954) In *Between Man and Man*, translated by Maurice Friedman, 209–24. New York: Macmillan, 1965.
———. "Author's Preface." (1913) In *Daniel: Dialogues on Realization*, translated by Maurice Friedman, 47. New York: Holt, 1964.
———. "Autobiographical Fragments." (1960) In *The Philosophy of Martin Buber*, translated by Maurice Friedman, edited by Paul Arthur Schilpp and Maurice Friedman, 3–39. LaSalle, IL: Open Court, 1967. Originally published as *Begegnung: Autobiographische Fragmente*. Edited by Paul Arthur Schilpp and Maurice Friedman. Stuttgart: Kohlhammer, 1960.

———. "The Baal-Shem-Tov's Instruction in Intercourse with God." (1928) In *Hasidism and Modern Man*, edited and translated by Maurice Friedman, 177–222. New York: Harper, 1958. Originally published as *Des Rabbi ben Elieser genannt Baal-Schem-Tow Unterweisung im Umgang mit Gott, das ist Meister vom guten Namen Unterweisung im Umgang mit Gott*. Berlin: Schocken, 1935.

———. "The Beginnings." (1943) In *The Origin and Meaning of Hasidism*, edited and translated by Maurice Friedman, 24–57. New York: Harper, 1960.

———. *A Believing Humanism: My Testament, 1902–1965*. Translated and edited by Maurice Friedman. New York: Simon & Schuster, 1967.

———. "Bergson's Concept of Intuition." (1943) In *Pointing the Way: Collected Essays*, edited and translated by Maurice Friedman, 81–86. New York: Harper, 1957.

———. "Biblical Humanism." (1941) In *On the Bible: Eighteen Studies*, translated by Michael A. Meyer, edited by Nahum N. Glatzer, 211–16. New York: Schocken, 1968.

———. "Biblical Leadership." (1933) In *Israel and the World: Essays in a Time of Crisis*, 2nd ed., translated by Greta Hort, 119–33. New York: Schocken, 1963.

———. *Briefwechsel aus sieben Jahrzehnten* [The Letters of Martin Buber: A Life of Dialogue]. Edited by Grete Schaeder. 3 vols. Heidelberg: Lambert Schneider, 1972–75.

———. "Buddha." (1907) In *Ereignisse und Begegnungen*, 3–9. Leipzig: Insel Verlag, 1920. http://archive.org/details/ereignisseundbegoobubeiala.

———. *Chinese Tales: Zhuangzi, Sayings and Parables and Chinese Ghost and Love Stories*. (1911) Translated by Alex Page. Amherst, NY: Humanity, 1998.

———. "The Commentary, 'Afterword.'" (1910) In *I and Tao: Martin Buber's Encounter with Chuang Tzu*, translated by Jonathan R. Herman, 69–96. Albany: State University of New York Press, 1996. Originally published as "Nachwort." In *Reden und Gleichnisse des Tschuang Tse*, 82–122. Leipzig: Insel-Verlag, 1910.

———. *Daniel: Dialogues on Realization*. (1913) Translated by Maurice Friedman. New York: Holt, 1964.

———. "Das Epos des Zauberers." (1914) In *Die Rede, die Lehre, und das Lied: Drei Beispiele*, 95–126. Leipzig: Insel-Verlag, 1917. https://archive.org/details/dierededielehreuoobube/page/n6.

———."Dialogue." (1929) In *Between Man and Man*, translated by Ronald Gregor Smith, 1–39. New York: Macmillan, 1965. Originally published as "Zwiesprache." In *Das dialogische Prinzip*, 139–96. (Heidelberg: Lambert Schneider, 1973).

———. "The Dialogue between Heaven and Earth." (1951) In *On Judaism*, edited by Nahum N. Glatzer, 214–25. New York: Schocken, 1967.

———. "Distance and Relation." (1950) In *The Knowledge of Man: A Philosophy of the Interhuman*, translated by Ronald Gregor Smith, 59–71. New York: Harper, 1965.

———. "Ecstasy and Confession." (1909) In *Ecstatic Confessions: The Heart of Mysticism*, collected and introduced by Martin Buber, translated by Esther Cameron, edited by Paul Mendes-Flohr, 1–11. New York: Harper, 1985.

———. *Ecstatic Confessions: The Heart of Mysticism*. (1909) Collected and introduced by Martin Buber. Edited by Paul Mendes-Flohr. Translated by Esther Cameron. New York: Harper, 1985.

———. "Education." (1926) In *Between Man and Man*, translated by Ronald Macgregor Smith, 83–103. New York: Macmillan, 1965.

———. "Elements of the Interhuman." (1954) In *The Knowledge of Man: A Philosophy of the Interhuman,* translated by Ronald Gregor Smith, 72–88. New York: Harper, 1965. Originally published as „Elemente des Zwischenmenschlichen." In *Das dialogische Prinzip,* 271–98. (Heidelberg: Lambert Schneider, 1973).

———. *Ecstatic Confessions: The Heart of Mysticism.* Collected and introduced by Martin Buber. Edited by Paul Mendes-Flohr. Translated by Esther Cameron. New York: Harper, 1985.

———. "The Faith of Judaism." (1928) In *Israel and the World,* 2nd ed., translated by Greta Hort, 13–27. New York: Schocken, 1963.

———. "Foreword." (1957) In *Pointing the Way: Collected Essays,* translated and edited by Maurice Friedman, xv–xvi. New York: Harper, 1957.

———. "Foreword to the New Edition." (1953) *For the Sake of Heaven,* 2nd ed., translated by Ludwig Lewisohn, vii–xiii. New York: Harper, 1953.

———. "The Foundation Stone." (1943) In *The Origin and Meaning of Hasidism,* edited and translated by Maurice Friedman, 60–88. New York: Harper, 1960.

———. "Fragments on Revelation." (1964) In *A Believing Humanism: My Testament, 1902–1965,* translated by Maurice Friedman, 113–16. New York: Simon & Schuster, 1967.

———. "God and the Spirit of Man." (1951) In *Eclipse of God: Studies in the Relation between Religion and Philosophy,* translated by Maurice Friedman, 123–29. Amherst, NY: Amity, 1999.

———. *Good and Evil: Two Interpretations.* (1952) Translated by Ronald Gregor Smith. New York: Scribner's, 1993.

———. [*The Great Maggid and His Disciples*] *Der Grosse Maggid und seine Nachfolge.* (1922) Frankfurt am Main: Rütten & Loening, 1922.

———. "Hasidism and Modern Man." (1957) In *Hasidism and Modern Man,* edited and translated by Maurice Friedman, 21–43. New York: Harper, 1958.

———. "Hebrew Humanism." In *Israel and the World: Essays in a Time of Crisis,* translated by Olga Marx, 240–52. New York: Schocken, 1948.

———. "Herut: On Youth and Religion." (1919) In *On Judaism,* translated by Eva Jospe, edited by Nahum N. Glatzer, 149–74. New York: Schocken, 1967. Originally published as *Cheruth: Eine Rede* über *Jugend und Religion.* (Vienna and Berlin: Löwit, 1919).

———. "The Holy Way." (1919) In *On Judaism,* translated by Eva Jospe, edited by Nahum N. Glatzer, 108–48. New York: Schocken, 1967.

———. "Hope for this Hour." (1952) In *Pointing the Way: Collected Essays,* edited and translated by Maurice Friedman, 220–29. New York: Harper, 1957.

———. "The How and Why of Our Bible Translation." (1938) In *Scripture and Translation,* edited and translated by Lawrence Rosenwald, 205–19. Bloomington: Indiana University Press, 1994.

———. *I and Thou.* Translated by Walter Kaufmann. New York: Scribner's, 1970.

———. *I and Thou.* 2nd ed. Translated by Ronald Gregor Smith. New York: Scribner's, 1958.

———. *Ich und Du.* (1922) Gütersloh: Gütersloher Verlagshaus, 1974.

———. "In the Midst of History." (1933) In *Israel and the World: Essays in a Time of Crisis,* 2nd ed., translated by Olga Marx, 78–82. New York: Schocken, 1963.

———. "Interpreting Hasidism." (1963) *Commentary* 33.3 (September 1963) 218–25.

———. "Interrogation of Martin Buber." In *Philosophical Interrogations*, edited by Sidney C. Rome and Beatrice K. Rome, 14–117. New York: Holt, 1964.

———. "Introduction." (1907) In *The Legend of the Baal-Shem*, translated by Maurice Friedman, 9–13. Princeton: Princeton University Press, 1995.

———. "Jewish Religiosity." (1913) In *On Judaism*, translated by Eva Jospe, edited by Nahum N. Glatzer, 79–94. New York: Schocken, 1967.

———. "Judaism and Civilization." (1951) No translator given. In *On Judaism*, edited by Nahum N. Glatzer, 191–201. New York: Schocken, 1967.

———. "Judaism and Mankind." (1910) In *On Judaism*, translated by Eva Jospe, edited by Nahum N. Glatzer, 22–33. New York: Schocken, 1967.

———. "Judaism and the Jews." (1909) *On Judaism*, translated by Eva Jospe, edited by Nahum N. Glatzer, 11–21. New York: Schocken, 1967.

———. "Landauer und die Revolution." *Masken: Halbmonatschrift des Düsseldorfer Schauspielhauses* 14.18–19 (1919) 282–91.

———. "The Land of the Jews." (1910) In *The First Buber: Youthful Zionist Writings of Martin Buber*, edited and translated by Gilya Gerda Schmidt, 206–8. Syracuse, NY: Syracuse University Press, 1999.

———. *The Legend of the Baal-Shem*. (1908) Translated by Maurice Friedman. Princeton, NJ: Princeton University Press, 1995.

———. "The Life of the Hasidim." (1908) In *Hasidism and Modern Man*, edited and translated by Maurice Friedman, 71–122. New York: Harper, 1966.

———. "Man and His Image-Work." (1963) In *The Knowledge of Man: A Philosophy of the Interhuman*, translated by Maurice Friedman, edited by Maurice Friedman, 149–65. New York: Harper, 1965.

———. *Meister Eckharts mystische Schriften*. Edited and translated by Gustav Landauer. Berlin: Schnabel, 1903.

———. *Moses: The Revelation and the Covenant*. (1944) Amherst, NY: Humanity, 1998.

———. "My Way to Hasidism." (1918) In *Hasidism and Modern Man*, edited and translated by Maurice Friedman, 47–69. New York: Harper, 1960. Originally published as "Mein Weg zum Chassidismus: Errinerungen." (Frankfurt: Rütten & Loening, 1918).

———. "Nachwort: Zur Geschichte des dialogischen Prinzips" [Afterword: The History of the Dialogical Principle]. In *Das dialogische Prinzip*, 301–19. Heidelberg: Lambert Schneider, 1973.

———. "On the Psychologizing of the World." (1923) In *A Believing Humanism: My Testament, 1902–1965*, translated by Maurice Friedman, 144–52. New York: Simon & Schuster, 1967.

———. "On the Suspension of the Ethical." (1951) In *Eclipse of God: Studies in the Relation between Religion and Philosophy*, translated by Maurice Friedman, 115–20. Amherst, NY: Amity, 1999.

———. *Paths in Utopia*. (1947) Translated by R. F. C. Hull. London: Routledge, 1949.

———. "People and Leader." (1919) In *Pointing the Way: Collected Essays*, translated and edited by Maurice Friedman, 148–60. New York: Harper, 1963.

———. "People Today and the Jewish Bible: From a Lecture Series." (1926) Translated by Lawrence Rosenwald. In *Scripture and Translation*, edited by Martin Buber and Franz Rosenzweig, 4–21. Originally published as "Der Mensch von heute und die jüdische Bibel." In *Die Schrift und ihre Verdeutschung*, 13–45. (Berlin: Schocken, 1936).

———. "Philosophical and Religious World View." (1928) In *A Believing Humanism: My Testament, 1902-1965*, translated by Maurice Friedman, 130-35. New York: Simon & Schuster, 1967.

———. "Postscript." (1957) In *I and Thou*, translated by Ronald Gregor Smith, 121-37. New York: Scribner's, 1958. Originally published as "Nachwort, Oktober 1957." In *Ich und Du*, 145-60. (Gütersloh: Gütersloher Verlagshaus, 1974).

———. "Preface to the 1923 Edition." (1923) In *On Judaism*, translated by Eva Jospe, edited by Nahum N. Glatzer, 3-10. New York: Schocken, 1967. Originally published as "Vorwort" in *Reden über das Judentum*. (Frankfurt am Main: Rütten & Loening, 1923).

———. "The Prejudices of Youth." (1937) In *Israel and the World: Essays in a Time of Crisis*, 2nd ed., translated by Olga Marx, 41-52. New York: Schocken, 1963.

———. "Prelude: Report on Two Talks." (1932) In *Eclipse of God: Studies in the Relation between Religion and Philosophy*, translated by Maurice Friedman, 3-9. Amherst, NY: Humanity, 1999.

———. "Productivity and Existence." (1914) In *Pointing the Way: Collected Essays*, edited and translated by Maurice Friedman, 5-10. New York: Harper, 1957.

———. *The Prophetic Faith*. Translated by Carlyle Witton-Davies. New York: Harper, 1960.

———. "The Question to the Single One." (1936) In *Between Man and Man*, translated by Ronald Gregor Smith, 40-82. New York: Macmillan, 1965. Originally published as "Die Frage an den Einzelnen." In *Das dialogische Prinzip*. 197-267. (Heidelberg: Schneider, 1973).

———. "Religion and Ethics." (1951) In *Eclipse of God: Studies in the Relation between Religion and Philosophy*, translated by Eugene Kamenka and Maurice Friedman, 95-111. Amherst, NY: Humanity, 1999.

———. "Religion and Modern Thinking." (1951) In *Eclipse of God: Studies in the Relation between Religion and Philosophy*, translated by Eugene Kamenka and Maurice Friedman, 65-92. Amherst, NY: Humanity, 1999.

———. "Religion and Philosophy." In *Eclipse of God: Studies in the Relation between Religion and Philosophy*, translated by Eugene Kamenka and Maurice Friedman, 27-46. Amherst, NY: Humanity, 1999.

———. "Religion as Presence" Lectures. (1922) In *Buber's Way to "I and Thou": The Development of Martin Buber's Thought and his "Religion as Presence" Lectures*, edited by Rivka Horwitz and Martin Buber, 19-129. Philadelphia: Jewish Publication Society, 1988. Originally published as "Religion als Gegenwart." In Rivka Horwitz and Martin Buber. *Buber's Way to "I and Thou": An Historical Analysis and the First Publication of Martin Buber's Lectures "Religion als Gegenwart."* 43-152. (Heidelberg: Schneider, 1978).

———. "Renewal of Judaism." (1910) In *On Judaism*, translated by Eva Jospe, edited by Nahum N. Glatzer, 34-55. New York: Schocken, 1995.

———. "Replies to My Critics." (1963) In *The Philosophy of Martin Buber*, edited by Paul Arthur Schilpp and Maurice Friedman, 689-744. The Library of Living Philosophers series 12. La Salle, IL: Open Court, 1967.

———. "Spinoza, Sabbati Zvi, and the Baal-Shem." (1927) In *The Origin and Meaning of Hasidism*, edited and translated by Maurice Friedman, 90-112. New York: Harper, 1960. Originally published as "Geleitwort zur Gesamtausgabe: Franz Rosenzweig gewidmet." In *Die Chassidische Bücher*, xi-xxxi. (Berlin: Schocken, 1927).

———. "Spirit and Body of the Hasidic Movement." (1921) In *The Origin and Meaning of Hasidism*, edited and translated by Maurice Friedman, 113–49. New York: Harper, 1960. Originally published as "Geleitwort." In *Der Grosse Maggid und seine Nachfolge*, xiii–xcvi. Frankfurt am Main: Rütten & Loening, 1922.

———. "The Spirit of the Orient and Judaism." (1912) In *On Judaism*, edited by Nahum N. Glatzer and translated by Eva Jospe, 56–78. New York: Schocken, 1967.

———. "Supplement: Christ, Hasidism, Gnosis." (1954) In *The Origin and Meaning of Hasidism*, translated by Maurice Friedman, 241–54. New York: Harper, 1960. Originally published as "Christus, Chassidismus, Gnosis." *Merkur* 8.10 (October 1954) 923–29.

———. "Symbolic and Sacramental Existence." (1934) Edited and translated by Maurice Friedman. In *The Origin and Meaning of Hasidism*, 152–81. New York: Harper, 1960.

———. *The Tales of Rabbi Nachman*. (1906) Translated by Maurice Friedman. New York: Horizon, 1956.

———. *Tales of the Hasidim: Book One: The Early Masters*. (1947) Translated by Olga Marx. New York: Schocken, 1991.

———. *Tales of the Hasidim: Book Two: The Later Masters*. (1948) Translated by Olga Marx. New York: Schocken, 1991.

———. "The Teaching of the Tao." In *Pointing the Way: Collected Essays*, edited and translated by Maurice Friedman, 31–58. New York: Harper, 1957.

———. *Two Types of Faith*. (1951) Translated by Norman P. Goldhawk. Syracuse, NY: Syracuse University Press, 2003.

———. "Über Jakob Boehme." *Wiener Rundschau* 5.12 (15 June 1901) 251–53. http://pegasus.cc.ucf.edu/~janzb/boehme/wienrund.htm.

———. "The Way of Man, According to the Teachings of Hasidism." (1948) In *Hasidism and Modern Man*, edited and translated by Maurice Friedman, 126–76. New York: Harpers, 1966.

———. "What is Common to All." (1956) In *The Knowledge of Man: A Philosophy of the Interhuman*, translated by Maurice Friedman, 89–109. New York: Harper, 1965.

———. "What is Man?" (1938) In *Between Man and Man*, translated by Ronald Gregor Smith, 118–208. New York: Macmillan, 1965. Originally published as *Das Problem des Menschen*. (Heidelberg: Schneider, 1948).

———. "What is to be Done?" (1919) In *Pointing the Way: Collected Essays*, translated and edited by Maurice Friedman, 109–11. New York: Harper, 1963.

———. "With a Monist." (1914) In *Pointing the Way: Collected Essays*, edited and translated by Maurice Friedman, 25–30. New York: Harper, 1957.

———. "Zueignung" [Dedication]. In *Die Geschichten des Rabbi Nachman* [*The Tales of Rabbi Nachman*], edited by Martin Buber, n.p. Frankfurt: Rütten & Loening, 1906.

Buber, Martin, ed. *Meister Eckhart's mystische Schriften: In unsere Sprache übertragen von Gustav Landauer*. Berlin: Schnabel, 1920.

Buber, Martin, and Carl R. Rogers. "Dialogue between Martin Buber and Carl R. Rogers." (1957) In *The Knowledge of Man: A Philosophy of the Interhuman*, 166–84. New York: Harper, 1965.

Buber, Martin, and Franz Rosenzweig. *Die Schrift: Verdeutscht von Martin Buber gemeinsam mit Franz Rosenzweig*. Revised 1954 edition. Gütersloh: Gütersloher Verlagshaus, 1992.

———. "Revelation and Law." In *On Jewish Learning*, translated and edited by Nahum N. Glatzer, 109–18. New York: Schocken, 1955.

Buber, Paula Winkler. "Betrachtungen einer Philozionistin [Reflections of a Philo-Zionist]." *Die Welt* 5 (September 6, 1901) 4–6. http://sammlungen.ub.uni-frankfurt.de/cm/periodical/pageview/3399685.

Buddhist Text Translation Society. *The Śūraṅgama Sūtra*. Ukiah, CA: BTTS, 2009. http://www.buddhisttexts.org/uploads/6/3/3/1/6331706/surangama_new_translation.pdf.

Bultmann, Rudolf. *New Testament and Theology*. New York: Scribner's, 1951.

Casper, Bernhard. "Franz Rosenzweig's Criticism of Buber's *I and Thou*." In *Martin Buber: A Centenary Volume*, edited by Hayim Gordon and Jochanan Bloch, 139–59. New York: KTAV, 1984.

Corrigan, Kevin. *Reading Plotinus: A Practical Introduction to Neoplatonism*. West Lafayette, IN: Purdue University Press, 2005.

Dante. *Purgatory and Paradise*. Translated by Henry Francis Cary. Chicago: Thompson & Thomas, 1901.

"Dhammacakkappavattana Sutta: Setting the Wheel of Dhamma in Motion." Translated by Thanissaro Bhikkhu, 1993 [SN 56.11 PTS: S v 420] http://www.accesstoinsight.org/tipitaka/sn/sn56/sn56.011.than.html.

Downing, Christine. "Meetings and Mismeetings: A Return to Martin Buber." In *The Luxury of Afterwards*, edited by Christine Downing, 81–92. New York: iUniverse, 2004.

Eber, Irene. "Introduction." In *Chinese Tales: Zhuangzi: Sayings and Parables and Chinese Ghost and Love Stories*, by Martin Buber, ix–xxiii. New Jersey: Humanities Press International, 1991.

———. "Martin Buber and Taoism." *Monumenta Serica* 42 (1994) 445–64.

Eckhart, Meister Johannes. *Breakthrough: Meister Eckhart's Creation Spirituality in New Translation*. Edited and translated by Matthew Fox. New York: Doubleday, 1991.

———. *Meister Eckhart: A Modern Translation*. Translated by Raymond Blakney. New York: Harper, 1957.

———. *Meister Eckhart: Selected Treatises and Sermons*. Edited and translated by James M. Clark. London: Faber, 1958.

———. *Meister Eckhart: Selected Writings*. Edited and translated by Oliver Davies. London: Penguin, 1994.

———. *Meister Eckharts mystische Schriften*. Edited and translated by Gustav Landauer. Berlin: Schnabel, 1903.

Ellenberger, Henri F. "The Concept of 'Maladie Créatrice.'" [1964] In *Beyond the Unconscious: Essays of Henri F. Ellenberger in the History of Psychiatry*, edited by Mark S. Micale, 328–40. Princeton, NJ: Princeton University Press, 1993.

———. *The Discovery of the Unconscious: The History and Evolution of Dynamic Psychiatry*. New York: Basic, 1970.

Eller, Vernard. *Kierkegaard and Radical Discipleship*. Princeton: Princeton University Press, 1968.

Fabry, Heinz.-Josef. "šûb." In *Theological Dictionary of the Old Testament*, edited by Gerhard Johannes Botterweck et al., 14.461–522. 16 vols. Grand Rapids: Eerdmans, 2004.

Ferguson, Margaret W. "Saint Augustine's Region of Unlikeness: The Crossing of Exile and Language." *Georgia Review* 29.4 (Winter 1975) 842–64.

Feuerbach, Ludwig. *Principles of the Philosophy of the Future.* Indianapolis: Bobbs-Merrill, 1966.

Finley, James. *Merton's Palace of Nowhere: A Search for God through Awareness of the True Self.* Notre Dame: Ave Maria, 1978.

Fox, Matthew. "Introduction, Commentary and Notes." In *Breakthrough: Meister Eckhart's Creation Spirituality in New Translation,* by Johannes, Eckhart, edited and translated by Matthew Fox, 1–51. New York: Doubleday, 1991.

Friedman, Maurice. "The Bases of Buber's Ethics." In *The Philosophy of Martin Buber,* edited by Paul Arthur Schilpp and Maurice Friedman, 171–200. The Library of Living Philosophers 12. La Salle, IL: Open Court, 1967.

———. *Encounter on the Narrow Ridge: A Life of Martin Buber.* New York: Paragon, 1991.

———. "Introduction." In *Meetings,* by Martin Buber, 7–19. La Salle, IL: Open Court, 1973.

———. "Introduction to the Torchbook Edition." In *Pointing the Way,* by Martin Buber, vii–xiii. New York: Harper, 1963.

———. "Martin Buber and Asia." *Philosophy East and West* 26.4 (October 1976) 411–26.

———. "Martin Buber's Encounter with Mysticism." *Human Inquiries* 10 (1970) 43–81.

———. *Martin Buber's Life and Work.* Vol. 1. *The Early Years, 1878–1923.* New York: Dutton, 1981.

———. *Martin Buber's Life and Work.* Vol. 2. *The Middle Years, 1923–1945.* New York: Dutton, 1983.

———. *Martin Buber's Life and Work.* Vol. 3. *The Later Years, 1923–1945.* New York: Dutton, 1983.

Gennep, Arnold van. *The Rites of Passage.* Chicago: University of Chicago Press, 1960.

Goethe, Johann Wolfgang von. *Faust.* Erster Teil. Halle, Germany: Verlag Otto Hendel, 1900.

———. *West-östliche Divan.* Vienna: Armbruster, 1820.

Gregory of Nyssa. *The Life of Moses.* Classics of Western Spirituality. Mahwah, NJ: Paulist, 1978.

Henderson, Joseph L. *Thresholds of Initiation.* Middletown, CT: Wesleyan University Press, 1967.

Heraclitus of Ephesus. *The Cosmic Fragments.* Translated by G. S. Kirk. Cambridge: Cambridge University Press, 1978.

Herman, Jonathan R. *I and Tao: Martin Buber's Encounter with Chuang Tzu.* Albany: State University of New York Press, 1996.

Hodes, Aubrey. *Martin Buber: An Intimate Portrait.* New York: Viking, 1973.

Hölderlin, Friedrich. *Gesammelte Werke.* Zweiter Band. Leipzig: Diederichs, 1905.

Homans, Peter. *Jung in Context: Modernity and the Making of a Psychology.* Chicago: University of Chicago Press, 1979.

Horwitz, Rivka. *Buber's Way to "I and Thou": The Development of Buber's Thought and his "Religion as Presence" Lectures.* Philadelphia: Jewish Publication Society, 1988. Originally published as *Buber's Way to "I and Thou": An Historical Analysis and the First Publication of Martin Buber's Lectures Religion als Gegenwart.* (Heidelberg: Schneider, 1978).

Huston, Phil. *Martin Buber's Journey to Presence.* Abrahamic Dialogues 7. New York: Fordham University Press, 2007.

"Itivuttaka: The Group of Ones." Translated by Thanissaro Bhikkhu, 2001 [KN Iti 1-27 PTS: Iti 1-19] http://www.accesstoinsight.org/tipitaka/kn/iti/iti.1.001-027.than.html.

Jaspers, Karl. *The Origin and Goal of History*. Translated by Michael Bullock. London: Routledge, 1953.

Kant, Immanuel. *Groundwork of the Metaphysics of Morals*. Translated by James W. Ellington. 3rd ed. Indianapolis: Hackett, 1993.

"Karaniya Metta Sutta: Loving-Kindness." Translated by Nanamoli Thera, 1995. [SN 1.8 PTS: Sn 143-152] http://www.accesstoinsight.org/tipitaka/kn/snp/snp.1.08.nymo.html.

Kaufmann, Walter. "Buber's Religious Significance." In *The Philosophy of Martin Buber*, edited by Paul Arthur Schilpp and Maurice Friedman, 665–85. The Library of Living Philosophers 12. La Salle, IL: Open Court, 1967.

———. *I and Thou: A New Translation with a Prologue "I and You" and Notes*. New York: Scribner's, 1970.

———. "I and You: A Prologue." In *I and Thou*, translated by Walter Kaufmann, 9–48. New York: Scribner's, 1970.

———. "Introductory Essay: The Inevitability of Alienation." In *Alienation*, by Richard Schacht, xiii–lvi. Garden City, NY: Doubleday, 1970.

Keating, Thomas. *Invitation to Love: The Way of Christian Contemplation*. New York: Continuum, 1996.

Kepnes, Steven. *The Text as Thou: Martin Buber's Dialogical Hermeneutics and Narrative Theology*. Bloomington: Indiana University Press, 1992.

Kierkegaard, Søren. *Concluding Unscientific Postscript*. Edited and translated by Walter Lowrie and David F. Swenson. Princeton, NJ: Princeton University Press, 1992.

———. *Either/Or*. 2 vols. Translated by Walter Lowrie. Garden City, NY: Anchor, 1959.

———. *Fear and Trembling*. Translated by Alastair Hannay. London: Penguin, 1985.

———. *The Sickness unto Death: A Christian Psychological Exposition for Upbuilding and Awakening*. Translated by Howard V. Hong and Edna H. Hong. Princeton: Princeton University Press, 1980.

Kirsch, Thomas, et al., eds. *Initiation: The Living Reality of an Archetype*. East Sussex, UK: Routledge, 2007.

Kohn, Hans, and Robert Weltsch. *Martin Buber: Sein Werk Und Seine Zeit: Ein Beitrag Zur Geistesgeschichte Mitteleuropas, 1880–1930*. Cologne: Melzer, 1961.

Lao Tzu. *The Sayings of Lao Tzu* [The Tao Te Ching]. Translated by Lionel Giles. London: Murray, 1905.

Lovejoy, Arthur O. *The Great Chain of Being: A Study of the History of an Idea*. New York: Harper, 1960.

Lunn, Eugene. *Prophet of Community: The Romantic Socialism of Gustav Landauer*. Berkeley: University of California Press, 1973.

McDonald, William. "Søren Kierkegaard." In *Stanford Encyclopedia of Philosophy*. Edited by Edward N. Zalta. Winter 2017. https://plato.stanford.edu/archives/win2017/entries/kierkegaard/.

Mendes-Flohr, Paul. *From Mysticism to Dialogue: Martin Buber's Transformation of German Social Thought*. Detroit: Wayne State University Press, 1989.

———. "Martin Buber's Conception of God." In *Divided Passions: Jewish Intellectuals and the Experience of* Modernity, edited by Paul Mendes-Flohr, 237–82. Detroit: Wayne State University Press, 1991.

Napoleon, and R. M. Johnston. *The Corsican: A Diary of Napoleon's Life in His Own Words, Compiled by R. M. Johnston*. Boston: Houghton Mifflin, 1930.
The New Testament in Hebrew and English. [Salkinson-Ginsburg translation] London: Society for the Distribution of Hebrew Scriptures, 2000.
"Nibbāna Sutta: Unbinding (3)." Translated by Thanissaro Bhikkhu, 2012 [Ud 8.3 PTS: Ud 80] http://www.accesstoinsight.org/tipitaka/kn/ud/ud.8.03.than.html
Nietzsche, Friedrich. *The Birth of Tragedy and the Genealogy of Morals*. Translated by Francis Golffing. Garden City, NY: Doubleday, 1956.
Ong, Walter. "World as View and World as Event." *American Anthropologist* 71 (1969) 634–47.
Ortega y Gasset, José. *The Revolt of the Masses*. New York: Norton, 1957.
Osborne, Arthur. *Ramana Maharshi and the Path of Self-Knowledge*. New York: Weiser, 1970.
Paracelsus, Theophrastus Bombastus von Hohenheim. *Die große Wundarznei*. Vol. 10 in *Paracelsus Sämtliche Werke*. Ed. Karl Sudhoff. Munich: Oldenbourg, 1928.
Pascal, Blaise. *Pensées*. New York: Dutton, 1958.
Perkins, Robert L. "Buber and Kierkegaard: A Philosophic Encounter." In *Martin Buber: A Centenary Volume*, edited by Hayim Gordon et al., 275–303. New York: Ktav, 1984.
Petuchowski, Jakob J. "The Concept of 'Teshuvah' in the Bible and the Talmud." *Judaism* 17.2 (Spring 1968) 175–85.
Plato. *Letters*. Translated by Glenn R. Morrow. In *Plato: Complete Works, 1634–76*. Edited by John M. Cooper and D. S. Hutchinson, 1634–76. Indianapolis: Hackett, 1997.
Plotinus. *The Enneads*. Translated by Stephen McKenna. Burdett, NY: Larson, 1992.
———. *The Essential Plotinus: Representative Treatises from the Enneads*. Translated by Elmer O'Brien. Indianapolis: Hackett, 1964.
Ricoeur, Paul. "The Hermeneutical Function of Distanciation." In *Hermeneutics and the Human Sciences: Essays on Language, Action, and Interpretation*, edited and translated by John B. Thompson, 131–44. Cambridge: Cambridge University Press, 1981.
"Rohitassa Sutta." In *Samyutta Nikaya: An Anthology*, translated by Bhikkhu Ñanananda, SN 2.26. 2007. http://www.accesstoinsight.org/lib/authors/nanananda/wheel183.html#fnt-26.
Rosenzweig, Franz. "The Builders: Concerning the Law." In *On Jewish Learning*, translated and edited by Nahum N. Glatzer, 72–92. New York: Schocken, 1955.
———. "Scripture and Luther." In *Scripture and Translation*, by Martin Buber and Franz Rosenzweig, edited and translated by Lawrence Rosenwald, 47–69. Bloomington: Indiana University Press, 1994.
———. *The Star of Redemption*. New York: Holt, Rinehart and Winston, 1971.
Rosenzweig, Franz, and Nahum N. Glatzer. *Franz Rosenzweig: His Life and Thought*. New York: Schocken, 1961.
Rosenzweig, Franz, et al. *Briefe*. Berlin: Schocken, 1935.
Rousseau, Jean-Jacques. *Discourse on the Origins of Inequality*. Indianapolis: Hackett, 1992.
"Sabbasava Sutta: All the Fermentations." Translated by Thanissaro Bhikku, 1997 [MN 2 PTS: M i 6] http://www.accesstoinsight.org/tipitaka/mn/mn.002.than.html.

Schaeder, Grete. *The Hebrew Humanism of Martin Buber*. Detroit: Wayne State University Press, 1973.

———. "Martin Buber: A Biographical Sketch." In *The Letters of Martin Buber*, translated by Richard Winston et al., 1–62. New York: Schocken, 1991. Originally published as "Martin Buber: Ein biographischer Abriß." In Martin Buber, *Briefwechsel aus sieben Jahrzehnten*, 1.19–141. Edited by Grete Schaeder. (Heidelberg: Lambert Schneider, 1972).

Schilpp, Paul Arthur, and Maurice Friedman, eds. *The Philosophy of Martin Buber*. The Library of Living Philosophers 12. La Salle, IL: Open Court, 1967.

Schopenhauer, Arthur. *The World as Will and Representation*. Cambridge: Cambridge University Press, 1914.

Shapira, Avraham. *Hope for Our Time: Key Trends in the Thought of Martin Buber*. Albany: State University of New York Press, 1999.

Silberstein, Laurence W. *Martin Buber's Social and Religious Thought: Alienation and the Quest for Meaning*. New York: New York University Press, 1989.

Stein, Murray. "On Modern Initiation into the Spiritual." In *Initiation: The Living Reality of an Archetype*, edited by Thomas Kirsch et al., 85–102. East Sussex, UK: Routledge, 2007.

"A Study of History." *Life* (23 Feb. 1948) 119+.

Tillich, Paul. "The Two Types of Philosophy of Religion." In *Theology of Culture*, edited by Robert C. Kimball, 10–29. New York: Oxford University Press, 1959.

Toynbee, Arnold, and Edward D. Myers. *A Study of History. Vol. 3, The Growth of Civilizations*. 12 vols. London: Oxford University Press, 1948.

Talmud: Niddah 30b:18–23. Sefaria, https://www.sefaria.org/Niddah.30b?lang=bi.

The Upanishads. 4 vols. 2nd ed. Translated and edited by Swami Nikhilananda. New York: Ramakrishna-Vivekananda, 1979.

Wasserstrom, Steven M. *Religion after Religion: Gershom Scholem, Mircea Eliade, and Henry Corbin at Eranos*. Princeton: Princeton University Press, 1999.

Wheelwright, Philip. "Buber's Philosophical Anthropology." In *The Philosophy of Martin Buber*, edited by Paul Arthur Schilpp and Maurice Friedman, 69–95. LaSalle, IL: Open Court, 1967.

Winokuer, Howard R., and Darcy L. Harris. *Principles and Practice of Grief Counseling*. New York: Springer, 2012.

Wolfson, Elliot. "The Problem of Unity in the Thought of Martin Buber." *Journal of the History of Philosophy* 27.3 (July 1989) 423–44.

Wood, Robert E. *Martin Buber's Ontology: An Analysis of "I and Thou."* Evanston, IL: Northwestern University Press, 1969.

Würthwein, Ernst. "Repentance and Conversion in the Old Testament." In *Theological Dictionary of the New Testament*, edited by Gerhard Kittel et al., and translated by Geoffrey W. Bromiley, 4.980–89. 10 vols. Grand Rapids: Eerdmans, 1964.

Zhuangzi. *Chuang-tzŭ: The Inner Chapters*. Translated by Angus C. Graham. Indianapolis: Hackett, 2001.

Index

Note: Apart from foreign words and titles, index terms which are in italics are indexed only where they have the distinctive existential, metaphorical or spiritual meanings they carry within Buber's discourse.

1. Persons

Abraham, 95, 135 n 83, 250–51, 264, 293
Adam, 22n39, 230, 242
Amos, 247
Angelus Silesius, 70
Asoka, 286
Augustine of Hippo, 180, 211, 239
Avnon, Dan, 4, 21, 22, 95, 125, 126, 130, 176, 181, 208, 269, 293

The Baal-Shem-Tov, Israel ben Eliezer, xx, 3, 10, 16, 19–21, 23–25, 34, 39, 41, 46, 54, 61, 67, 109, 130, 135–36, 225, 227, 249, 268, 278–79, 293–94, 296, 297
Bergmann, Hugo, 65, 66, 116
Boehme, Jacob, xx, 58, 107–08, 125, 148, 298
Borges, Jorge Luis, 201, 202, 293
Bourgeault, Cynthia, 153, 293
Breslauer, S. Daniel, 26, 293
Buber, Adele, 59–61
Buber, Carl, 62–63
Buber, Elise Wurgast, xix, 10, 28–29, 57–59, 64–65, 68
Buber, Eva, 63

Buber, Paula, 10, 19, 28, 35, 57, 63–70, 79–80, 299
Buber, Rafael, xiv, 63
Buber, Salomon, 10, 59–61
The Buddha, 116, 134, 139, 178, 224, 226, 227, 231–34, 258, 260, 271, 285–88, 294

Chuang-Tzu (Zhuangzi), xx, 7, 109, 117, 121, 128, 134, 140, 142, 168, 286, 294, 299, 300, 303
Confucius, 14
Corrigan, Kevin, 245, 299

Daniel, 71–72
Dante Alighieri, 51, 180, 240, 299
Descartes, Rene, 95, 187
Diamond, Malcolm, 47
Dilthey, Wilhelm, 58, 108–10, 112, 113
Downing, Christine, 57, 299

Eckhart, Meister Johann, xvi, 32, 58, 70, 97, 104, 107, 123, 138–39, 142, 217, 224, 226–28, 235, 270, 296, 298, 299, 300
Einstein, Albert, 181
Eliade, Mircea, 15–16, 303
Elijah, 249, 251, 282

INDEX

Ellenberger, Henri, 14, 26–27, 32–33, 35–38, 299
Eller, Vernard, 191, 299
Eve, 242

Fabry, H.-J., 195, 299
Feuerbach, Ludwig, 37, 70, 108, 150, 179, 300
Finley, James, 153, 300
Fox, Matthew, 217, 299, 300
Francis of Assisi, 5, 108
Freud, Sigmund, 14, 38, 167, 186
Friedman, Maurice, xiii, 2, 23, 27–30, 39, 44–45, 47, 56, 58, 59, 61, 62, 64, 65, 66, 68, 69–70, 73, 75, 78–79, 82, 92, 98, 109, 110, 116, 117, 121–22, 126, 139, 208, 265, 268, 293–98, 300, 301, 303

Gennep, Arnold Van, 13–14, 300
Glatzer, Nahum, 82, 293–99, 302
Goethe, Johann Wolfgang von, 50, 51, 68, 162, 190, 214, 300
Gregory of Nyssa, 223, 253, 300

Hafez, 68
Hallo, Rudolf, 80, 81, 83, 93
Harris, Darcy L., 31, 32, 35, 303
Hechler, The Rev. William, xx, 10, 57, 71–72
Hegel, Georg Friedrich Wilhelm, 58, 179
Heidegger, Martin, 180
Henderson, Joseph, 13–14, 300
Herman, Jonathan R. 7, 117, 121, 126, 129, 294, 300
Heraclitus, 200, 206–07, 215, 217, 300
Herzl, Theodor, xx, 7, 17–19, 67, 71
Hölderlin, Friedrich, 51, 58, 150, 217, 300
Homans, Peter, 147, 300
Horwitz, Rivka, 38, 72, 82–83, 85, 93, 159–60, 297, 300

Isaac, 95, 103, 250–51
Isaiah, Deutero-Isaiah, 92, 152, 207, 221, 250, 268, 271, 289

Jacob, xi, 95, 132, 242, 249, 251, 289
Jaspers, Karl, 135, 301
Jesus, 30, 50, 132, 134, 138, 156, 178, 190, 195, 214, 224, 226, 227, 234, 258, 260, 271, 285–86, 290
Job, 27, 160, 259, 280
Jonah, 277
Jung, Carl Gustav, 14, 38, 147, 273, 300

Kant, Immanuel, 46, 148, 149, 152, 155, 156, 180, 234, 239, 301
Kaufmann, Walter, xiii, xiv, xv–xvii, 2, 9, 49, 68, 100, 116, 147, 151, 172, 179, 186, 187, 189, 203, 237, 259, 293, 295, 301
Keating, Thomas, 153, 301
Kepnes, Steven, 9, 56, 301
Kierkegaard, Søren, 12, 37, 43, 50, 96, 98–101, 103, 106, 139, 141, 186, 189–93, 199, 202, 203, 208, 219, 221, 238, 246–49, 299, 251, 301, 302
Kipling, Rudyard, 66
Kohn, Hans, 1, 8, 301

Landauer, Gustav, xix, xx, 7, 10, 18, 26–32, 35–36, 38, 46, 48, 55, 57–58, 75–79, 82, 93, 107, 115, 138, 147, 151, 296, 298–99, 301
Lao Tzu, 220, 227, 238, 258, 260, 285, 286, 301
Leib the Wanderer, 54
Locke, John, 185
Lovejoy, Arthur O., 235, 301
Lunn, Eugene, 28, 78, 301

Mauthner, Fritz, 28
Mayer, Eugen, 93
Mc Donald, William, 43, 301
Mehe, xx, 10, 29, 57, 73–74, 78, 107, 112, 119–20, 131
Mendelssohn, Moses, 151
Mendes-Flohr, Paul, 2, 7, 31, 78, 130, 147–49, 151, 181, 294, 295, 301
Moses, xxi, 6, 14, 132, 135, 151, 176, 207, 220, 223, 249, 251–53, 259, 271, 279, 289, 296, 300

Munk, Georg [Paula Buber's pen name], 67

Napoleon, 50, 189–90, 214, 302
Nicholas of Cusa, xx, 58, 107, 148
Nietzsche, Friedrich, 113, 148, 160–61, 254, 279, 302

Ortega y Gasset, José, 216, 302
Osborne, Arthur, 203, 302
Otto, Rudolf, 12, 219, 224

Pascal, Blaise, 95–96, 173, 180, 302
Paul, 271, 286
Perkins, Robert L., 189, 302
Petuchowski, Jakob J., 195, 302
Plato, 14, 39, 180, 203, 235, 302
Plotinus, 74, 107, 137, 168, 172, 181–82, 194, 196, 203–04, 229, 238, 245, 248, 299, 302
Pseudo-Dionysius, 107

Ricoeur, Paul, 44, 302
Rogers, Carl, 27, 29, 32, 298
Rosenzweig, Franz, xxi, 10, 17, 36, 57, 60, 62, 79–93, 116, 151, 160, 242, 248, 250, 259, 263, 272, 296–99, 302
Rousseau, Jean-Jacques, 161, 302
Ruth, 69

Schaeder, Grete, 7–8, 13, 20, 29, 31, 42, 59, 63, 64, 66–69, 75, 81, 101, 131, 294, 303
Scheler, Max, 12, 50, 219, 246–47
Schleiermacher, Friedrich, 12, 219, 224
Schopenhauer, Arthur, 148–49, 303
Shoishar, Aharon, 268
Silberstein, Laurence, 146–47, 303
Simmel, Georg, 113, 123, 147
Smith, Ronald Gregor, xiii–xvii, xxi, 151, 183, 186–87, 189, 203, 221, 265, 287–88, 294–95, 197–98
Socrates, 50, 187, 190–91, 214
Spinoza, Baruch, 233
Spitteler, Carl, 77
Stein, Murray, 19, 32, 303
Stirner, Max, 186

Susya, Rabbi, 40
Symeon the New Theologian, 245–46

Tillich, Paul, 97, 303
Tönnies, Ferdinand, 7
Toynbee, Arnold, 14, 27, 303

Weltsch, Robert, 1, 8, 131, 301
Wheelwright, Philip, 186, 191, 303
Winokuer, Howard R., 31–32, 35, 303
Wolfson, Elliott, 137, 303
Wood, Robert E., xiii, 49, 52, 92, 186, 303
Würthwein, Ernst, 195, 303

2. German terms

Abgeschiedenheit, 138, 142
All, das All, Allwesen, 121, 229, 243
Alp, 189, 194
Angst, 98
Angesicht, 248

Bahn, 263–265
Baumeister, 130, 181
Begegnen, Begegnung, xiii, 44, 71, 110–11, 154, 197, 210, 281, 293, 294
Bestimmung, 111, 203
Bewahren, 214
Bewähren, 214
Beziehung, 85, 110, 115, 191, 212, 223, 232

Das Du an sich, 46, 149
Dasein, Krasse Dasein, 70, 231
Dazwischen, 157, 214
Ding an sich, 46, 148–49, 152, 239
Du, 49, 52, 150–51, 172, 174, 215, 280
Durchbruch, 217

Eifer, 20
Eigensein, 175
Eigenwesen, 179, 185–87, 189–92, 194, 196, 199, 208
Das Eine, 137, 200, 209
Die Eine Wirklichkeit, 249

Einzelne, 190, 191
Einzige, 186
Einzigkeit, 251
Entwirklichung, 177, 179, 185, 189
Erlebnis, 11, 76–78, 107–13, 115, 117–19, 121, 123, 125, 148–49, 184, 188, 230
Das Erlebte Konkret, 275
Erlösung, 260
Der Ewige, 151

Gegenstand, 49, 168
Gegenüber, das Gegenüber, 46, 149
Gegenwart, 49, 168, 196, 297, 300
Gelassen, Gelassenheit 102, 104, 203, 224
Gelebte Wirklichkeit, 101, 121, 230
Gemeinschaft, 7, 31, 75–76, 78–81, 107, 181
Gestalt, 159–60, 165, 243–44, 258–59, 261–63
Gleichnis, 128, 242, 294

Haltung, 152
Harren, 221
Heil, 252
Heilsleben, 231

Kehre, kehren, umkehren 195

Lebensphilosophie, 113

Meister, 60, 127

Nichttun, 222

Person, 185–86, 190

Schicksal, 203, 211
Sehnsucht, 164, 167, 242
Sein, 70, 141, 169, 187, 191, 213
Selbstbehauptungstrieb 187, 222
Selbsterscheinung, 188
Sosein, 187

Umgang, 23
Umkehr, 175, 195–96
Ungeschmälert, 198

Urchristentum, 285
Urgrund, 11, 45, 70, 97, 142, 175
Urjude, 268
Urzeit, 267

Verbundene, 237
Verbundenheit, 175
Verbundensein, 250
Verfremdung, 147
Vergegnung, 10, 57–58, 71
Verwirklichen, Verwirklichung, 141, 200, 202
Verzweiflung, 193
Der Vollendete, 126–29, 132, 141, 209, 231
Vollkommen, vollkommene, 21, 141, 223, 269

Wahrheit, 70
Wechselwirkung, 197
Weg, 38, 210, 216
Weisung, 125
Weltkonkretum, 101
Wesensakt, 176, 180
Wiedererkennen, 196
Der willkürliche Mensch, 188
Wirken, Wirkend, Wirkung, 176, 197, 207, 212–13
Wirklichwerden, 201
Wirklichkeit, 70, 101, 197, 213, 230, 249

Zeugen, 20
Zurückbiegung, Rückgebogen, 157, 187, 195, 232

3. Hebrew terms

Am-haaretz, 127
Aggadah, 5–6, 60
Akedah, 250, 290
Atah, 151

Erev, 90

Galut, 266–68

Halakha, 5, 81
Haskalah, 10, 60
Hasidut, 21–22
Hitlahavut, 201, 207

Kavana, 104

Mashal, 128
Miqra, 17
Mitzva, Mitzvot 88, 90

Olam, 242

Panim, 248

Qavah, 221

Re'ah, 158
Rebbe, 130
Ruach Elohim, 151

Shalom, 267
Shekinah, 70, 140, 144
Shema, 263
Sheol, 28
Shul, 152

Tefillin, 62
Teshuvah, 11, 16–17, 21, 40, 44, 53, 141, 175, 192–97, 199–200, 202, 205–09, 212, 216–17, 240, 247, 249, 257–59, 262, 265, 269, 289, 302
Tohu wa Bohu 152
Torah, 6, 54, 60, 125, 130, 157

Urim and t(h)ummim 6, 282

Yada, 242
Yichud, 139, 142, 145, 198
Yom Kippur, 40, 62, 90

Zerizut, 20–21, 203, 206

4. The Hebrew Scriptures and the New Testament

Genesis 1:1, 162
Genesis 1:2, 152, 211
Genesis 3:8, 144
Genesis 4:1, 242
Genesis 4:6–7, 190
Genesis 22:1–19, 251
Genesis 22:9, 103
Genesis 32:24–30, 249
Genesis 49, 69
Genesis 49:26, 242

Exodus 3, 207
Exodus 3:1–6, 259
Exodus 3:14, 220, 252
Exodus 3:1–4:17, 249
Exodus 28:30, 283

Leviticus 19:18, 157

Deuteronomy, 176
Deuteronomy 6:4–5, 262–63

Judges 11–12, 186

I Kings 19:11–18, 249

Job 4:16, 160, 259
Job 4:12–21, 160
Job 19:25, 280

Psalm 73:23–24, 280

Isaiah 6, 152, 207
Isaiah 6:1, 152
Isaiah 40:31, 221, 250
Isaiah 66:18–20, 271–72

Jeremiah 2:13, 248
Jeremiah 4:1, 195

Daniel, 71–72

Hosea 6:1, 195

Jonah, 277

Matthew 4:17, 195
Matthew 6:24, 246

Luke 8:26–51, 156
Luke 10:42, 137–38

Gospel of John, 227
John 1:1, 162
John 10:30, 226
John 13:22, 156

Romans 8:18–23, 235

Philippians 3:13, 223

I John 3:9, 213

5. General

A Priori of Relation, 161, 164, 166
The Absolute, 3, 6, 46, 70–71, 95, 99–100, 102–04, 106, 117, 128, 132, 138–39, 141, 152, 200–03, 205, 209, 223–25, 246–47, 267, 272–73, 285, 290
Absorb, Absorption Mysticism, 12, 50, 110, 113–14, 118, 219, 226–34, 245, 257, 275
The Abstract, Abstraction, Abstracting, 41, 45, 76, 95, 100, 102–03, 107–08, 115, 152, 156, 169, 180, 192, 198, 221, 276
Abyss, 5, 35, 59, 71, 99–100, 142, 185, 199, 200, 209, 215–16, 245, 277, 279
Accept, Acceptance, 36, 81, 101, 105–06, 150, 216, 222, 251, 273, 276, 280
Access, Accessible, 34, 37, 40–42, 92, 95, 104, 112, 124, 136, 145, 157, 185, 211, 254, 261, 268, 270, 276
Act, Action, Enact, 3, 19, 21–22, 24, 30, 44–45, 48, 50–55, 77, 82, 88, 91, 95, 104–05, 111, 114–15, 119–20, 122–24, 135–39, 144, 152, 154–56, 158–60, 162–63, 165–66, 175–78, 180, 187–88, 190–91, 195–202, 206–11, 214, 222, 225–28, 230, 235, 237–40, 243, 245, 247–53, 256, 259, 264, 274–77, 283
Act of Being, Being-Act, 135, 176, 178, 180, 240, 250, 256
Active vs. Receptive, 55, 66, 102, 105, 154–56, 194, 199, 221, 245, 262–63, 279
Actual, Actuality, Actualize, 3, 6, 22, 25, 47, 76, 78–79, 86, 89, 91, 101–02, 104, 112, 130, 135, 156, 158–59, 161–62, 165, 169, 180, 184, 189, 192, 202–03, 209–12, 214, 227–28, 233–34, 239–40, 248, 250, 257–58, 269, 273–74, 275–76, 291
The Adamic Task, 230
Address, 5, 16–17, 23–24, 30, 33, 47, 49, 55–56, 59, 65–66, 73–74, 81, 84, 89, 91, 98, 102–04, 124, 134–35, 146–47, 150–56, 158–59, 165–66, 169–72, 187, 194, 196, 219–21, 224–25, 234, 237, 241–43, 246–47, 255, 275, 280, 291; see also *Call*
Advaita, 108, 229–30
Affirmation, 48, 62, 73, 77, 88–90, 94, 120, 141, 150, 171, 209, 230, 238, 251–52, 262–63, 276
Agon, 11, 53, 265, 289
Ahamkara, 187, 222
Alienation, 11, 17, 146–49, 153, 161, 167, 170–71, 174, 177–79, 181–83, 185, 187, 190, 194, 215, 232, 234, 240, 244, 247, 263, 267, 279, 301, 303
The All, 111, 118, 122, 145, 148–49, 155, 198, 200, 202, 229–30, 235, 243, 262–63
Anguish, 35, 52, 58–59, 115, 215, 239, 249, 281
Anthropology, 34, 83, 147, 160–61, 163, 167, 186, 191, 220, 227, 261, 266, 303; *Anthropological Thought* 96, 147

Apollonian vs. Dionysian, 113, 148, 291
Apophatic, 103, 203, 222, 246, 255, 261
Apostle, 55, 137, 271
Apperception, 41, 95, 124, 149, 154, 259
Appropriate, 44, 124, 187, 188, 191, 212–13, 221, 222; *Self-Appropriation* 187, 188, 191, 213, 222; see also *Participate, Participation*
Archetype, 13, 14, 57, 174, 195, 204, 217, 239, 250, 251, 301, 303
Art, The Arts, 2, 30, 58, 67, 135, 148, 159, 160, 226, 235, 244
Ascesis, 23, 33, 37, 139, 245
Assimilation, Jewish, 31, 102
Atheism, Atheist, 51, 221, 248
Atman, 134, 286; *atmanam vidhi* 203
Attachment, 203, 211, 245
Attain, Attainment, 20, 22, 34, 37, 42, 104, 105, 131, 182, 203, 204, 273, 276; *Attained Oneness* 127, 141, 144, 239
Attestation, 42, 47, 264; *Inner Attestation* 41–43; see also *Confirm, Confirmation*
Authenticate, Authentication, 44, 45, 69, 133, 181, 283
Authentic, 5, 25, 37, 45, 49–50, 53, 55, 58, 63, 89, 90, 92, 98, 122–26, 128, 136, 138–39, 141, 146, 157, 174, 190, 193, 213–15, 234, 256–57, 263, 271–72, 274–77, 280–81, 283; *Authentic Dialogue* 50, 55, 63, 276; *Authentic I, Authentic Self* 146, 190, 193, 213, 283; *Authentic Life, Living* 92, 98, 123–26, 128, 136, 138–39, 141, 271; *Authentic Subjectivity* 213; *Authentic Participation in Being* 37; *Authentic Subjectivity* 213; *The Authentic Way* 5, 272; see also *Genuine*
Authenticity, 5, 31, 45, 53, 58, 90, 125, 128, 174, 215, 234, 277, 280, 283
Autonomous I, Autonomous Individual, Autonomous Self, 104, 165, 179, 186, 187, 192
Autonomous Reason, 41, 95, 97, 102

Autonomy, 95, 104, 106, 147, 166, 175, 187, 210
Await, Awaiting 155, 178, 203, 207, 210, 221, 252
Awakening, 15, 17, 21, 23, 40, 44, 133, 163, 196, 202, 218, 222, 231, 247; Buber's spiritual awakening xx, 8, 10, 17, 21–23, 26, 32, 33, 34, 38, 40, 48, 51, 130, 267, 269
Awareness, Double Awareness, 102, 202, 204, 213, 253, 268; *I Awareness* 162, 165, 166, 200; *Self-Awareness* 165, 188, 213, 237; see also *Conscious, Consciousness*
Axial, Axial Period, 102, 135, 178, 270

Bear Witness, 22, 26, 34, 40–43, 220, 254, 282 ; see also *Witness, Testify*
Becoming, 21–22, 32, 37, 66, 84, 93, 99, 103, 106, 142, 144, 150, 160, 162, 163, 171, 198, 212–14, 216, 221–22, 227, 230, 236, 240, 247, 253, 260, 264, 269, 276, 285; *Becoming One*, 198, 227, 230
Being [as general existence], 3, 5, 18, 23, 25, 27, 36–37, 39, 47, 70, 74, 95–96, 98, 103, 109–14, 117–22, 125, 131, 133, 135, 136, 139, 141, 143, 145, 153–55, 158, 170–71, 175, 178–79, 188, 190–92, 205, 209–10, 212–13, 223, 227, 229–30, 232–33, 237–39, 243, 252, 273–74, 280
Being [as individual existence], 3, 8, 16–17, 21, 27, 40, 55, 59, 64–65, 68, 89, 91, 102, 110–11, 120, 122, 129, 131, 133–34, 136, 138, 150, 152–54, 156–57, 159, 168, 176, 186, 188, 191–92, 195–201, 203–05, 207–210, 212, 221–23, 228, 231–33, 236–37, 239, 242, 244, 250–51, 257–59, 262, 264, 273–74, 276, 278, 280
Belief vs. Faith or Trust, 105, 209, 256

INDEX

Bend Back, Bend Backward, [*Zurückbiegen*], 187, 195, 232, 233
Berlin, xix, xx, 18, 19, 58, 63, 67, 71, 75, 76, 108, 113, 123, 147
"The Between," ["*das Inzwischen*"], 3, 31, 36, 37, 47, 68, 69, 78, 89, 144, 156–58, 171, 178, 184, 212, 214, 225, 226, 227, 237, 244, 262, 265
Bhagavad Gita, 187, 222
Bodhisattva, 230
[Human] Body, 29, 129, 162–66, 189, 195, 233, 251, 287, 288
Biblical Humanism, Hebrew Humanism, 12, 60, 113, 290, 292
Binding, 31, 58, 95, 102, 103, 106, 117, 164–67, 176, 196, 213, 241, 250–51, 263, 272
Bond, 40, 103, 106, 165, 166, 196, 206, 263, 267; *Bond of Connection and Separateness* 213; *Cosmic Bond* 164, 166, 167; *Natural Bond* 164, 166; *Spiritual Bond* 167
Bourgeois, Bourgeoisie 148, 161, 185
Brahman, 162, 229, 286
Breakthrough [*Durchbruch*], 102, 176, 178, 193, 194, 200, 205, 209, 211, 217, 222, 247
Breath [of God], 6, 151, 191, 212, 242
Buber's Conversion to Hasidism, 23, 25, 269
The Buddha, 116, 134, 139, 178, 224, 226–27, 231–34, 258, 260, 271, 285–88
Buddhist, Buddhism, 5, 12, 15, 50, 132–33, 219, 230–32, 287–88
Butterfly and Chrysalis, 49, 168, 175–76, 240, 257–58

Call, Calling Forth, 5, 8–10, 12, 17, 19–23, 25, 32, 34, 41–42, 46, 48, 65, 79, 92, 113, 120, 133, 145, 152, 157, 159, 168, 174, 178, 195–96, 203, 207, 210, 218, 233, 243, 249, 260–61, 265, 267–69, 271, 277–79, 281–89
"Cannot be Taught", 247

Carve, Uncarved Block or Log or Marble, 237–38
Cat, 9, 51, 155, 236
Causal Nexus, 138, 149, 163, 170, 177, 179, 182–84, 189, 194, 205–06, 208, 215
Causality, 159, 177–78, 182–83, 203, 212
Center, 5, 17, 59, 180–81, 195–96, 200, 220, 222, 224, 240, 257, 265; *Center of the Person* 17, 59, 222; *The Centered Life* 200; *Centerless* 200; *Human-Centered* 70, 96, 125, 141; *Image of the Center* 5, 220; *The Living Center of Community* 130–31, 181; *The Transcendental Center* 182, 196, 200, 224, 240, 257, 265
Central Person, 22, 126–28, 130, 133–34, 142–43, 222, 286
Chain of Being, 235–36
Chih-jen, 126
Choice, Choose, 11, 43, 49, 52, 72, 75, 94, 136–38, 144, 146, 152–54, 168, 172, 192–93, 198–202, 206, 214, 216–18, 221, 229, 264, 268, 273, 277
Christian, Christianity, 5, 12, 15, 50, 71–72, 100, 107, 132–33, 153, 164, 219, 226, 235, 285–86, 289–90; see also Primal Christianity
Circumstance, Circumstances, 11, 13, 21, 35, 37, 105–06, 120, 139, 152–53, 188, 198, 200–02, 210, 253, 273, 276, 278–79
Cognition, Cognitive, 95, 123–24, 136, 196
Community [*Gemeinschaft*], 7–8, 15, 21–22, 31, 42, 60–62, 75–77, 82, 123, 126–27, 130–31, 135, 147, 158, 176–77, 180–82, 241, 247, 256–58, 261; *Hasidic Community* 8, 60, 61, 82, 123, 131, 181
Compassion, 129, 156, 158, 230, 232; see *Love*
Completed Man, Completed Person, 22, 25, 126, 222–23

complexio oppositorum, 43
Concentrate, Concentration, 141, 154, 194, 198–99, 227–28, 230, 237–38, 256; see also *Becoming One*
Conceptual Thought vs. Non-Conceptual Intuitive Immediacy, 42, 43, 45, 86, 95, 96, 102, 123, 169, 209, 234
The Concrete [The Concreteness of an individual lived human life or moment embedded in a historical context], 3, 13, 22–23, 38, 41, 45–47, 54–56, 59, 68, 73, 78, 93–97, 99–106, 108, 112, 114–17, 119, 121, 125, 133, 135–36, 143, 154, 156, 159, 163, 172, 174, 192, 209, 215, 232, 243, 251, 259, 263, 275–79, 291
"The Condition of Nothing", 143
Conditional Being, 223
Confessional Stance, 290
Confirm, Confirmation [to confirm self and other in dialogue/action], 69, 105, 150, 171, 181, 191, 209, 251, 256, 257, 276, 285; *Confirmation from Within* 45
Confront, Confrontation, 9, 49, 97, 101, 134, 144, 152–53, 159–60, 165, 170, 193–94, 199, 211, 259, 278, 281
Conscious, 21, 22, 108, 163, 166–67; *I-Conscious* 163, 165
Consciousness, 24, 78, 106, 108, 150, 153, 163, 183; *Self-Consciousness* 187, 191, 204, 213
Constancy, Steadiness, 50, 51, 111–12, 117, 122, 125, 143, 199, 214, 222, 256–57
Consume, Consumer, Consumerism, 50, 188
Contingency, 59, 74–75, 110, 113–15, 150, 166, 204, 206, 239, 266, 275
Conversation, 33, 44, 72–74, 80, 88, 93, 100, 157
Cosmic, 161, 163, 164–68, 171, 174, 200, 215–16, 219, 235, 236, 251, 257; *Cosmic Alienation, Homelessness* 147, 174, 179, 180–82; *Cosmic Bond* 164–67; *Cosmic Erlebnis, Subjectivity* 78, 162; *Cosmic Gyre, Cycle* 174–78, 192, 216, 219, 255, 257–65; *Cosmic Mediator* 131; *Cosmic Musical Score* 51; *Cosmic Primal Meaning* 104, 144; *Enoch the Cosmic Cobbler* 45; see also *Metacosmic*
Cosmology, Cosmological Thought, 97, 147, 180, 183
Cosmos, 176–77, 180, 241, 244, 257, 263
Cosmos as Home, 146, 177, 180, 241, 244; *Cosmic Homelessness* 146–47, 179, 180–82
Covenant, 6, 106
Creative Withdrawal, 9, 27, 33, 35–36, 38
Creative Illness, 14, 26–38
Creativity, Realm or Sphere of Creativity, 55, 66–67, 84, 155, 159–60, 188, 225, 235, 243–45
Creation, The Created Order, 21, 73, 84, 102, 112, 144, 152, 164–65, 168, 171, 219, 225, 230, 233–35, 241, 243, 247–49, 260, 263, 289
The Creator, 21, 103–04, 114, 144, 182, 202, 204, 225, 232, 235, 243, 247, 263, 283; *Co-Creator* 21
Crisis, 7, 11, 19, 26, 74, 110, 171, 174, 176–78, 193–99, 214–17
Culture, 2, 4, 12, 20, 58, 60, 70, 95–96, 108, 126, 134–35, 145, 147–48, 162, 173–74, 180, 269, 279, 290
Cycle, 174, 176–79, 216, 219, 231, 255

Death and Rebirth, 15, 24, 178, 193, 204, 217–18, 291
Death of Landauer, xx, 7, 18, 26–32, 35–36, 38–39, 46, 48, 75, 78, 115, 138, 147
Decide, 138, 150, 154, 193, 199–201, 203, 209, 212, 214–18, 268; see also *Choose*
Decision, 49, 52, 69, 73, 136–37, 152, 158, 170, 198, 200–01, 203, 205, 209, 212, 216, 218, 228, 232–33, 249, 277, 283; see also *Choice*

Decisive, Decisiveness, 24, 29, 32, 37, 39, 56, 58, 65, 68–69, 72, 74, 75, 79, 93, 99, 104, 136, 198, 200, 204, 209–10, 217, 244, 267, 275

Der Jude xx, 91

Defining Purpose, Destined Purpose, 138, 202–03, 204, 207, 209–10, 212, 257, 278

Depth, Depths, 7, 9, 10, 11, 14, 26, 30, 35, 40, 41, 45, 63, 64, 73, 79, 86, 91, 112, 114, 123, 132, 145, 147, 159, 168, 171, 193, 197, 199, 200, 203, 204, 215, 217, 230, 232, 236, 249, 268, 270, 278, 280, 291

Desire, 20, 64, 77, 108, 118, 129, 132, 140, 164, 169, 178, 188, 196, 204, 207, 213, 231, 245, 251, 256

Despair, 73, 173, 184, 192–94, 216

Destiny, Destined, 18, 30, 32, 73, 79, 103–05, 119, 120, 129, 132, 136, 142, 154, 157, 177–78, 189, 193, 199, 201–05, 207, 209–12, 215, 228, 233, 247, 276

The Detached I, 166

Detach, Detachment, 30, 119, 129, 138–39, 142, 163–67, 170, 203, 228, 245, 247, 291

Devotio, 113–15, 127

The Dialogical Community, 123, 126, 127, 130, 131

The Dialogical Moment, 17, 49, 102, 114, 250, 254, 276

The Dialogical Person, 120, 135, 278

Dialogical Reality, 12, 35, 48, 56, 86, 90, 101, 218, 219, 220, 253

Differentiation, 122, 150, 162–63, 175, 187, 235, 238

Das Ding an sich, 46, 148–49, 152, 239

Direct, 26, 41, 55, 56, 95, 102, 141, 149, 154, 168, 191, 199, 213, 246; see also *Immediate, Unmediated*

Divide, 128, 136, 148; Creator vs. Creature 232, 235; Divided Self 268; Buber's Mystical vs. His Dialogical Phase 2–3, 118, 122, 145, 198; The Mystical vs. The Everyday 73–74, 119, 120, 122, 227; The Orient vs. the Occident 270; Self vs. The Other 149, 187

The Divine, 2, 6, 21, 25, 31, 68, 111, 114, 115, 131, 132, 140, 142, 152, 176, 198, 201, 203, 207, 219–20, 226, 229, 231, 251–56, 258–62, 264, 279–80; Divine Countenance, Presence 68, 203, 240, 248, 250, 262–64; Divine-Human Relationship 24, 25, 27, 53, 103–05, 175, 219–20, 223, 225–27, 234, 239–40, 242, 245, 248, 258–59, 262, 275; Divine Other 140, 253, 254

Dogma, Dogmas of modernity, 179, 182–83, 189, 193, 194, 205–06; Creedal Dogmatists 170; Dogmatists of the Law 5

Double Nature of Humanity, 236

Duality—the absolute and the conditional 141; duality of choice 192; duality of human nature 236; duality vs. mystical experience of oneness 227–28; *I-Thou* vs. *I-It* 46, 211; *I* vs. not-*I* 50; *I* vs. *Thou* 162, 241; inner duality 136; knowledge and law vs. teaching 124; self vs. openness to the Other 91, 103, 149, 197; the-two-and-the-one 158

Duty, Absolute Duty, Supreme Duty, 39, 100, 103, 137, 139, 198, 228

Eclipse of God, xxii, 45, 102, 277, 279

Effective Action, 135, 190, 199, 230

Ego cogito of Descartes, 187

Either/Or, 115, 168, 245

Encounter, xiii, 6, 7, 9, 16, 20, 22–23, 25, 29–30, 32, 34, 41–47, 54–55, 57–59, 61, 71, 73–74, 78–79, 94, 97, 101–05, 107, 110–12, 120, 125, 131, 135, 149–50, 154, 156–57, 159–60, 165, 169, 171, 176, 178, 184, 195, 197–98, 202–05, 209–10, 214, 219, 221–22, 225, 228, 231, 234, 236–39, 241, 243–45,

248–53, 255–59, 261–63, 265–
66, 273, 276, 281–82, 285–86
The Enduring, 71, 99, 209
Epektasis, 223, 253
Erlebnis-mysticism, 78, 119
Eros, 228, 241
Estrangement—see Alienation
The Eternal Feminine, 69
Eternal, 61, 69, 99, 137, 138, 141–45,
191, 201–02, 212, 226, 230–31,
239, 242, 249, 252, 258, 263,
271, 278; The Eternal [God]
92, 97, 114, 151, 246, 253,
264; Eternal Life 191, 212, 239;
The Eternal Tao 143, 220; The
Eternal Thou xi, 9, 11, 20, 22,
74, 91, 93, 103–04, 106, 110–12,
135, 144, 151, 174, 179, 181,
193–94, 198, 202–05, 212,
219–21, 223–25, 227, 229, 231,
234–35, 239–42, 247, 249–50,
252–57, 259, 261–64, 273, 275,
277–79, 282–83, 285, 289, 291
Ever Anew, 99–100, 208, 214, 245; "Ever
Anew" vs. "Once for All" 170
The Everyday, 3, 35, 65, 68, 73–74, 78,
105, 109, 114, 119–20, 143, 153,
154, 170, 172, 214–15, 227–29,
263, 267
Exclusivity, 110, 118, 145, 155–56, 159,
166, 168, 223, 238, 240, 248
Exemplum, 55, 128
Exile, 12, 21, 266–68, 271–72
Existence [existential, concrete human
reality], 11–12, 23–26, 34, 39,
41–44, 47, 70, 96–101, 103–05,
112, 115, 119–20, 124–26, 128,
134, 138, 141, 143–44, 152, 156,
160, 162–64, 167, 170, 174, 182,
185, 191–93, 196, 204, 208–13,
217, 230–32, 236, 240, 243, 252,
257, 267–69, 275–76
Existential, 2, 6, 8, 10–11, 34, 38, 43,
58–59, 68, 71, 72, 94, 96, 98, 99,
100, 105–06, 110, 115, 125, 132,
136, 139, 147, 149, 152, 192,
220, 222, 228
Experience, 11, 18, 24, 27, 29–30, 42,
46, 54, 46–59, 62, 73, 97, 100,
107–12, 118–21, 131, 147,
153–54, 159, 161, 162, 163, 166,
169, 175, 182, 184, 188, 192,
195, 218, 220, 222, 227–29, 233,
237–39, 244–45, 254, 257, 259,
273, 276, 280

The Face [the presence of God], 6, 24,
103–07, 135, 202–03, 207, 212,
226, 248–49, 264, 289
Faith, 15, 18, 27, 42, 59, 96–100, 103,
105–06, 114, 196, 203, 210, 220,
224–25, 244, 253, 269, 281
Fate, 52, 104, 144, 159, 168, 177–79,
182–83, 193, 204, 263, 265, 275
Fear of God, 105
Feeling, 29, 30, 119, 152, 156, 175,
183–85, 188, 216, 224–25, 228,
237, 238
Fervor, 20–21, 23, 60–61, 246; see also
Readiness.
Fin de Siècle, 75–76, 146
Fire, Flame, 39–40, 95, 130, 200–02,
206–07, 252–53, 261, 264
First World War, 3–4, 7–8, 10, 17, 20,
26–29, 37, 57, 70–73, 75–79,
83–84, 93, 99, 107, 109–10, 115
Fleeting, 121, 168, 169, 171, 198, 230,
239
Forgetting [as a spiritual act], 24, 203–
04, 217
Founder, Founding, 10, 14, 16, 17, 20,
23, 134–35, 164, 176, 200, 252,
258, 260, 285
Fragment, Fragmentation, 112, 121, 128,
179, 244, 279
Frankfurt, xxi, 30, 36, 75, 80, 92, 101,
116
Frankfurt Lehrhaus [Freies Jüdisches
Lehrhaus], 36, 50, 81–84, 111,
290

Free, 40, 104, 129, 139, 157, 158, 173, 177, 186, 189, 203, 205–09, 212, 223, 225, 246, 249, 253, 264, 267; *Free Person* 173, 186, 189, 207, 208, 209; see also *Self-Willed Person*.

Freedom, 129, 178, 194, 202–06, 208–10, 212, 234

Fulfill, 125, 128, 138, 145, 160, 204, 257, 292; *Fulfilled* 99, 103, 142, 169, 189, 211, 220, 223, 231, 256, 292; *Fulfilling* 88, 124, 126, 127, 128, 133, 224, 228, 257, 286; *The Fulfilling Person* 127, 128; *Fulfillment* 69, 106, 126, 134, 141, 184, 204, 219, 226, 256, 285, 286

Fullness, 23, 37, 74, 103, 120–21, 127, 133, 141, 166, 177, 187, 190, 194, 204, 207, 214–18, 243, 248, 250, 290, 292

Gaze, 46, 58, 73, 101, 151, 155, 203–04, 236–38, 261

Genealogy, 49, 146, 160–68

Gift, 68, 165, 221, 222, 230, 254, 257, 280, 281

Gnosis, Gnostic, Gnosticism, 107, 113–15, 170, 205

Go, Go Forth, Go Out, 18, 64, 105, 120, 194–95, 198–99, 203–04, 207, 209–10, 217, 221–23, 228, 230, 234, 252, 256–58, 264, 269; see also *Step, Step Forth*

The Godhead, 70, 228

God-Talk, 257

Golem, 66, 290

Grace, 16, 54, 68, 114, 154, 155, 158, 169, 189, 201, 202, 204, 221–22

Grasp, 20, 21, 97, 124, 128, 141, 166, 171, 172, 180, 194, 200, 201, 207, 210, 217, 253, 257, 267, 274, 280, 283

The Great Mother, 164, 166–67; see also Mother Goddess

Grief, 27–28, 31–36, 48, 58, 78, 147

Ground, Grounding, 5, 27, 37, 45–46, 51, 70, 86, 91, 94–98, 101–02, 110–12, 114, 125, 147, 154, 158, 162, 164, 178, 191, 193, 212, 219, 220, 222, 231, 261, 275, 292

Gyre, 174–78, 255, 257–65

Hallow, 3, 105, 181, 221, 223–25, 229, 248–49, 263

Hasid, xxi, 6, 23, 25, 45, 60, 68, 69, 128, 130, 140, 142, 144, 181, 201, 269

Hasidic, 4, 6–8, 11, 13, 16–17, 19–22, 25, 26, 33, 39–40, 45–46, 58, 60–62, 67–68, 75, 80, 82, 100, 117, 123, 128–33, 139, 142, 145, 181, 200, 204, 220, 235, 246, 253, 268–70, 290

Hasidism, xx, 5, 7, 8, 10, 20, 22–23, 25, 32, 34, 41, 56, 60, 62, 63, 70, 79, 109, 116, 122–23, 126, 130, 132–34, 139, 142–43, 145, 164, 233, 258, 267–69, 272, 281, 290

Haskalah, 10, 60

Hearken, 24, 209, 210

Heart, 6, 17, 40, 51, 57, 61, 62, 85–87, 90, 91, 221, 224, 239, 246, 260, 263, 282, 283

Hearth, 180, 241

Hebraic, xi, 265, 289–92

Hebrew Language, 17, 20, 22, 90, 92, 125, 128, 145, 151, 158, 175, 186, 195, 220, 221, 242, 248, 252, 267, 289, 290, 291

Hebrew Scriptures, 60–61, 81, 92, 125, 152, 186, 220, 253, 259, 268–69, 281–82, 289, 291

The Hebrew University, xxi, 70, 157, 266

Help, 23, 25, 61, 74, 129, 132, 133, 158, 181, 269, 277–78; *Helper* 18, 25, 120, 130–32

Heppenheim, xx, 35, 75, 80, 82, 88, 93

The Hidden, 44–45, 71, 99, 157, 178, 192, 196, 200, 207, 209, 250, 252, 265, 269–70; *Hidden History* 208, 289; see also *Conceal, The Between*

Hindu, Hinduism, 50, 136, 148, 219, 229–30, 234, 285

History, 5, 24, 30, 33, 58, 72, 95, 102, 104, 107, 114, 117, 132, 135–37, 144, 146, 148, 160, 163, 173, 174–79, 185, 186, 206, 253,

255–65, 267, 271, 272, 276, 278, 282–83, 289; *Hidden History* 208, 289; see also *Cycle, Gyre*
Holy Insecurity, 98–99, 101, 256, 264
Home, At home in the It-world 51, 52, 169, 171–72; *Homecoming* 122, 267–68; *Homeland* 267–68; *Homelessness, Cosmic*, 146–47, 179, 180–82
Hope, 61, 193, 215–17, 221, 272, 278, 279
Human-centered limits of Buber's thinking, 70, 96, 97, 125, 141, 147, 220
Humanism, 7, 60, 290; *Biblical Humanism* 290–92; *Hebrew Humanism* 7–8, 12, 113, 290

"I Martiri dell'Ararat", 30
I-in-Itself, 169
The I of Relation, 163, 222
Idealism, Idealistic Philosophy, 76–77, 107–08
Identity of Being, 109
Ideology, 76–77, 183, 185, 188, 193, 206
Idol, Idolatry, 112, 188, 190, 196, 219, 246–47, 280
Illusion, 3, 148, 184, 188, 190, 192–93, 221, 222, 226, 230, 232, 288
Image of God [*Tselem Elohim, Imago Dei*], 21, 22, 225, 253, 269
Imitation of God, 6, 104, 144
Immediate, 20, 21, 30, 41, 133, 136, 158, 165, 176, 181, 219, 286; see also *Direct, Unmediated*
I-ness, 163, 166
The I of I-It, 152–53, 166–67, 169, 186–87, 189–90, 192–93, 196, 199, 201–02, 207, 213, 222
The I of I-Thou, 152–54, 166, 186–87, 190–93, 196, 201, 213–14, 222, 238, 283
The I-Thou Relation, 7, 43, 45, 46, 51, 66, 101, 126, 155, 158, 161, 180, 184, 191, 197, 208, 219, 224, 225, 227, 232, 238, 240, 242, 247, 262, 275, 279
Imagination, Imagine, 24, 66, 106, 152, 159, 162, 166–67, 169–70, 181,

183, 194, 204, 217, 221, 243–45, 261
Imagining the real, 27, 29–30
Immediacy, Immediate, 3, 6, 8, 16, 20–21, 24, 30, 39, 41, 55, 95–96, 101–03, 105–08, 123, 131, 133, 136, 144, 158, 165, 169, 176, 181, 219, 256, 259, 275–77, 280, 282, 286, 291–92
Imitation, Imitating, 104, 144
In-breaking, 119, 136, 177, 240
Inborn Thou, 164–67, 174, 184, 192, 194, 220, 224
Individualism, ix, 107, 185, 188
The Individualist, 185–89, 191, 194, 205; see also *The Person*
Individuation, xx, 58, 146–49
The Infinite, 5, 46, 114, 159, 200, 202, 204, 246, 249, 264
Initiation, 6, 8–42, 51, 61, 96, 203, 206, 225, 249, 253, 267, 278
Indirect Communication 40, 43, 47, 48
Inner, 8, 9, 11, 13–15, 17–19, 32–35, 42–43, 55, 56, 65, 77, 108, 113, 126, 131, 136, 139, 153, 156, 159, 175, 183–85, 188, 194, 197–98, 203–04, 206, 215, 225, 230, 238, 246, 256–57, 262, 267–68, 280, 282; *Innermost* 6, 33, 62, 90, 114, 137, 150, 217, 232, 268, 280, 282; see also *Inward, Inwardness*
Inner Corroboration 36–37, 42–43, 47; see also *Attestation, Confirmation*
Instinct, 165, 183, 188, 198, 205–06, 210, 230
Intend, 17, 38, 198, 200, 202, 205, 221, 228, 251, 280; *Intent* 182, 244, 292; *Intention* 42, 47, 60, 104, 152, 155, 169, 196, 205, 228, 251, 279
Intentness, 20–21, 61, 206; see also *Eifer, Fervor, Readiness, Zerizut*
Interaction, 123, 130, 157, 165, 191, 197, 230, 232
Interlocutor, 2, 42, 44–45, 48–50, 52, 59, 82, 102, 197, 238, 245, 280, 292
Interpersonal, 29–30, 56, 59, 63, 78, 90, 155, 184, 241; Inter-Human 55

Intuit, 36, 51, 96, 193, 198, 228; *Intuition* 95, 109, 123–24
Inward, Inwardness, 25, 43, 74, 183–85, 221, 232–33, 247–48, 271, 282
Irony, 43, 170, 257

Jerusalem, xxi, xxii, 70, 122, 146, 268, 271, 272
Journey metaphor, 11, 14, 100, 108, 133, 174, 209
Judaism, xx, 4–5, 10, 18, 20–22, 58–59, 62–64, 90, 109, 116–17, 122, 124–25, 132, 134–37, 144, 195, 266–72, 289–90

Kabbala, 66, 72, 100, 127, 142
The Kalevala, 58, 109
Kinetic, 30, 162, 195, 251, 270
Kingdom [of God], xxi, 88, 99, 134, 178, 195, 260, 265, 285–86

Layers: The Outer Psychic Layer vs. *The Inner Factual Layer*, 256–65
"Lectures on Judaism", 58–59, 90, 109, 117, 122, 136, 290
Let Go, 15, 24, 124, 139, 164, 167, 196, 202–04, 207, 217, 222–23
Listen, 2, 5, 20, 23–24, 44, 49, 100, 119, 133, 138, 161, 165, 172, 226–27, 281, 292
Lived, 17, 101, 124, 126, 132, 144–45, 154, 162, 169, 227; *Lived All* 74, 121; *Lived Concrete* 38, 45, 56, 59, 68, 73, 96, 101, 103–04, 106, 108, 115, 251, 275–77; *Lived Experience* 3, 24, 36, 54, 68, 73, 94, 107–08, 121, 192, 238–39, 273; *Lived Life* 5, 24, 45, 54, 55, 101–02, 105–06, 114–15, 123, 134, 138, 149, 170, 209, 210, 218; *Lived Reality* 43, 97, 108, 169, 230, 231, 234, 260; see also *Actual, Concrete*
Logic, 43, 97
Logos, 241, 243, 292
Longing, 51, 57, 64, 69, 88, 164–65, 167, 169, 232, 242, 275

Lord of the Voice, 24, 204, 218
Loss, 10, 17, 19, 26, 32, 34, 35, 47, 178, 180, 184; of identity 268; of *I-Thou* 279, 282; of Landauer 10, 26–32, 35, 55, 75, 78–79, 115; of Buber's mother 10, 29, 56–59; of the Presence 239; of reality 177, 179; of selfhood 192; of true being 179; see also *Grief*
Love, 50, 60–61, 63–64, 68–70, 92, 105–06, 109, 111, 114, 129, 153, 156–58, 225, 27, 233, 240–44, 249, 262–63, 288; see also *Compassion*

Make Visible, 47, 88, 128, 270
Making One, 139, 142, 145; see also *Yichud*
Making Present, 16, 37, 46, 114, 150, 245, 276
Making Real, 200; see also *Realization*
Mana, 49, 162, 289
Marcionite, 247
The Margin, 229
Master, 11, 15–17, 20–23, 39–40, 54–55, 109, 116, 123–36, 138, 141–43, 164, 176, 181, 190, 214, 222, 224, 226–27, 231, 246, 258, 266, 270, 281
Master-Builder, 130, 135, 181–82
Materialism, Materialist, 167, 170, 179
Meaning [existential meaning as opposed to meaninglessness], 74, 95, 102, 103–05, 108, 125, 132, 137, 141, 144, 177, 191, 204, 210–11, 232, 238, 241, 243, 250, 251, 256, 257, 258, 262, 271, 272, 276, 279
Mediated [vs. unmediated, immediate], 95–96, 106, 123, 153, 169, 189, 209, 224, 277
Mediator, 131, 133, 269
Meet, Meeting, xiii, 18, 20, 23, 27, 30, 45–47, 55, 57, 58, 65, 87, 94, 97, 99, 103–05, 109–10, 120, 141–42, 150, 157, 165, 189–90, 194, 199, 207, 220, 222–24, 239,

244, 266, 273–74, 275, 281, 283; see also *Encounter*
Messianic, 88, 178
Metacosmic, 167, 175, 235, 257
Metaphor, 3, 11, 30, 32, 87–88, 106, 156, 198, 206, 219, 235, 247–48, 260, 266, 279; metaphor of the center 181–82, 240; metaphor of commensalism 150, 191, 276; metaphor of chrysalis and butterfly 175; metaphor of the covenant 106; metaphor of the Face 289; metaphor of the journey 11; metaphor of music 106, 168, 266; metaphor of the narrow ridge 99; metaphor of pointing 10, 43, 44, 47; metaphor of smelting 259; metaphor of the sun 144
Mica, Buber's Encounter With, 52, 155, 237–39, 265
Mighty Revelations, 176
Mis-meeting, 10, 29, 54–57, 68, 71–74, 94
Monism, Monist, Oneness, 108, 125, 135, 145, 149, 171
Mother xix, 10, 28–29, 57–59, 64, 65, 68, 164, 166–67, 194, 220
Mother Goddess, 194
Mourning, 30, 32, 79; see also Grief
Music, 51, 106, 154, 168
Muslim, 15, 133
Mutual, Mutuality, 7, 41–42, 54, 63, 69, 80, 93, 130, 150, 154–55, 166, 171, 181, 189, 197, 221, 225, 236, 240, 275–76, 292
Mystery, 40, 42, 74, 83, 105, 135, 154–55, 169, 198, 199, 202, 203, 205, 223, 228, 231, 236, 239, 241, 243
Mystic, 50, 119, 120, 131, 227, 235, 258
Mystical Absorption, 50, 219, 226, 229, 231, 234
Mysticism, 3, 7, 24, 31, 58, 70, 75–78, 93, 107, 110, 112–15, 117–19, 121, 125, 130, 132–33, 139, 148–49, 181, 226–27, 229, 232, 234, 245

Myth of I and Thou, 34, 46

The Name, 220–21
The Nameless Way, 134, 216–17, 224, 278
The Narrow Ridge, 59, 71, 98, 99–100, 157, 209, 211, 264, 266, 290
Neighbor, 157–58
Noetic, 241, 243, 251
Nonbeing, 143, 231
Non-Dualism, 108, 229
Noumena vs *Phenomena*, 148–49

Objectify, 96, 185, 208, 264; see also Reify
Obligation, 91, 93, 123–24, 254
Occident, 270–72
Occidental Dualism, 31, 102
The One [God], 6, 24, 74, 103, 114, 137, 172, 178, 182, 194, 196, 204, 218, 223, 224, 234, 235, 241, 243, 248–49, 263, 264, 280
The One Thing Needful, 11, 18, 74, 95, 113, 120, 124, 126, 134, 137–41, 195, 196, 200–02, 205, 207, 209, 210–11, 219, 222, 224, 234, 251, 271, 278, 285, 290
The One vs. The Many, 138–39, 143, 172, 200, 234
Oneness, 50, 77, 78, 102, 108, 109–10, 112–14, 117, 120–22, 124–29, 133–34, 137–38, 141, 143, 148–49, 158, 162, 215, 227, 229, 238, 251, 273–74, 285–86
Ontology, Ontological, 22, 36, 95, 118, 120, 149, 150, 156–57, 177, 179, 212, 213, 227, 235, 268
Open, 1, 9, 12, 21, 22, 24, 26, 27, 35, 36, 41, 44, 55, 79, 84, 91, 93, 98, 99, 100, 104, 105, 114, 125, 135–36, 139, 145, 146, 150, 155, 156, 161, 164, 171, 173, 180, 194, 204, 212–13, 215, 217, 219, 221, 222, 223, 224, 232, 240, 241, 250, 253, 259, 261, 264, 269, 271, 276, 277, 280, 282, 283, 292

Openness, vi, 19, 65, 84, 86, 90, 95, 98, 110, 150, 154, 191, 196, 199, 202, 203, 206, 210, 212, 214, 224, 240, 273, 275, 276, 281, 283
Ordered World vs. World Order, 168, 170, 242
Orienting vs. Realizing, 46, 153, 165, 186
Originating Relational Event, 135, 176
Otherness, 69, 98, 150, 158, 184, 204, 253–54, 273, 276
Over-Against, 18, 46, 109–10, 113–15, 119–20, 149–50, 166, 191, 212, 220, 223–24, 228, 231, 236, 239, 259, 273–74
The Overwhelming, 46

The Pali Canon, 231–33, 287
The Pantheon in Rome, 88
Parable, xx, 109, 117, 121, 127–28, 134, 286
Paradox, 45–46, 126
Participate, Participation, 15, 37, 191, 212–14, 250, 256, 276; see also *Appropriate*
Passivity, 110, 154, 199, 210, 230, 259; see also *Receptivity*
Path, 4, 11, 23, 32, 38, 87, 99–100, 104, 134–35, 144, 158, 164, 174, 187, 192, 194, 198, 200, 205, 208, 209–10, 215–17, 224, 230, 245, 254–56, 259, 263–64, 269, 277–78, 280–81, 283, 285
Patriarch, 103, 242, 250, 278
The Perfect, Perfected [person], 8, 21–22, 126, 130–32, 135, 141, 143, 145
Perfection, 104, 144, 245, 292
The Person, 185–86, 190–92; see also *The Individualist*
Philosophy of Dialogue, 1–3, 6–7, 32, 54, 69, 78–79, 82, 94, 109, 117, 131, 146–47, 157, 283, 285
Philosophy of Realization, 4, 99, 117, 124
Pointing, 10, 40, 42–45, 47–48, 100, 218
Portal, 141, 180, 241–43, 245
Possess, 74, 101, 120, 143, 156, 177, 188, 190, 196, 211, 222, 246–47, 273, 278

Prague, xx, 267, 270, 271
Prayer, 83, 158, 207, 225–26, 240, 245, 256, 264
Presence, vi, xxi, 9, 11, 16, 49, 51–52, 54–55, 64–65, 69, 74, 95–96, 102, 149, 154, 156, 159, 160, 162, 168, 169, 171, 176, 184, 196–97, 208, 211–12, 219, 221–22, 241, 242, 245, 252, 256, 266, 274, 276–77, 279
The Presence [God], 9, 21, 34, 51, 68, 104, 106, 115, 144–45, 151, 197, 202–04, 206, 207, 220, 223, 224, 229, 234, 235, 239, 240, 241, 246, 248, 250, 251, 252, 253, 255, 257, 259–60, 262–64, 279, 289
Present, 6, 8, 11, 16, 18, 27, 32, 37, 43, 44, 46, 54–55, 73, 74, 78–79, 89, 91, 101, 114, 117, 143, 144, 150, 151, 154, 159, 162, 168–69, 171, 173, 182, 200, 204, 210, 221, 222, 223, 224, 241, 243, 245, 248, 249–50, 252–53, 259, 261, 263–64, 273, 274, 276, 280, 281, 282, 291
Primal Christianity, 164, 285
Primary Words [*I-Thou, I-It*], 44, 152–53, 161, 170, 175, 183, 185–87
Principium Individuationis, 118, 148
Proclaim, Proclamation, 4, 8, 10, 21–22, 25–26, 34, 36, 39, 41, 55, 98, 125, 136, 144, 170, 231, 243
Prophet, 42, 71, 78, 113, 125, 132, 135, 152, 195, 207, 247, 250, 258, 260, 277–83
Prophetic, xxi, 12, 100, 113, 125, 135, 266, 277–82, 291
Proof, Prove, 41, 45, 51, 126, 208, 211, 214, 245, 251, 256, 291, 292
Psychology, Psychologizing, 107, 110–12, 184, 190, 195, 232, 247, 253; *Psychologizing of the World* 107, 112, 184
Pure Effective Action, 135, 190

Readiness, 19, 21, 32, 178, 206, 263–64, 278; see also *Fervor, Intentness*

INDEX

Reading, 15–17, 20–21, 23–25, 37, 39, 41, 44, 86–88, 118, 121, 248, 259

Realization, 4, 8, 11, 15, 25, 31, 99, 109, 117, 124, 126, 132, 135, 191, 200, 212, 214, 224, 226, 229, 269, 274; *De-Realization* 190, 240; *Self-Realization* 257

Realizing, 8, 21–22, 25, 34, 46, 51, 55, 65, 70, 77, 98–99, 124, 126–27, 133, 141–42, 154, 174, 178, 190, 201, 209, 213, 215, 220, 223–25, 245, 256, 269

Realm of Thou, 51–52, 76, 112, 140, 151, 153–54, 159, 167, 171–72, 175, 190, 208–09, 211, 269

Reason, Logic, 41, 43, 97, 102, 140

Rebirth, 15, 24, 67, 178, 193, 204, 217–18, 291

Receive, 8, 16, 19, 24, 26, 32, 34, 42, 46, 54, 68, 113, 127, 134, 155–56, 202, 204, 218, 222–23, 239, 242, 244, 250–55, 270, 273–74, 277

Receptivity, 55, 66, 102, 105, 154, 155, 159, 194, 199, 221, 245, 262, 279

Recipient, 245, 251, 253–55, 257–61, 277

Reciprocity, 3, 36, 66, 103, 158, 165, 169, 207, 212, 238, 241, 250, 271, 274

Reduce, 45, 101, 124, 167, 177, 188–90, 195, 215, 221, 224, 241, 246, 248, 255, 257, 263, 278

Reduction, 48, 110, 112, 167, 179, 184–85, 190, 219, 232, 234, 241

Reify, 37, 46, 163, 169, 188, 222, 241; see also *Objectify*

Relation, 3, 7, 11, 25, 36, 43, 44, 55, 85, 100, 113–14, 130, 131, 150–51, 153–55, 158–160, 162–67, 169, 174–75, 177–82, 184–85, 187, 191–92, 194–98, 203, 210, 212–15, 220–28, 232–33, 235–36, 238–48, 250–52, 256–57, 262–64, 269, 274–77, 279, 282, 292; *The Absolute Relation* 100, 103, 139, 202, 223, 225, 247; *Complete Relation* 223; *The I of Relation* 163, 222; *The Thou of Relation* 165, 166; *Pure Relation* 214, 223, 225–27, 240, 250, 256; *Unconditional Relation* 213, 223; see also *I-Thou Relation*

Relation-Oriented Life, 180, 257

Religiosity, 21–22, 100, 113, 115

Renaissance, 67, 76, 267, 290

Renewal, 11, 31, 67, 113, 141–42, 164, 175, 178, 192–93, 196, 214, 217, 267–68, 271, 290

Resolve, 74, 100, 148, 149, 205, 209, 210, 221, 230, 234

Response, 10, 21, 25, 27–29, 31–32, 41, 50, 55–56, 65, 71, 74–75, 78–79, 81, 85–93, 98, 106–07, 112–14, 116, 119–20, 135, 146–47, 154, 176, 178, 180, 183, 190, 198, 200, 204, 211, 218, 230, 236–37, 243, 246–49, 253, 257, 261–61, 277, 280, 282–83, 292

Responsibility, 26, 30, 35, 43, 66, 74, 99, 113, 121, 131–32, 137, 139, 156, 158, 164, 198, 222, 243, 249

Revelation, 12, 23, 25, 92, 101, 134, 139, 176, 194, 205–07, 219, 225, 233, 249–55, 257–63, 279; *Eternal Revelation* 249, 254, 258; *Great/Small Revelations* 254–55, 258, 261

Rhetoric, 10, 41–53, 100, 174, 216, 291; Rhetorical Question 217, 227; Rhetorical Task 42; Rhetorical tools 40, 43, 48

Risk, 16–17, 52, 55, 70, 89, 98–99, 159, 198, 209, 218, 276

Romantic, 7, 58, 60, 161, 189, 245

Sacred, 15, 98, 133, 152, 180, 202, 207, 221, 226, 230–31, 271; Sacredness 158, 159, 211

Sacrifice, 158–59, 180, 189, 193, 196, 202–11, 215, 225–26, 241, 247, 250–51

Secret, 15, 56, 127, 147, 164, 239, 292; Secret Dialogue 92, 104, 275

Self—Apparent Self 193; *False Self* 153, 193; *True Self* 153, 193

Self-Appropriation, 187, 188, 213

Self-Awareness, 165, 188, 213, 237

Self-Construction, 187–88

Self-Contradiction, 184
Self-Deception, 110, 188, 189, 193
Self-Emptying, 142
Self-Image, 188
Self-Willed Person, 173, 212
Send, 23, 24, 198, 227, 236, 243, 257–61
Sense of Unity, 77, 107, 110
Separate, 13, 16, 18, 123, *153*, 163, *184*, 187, 199, 213, 234, 268, 275
Separation, 28, 57, 149, *153*, 163–67, 213, 222
Servant, 114, 136, 207, 246, 278
Serve, 97, 99, 114, 115, 120, 131, 143, 159, 201, 246, 247
Service, 61, *114–15*, 127, 133, 144, *155*, 158, 211, 224, 233, 241, 243
Setting at a Distance, 150, 274
Sickness, 120, 173, 178; *The Sickness of Our Age* 175, 179, 180
Sign, 24, 73, 102, 106, 204, 210, 218, 252, 253, 254, 264, 283
Silence, Silent, 43, 51, 88, 90, 119, 127, 142, 143, 160, 168, 177, 202, 231, 232, 241, 246, 249, 251, 259, 264, 280, 282
The Simple Person, 127, 129, 131
The Single One [Danish: *den enkelte*], 139, 190, 191, 247; *den enkelte* 190–191
Singleness, 61, 251
Smelting, 252, 258, 259, 261
Solidarity, 171, 191
Solitude, 35, 82, 83, 127, 147, *245–46*, 264
Span of Relation, 150, 226, 232, 274
Spark, 39, 208, 211
Speak, 4, 5, 24, 41–42, 47, 88, 132, 127, 150, 152, 169, 207, 212, 220, 236, 246, 253, 279, 280, 282; *God Speaks* 6, 9, 24, 74, 198, 243, 254, 291
Speech, 8, 23, 24, 33, 43, 51, 101, 131–33, 152, 235, 241; *Divine Speech* 24, 33, 101, 235, 243; see also *Utterance*

Spoken, 16, 17, 22–23, 58, 66, 89, 140, 163, 197, 220, 281; *Spokenness* 16, 281, 291; see also *Utterance*
Spiritual Awakening, xx, 8, 10, 17–26, 32–34, 38, 40, 48, 51, 130, 267, 269
Spiritual-Intellectual Entities, 235, 243–45
Splitting, 31, 73, 78, 102, 119, 125, 163, 227; see also Dividing in two
Stammering, 95, 236, 279, 280
Stance, 4, 5, 85, 93, 96, 98, 194, 222, 230, 266, 268, 276, 278, 290; *Being Stance* 18, 41; *Choice of Stance* 233; *Devotio Stance* 114–15, 138; *Existential Stance* 71–72, 100, 110, 125, 220; *I-It Stance* 11, 187, 199; *I-Thou Stance* 44, 51, 102, 119, 122, 129, 153–54, 159, 191, 210, 221–22, 247, 249, 251, 276; *I-Thou vs. I-It Stance* 37, 46–48, 59, 52–53, 95, 152, 212–13; *"Waiting" Stance* 221
Stand, 1, 15, 18, 23, 26, 27, 37, 59, 91, 98, 106, 112, 118–20, 129, 130, 135, 153, 158, 159, 165, 176, 181, 195, 198, 200, 223, 228, 231, 233, 258, 260, 268, 280; *Stand Fast* 278, 292; *Stand Firm* 105, 276, 278, 280; *Stand Forth* 47, 223; *Stand in Relation* 199; *Stand One's Ground* 91, 171; *Stand Over Against* 113, 150, 166, 212, 223, 228, 231, 257; *Stand Ready* 9, 21, 91, 135–36; *Stand the Test* 126, 262, 263; *Stand Toward God* 114, 195, 219, 234; *Stand Up To* 46, 114, 215, 278; *Stand With* 114, 246, 281; *Take One's Stand* 152, 183, 190, 212–13, 246, 247
Step, Step Forth, 36, 55, 87, 105–06, 114–15, 152, 154, 155, 195, 199, 203, 209–10, 212–13, 222–23, 226, 228, 248–49, 274, 279; see also *Go, Go Forth, Go Out*
Stimulus-Image vs. Object-Image, 162

Stripping, 24, 142, 203, 204, 206
The Subject, 24, 47, 107, 166, 185, 187–88, 204, 225, 230, 240
Subject-Object, 47, 107, 108, 124, 153, 175, 163, 179, 184–85, 191, 215, 237, 238, 242, 264
Subjective, Subjectivity, 37, 47, 76, 78, 93, 107–08, 111–13, 131, 153, 156–57, 162, 175, 179, 183–85, 190–91, 206, 212–13, 221, 225, 264
Suffering, 29, 35–36, 72, 105, 110, 115, 134, 231, 267–68, 276, 281, 285
Sufism, 5, 68, 132
Summons, 23, 25, 47, 92, 147, 253, 257, 269, 277; see also *Call, Send*
Supreme, 232, 246; *The Supreme* 182, 196, 262; *Supreme Duty* 198, 228; *The Supreme Encounter, Meeting* 20, 23, 199, 205–08, 219, 222, 248, 249–53, 256; *The Supreme Moment* 202; *The Supreme Relationship* 214
Surrender, 15, 104, 111, 114, 120, 159, 239, 248, 253, 262, 283, 286
Symbol, Symbolic, 15, 74, 111, 134, 161, 196, 242, 252–53, 255, 258, 260–63
Symphony, 106, 168, 266

Tao, 104, 120, 128–29, 134–35, 140–41, 143–45, 154, 168, 199, 210, 217, 220, 241, 155, 160, 265, 285–86
Taoism, 7, 11, 70, 84, 116–17, 121–22, 125, 129, 139, 144, 164, 289
The *Tao Te Ching*, 121, 129, 140–42, 220, 238
Task, 3, 21–22, 26, 31, 35, 37, 40–43, 47–48, 84–85, 92, 99, 145, 198, 200, 208, 216, 222, 230, 238, 240, 249, 253, 268–70, 275, 277–79, 281–82
Tat Tvam Asi, 148
The Teaching, 4, 11, 23, 25, 40, 47, 55, 70, 102, 108, 116, 122–26, 128–29, 132–34, 137, 140, 176, 201, 231, 260, 270–72, 286

"The Teaching of the Tao", 3, 22, 116–25, 128, 130, 132–36, 139–40, 143, 145, 153, 209, 222, 231, 258, 260, 285
Teaching Story, 5, 56, 60, 109, 117, 128, 130, 132–34, 138, 270; see also *Parable*
Telos, 203, 210
Tension, 99, 102, 113, 115, 158, 171, 232, 248, 253, 255, 263, 268, 274, 275, 278
Testament, 10, 32, 41, 90; *I and Thou* as Testament 7, 9, 32, 41, 48, 51, 282–83
The Testament of Rabbi Israel Ben Eliezer, 3, 10, 16, 20, 21, 23, 41, 135, 225, 249
Testify, 17, 20, 21, 41, 43, 48, 234, 269, 278
Testimony, 16, 41, 50, 54, 95, 199–202
The Tetragrammaton, 151, 252
Text as *Thou*, 9, 23, 44
Theism, 108, 221
Theological Talk, 220
Theonomous, 271
Theophany, 157, 160, 178, 212, 220, 249, 252–53, 259–60, 262, 265, 289
This-worldly, 29, 251
The *Thou [Du]* of Direct Address to the Reader, 49, 52, 172, 215, 280
Threshold, 4, 153, 155, 208, 210, 211, 235–36, 239, 265
Transformation, 3, 7, 8, 9, 13–15, 19–22, 24–25, 32, 37, 39, 44, 51, 53, 55–57, 99, 118–19, 140–43, 174, 195–96, 201, 204, 207–08, 212, 217, 238–39, 244, 249, 252, 255, 258–59, 265, 280, 291
Transcendent, 19, 32, 43, 45, 73, 124, 128, 137, 202–04, 211, 219, 251, 272, 275; *The Transcendent* 101, 102, 107, 114, 144, 182, 235, 277, 279; *Transcendent Compassion* 232; *Transcendent Dimension of Thou* 152, 209
Transmission, 15–16, 23, 38, 40, 123–24, 128, 132–33, 250–51, 281
Tree, 9, 51–52, 155, 158, 163, 238–39

INDEX

Turn, Turning, 11–12, 16–17, 21, 24, 29, 40, 44, 52, 53, 74, 78, 94, 95, 114, 117, 141, 150, 157, 173–76, 178, 192–208, 212, 215–17, 219, 222, 240, 249, 257–59, 265, 269, 271, 274–75, 277, 280–81, 283, 289, 290; Return 136, 150, 174,192, 195, 207–08, 247, 257, 258, 263, 271

The Turn Inward, 183–84, 232–33

Turning Points of the Ages, 176, 258

The two-and-the-one, 274–75

Uncertainty, 98, 99, 177, 204, 217, 221, 267

The Unconditional, 27, 46, 103, 110–11, 113, 115, 126, 128, 132, 138, 195, 213, 223, 248, 252, 259, 262; see also The Absolute

Unification, 48, 120, 128, 136, 137, 139, 142, 198, 226–28, 230–32, 234, 237, 249, 2259, 273, 285; see also Oneness

Unified, 120, 124–25, 128, 134, 137–41, 143, 154, 180, 198, 230, 232, 237, 251, 257, 280, 285–86; Unified Life 120, 125–27, 154, 280, 286; Unified Person 134, 143, 285–86; see also Oneness

Unitive [Mysticism], 71, 113, 115, 118, 226, 232, 234

Unity, 58, 70, 76–78, 99, 108, 109–10, 117, 118–20, 123, 125, 136–39, 141–45, 148, 156, 158, 162–63, 182, 198, 226–28, 230–31, 234, 237–37, 253, 262, 271, 273–75; see also Oneness

Unmediated, 45, 46, 91, 95, 96, 102, 154, 156, 160, 169, 210, 213, 224, 232, 256; see also Direct, Immediate

The Unnamable, 70, 134, 220

Unreality, 179, 184, 186

The Upanishads, 134, 229, 286, 289

Urim and Thummim, 6, 282

Utopian, 31–32, 75, 78

Utterance, Uttering, 4, 84, 88, 105, 132, 151, 220, 279; see also Speech

Values, 5, 29–30, 95, 99, 102, 115, 144, 161, 165, 215, 230, 235–36, 246, 269, 272

Vatic Voice, 31–32. 75, 78

Vedanta, Vedantic, 108, 125, 148

Verification, 45

Vienna, xix, 58, 60, 62, 63, 65, 108

Vocation, 15, 198, 202, 203

Voice, 9, 16–17, 20, 23–24, 31, 42, 48–49, 52, 64, 82, 92, 98, 150, 160, 169, 171, 197, 203–04, 218, 240, 249, 251, 252, 254–55, 259–60, 266, 277, 279–82, 291–92

Vulnerability, 55, 59, 64–66, 86, 89, 98, 110, 115, 150, 198, 203–04, 209

Wait, Await, 6, 68, 130, 155, 178, 203, 207, 210, 221, 224, 246, 250, 252, 278

Watershed, 18, 26, 38, 70–71, 115, 118, 149

The Way as Cosmic Process, 178

The Way of Being in the World, 209–10, 264

The Way of Dialogue, 36–37, 38, 113, 123, 195, 232–33, 275, 280

The Way of God, 6, 103, 144, 277

The Way of Man, 5, 25, 104–05, 124–25, 143, 195, 228, 255, 272

The Way of Salvation, 144–45, 231, 247, 264–65, 280–81

The Way of the Tao, 141, 210, 265, 285

Whole, 105, 128, 129, 131, 141, 156, 194, 196, 200, 214, 216, 221, 235, 243, 245, 249, 250; Becoming Whole 216

Whole Being / Existence / Person / Self, 3, 16, 21–22, 27, 44, 55, 64, 95, 110–11, 117, 120, 122, 125–26, 138, 153–54, 159, 176, 195, 197–200, 203, 205, 207, 209–10, 212, 221–23, 230–31, 253, 258, 259, 262, 264, 269, 273–74, 276, 278, 280

Wholeness, 16, 58, 129, 140, 153–54, 163–64, 169, 198–99, 228, 231, 234, 252, 257, 268, 274–75, 281

The Will, 16, 91, 104, 111, 125, 154–55, 183, 189, 195, 200–02, 209–10, 238, 248, 251, 259, 262–63, 275, 283; *Capricious or Arbitrary Self-Will* 104, 106, 135, 173, 186, 188, 189, 199, 205; *God's Will* 195, 280; *Higher Will* 189, 205, 209; *Little Will / Great Will* 205, 207, 209, 210; *Moral Will* 194; *Oneness or Unity of Will* 138, 227

Witness, 11, 26–27, 38, 41–42, 44–48, 95–97, 100, 106, 129, 199, 251, 154, 286; *Bear Witness* 22, 26, 34, 40–43, 220, 224, 282; *Inner Witness* 42; see also *Testify*, *Testimony*

Word, 4, 9, 17, 26, 44, 47, 66, 91, 133–35, 152, 155, 175–77, 179, 235, 241, 243, 248, 257–59, 262–64, 279, 281, 286, 291–92; *Primal or Primary Word / Word Pair* 44, 46–48, 152–54, 163, 170, 175, 179, 183, 185–87, 207

Worship, 207, 231, 256

Wu-wei, 117, 121, 153, 199, 210, 222, 230, 248, 249

Yom Kippur, 40, 62, 90

Zen Buddhism, 5, 132

Zionism, 17–18, 64, 67, 78

Zionist Congress, 19, 64–65, 67

Zürich, xix, 63, 108

www.ingramcontent.com/pod-product-compliance
Lightning Source LLC
Chambersburg PA
CBHW050615300426
44112CB00012B/1512